THE MONEY MUSEUM
OF THE DEUTSCHE BUNDESBANK

THE MONEY MUSEUM

OF THE DEUTSCHE BUNDESBANK

HIRMER

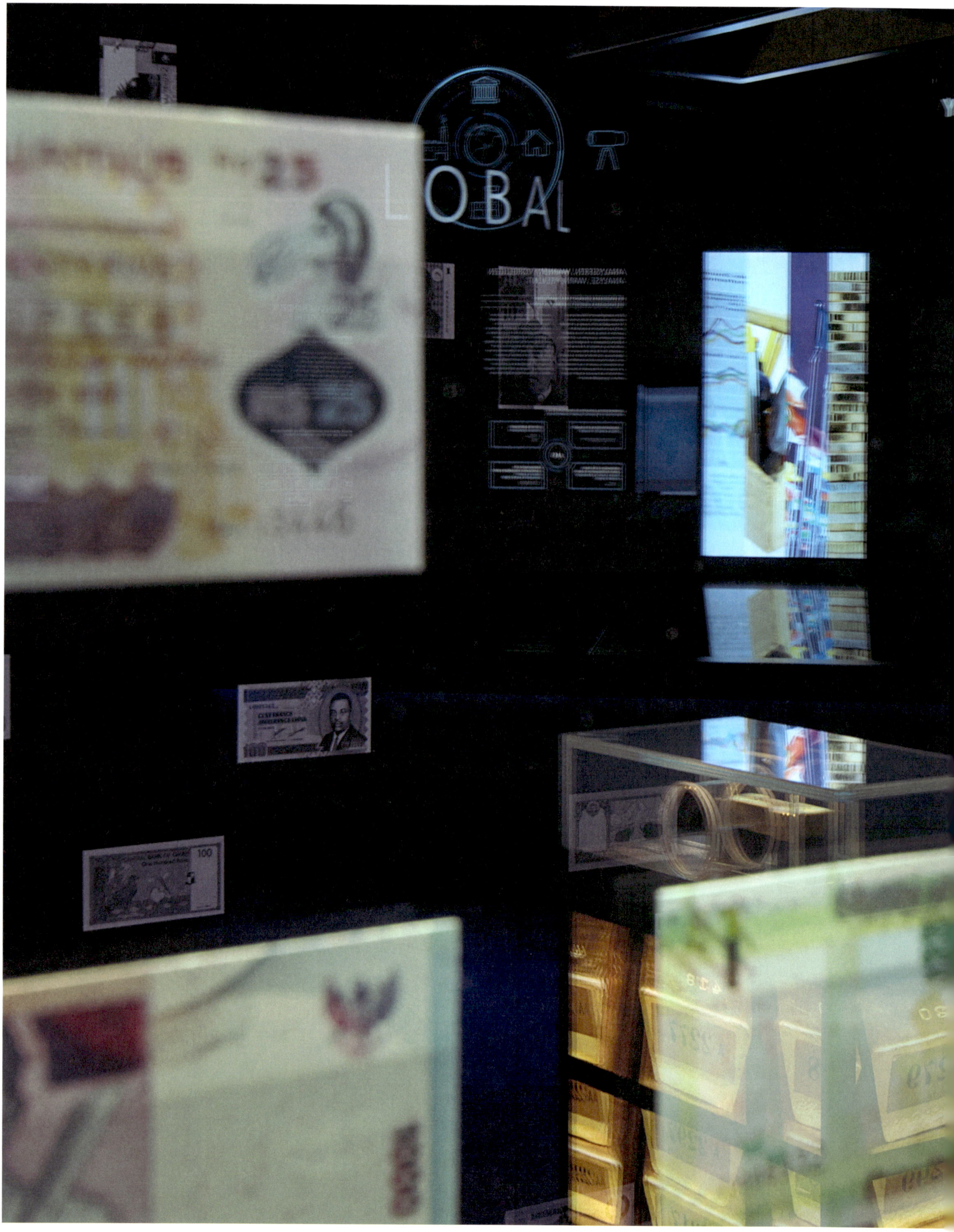
OBAL

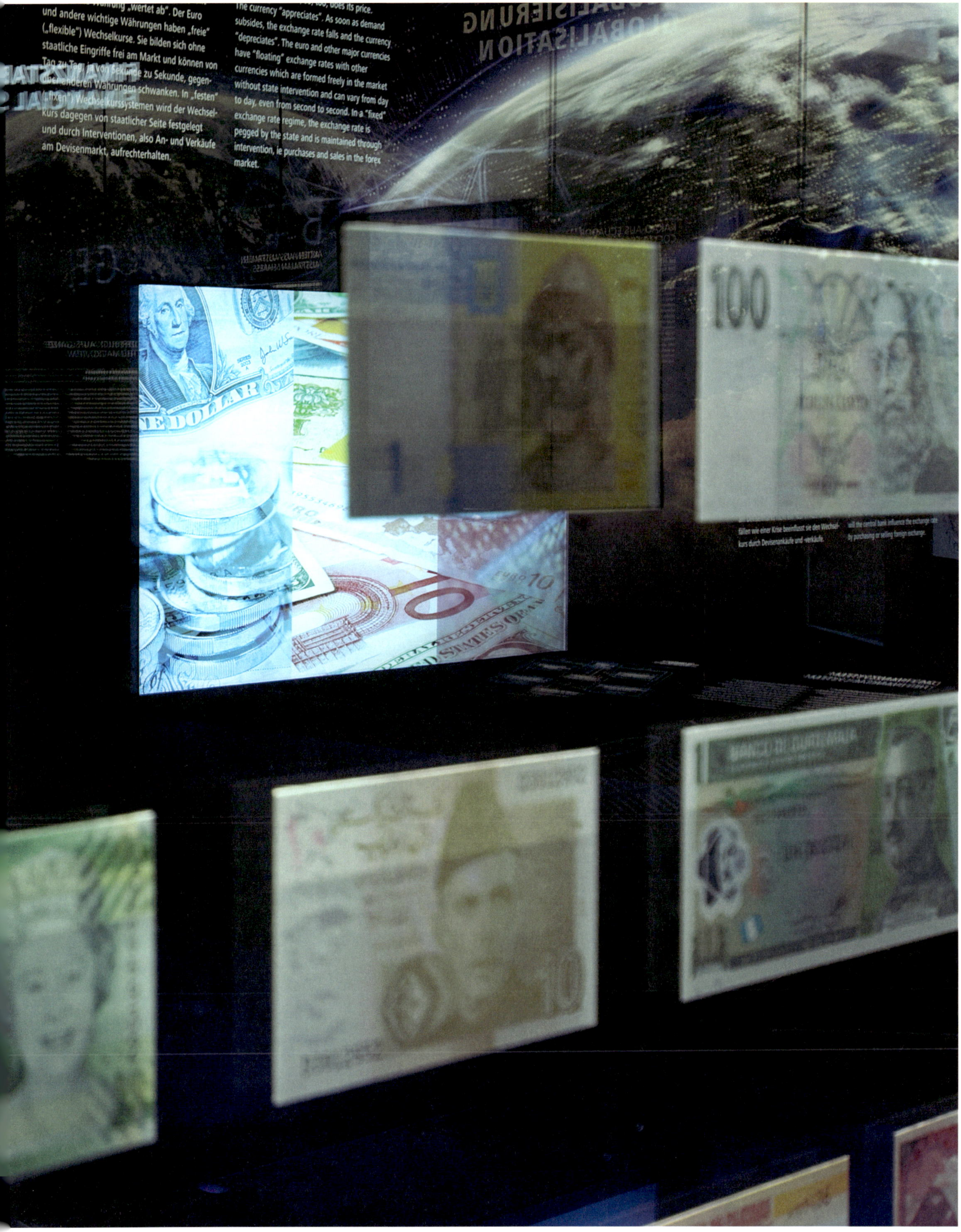
Währung „wertet ab". Der Euro
und andere wichtige Währungen haben „freie"
(„flexible") Wechselkurse. Sie bilden sich ohne
staatliche Eingriffe frei am Markt und können von
Tag zu Tag, ja von Sekunde zu Sekunde, gegen-
über anderen Währungen schwanken. In „festen"
(„fixen") Wechselkurssystemen wird der Wechsel-
kurs dagegen von staatlicher Seite festgelegt
und durch Interventionen, also An- und Verkäufe
am Devisenmarkt, aufrechterhalten.
The currency "appreciates". As soon as demand
subsides, the exchange rate falls and the currency
"depreciates". The euro and other major currencies
have "floating" exchange rates with other
currencies which are formed freely in the market
without state intervention and can vary from day
to day, even from second to second. In a "fixed"
exchange rate regime, the exchange rate is
pegged by the state and is maintained through
intervention, ie purchases and sales in the forex
market.
100

CONTENTS

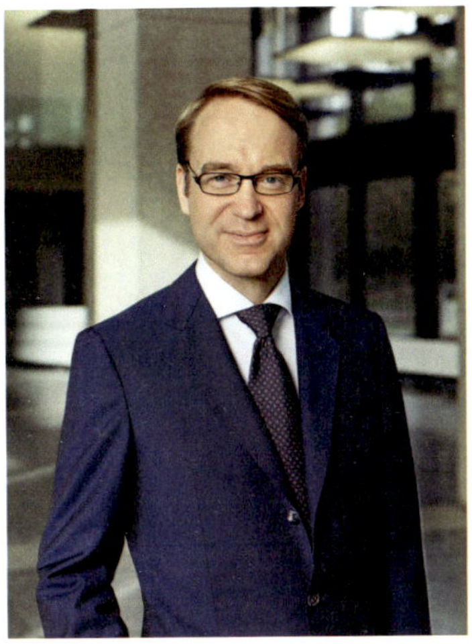

FOREWORD

The Money Museum of the Deutsche Bundesbank invites visitors to learn the basics about money and the tasks of a central bank. The exhibition covers a wide spectrum from the first coins to today's money held on a bank account, known as book money. Historical experience shows us that money can only function properly as a medium of exchange, unit of account and store of value if its value remains stable over time. And this requires a functioning monetary system and states and institutions with a commitment to stability.

As a central bank, we have a vested interest in ensuring that the general public not only has an abstract awareness of monetary stability but appreciates its specific benefits. Understanding a monetary policy which is oriented to price stability breeds confidence. It is public confidence in our stability policy which forms the basis for the backing we enjoy, and which is so important for our work. The exhibition will therefore explain central banks' tasks in a detailed and illustrative manner and show specifically what the Deutsche Bundesbank is doing at the national, European and global levels to further the cause of stable money.

This museum guide is not a replacement for a personal visit to the Money Museum. The experience of this venue for interactive learning and experience, with its exciting multidimensional stagings, cannot be compressed between the covers of a book. What this book can do, however, is document the exhibition's essential content. This makes it a richly illustrated, easy-to-understand guide which conveys experiences from the millennia-old history of money and explains how our money functions today.

I hope that this book will offer you, dear readers, many new things to discover, and that it will awaken your curiosity and interest in the world of money and encourage you to visit our Money Museum in Frankfurt am Main.

Frankfurt am Main, March 2017

Dr. Jens Weidmann
President of the Deutsche Bundesbank

GUIDE

ⓘ INFORMATION

1 STARTING POINT

2 **CASH**
— CASH TODAY
- - - CASH IN THE PAST
3 MONEY CABINET

4 **BOOK MONEY**
— BOOK MONEY TODAY
- - - BOOK MONEY IN THE PAST
5 THE LANGUAGE OF MONEY

6 **MONETARY POLICY**
— MONETARY POLICY TODAY
- - - MONETARY POLICY IN THE PAST
7 INFLATION IN 1923
8 GERMAN CENTRAL BANK

9 **GLOBAL MONEY**
— GLOBAL MONEY TODAY
- - - GLOBAL MONEY IN THE PAST
10 ECONOMIC AND MONETARY UNION (EMU)
11 CURRENT AFFAIRS WINDOW
12 "WORLDS OF MONEY" (360° CINEMA)

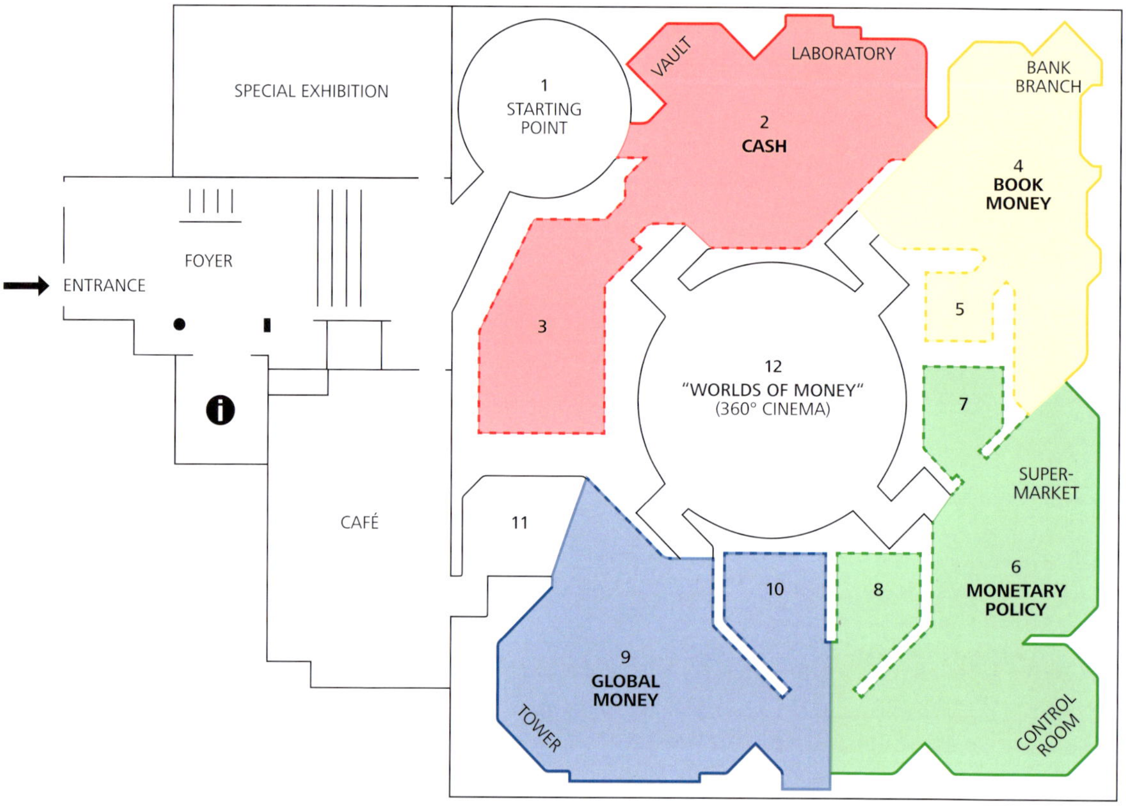

PRELIMINARY EDITORIAL REMARKS

This guide to the Money Museum is organised by room and accompanies the visitor on his or her tour through the museum's four modules: cash, book money, monetary policy and global money. At the beginning of each module, this guide introduces each theme area from a historical perspective. We then take a look at each respective cabinet before turning to the current aspects of each issue. Original texts from the museum impart economic and historical information and introduce the visitor to the world of money.

All exhibits shown here are numbered and listed in the directory of exhibits at the end of this guide.

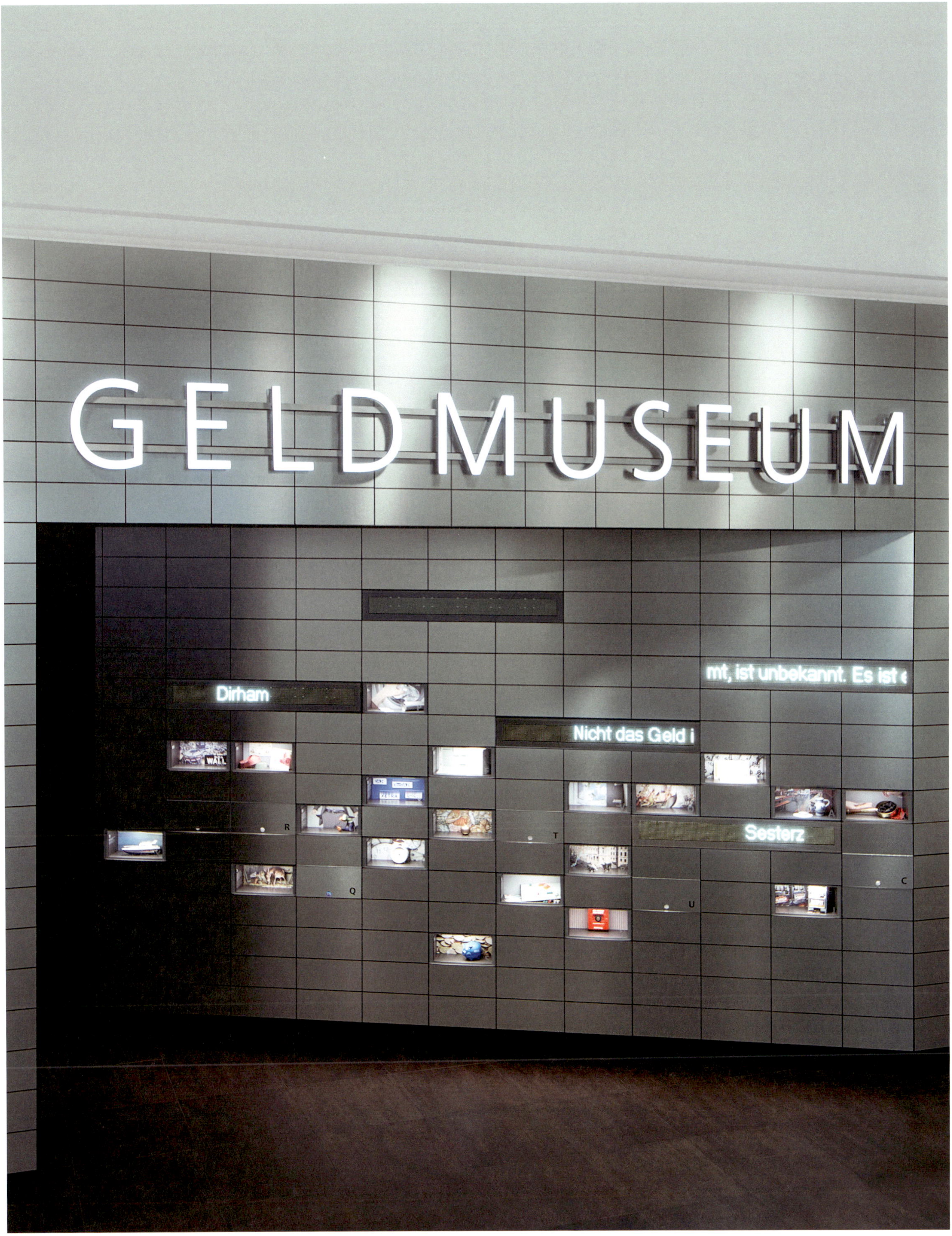
GELDMUSEUM
Dirham
mt, ist unbekannt. Es ist
Nicht das Geld i
Sesterz

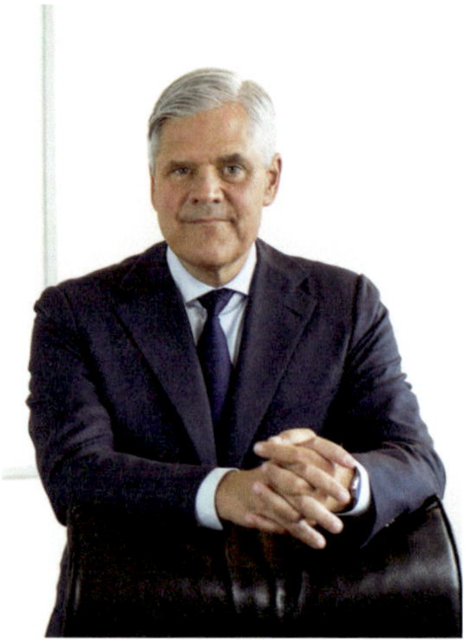

INTRODUCTION

The Bundesbank established the Money Museum back in 1999 as a venue dedicated to economic education. Its presentation of the topic of monetary policy and use of an attractive repertoire of multimedia were pioneering. After more than ten years of faithful service, however, the exhibition was slowly beginning to show its age, not just in terms of its content and design, but technically as well. This prompted the Bundesbank's Executive Board to decide in January 2010 that the Bank's Money Museum needed to be overhauled. In December 2013, following a public call for tenders, the Executive Board awarded a contract to Stuttgart-based museum planning specialists Milla & Partner to design and implement an exhibition space that best conveyed the Money Museum concept developed by the Bundesbank.

After three years of intense cooperation between Bundesbank experts and more than a dozen external firms, the Money Museum reopened its doors on 17 December 2016. I wish to thank all those who have contributed to the creation of this unique venue for learning and experience for their dedication and hard work.

The overriding message of the new exhibition is the importance of stable money for the economy and society at large. Visitors are invited to understand why stable money is so important and what a central bank does, and episodes from history encourage them to reflect critically on what they experience. A central bank's activities can be somewhat abstract, so the exhibition makes them more approachable by embedding them in everyday situations that visitors will probably encounter in real life (for example, a bank branch, an automated teller machine, a supermarket, a basket of goods and a bureau de change). Individual display cases bring money-related themes to life for children. More than 60 interactive media stations located throughout the exhibition are fun and entertaining features that provide in-depth information on particular topics.

Before visitors enter the exhibition itself, a number of small display cases and banners invite them to play an alphabetical word association game on the topic of money. They then enter the first part of the museum proper, a circular room which outlines the basic functions of money – information which is expanded upon later in the tour. The tour leads visitors through the four themed areas: "Cash", "Book money", "Monetary policy" and "Global money". In each one, a caption on the outer wall of the tour route explains the current and general context and illustrates the central bank's tasks in that particular field. The interior wall, meanwhile, explores the theme from a historical perspective.

The "Cash" area deals with banknotes and coins, and it displays the latest series of euro banknotes and euro coins. A laboratory challenges visitors to find the counterfeit and investigate whether banknotes are genuine or fakes. The "Book money" area, which is made up to look like a bank branch, covers the topic of non-cash money, payments and banks. It explains how banks create money and outlines banking supervision. The "Monetary policy" themed area is divided into two sections. The first uses a supermarket scene to illustrate prices, price developments and the importance of price stability. The second, which resembles a control room, encourages visitors to understand the monetary policy tasks, objectives and instruments of the Eurosystem. The fourth and final themed area, "Global money", takes a look at other currencies, exchange rates and reserve assets. It offers visitors insights into the international financial system and explains why international cooperation is so crucial for financial stability. At the centre of each themed area is what is known as a supersign, which offers a "speed read" of the key issues and messages in each area.

The museum boasts dedicated spaces (cabinets) which present individual topics in greater detail and provide an immersive ex-

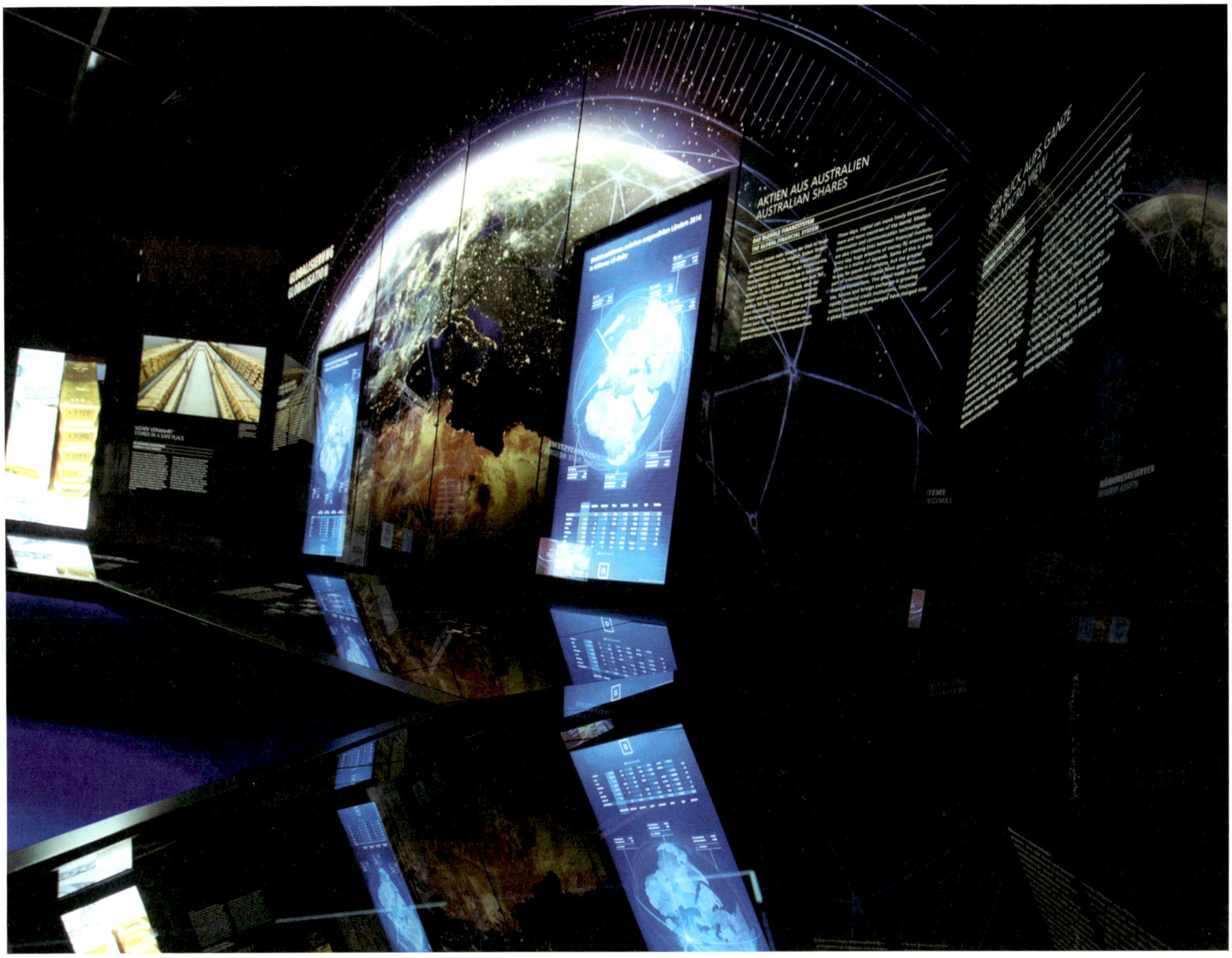

perience for visitors. One exhibition highlight is the money cabinet, which contains important and outstanding exhibits from the Bundesbank's collection of coins to document the history of money. The other cabinets explain the origins of the banking industry in the Middle Ages, Germany's encounter with hyperinflation in 1923, the history of German central banks and the road to European economic and monetary union.

Further highlights of the exhibition include the "banknote swarm", banknotes from all over the world encased in large glass walls, and a gold bar that visitors can touch. At the heart of the exhibition tour lies the 360° "Money Worlds" cinema. Three films use stimulating and thought-provoking elements to immerse visitors in different experiences and challenge them to reflect on, question and discuss what they see. The tour concludes with a large monitor (the "Current Affairs Window"), which flashes up the latest developments in the field of money and concerning the tasks of central banks. The exit then guides visitors into the café and museum shop.

The exhibition is ideal for self-directed visits. By arrangement, visitors can enhance their museum experience by making use of educational services such as guided tours, discovery tours and workshops, and financial literacy talks for school groups and students.

Dr. Andreas Dombret
Member of the Executive Board
of the Deutsche Bundesbank

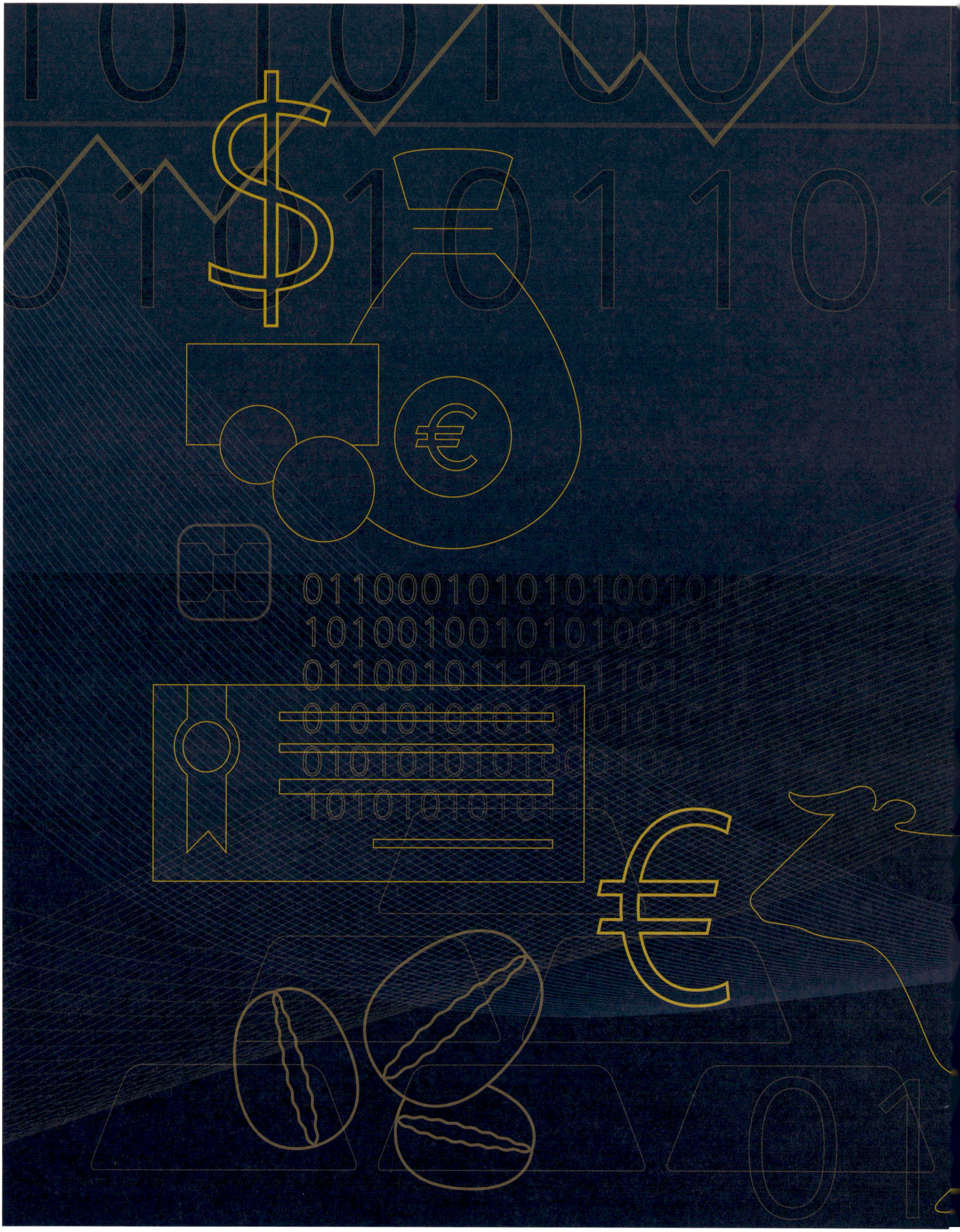

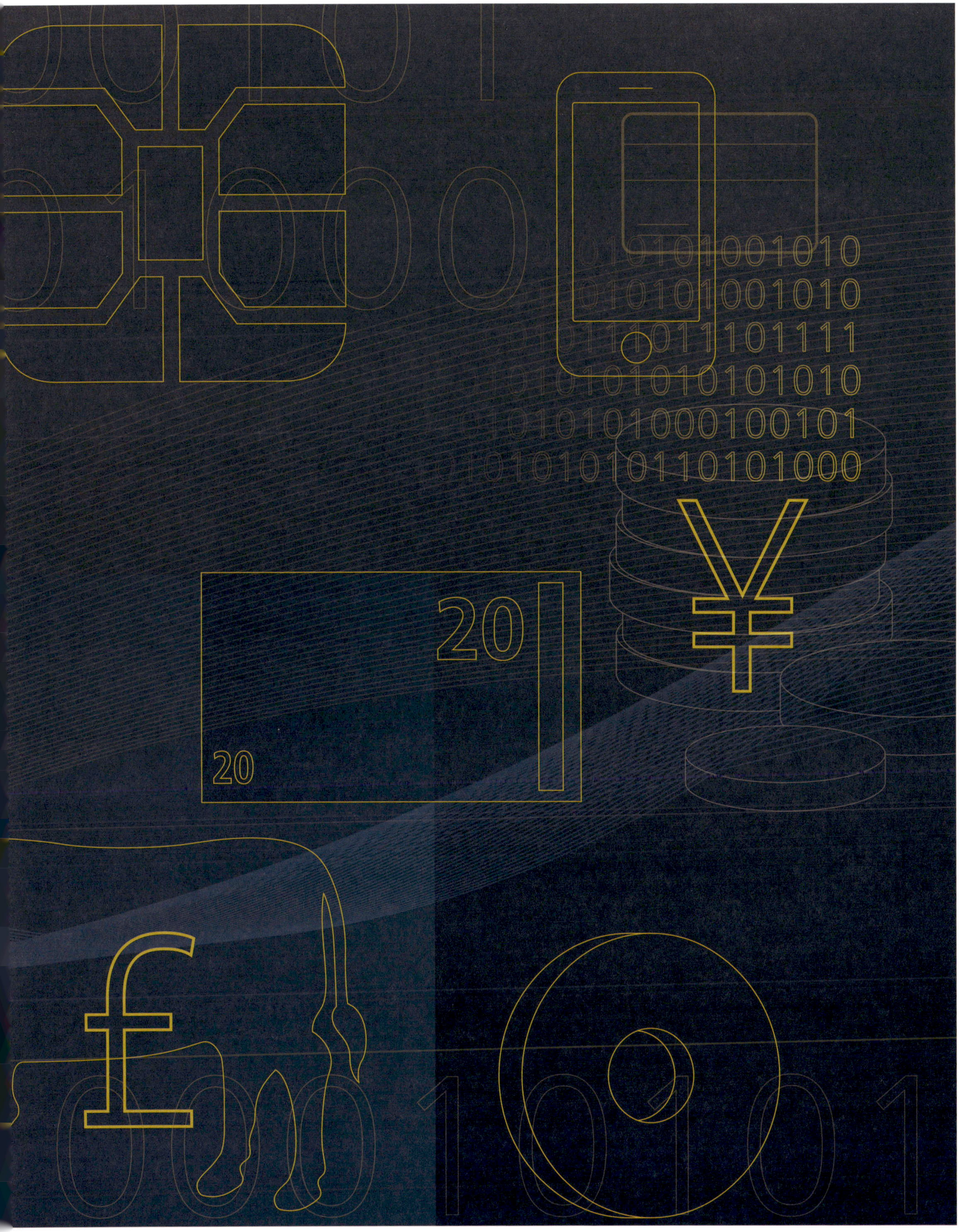

WHAT IS MONEY?

MONEY IS WHAT COUNTS

Money is something we meet in every corner of life. It's the generally accepted means of exchange and payment.

Little is known about the origins of money. Some experts believe it has its roots in religious offerings, others in barter trade. For centuries, valuables like gold, silver, salt or certain shells served as money. The coins and banknotes we use today have little material value of their own, while the money in our bank accounts consists of little more than bits and bytes.

It doesn't really matter what money is made of, or what form it takes. All that counts is that it is accepted as a medium of exchange, unit of account and store of value. This can only work if people trust money.

MEDIUM OF EXCHANGE

Before the days of money, people exchanged one good for another. But bartering, as it was known, wasn't easy. Unless a direct exchange could be found, barter chains sometimes got quite long before everyone got what they needed. Pretty soon, people came up with the idea of using money as a generally accepted medium for their trading. Money makes it easier to exchange goods, and it supports trade.

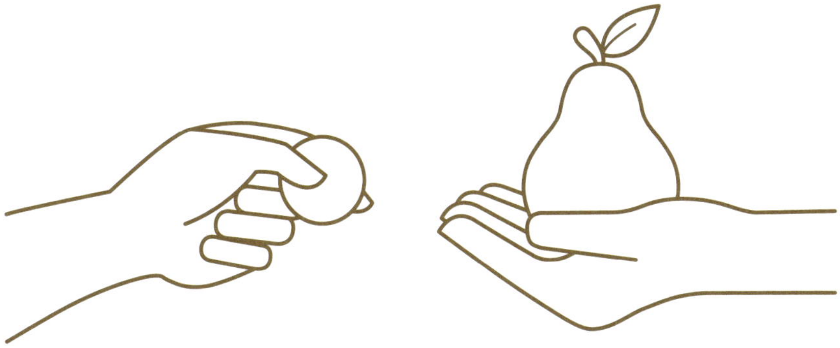

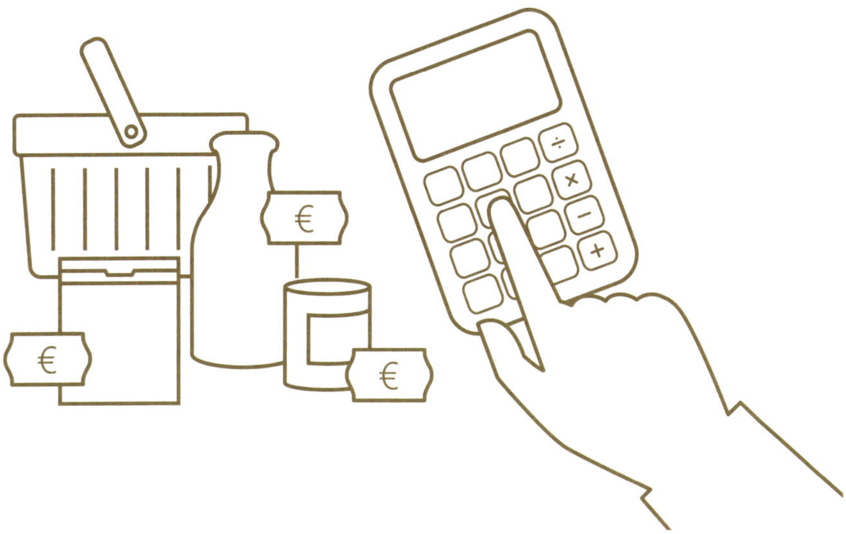

UNIT OF ACCOUNT

Money is vitally important in our economy because it is a unit of account that lets us compare the value of goods. A unit of account, moreover, lets us compare very different things – the price of labour with the price of a machine, say. Money can also be used to calculate the costs of manufacturing a car or a country's national product.

STORE OF VALUE

Some of us want to store money to spend it in the future or somewhere else. Money gives us the flexibility to do these things. It's the lubricant greasing our modern economy. To serve as a store of value, money needs to be durable and stable in value. Money nowadays has no material value, so it's all about maintaining the nominal value. It's the job of central banks to keep the value of money stable.

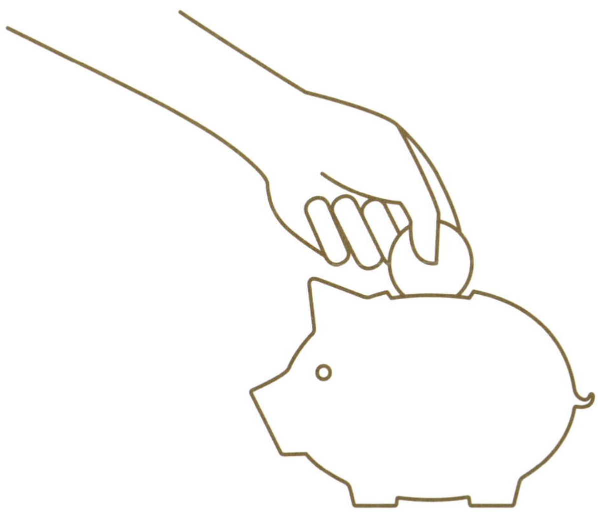

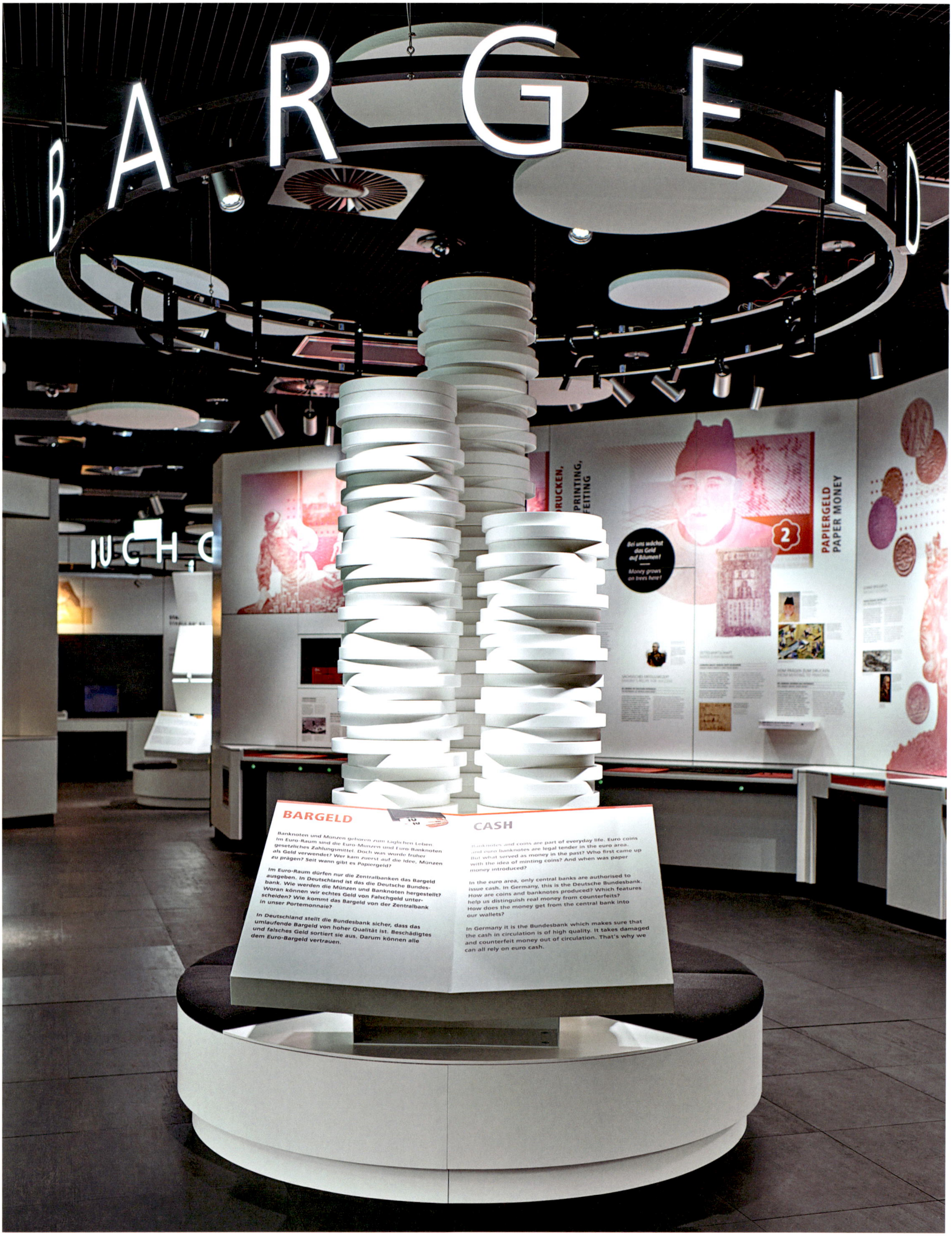
BARGELD
PAPIERGELD
PAPER MONEY
Bei uns wächst das Geld auf Bäumen!
Money grows on trees here!
BARGELD
Banknoten und Münzen gehören zum täglichen Leben.
Im Euro-Raum sind die Euro-Münzen und Euro-Banknoten
gesetzliches Zahlungsmittel. Doch was wurde früher
als Geld verwendet? Wer kam zuerst auf die Idee, Münzen
zu prägen? Seit wann gibt es Papiergeld?
Im Euro-Raum dürfen nur die Zentralbanken das Bargeld
ausgeben. In Deutschland ist das die Deutsche Bundes-
bank. Wie werden die Münzen und Banknoten hergestellt?
Woran können wir echtes Geld von Falschgeld unter-
scheiden? Wie kommt das Bargeld von der Zentralbank
in unser Portemonnaie?
In Deutschland stellt die Bundesbank sicher, dass das
umlaufende Bargeld von hoher Qualität ist. Beschädigtes
und falsches Geld sortiert sie aus. Darum können alle
dem Euro-Bargeld vertrauen.
CASH
Banknotes and coins are part of everyday life. Euro coins
and euro banknotes are legal tender in the euro area.
But what served as money in the past? Who first came up
with the idea of minting coins? And when was paper
money introduced?
In the euro area, only central banks are authorised to
issue cash. In Germany, this is the Deutsche Bundesbank.
How are coins and banknotes produced? Which features
help us distinguish real money from counterfeits?
How does the money get from the central bank into
our wallets?
In Germany it is the Bundesbank which makes sure that
the cash in circulation is of high quality. It takes damaged
and counterfeit money out of circulation. That's why we
can all rely on euro cash.

BANKNOTES AND COINS ARE PART OF EVERYDAY LIFE. EURO COINS AND EURO BANKNOTES ARE LEGAL TENDER IN THE EURO AREA. BUT WHAT SERVED AS MONEY IN THE PAST? WHO FIRST CAME UP WITH THE IDEA OF MINTING COINS? AND WHEN WAS PAPER MONEY INTRODUCED?

IN THE EURO AREA, ONLY CENTRAL BANKS ARE AUTHORISED TO ISSUE CASH. IN GERMANY, THIS IS THE DEUTSCHE BUNDESBANK. HOW ARE COINS AND BANKNOTES PRODUCED? WHICH FEATURES HELP US DISTINGUISH REAL MONEY FROM COUNTERFEITS? HOW DOES THE MONEY GET FROM THE CENTRAL BANK INTO OUR WALLETS?

IN GERMANY IT IS THE BUNDESBANK WHICH MAKES SURE THAT THE CASH IN CIRCULATION IS OF HIGH QUALITY. IT TAKES DAMAGED AND COUNTERFEIT MONEY OUT OF CIRCULATION. THAT'S WHY WE CAN ALL RELY ON EURO CASH.

CASH

"IF ANYONE IS CROESUS AROUND HERE, IT'S ME!"

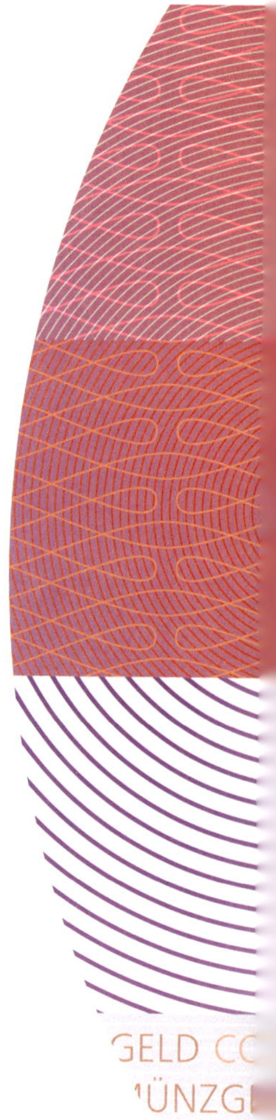

A LOOK BACK THROUGH HISTORY

The historical section of the exhibition begins with the birth of the coin in Asia Minor in the 7th century BC. It illustrates the time-honoured art of minting and, through numerous exhibits, presents an illustrative introduction to the history of coins up until the beginning of the modern era.

The history of paper money in Europe is much shorter. This continent only knew coins until into the 17th century, even though Marco Polo had already reported the invention of paper money in China. It was only the enormous weight of Swedish copper plate coins which caused a banker in Stockholm in 1661 to hit upon the following idea: to issue, in return for deposits of copper plates, paper vouchers – which were soon used as scrip. Advances in paper manufacturing and printing technology have made banknotes ever safer against counterfeiting over the centuries. However, wherever there is cash, counterfeits are never far away. The historical section is rounded out by spectacular cases of private and government counterfeiting.

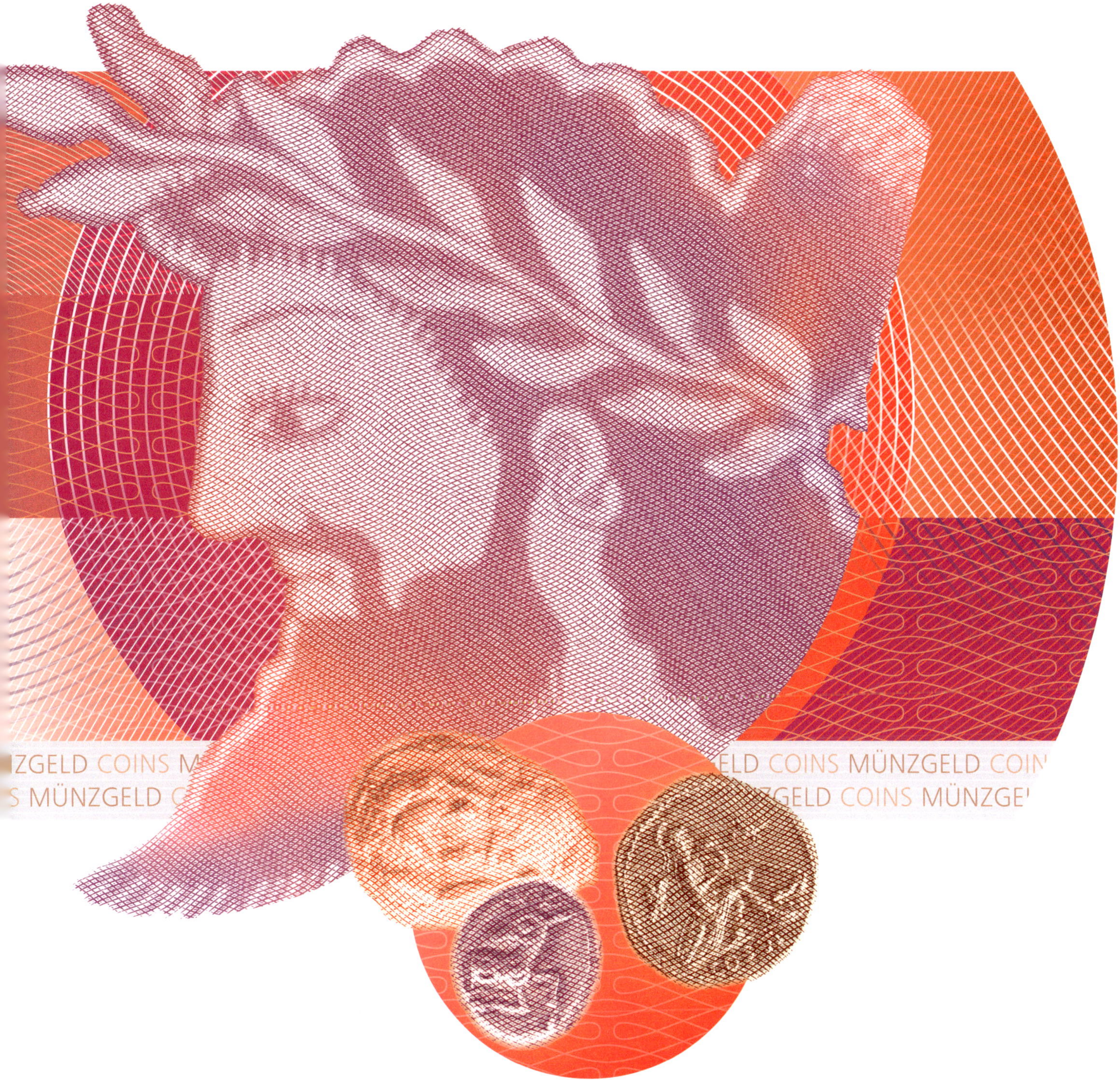
ZGELD COINS M
S MÜNZGELD C
ELD COINS MÜNZGELD COIN
ZGELD COINS MÜNZGE

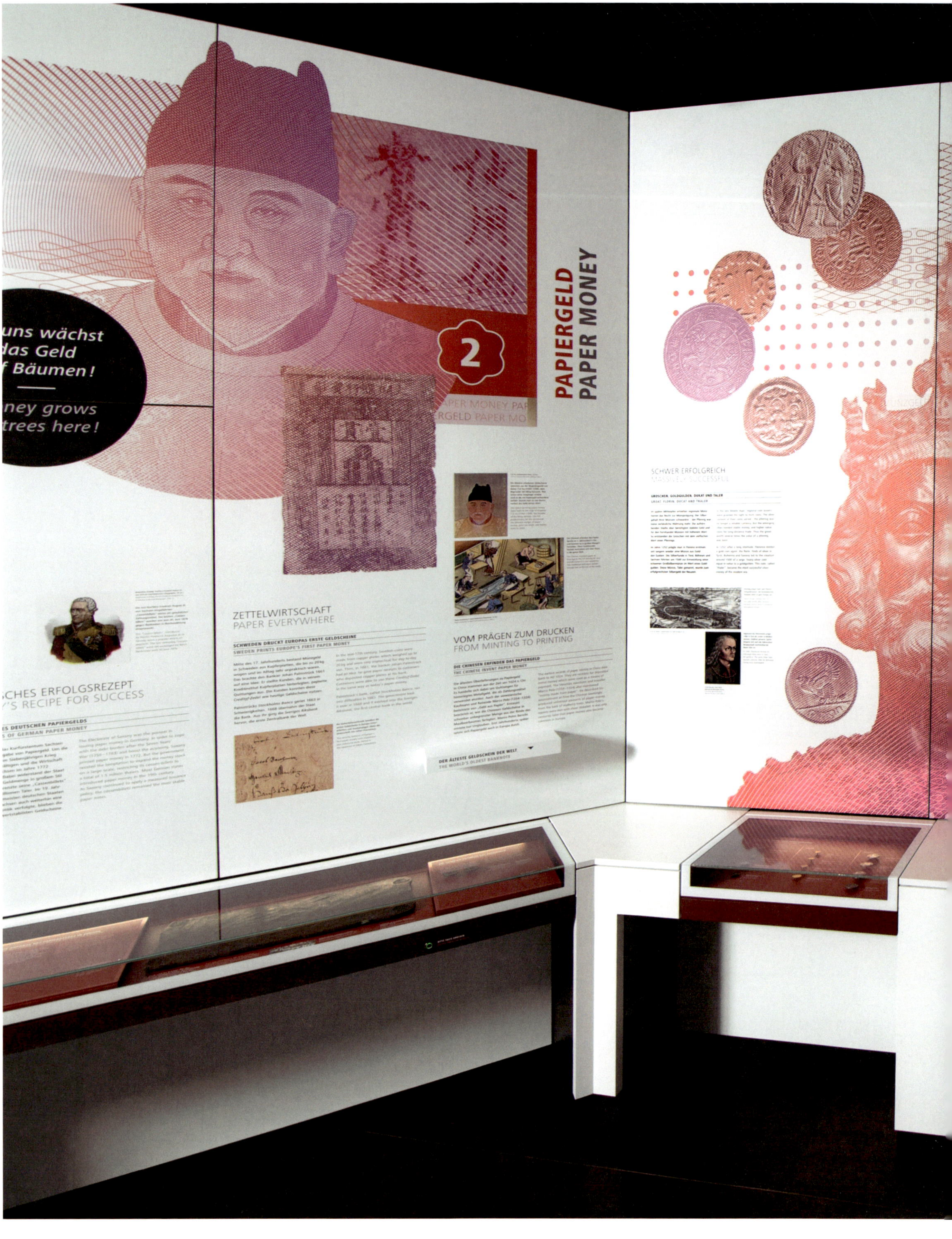
uns wächst
das Geld
f Bäumen!
ney grows
trees here!
2
PAPIERGELD
PAPER MONEY
SCHWER ERFOLGREICH
ZETTELWIRTSCHAFT
PAPER EVERYWHERE
VOM PRÄGEN ZUM DRUCKEN
FROM MINTING TO PRINTING
SCHES ERFOLGSREZEPT
Y'S RECIPE FOR SUCCESS

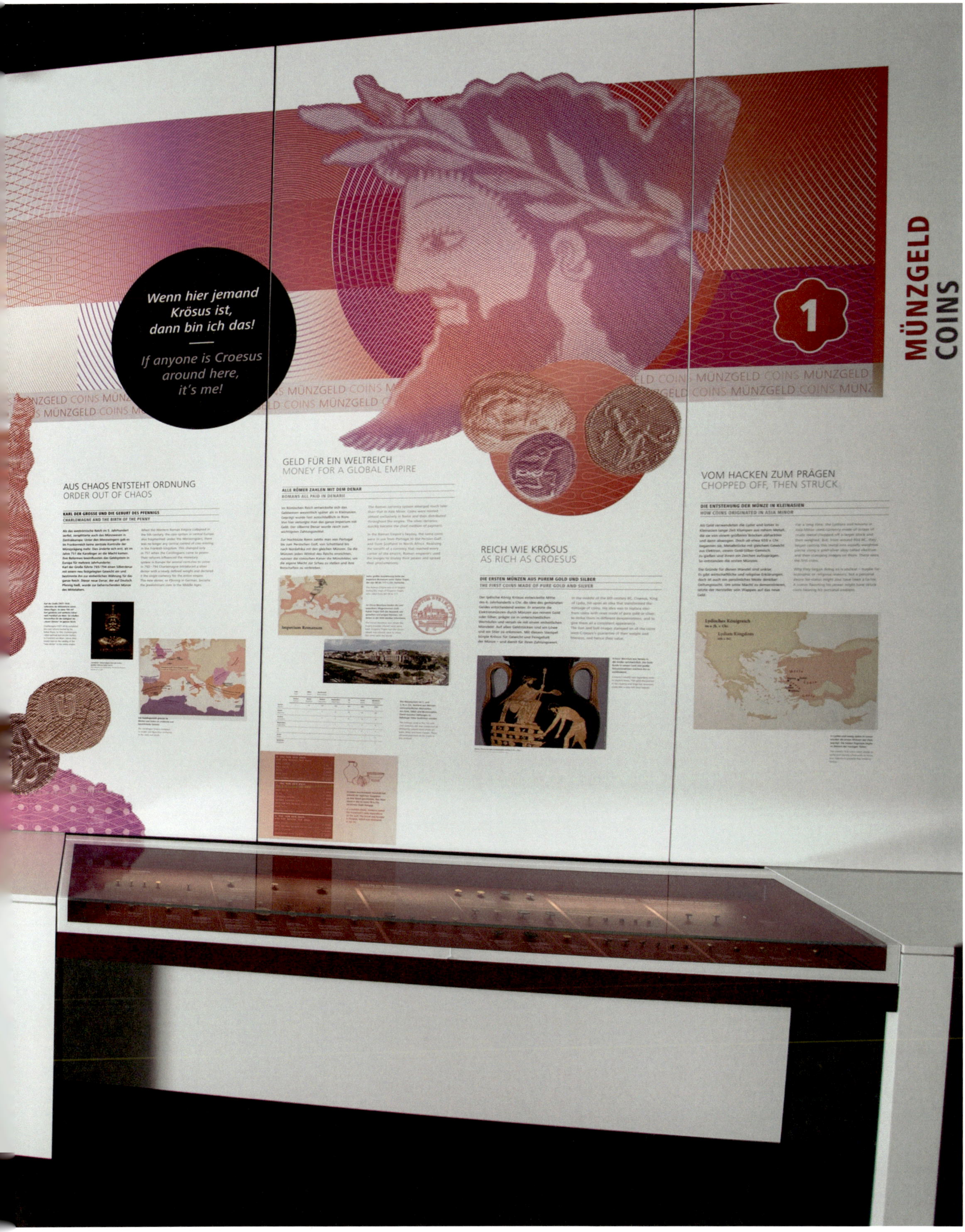
MÜNZGELD
COINS
1
Wenn hier jemand Krösus ist, dann bin ich das!
If anyone is Croesus around here, it's me!
MÜNZGELD COINS MÜNZGELD COINS
AUS CHAOS ENTSTEHT ORDNUNG
ORDER OUT OF CHAOS
KARL DER GROSSE UND DIE GEBURT DES PFENNIGS
CHARLEMAGNE AND THE BIRTH OF THE PENNY
GELD FÜR EIN WELTREICH
MONEY FOR A GLOBAL EMPIRE
ALLE RÖMER ZAHLEN MIT DEM DENAR
ROMANS ALL PAID IN DENARII
REICH WIE KRÖSUS
AS RICH AS CROESUS
DIE ERSTEN MÜNZEN AUS PUREM GOLD UND SILBER
THE FIRST COINS MADE OF PURE GOLD AND SILVER
VOM HACKEN ZUM PRÄGEN
CHOPPED OFF, THEN STRUCK
DIE ENTSTEHUNG DER MÜNZE IN KLEINASIEN
HOW COINS ORIGINATED IN ASIA MINOR

1 **ELECTRUM COIN**
CA 630 BC
(SCALE 3:1)

2 **½ STATER**
561 – 546 BC
(SCALE 3:1)

3 **⅓ STATER**
561 – 546 BC
(SCALE 3:1)

4 **DENARIUS**
148 – 149
(SCALE 2:1)

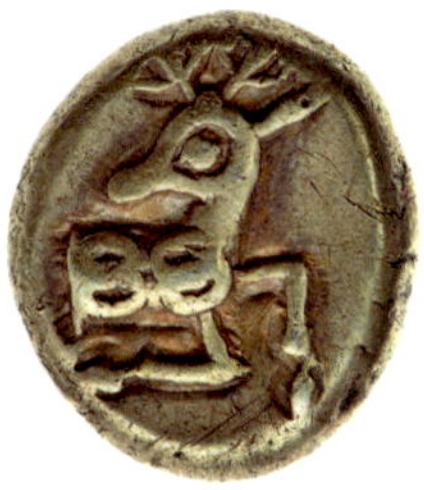

1

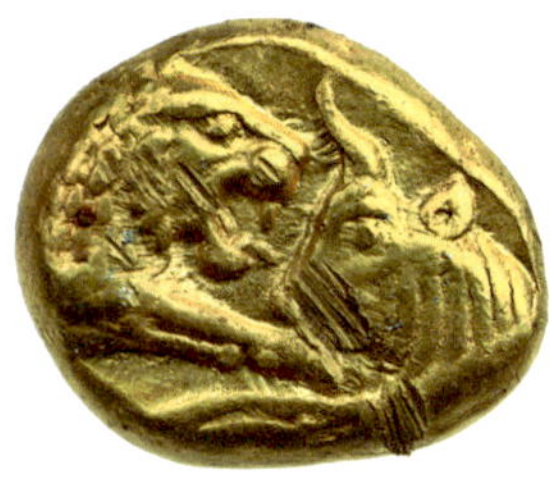

3

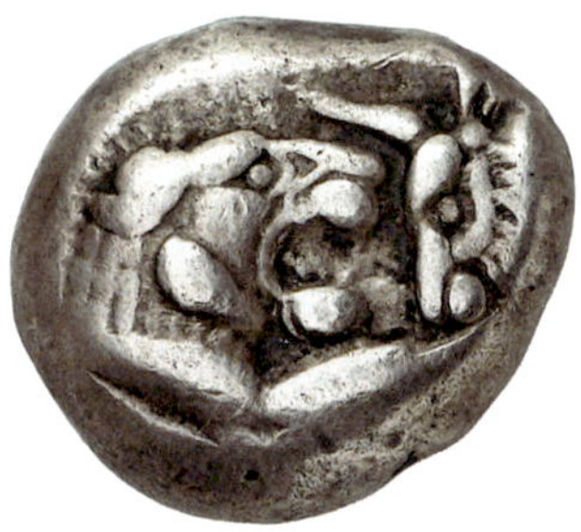

2

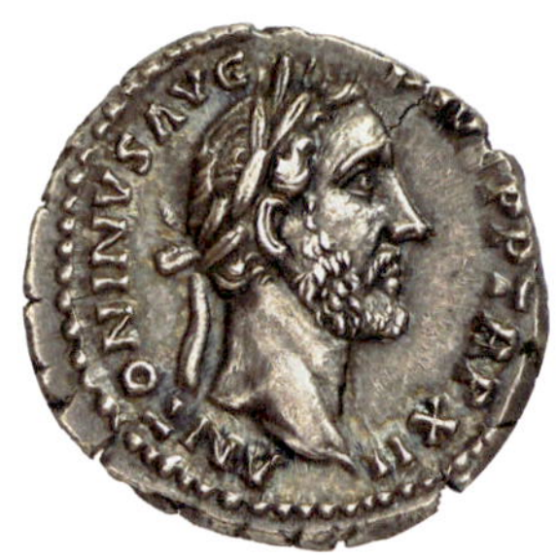

4

CHOPPED, THEN STAMPED

HOW COINS ORIGINATED IN ANATOLIA

For a long time, the Lydians and Ionians in Anatolia used currency made of scraps of crude metal chopped off a larger block and then weighed. But, from around 650 BC, they began casting this metal into equally weighted pieces using a gold-silver alloy called electrum and then stamping images on them. These were the first coins.

AS RICH AS CROESUS

THE FIRST COINS MADE OF PURE GOLD AND SILVER

In the middle of the 6th century BC, Croesus, King of Lydia, hit upon an idea that transformed the mintage of coins. His idea was to replace electrum coins with ones made of pure gold or silver, to strike them in different denominations, and to give them all a consistent appearance. The lion and bull images stamped on all the coins were Croesus's guarantee of their weight and fineness, and hence their value.

MONEY FIT FOR A GLOBAL EMPIRE

ROMANS ALL PAID IN DENARII

The Roman currency system emerged much later than that of Anatolia. Coins were minted almost exclusively in Rome and then distributed throughout the empire. The silver denarius quickly became the chief medium of payment. In the Roman Empire's heyday, denarii were in use from Portugal to the Persian Gulf, and from Scotland to North Africa.

ORDER OUT OF CHAOS

CHARLEMAGNE AND THE BIRTH OF THE PFENNIG

In 793–794 Charlemagne introduced a silver denier with a newly defined weight and declared it the single currency for the entire empire. This new denier, or pfennig in German, became the predominant coin in the Middle Ages.

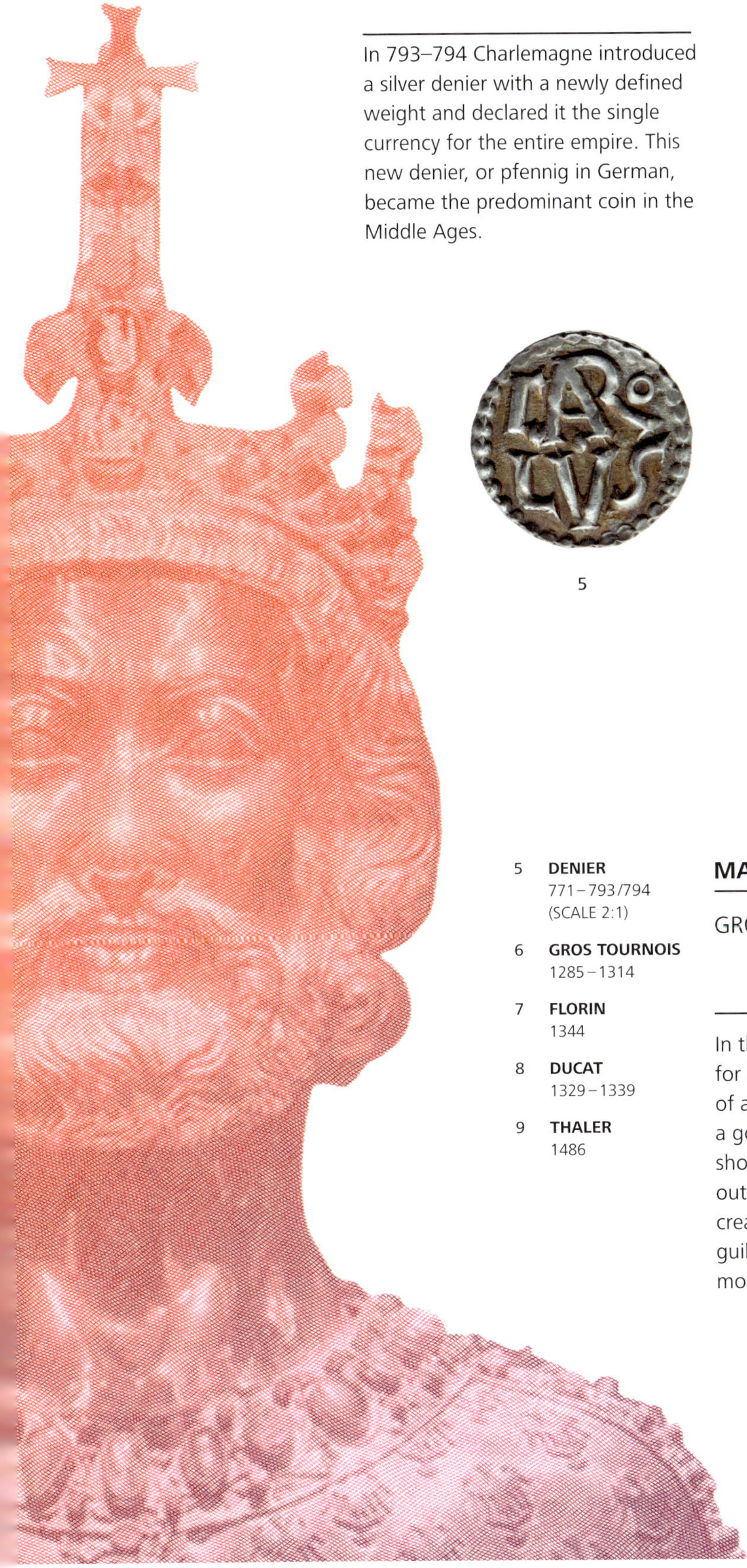

5

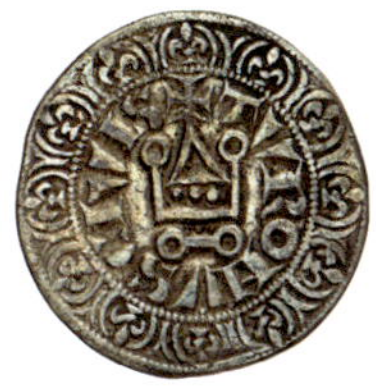

6

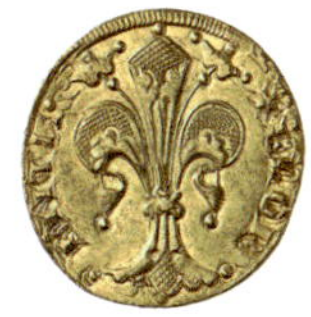

7

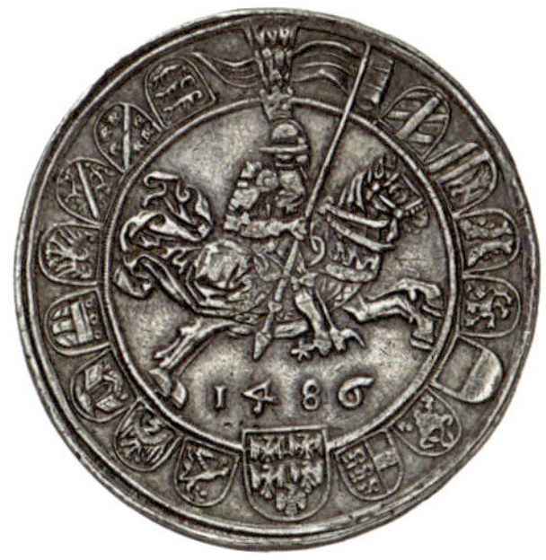

9

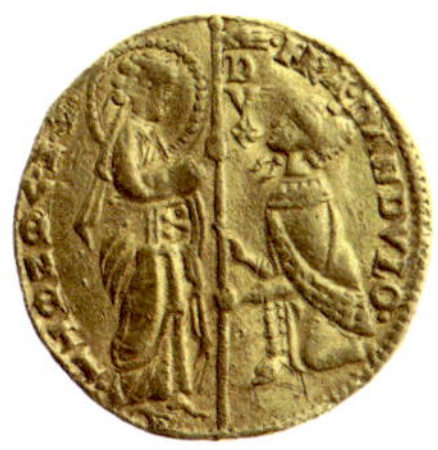

8

5 **DENIER**
771–793/794
(SCALE 2:1)

6 **GROS TOURNOIS**
1285–1314

7 **FLORIN**
1344

8 **DUCAT**
1329–1339

9 **THALER**
1486

MASSIVELY SUCCESSFUL

GROSCHEN, GUILDER, DUCAT AND THALER

In the late Middle Ages, the emerging cities needed higher-value coins for long-distance trade. Thus the groschen, worth several times the value of a pfennig, was born. In 1252, after a long interlude, Florence minted a gold coin again: the guilder. Venice began minting coins of fine gold shortly after Florence, and Venetian ducats were in circulation throughout Europe. Finds of silver in Tyrol, Bohemia and Saxony led to the creation in 1500 of a large, heavy silver coin equal in value to a gold guilder. These coins, called thalers, became the most successful silver money of the modern era.

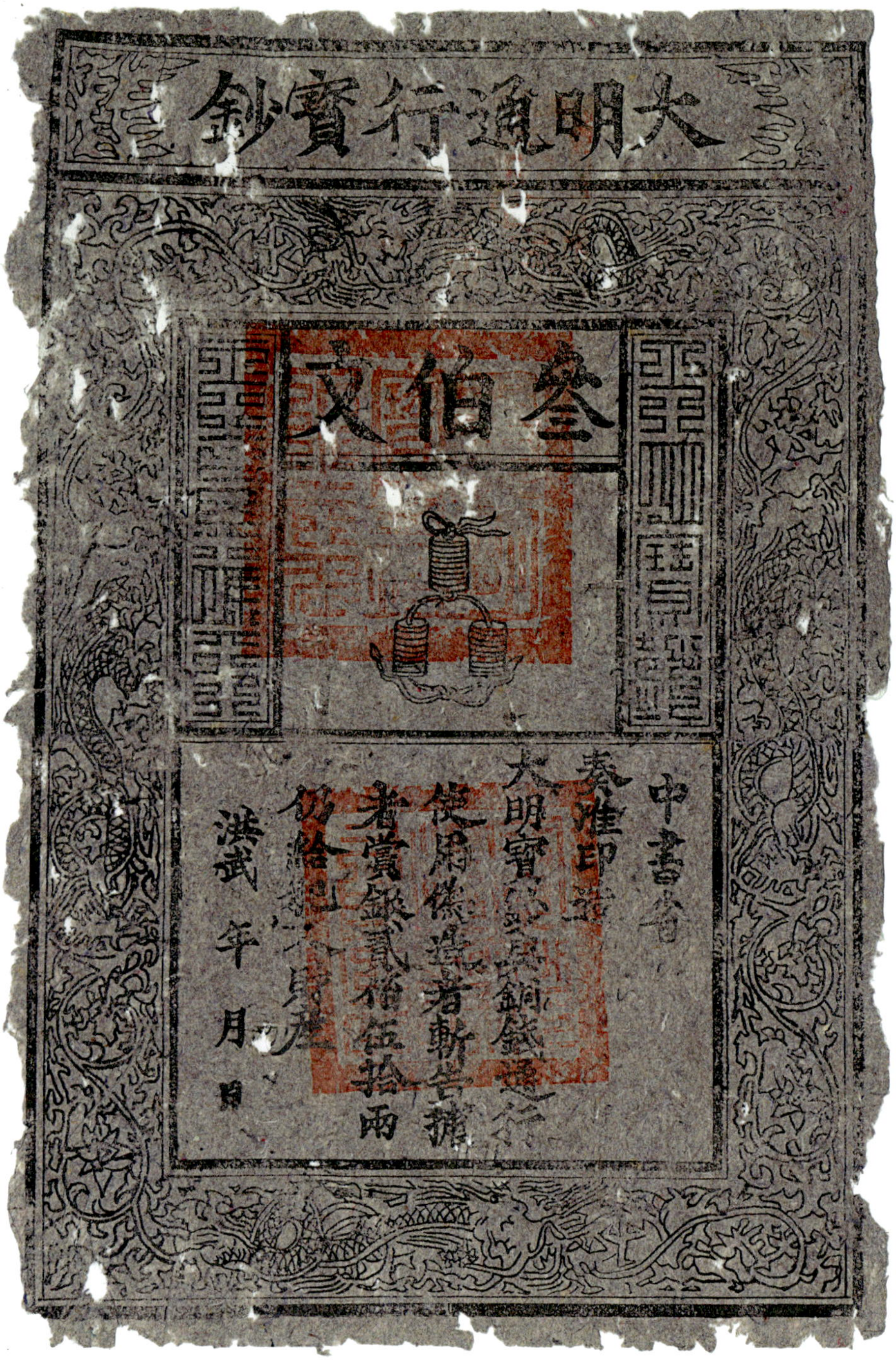

10 **300 CASH,** 1368 – 1399

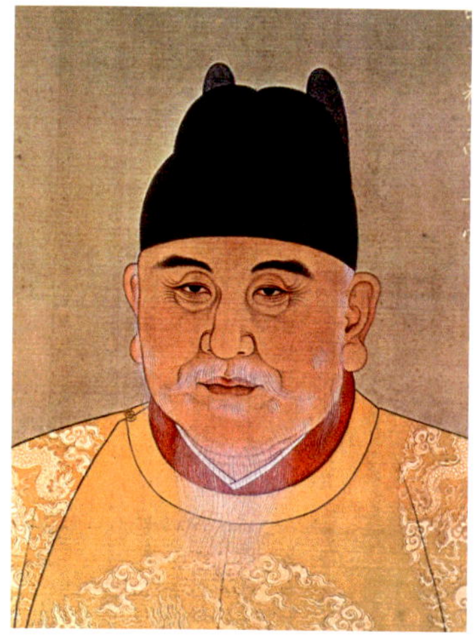

THE OLDEST SURVIVING PAPER MONEY DATES BACK TO THE REIGN OF EMPEROR T'AI TSU (1368–1398), THE FOUNDER OF THE MING DYNASTY.

FROM MINTING TO PRINTING

THE CHINESE INVENT PAPER MONEY

The earliest records of paper money in China date back to AD 1024. They are receipts for deposited metal money which were used as a means of payment. The Venetian merchant and traveller Marco Polo (1254–1324) also mentioned "money made from paper". He described his astonishment at how the Chinese seemingly produced unlimited amounts of paper money from the bark of mulberry trees. Marco Polo's reports were met with sheer disbelief. It was only centuries later that paper money also became common in Europe.

"MONEY GROWS ON TREES HERE!"

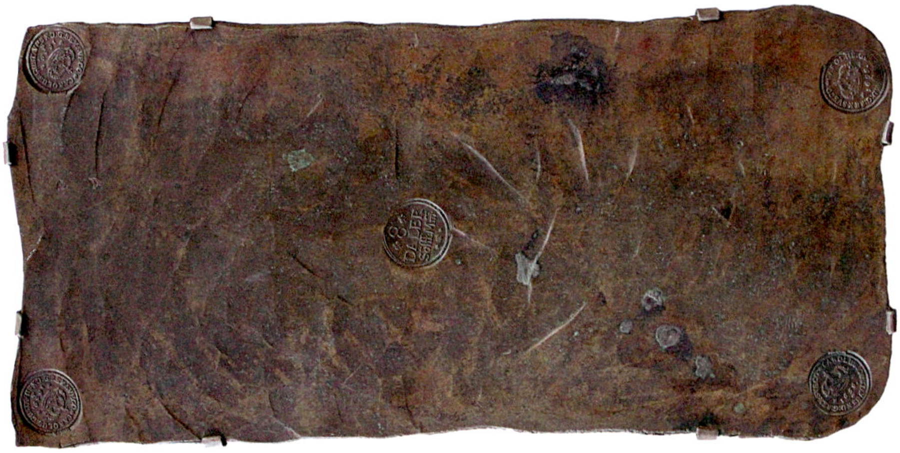

11 **8-DALER COPPER PLATE COIN**
1659, WEIGHT: 14.4 KG, SIZE 63 x 28 CM

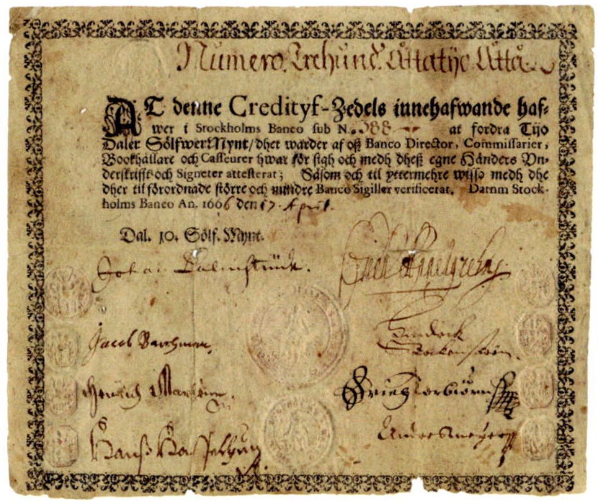

12 **10-DALER CREDITYF-ZEDEL**
1666

PAPER EVERYWHERE

SWEDEN PRINTS EUROPE'S FIRST PAPER MONEY

In the mid-17th century, Swedish coins were made from copper plates which weighed up to 20 kg and were very impractical for day-to-day use. Then, in 1661, the banker Johan Palmstruck had an idea: he gave paper receipts to customers who deposited copper plates at his bank. Customers were able to use these *Credityf-Zedel* in the same way as today's paper money. Palmstrück's bank, called Stockholms Banco, ran into difficulties in 1663. The government took it over in 1668 and it evolved into the Sveriges Riksbank, the first central bank in the world.

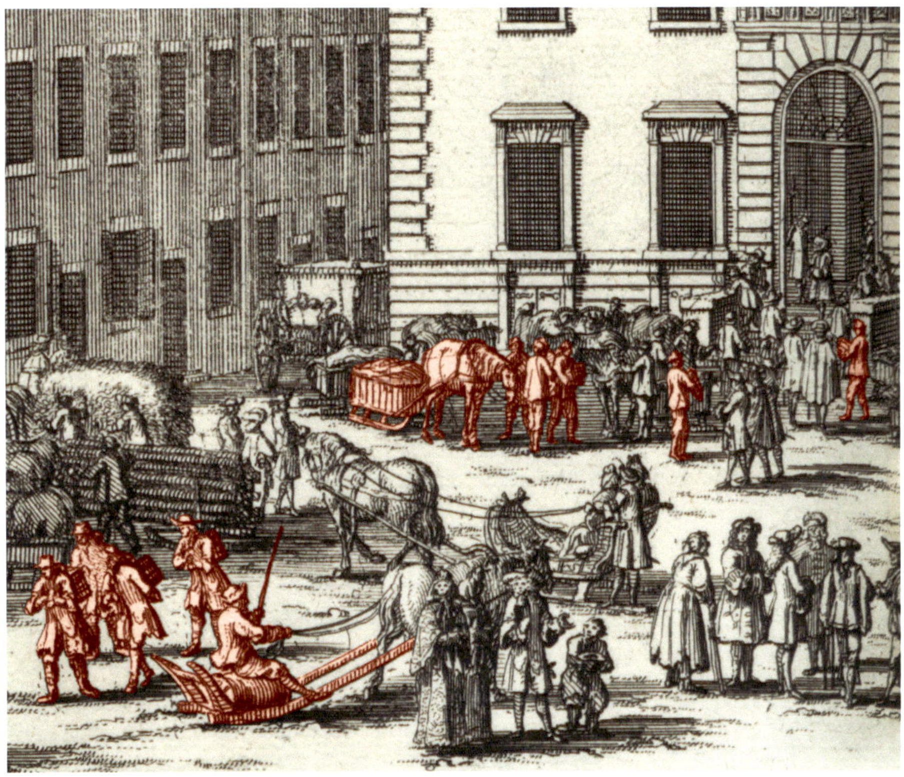

TOO BIG AND HEAVY FOR DAY-TO-DAY TRANSACTIONS: DELIVERY OF COPPER PLATE COINS TO SVERIGES RIKSBANK AT THE END OF THE 17TH CENTURY.

A 2,500 YEAR-OLD ART

THE MINTING OF COINS

The underlying principle of coin minting has not changed since antiquity: two dies with engraved images are pressed together to print a motif on a small metal plate, known as a flan or a planchet. There have, however, been a number of technological advances since then: for 2,000 years coins were minted by hand, but since the 16th century, machines have been used, making coin production invariably quicker, more precise and more counterfeit proof.

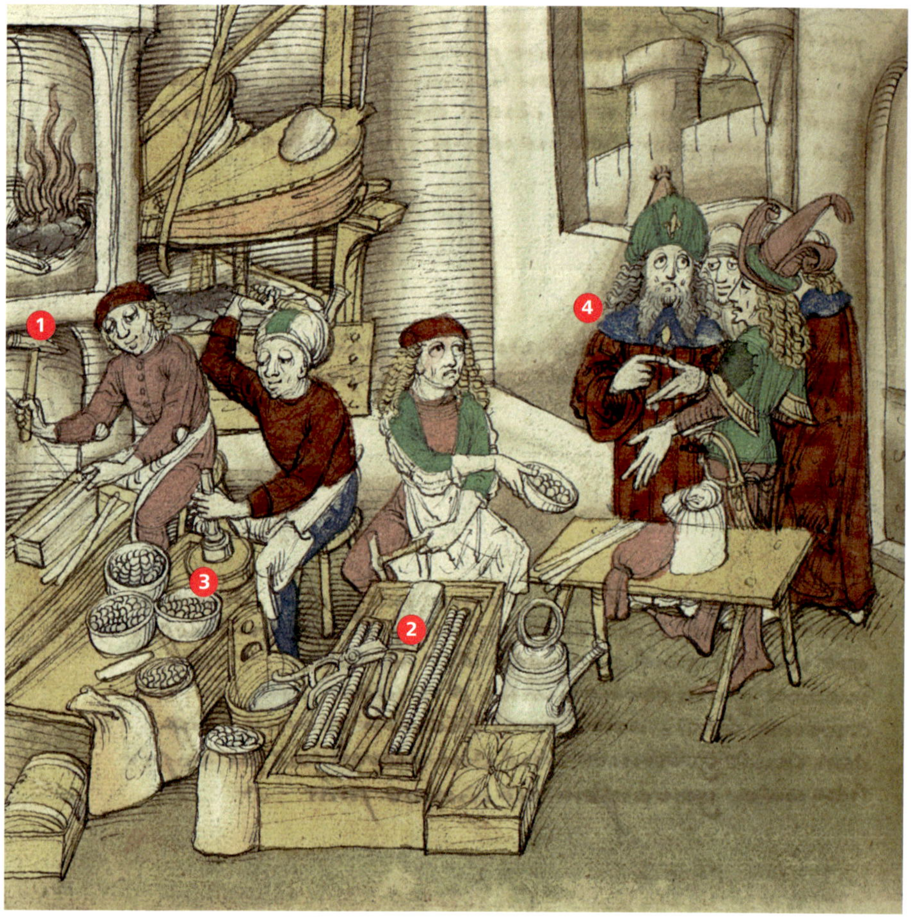

THE COIN METAL WAS CAST INTO BARS AND HAMMERED FLAT (1), FROM WHICH THE FLANS WERE CUT (2). ONCE THE COINS HAD BEEN MINTED (3), THE FINISHED COINS WERE THEN CHECKED (4).

BLOW AFTER BLOW

For centuries, coins were minted by hand. Minting coins using a hammer and anvil mostly required several people to work together: one to place the flan on the lower die – which was fixed into the anvil – and then to place the upper die on top of the flan, and another to strike the die forcefully with a hammer. Several blows were often needed.

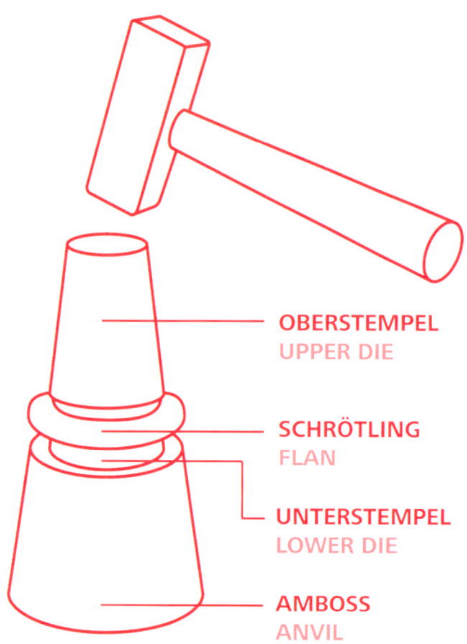

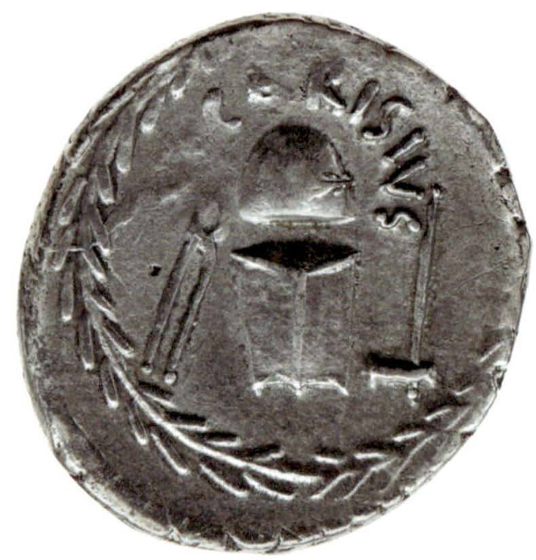

13 **THIS ROMAN DENARIUS FROM 46 BC SHOWS A SET OF MINTING TOOLS (TONGS, HAMMER AND ANVIL) AS WELL AS THE CAP OF VULCAN, GOD OF METALWORKING.**

MACHINES REPLACE MUSCLE POWER

The mid-16th century saw the emergence of the first automated coin manufacturing processes, heralding the end of the era of hand-minted coins. With the rotary press, rollers turning in opposite directions were used to imprint the coin images on metal strips. This allowed much faster minting than before. Screw presses, also known as balanciers, also emerged around this time. These worked by exerting very high pressure and were easier to operate. In the 18th century, they eventually became the norm. Industrial coin manufacturing was pioneered by Dietrich Uhlhorn with his toggle press in 1817.

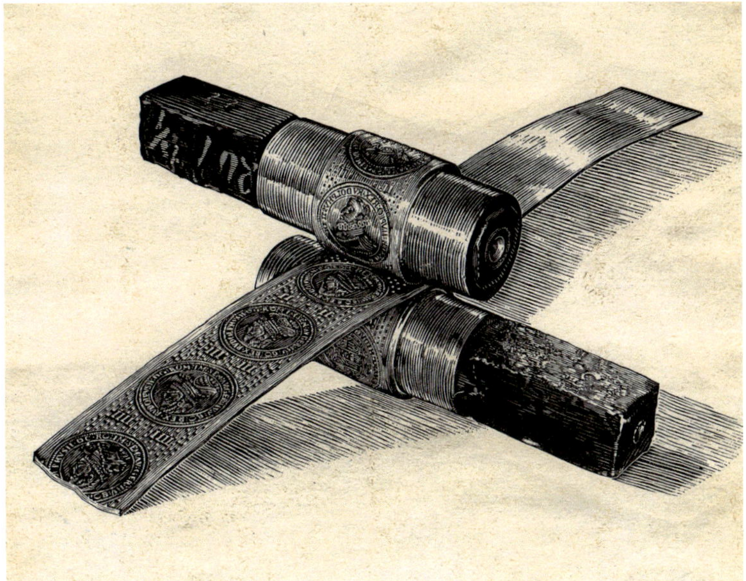

ROTARY PRESS

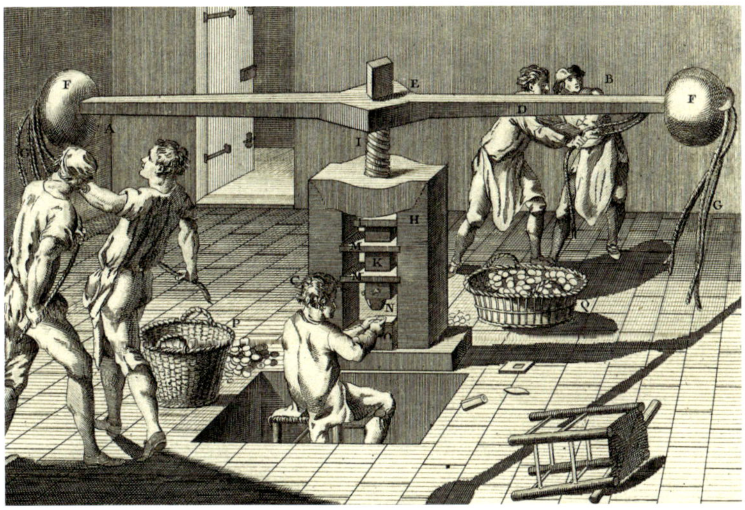

A NUMBER OF MEN ACCELERATING THE SWINGING ARM OF THE BALANCIER, WHICH TRANSFERS THE FORCE TO THE SPINDLE SCREW AND THE UPPER DIE.

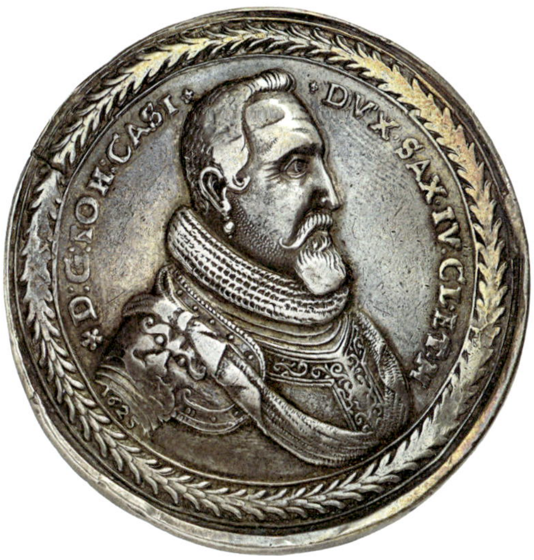

14 THIS DOUBLE THALER OF THE DUKEDOM OF SAXONY-COBURG FROM 1625 OWES ITS VERY HIGH RELIEF TO THE HIGH STAMPING PRESSURE OF THE BALANCIER. (SCALE 1,5:1)

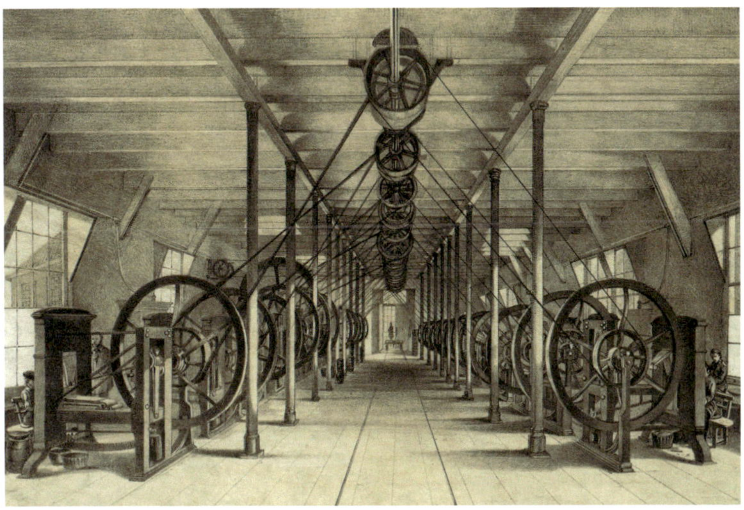

DIETRICH UHLHORN'S STEAM-POWERED TOGGLE PRESS

STEP BY STEP TOWARDS A MODERN BANKNOTE

In the race against counterfeiters, manufacturers have continuously refined paper money. In the 18th century, banknotes were still certified by means of seals and signatures. Since the 19th century, advances in paper production and printing technology turned banknotes into a highly sophisticated industrial mass product.

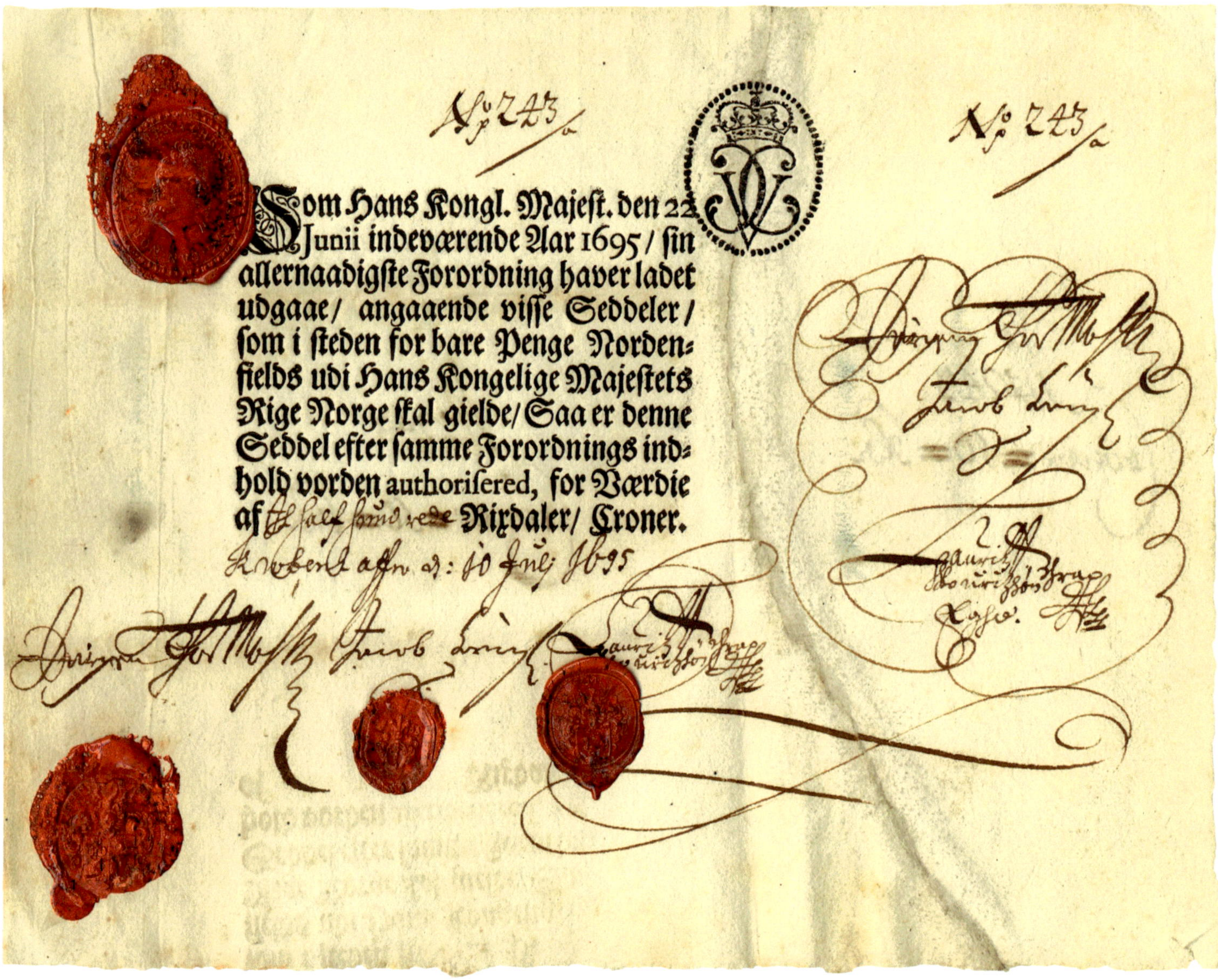

15 50 NORWEGIAN RIXDALER FROM 1695, WITH TALON RE-ATTACHED AT THE RIGHT

BANKNOTES ORIGINALLY DOCUMENTED A CLAIM TO GOLD OR SILVER COINS. TO PREVENT COUNTERFEITS, THE ISSUING BANK CUT OFF PART OF THE PRINTED EDGE OF ITS NOTES. THIS "TALON" WAS RETAINED BY THE BANK. IF SOMEONE BROUGHT THE NOTE BACK TO THE BANK, THE BANK CHECKED WHETHER THE "TALON" MATCHED THE NOTE.

AT THE END OF THE 18TH CENTURY, BANKNOTES BEGAN TO FEATURE COMPLEX ORNAMENTAL AND FIGURATIVE DESIGNS. WATERMARKS PROVIDED ADDITIONAL PROTECTION.

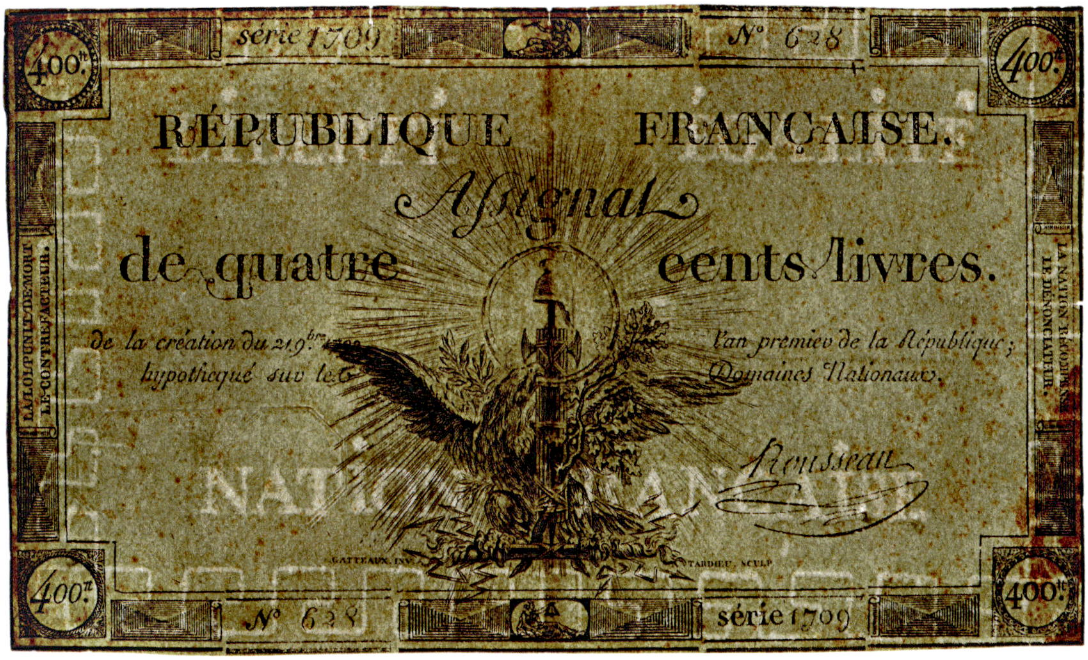

16 **FRANCE, 400 LIVRES**
1792, WATERMARK VISIBLE

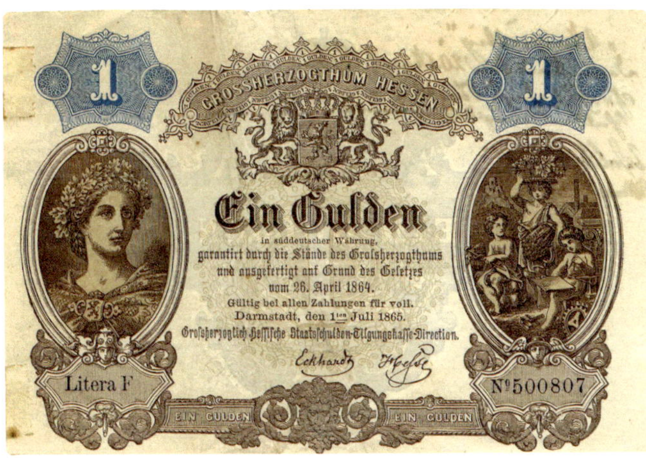

17 **HESSE, 1 GULDEN,** 1865 (FRONT)

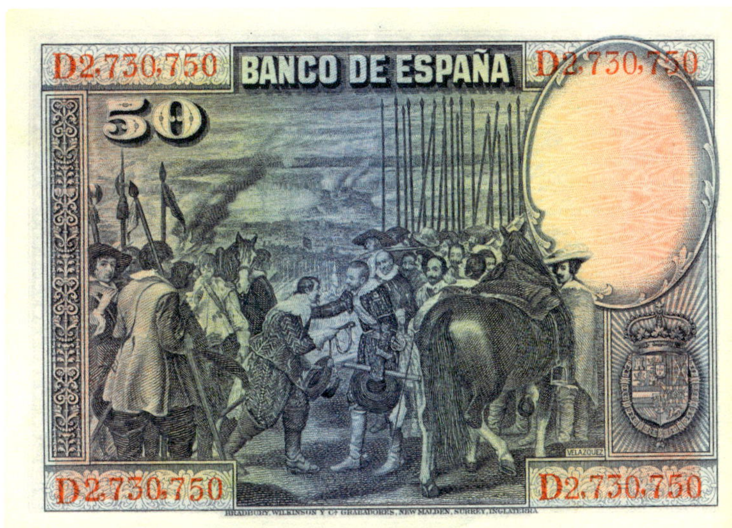

18 **SPAIN, 50 PESETAS,** 1928 (REVERSE)

WITH THE INTRODUCTION OF DIESTAMPING IN THE 19TH CENTURY, ENGRAVERS WERE ABLE TO INCORPORATE FINE ORNAMENTAL ELEMENTS, ESPECIALLY GUILLOCHÉ PATTERNS, INTO BANKNOTES. THEY EMPLOYED A VARIETY OF INKS AND ALSO PRINTED ELABORATE DESIGNS ON THE REVERSE SIDES.

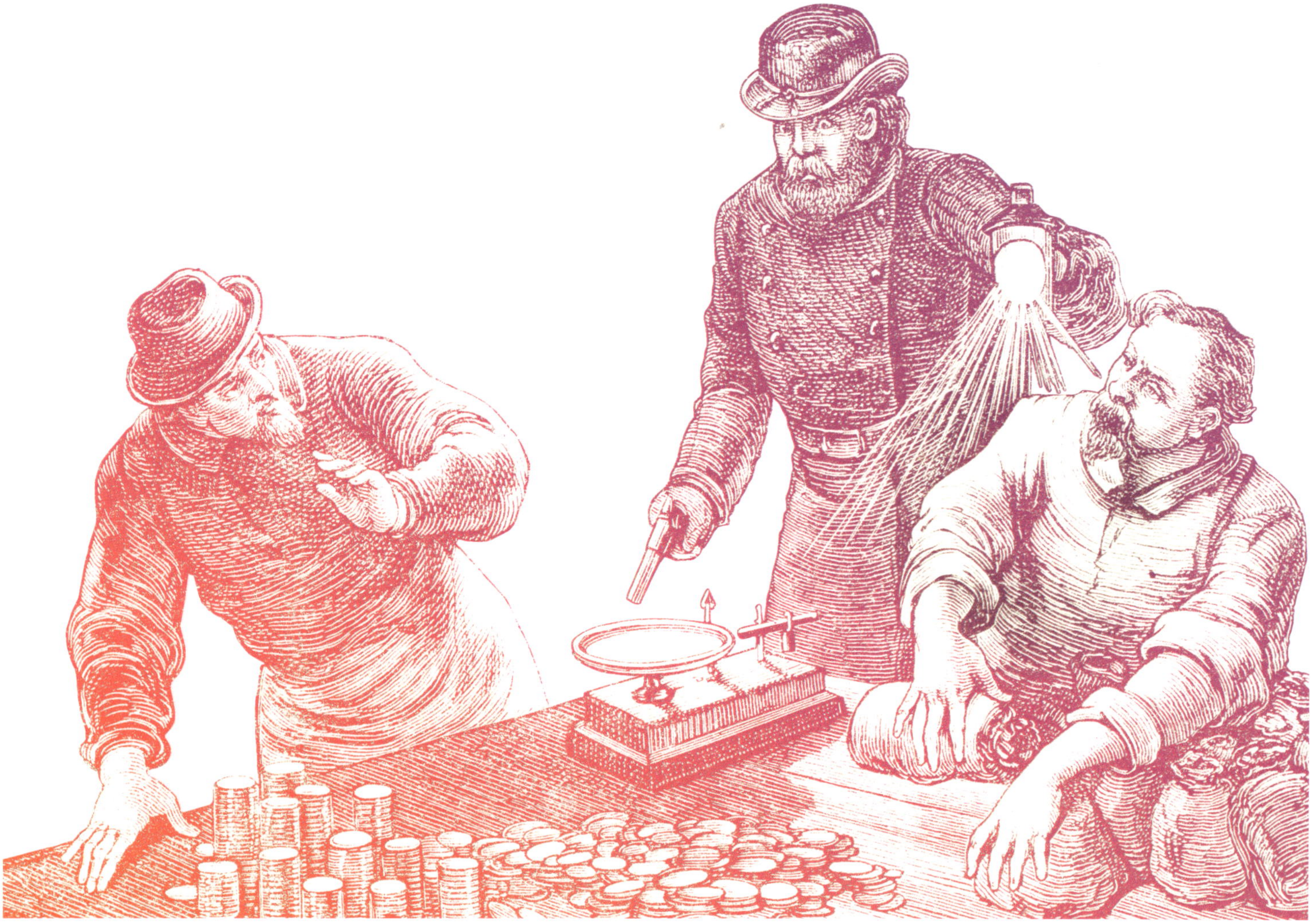

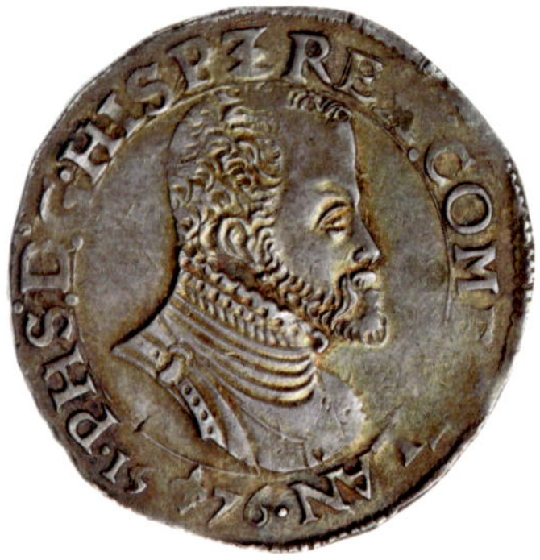

19
⅓ **PHILIPPSTALER**
INTACT WEIGHING 6.79 G
(SCALE 1.5:1)

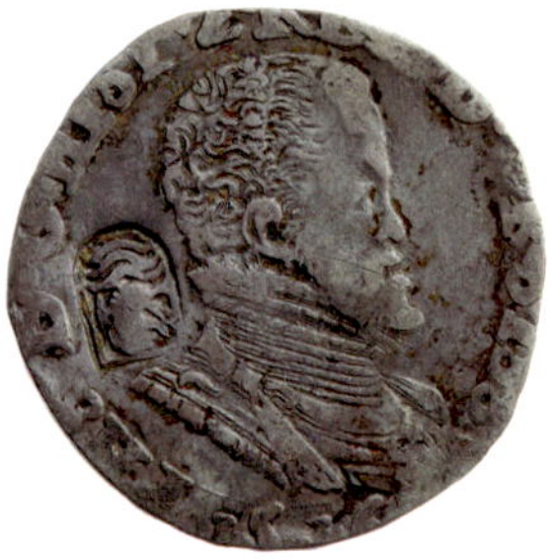

20
⅓ **PHILIPPSTALER**
HEAVILY CUT WEIGHING 5.27 G
(SCALE 1.5:1)

BE ON YOUR GUARD

COUNTERFEITING IS AS OLD AS MONEY ITSELF

Counterfeiters have been trying to copy money for as long as it has been in existence. Coins made of precious metal were counterfeited using cast copies made from poor-quality metals or by coating a piece of base metal with a thin layer of silver or gold and then striking the flan using a forged die. It was also a lucrative undertaking to file or cut off small quantities of precious metal from genuine coins. For centuries it was therefore common practice to weigh coins to check whether they were genuine. As for paper money forgeries, counterfeiters used to need a great deal of artistic skill as this involved engraving printing plates or reproducing individual notes by hand.

WHEN THE STATE STARTS COUNTERFEITING

Counterfeiting money isn't just something done by crooks looking to make a fortune. Throughout history, countries, too, have produced counterfeits – in times of war, say, to cripple the enemy's economy or replenish their own coffers. Napoleon did so against Austria, as did the British monarchy during the American War of Independence. In World War II, the German government had vast quantities of bogus British banknotes printed.

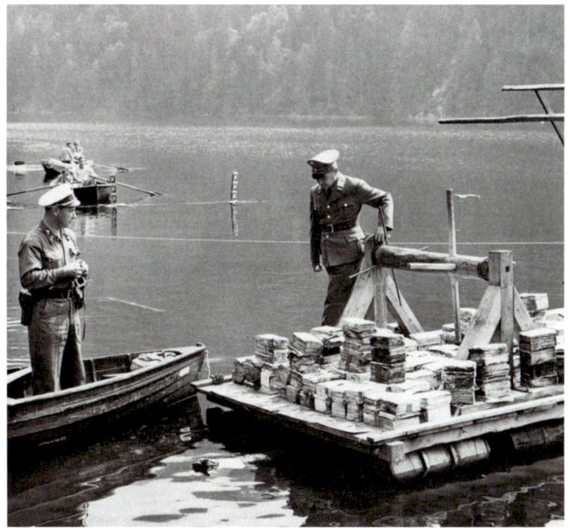

OPERATION BERNHARD

In 1942, the Nazis set up a secret printing works at the Sachsenhausen concentration camp. They forced inmates who had previously worked as artists, engravers or printers to forge millions of British banknotes. Their goal: to wage economic warfare on the UK, Germany's enemy in the war. Towards the end of the war, the Nazis dumped crates of forged notes and printing blocks in Lake Toplitz in Austria, from where they were later recovered.

HAND-DRAWN

Counterfeiters normally produce bogus banknotes using a variety of printing techniques, but not all of them do. In the 1970s, one counterfeiter drew remarkably exact 1,000DM banknotes by hand. They weren't quite identical, though, and they had no watermark or security thread. The counterfeiter was given a long prison sentence.

21 **HAND-DRAWN COUNTERFEIT 1,000-DM NOTE**

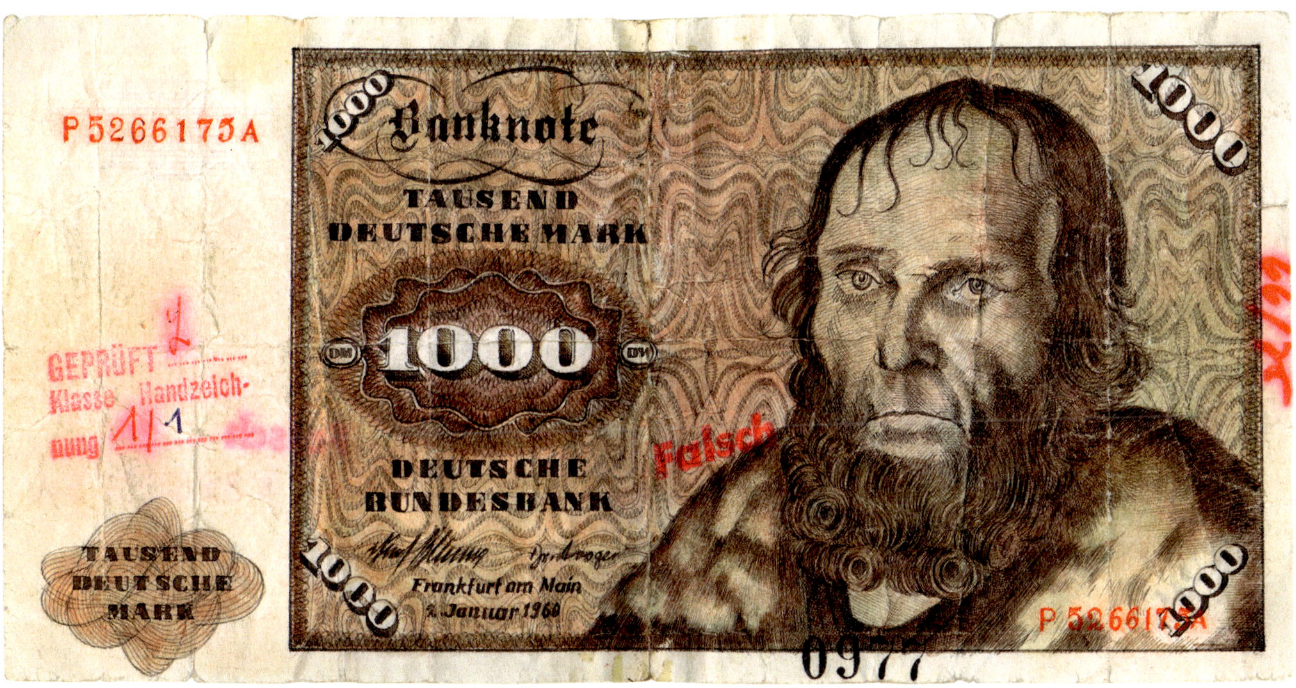

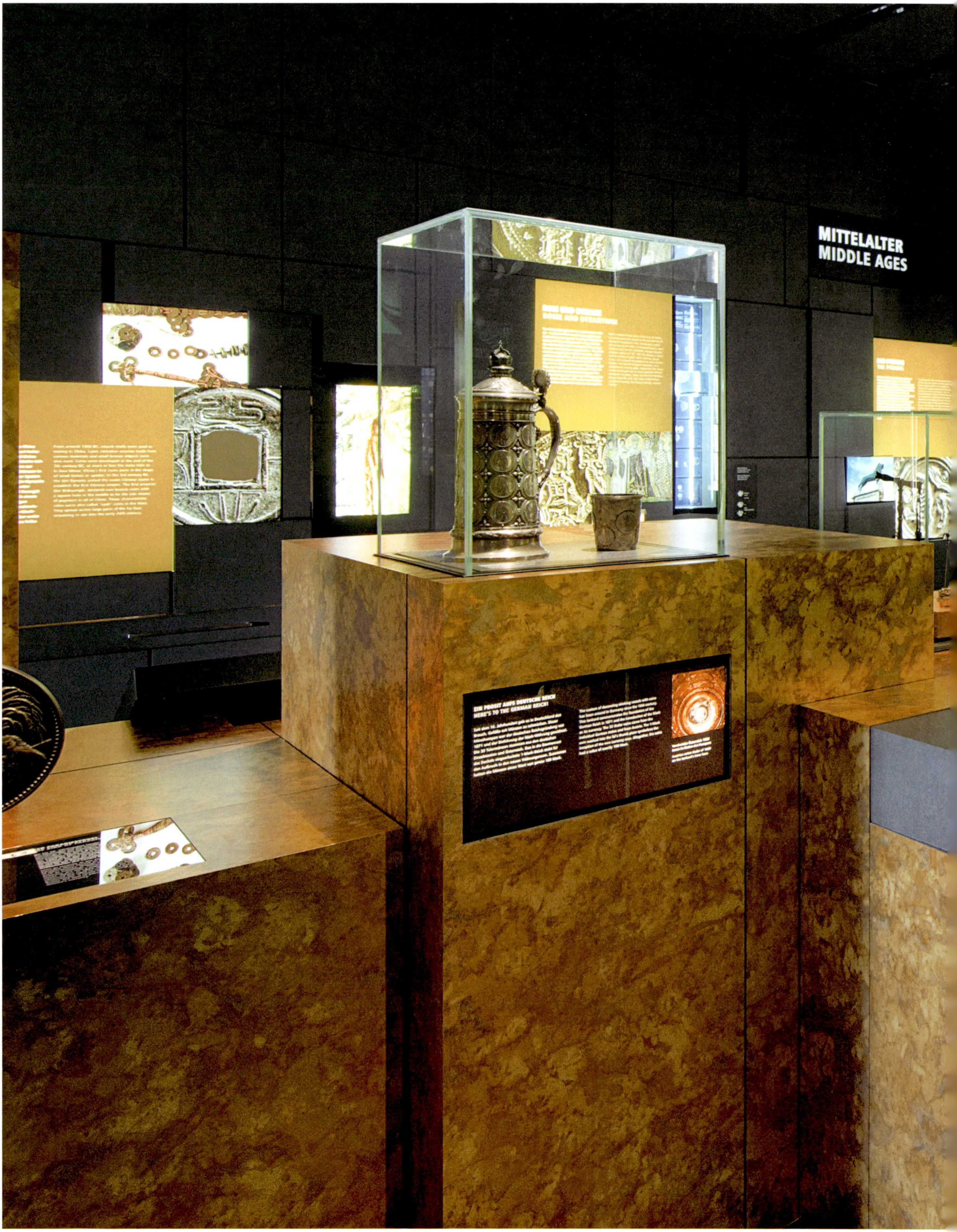
MITTELALTER
MIDDLE AGES

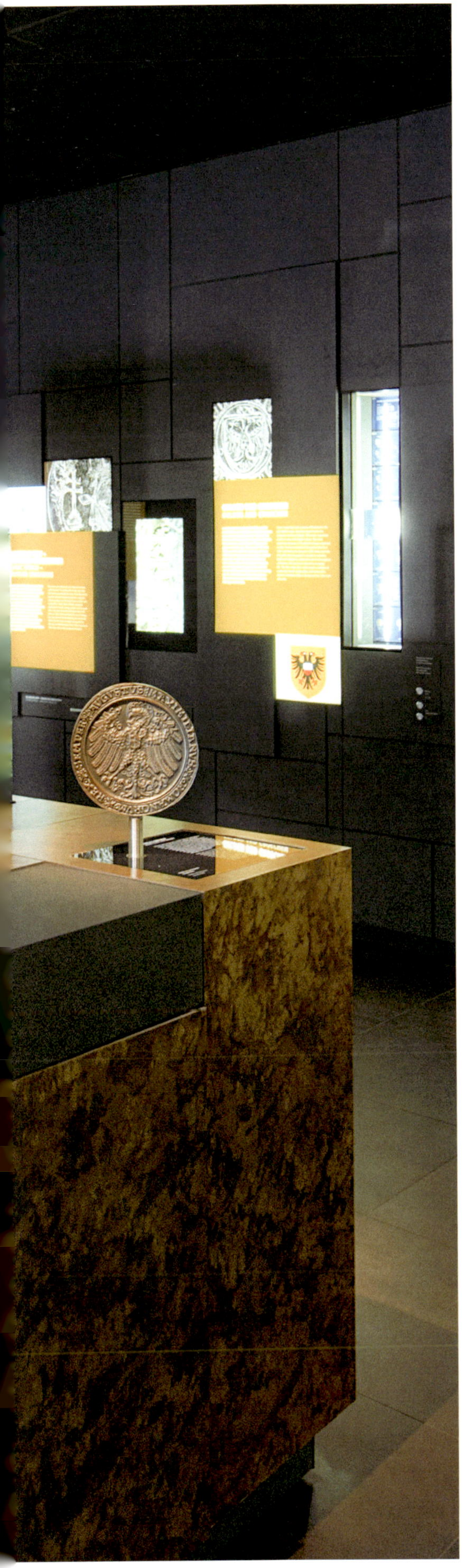

MONEY CABINET

The Deutsche Bundesbank's coin collection comprises not only traditional payment media but some 90,000 coins and 260,000 banknotes from every era.

The most precious treasures in this collection are slumbering in the twilight of the money cabinet, waiting to be discovered. They direct the observer's gaze beyond the borders of western culture and tell the story of money throughout every single continent. Selected items can also be viewed at interactive media stations in high resolution, just like under a microscope. Items such as cowrie shells, bars of salt or stone money illustrate the fact that traditional payment media are not the forerunners of cash but objects which have been used as money for centuries, and in some cases up to the present.

The heart of the money cabinet is the "hoard", an installation in the middle of the room made up of multiple display cases which impressively display the highlights of the collection – including the world's only extant gold coin minted by Brutus, the famous co-conspirator, after the assassination of Gaius Julius Caesar.

35

ANCIENT GREECE

The first coins were minted by the Lydians in Asia Minor during the 7th century BC. Shortly after, the idea of minting coins reached the Greek world. By the beginning of the 5th century BC, the coins had spread to the cities of the Aegean region and mainland Greece and were found almost throughout the entire Mediterranean area. Unlike the Lydians, the Greeks mainly used silver to make their coins. Each city-state in ancient Greece minted its own coins, bearing a characteristic motif: popular images were gods, animals and plants, referring to the mythical-religious or economic culture of the respective cities.

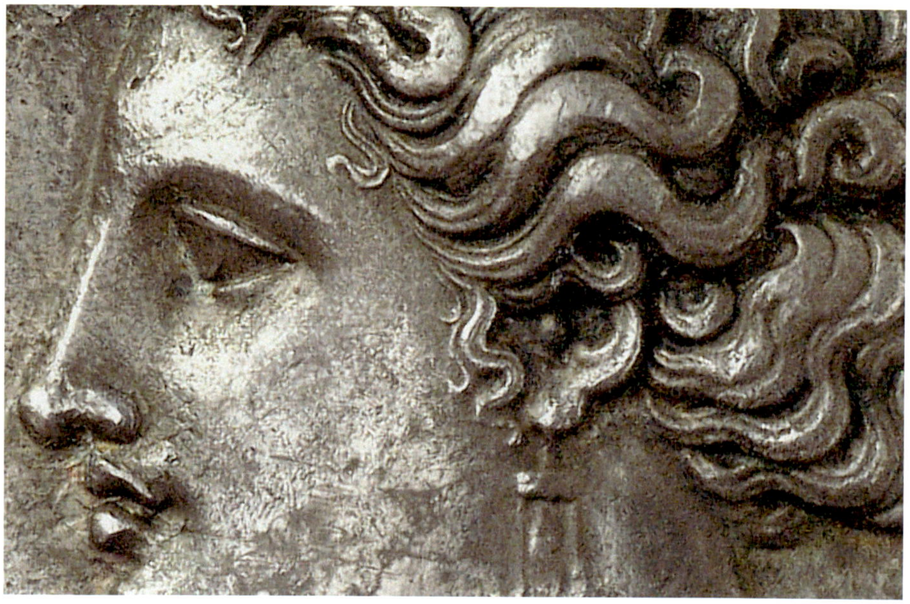

22 **IMAGE OF THE NYMPH ARETHUSA ON A DECADRACHM FROM SYRACUSE,** 400–395 BC (SCALE 6:1)

23

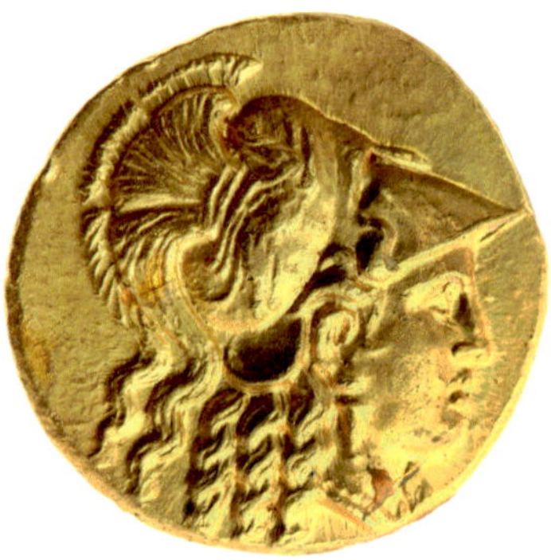

24

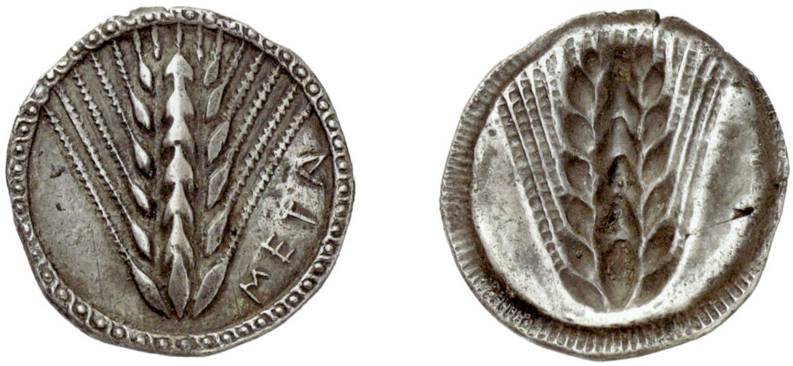

25

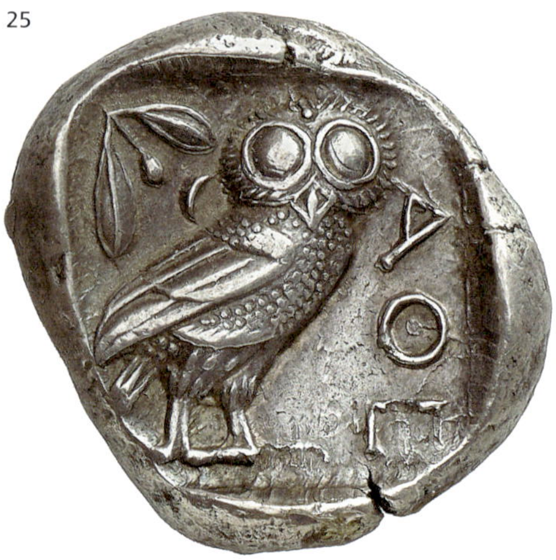

26

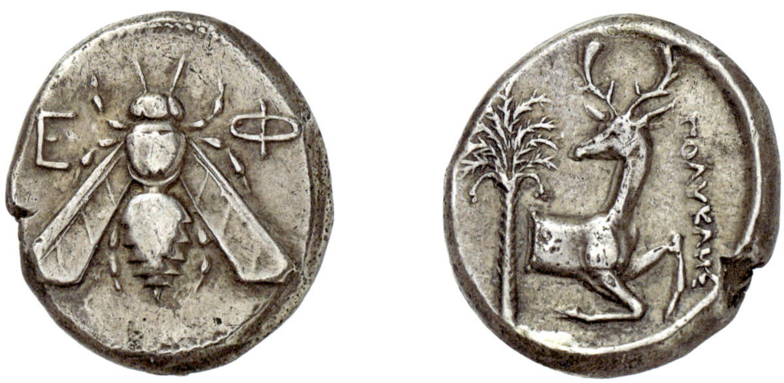

23 **IMAGE OF THE GODDESS ATHENE ON A GOLD STATER,** CA 311–305 BC (SCALE 2.5:1)

24 **METAPONTUM, NOMOS,** 6TH/5TH C BC (SCALE 2:1)

25 **ATHENS, TETRADRACHM,** 5TH C BC (SCALE 2.5:1)

26 **EPHESUS, TETRADRACHM,** 387–295 BC (SCALE 2:1)

CHINA

From around 1300 BC, cowrie shells were used as money in China. Later, imitation cowries made from various materials and small bronze objects were also used. Coins were developed at the end of the 7th century BC, at more or less the same time as in Asia Minor. China's first coins were in the shape of small knives or spades. In the 3rd century BC, the Qin Dynasty united the seven Chinese states to establish the first Chinese empire. The first emperor, Qin Shihuangdi, declared cast bronze coins with a square hole in the middle to be the sole means of payment in all of China. These characteristic coins were also called "cash" coins in the West. They spread across large parts of the Far East, remaining in use into the early 20th century.

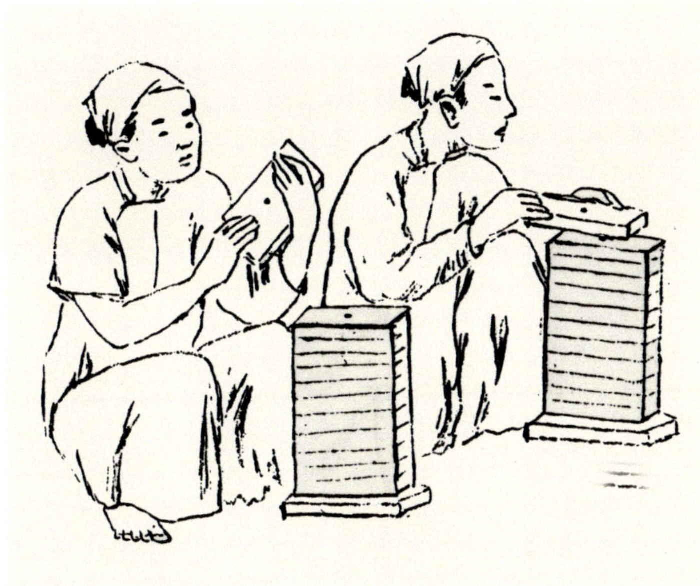

CASH COINS WERE NOT MINTED, BUT CAST. THE COIN MOULDS WERE MADE IN CLAY TABLETS. A CHANNEL FOR THE MOLTEN METAL JOINED SEVERAL STACKED CLAY TABLETS.

27

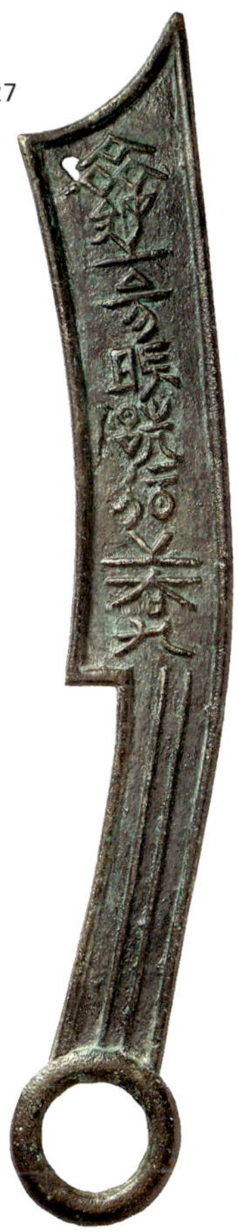

28

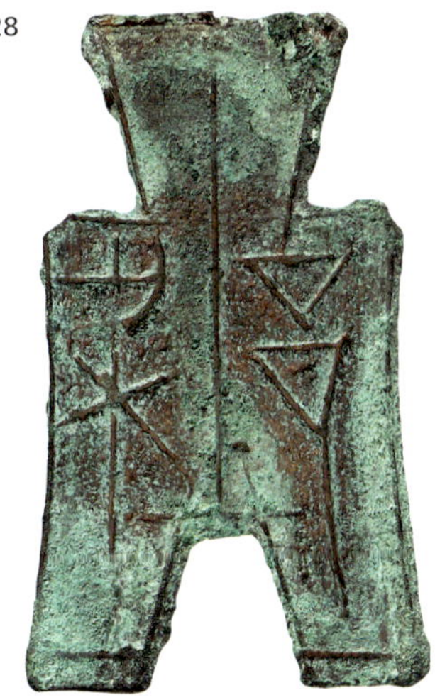

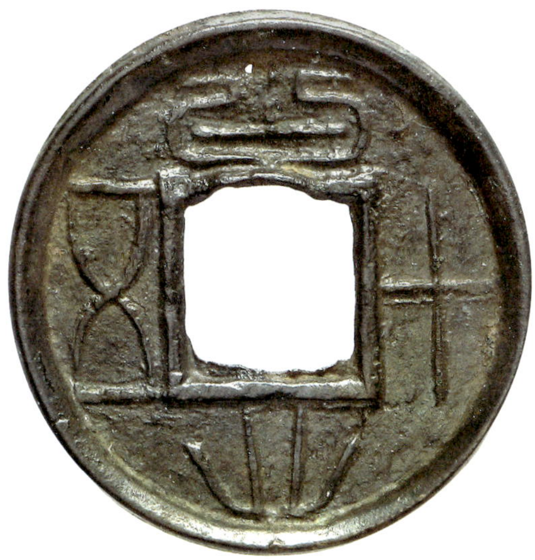

30

29

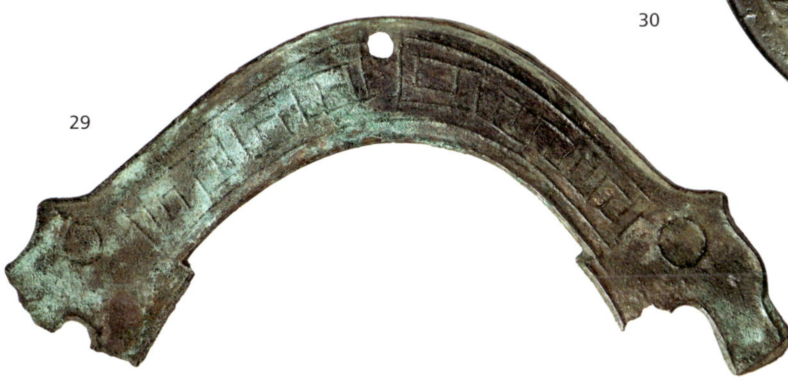

27 **KNIFE COINS** (SCALE 1:1.5)

28 **SPADE COINS** (SCALE 1.5:1)

29 **BRIDGE MONEY**

30 **CASH COIN,** AD 7–14 (SCALE 2.5:1)

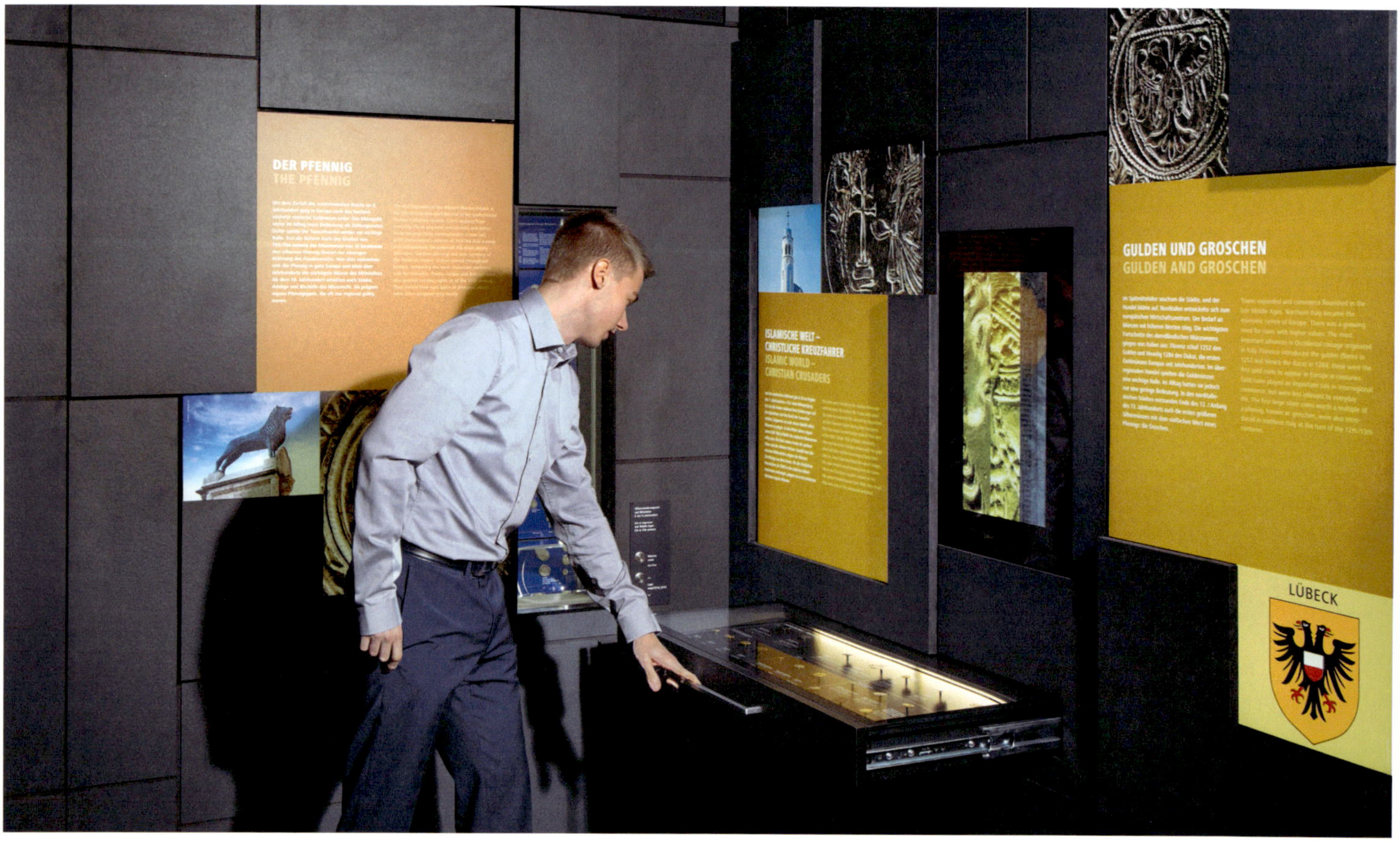

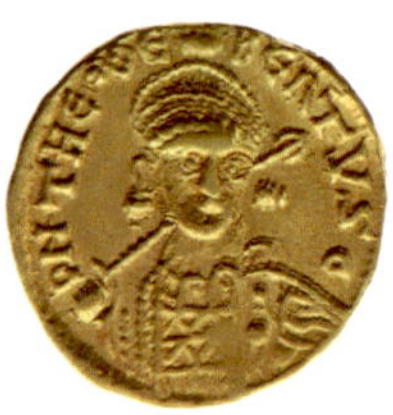

31

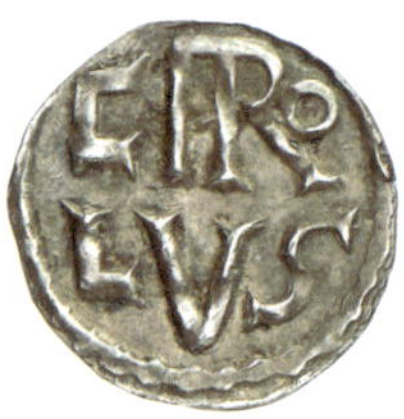

32

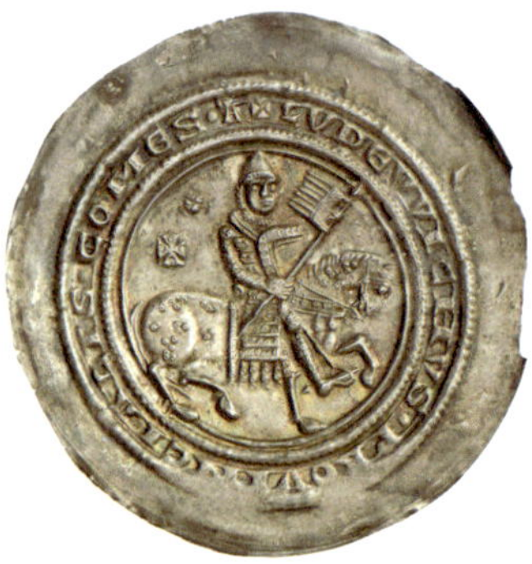

33

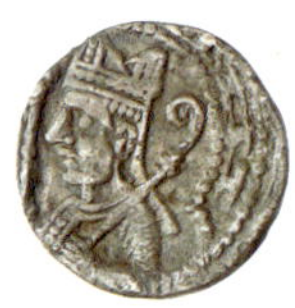

34

31 **MEROWINGIANS SOLIDUS,** 534–548 (SCALE 1.5:1)

32 **CAROLINGIANS DENIER,** 771–793/794 (SCALE 1.5:1)

33 **GOTHA, BRACTEATE** 1172–1190

34 **MAINZ, PFENNIG** 1183–1200 (SCALE 1.5:1)

THE PFENNIG

The disintegration of the Western Roman Empire in the 5th century also spelt the end of the sophisticated Roman monetary system. Coins receded from everyday life as payment instruments and barter trade became more commonplace. It was not until Charlemagne's reforms of 793/794 that coinage was reorganised. He ordained the silver penny (denarius, German pfennig) the sole currency of the Frankish empire. It then spread throughout Europe, remaining the most important medieval coin for centuries. Towns, nobles and bishops were also granted minting rights as of the 10th century. They minted their own types of pfennigs, which were often accepted only locally.

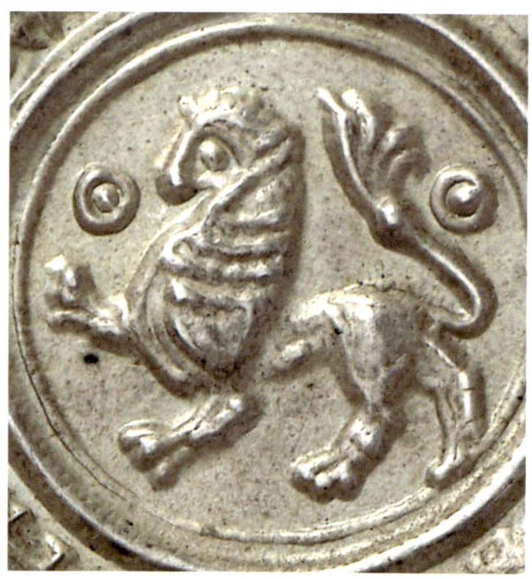

35 **HERALDIC ANIMAL OF HENRY THE LION ON A BRACTEATE FROM BRAUNSCHWEIG,** 1142–1180

ISLAMIC WORLD

No coins were minted on the Arabian Peninsula until the early 7th century AD. It was only when the Arabs encountered the coins of the Byzantines and the Sasanian Empire during their conquests that they began to mint similar coins of their own. In the 690s, Caliph ʻAbd al-Malik completely reformed the Arabic coinage system with the gold dinar and silver dirham becoming its basis from then on. Since Islam prohibited the use of images, the coins showed ornate lettering from the Quran.

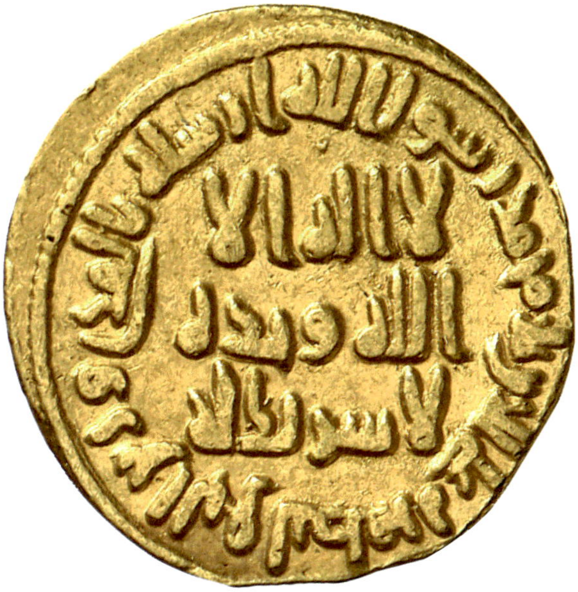

36

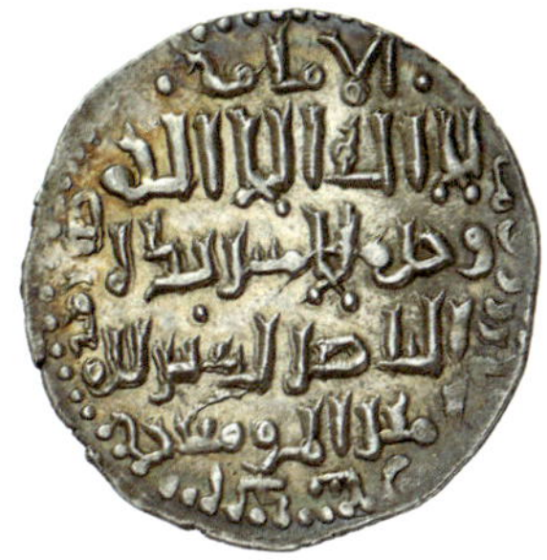

37

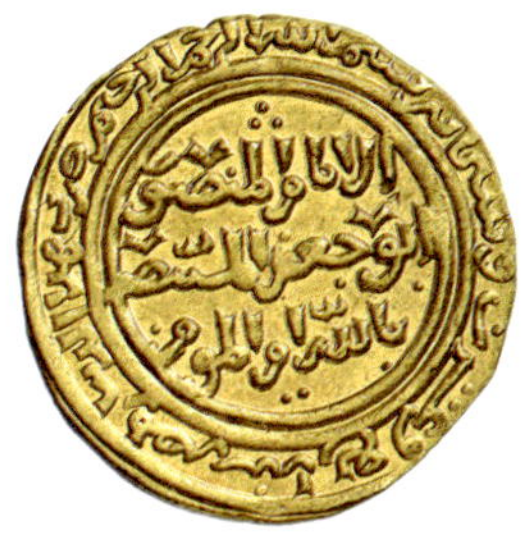

38

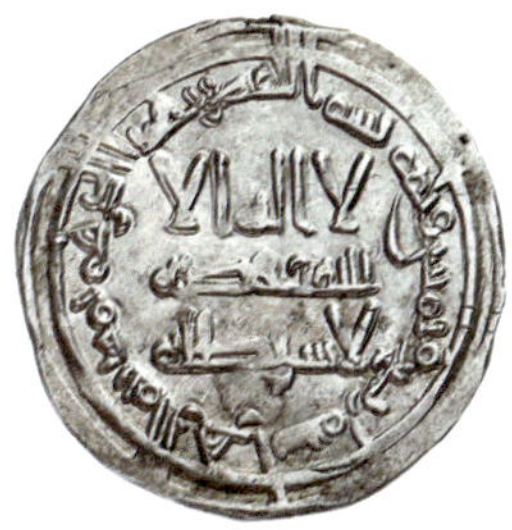

39

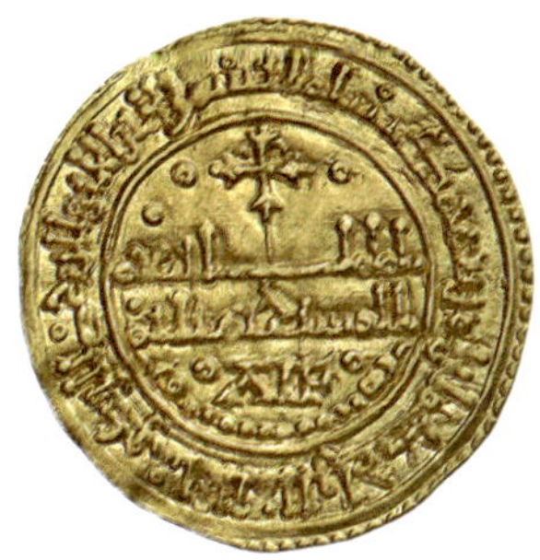

40

36 **IRAQ, DINAR,** 698/699 (SCALE 4:1)

37 **ANATOLIA, DIRHAM,** 1211/1212 (SCALE 1.5:1)

38 **EGYPT, DINAR,** 1226/1227 (SCALE 1.5:1)

39 **CORDOBA, DIRHAM,** 965 (SCALE 1.5:1)

40 **KING ALFONSO VIII, MORABITINO** 1187, MINTED AFTER AN ISLAMIC MODEL (SCALE 1.5:1)

CHRISTIAN CRUSADERS

When the Christian crusaders advanced into the eastern Mediterranean from 1096, they struck their own coins in the conquered territories.

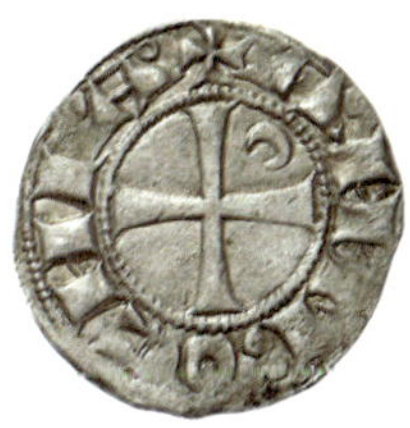

41

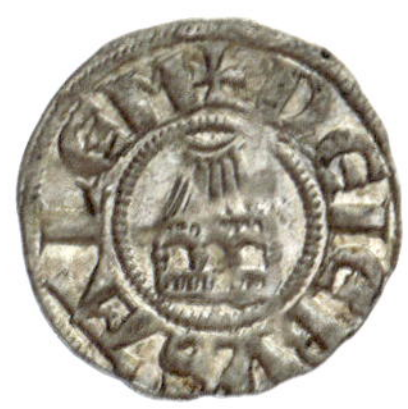

42

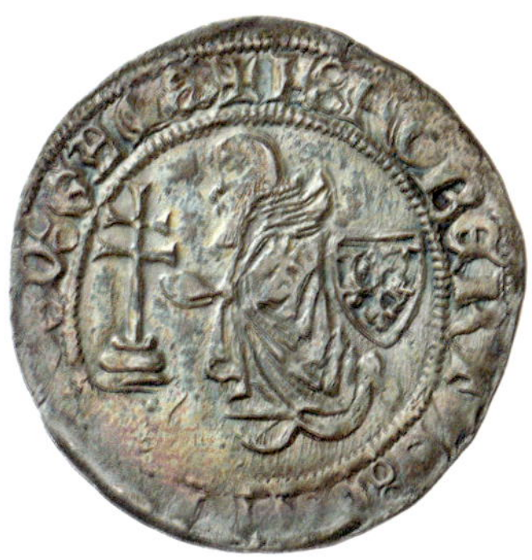

43

41 **ANTIOCH, DENIER,** 1163 – 1188

42 **JERUSALEM, DENIER,** 1163 – 1174

43 **ORDER OF ST JOHN ON RHODES GIGLIATO,** 1374 – 1376

(ALL SCALE 1.5:1)

THE THALER

Coinage in Europe changed fundamentally at the turn of the 16th century. The strong increase in the production of silver brought forth a new type of coin: the first large silver coins equal in value to a goldgulden were created in Tyrol in 1486. They were initially known as guldengroschen or guldiner. Later the name thaler was established, derived from the mint in the Bohemian town of Joachimsthal, where the counts of Schlick minted these coins in large quantities. Thaler coins became a cornerstone of the German monetary system and served as the model for coins minted by many other European countries.

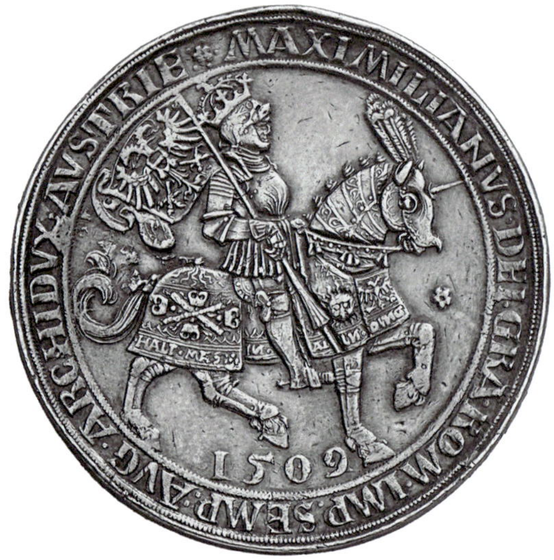

44

44 **SCHAUGULDINER**
1509 (SCALE 1.25:1)

45 **"FLAT CAP THALER"**
1500

46 **REICHSTHALER**
1629

47 **½ KONVENTIONSSPEZIESTHALER**
1782

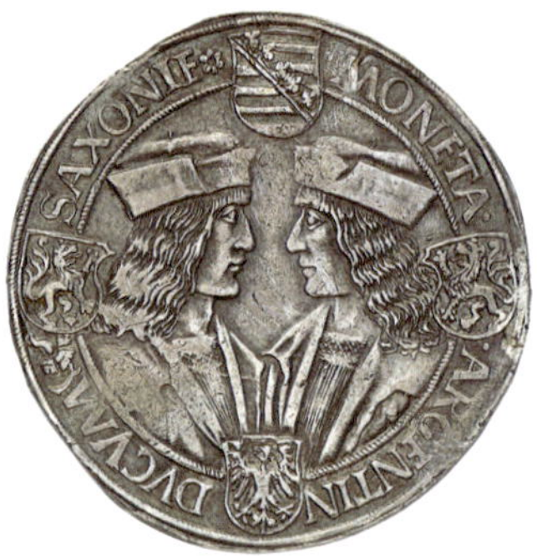

45

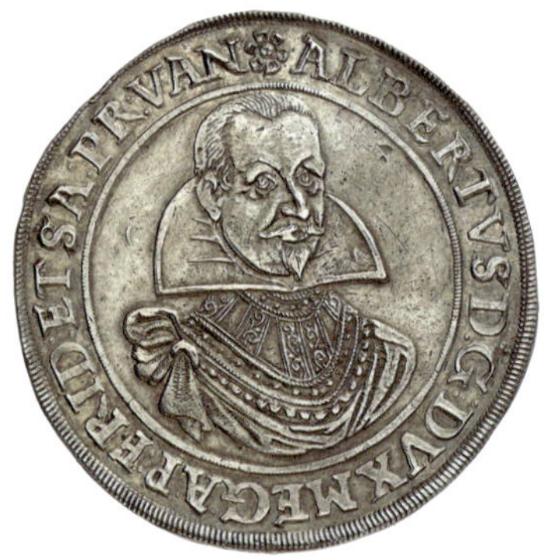

46

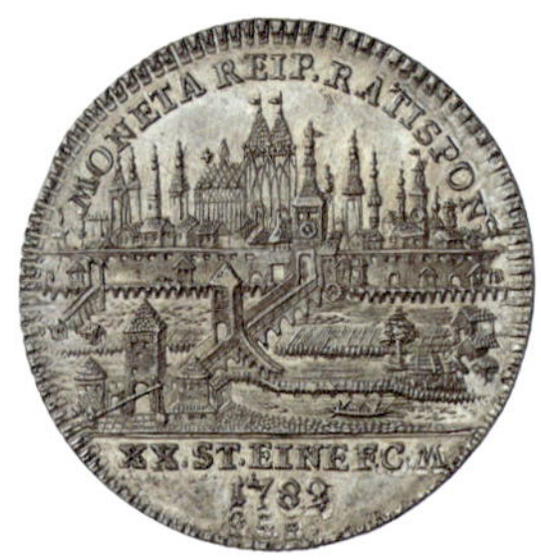

47

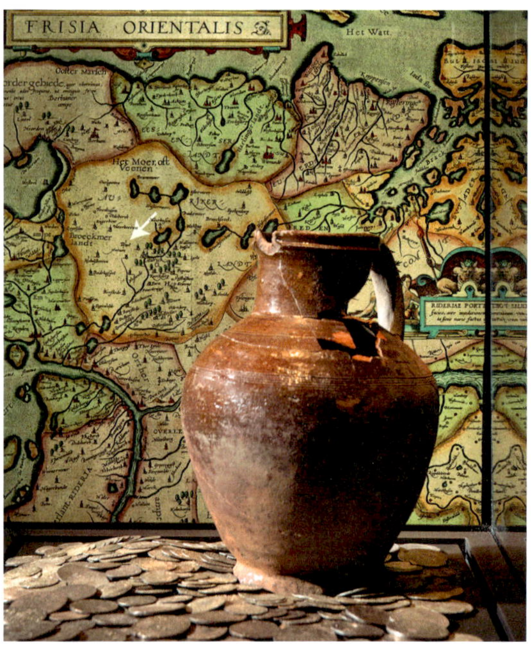

HOARD OF COINS FOUND IN WALLE

In 1971 a pot filled with 468 silver coins – around 2.2 kg of pure silver – was discovered near the East Frisian town of Walle. Discovered during extension of a farmhouse, it is thought to have been buried in the late 16th century. The coins originated from mints across Europe; one was even struck in Mexico.

48 **HOARD OF COINS FOUND IN WALLE**

JAPAN

A money-based economy was not established until relatively late in Japan, with barter trade predominating for a long time. At the end of the 16th century, the Tokugawa shoguns introduced a coin system based on gold, silver and copper. Cast bronze coins were the most important means of payment. The large oval gold plates (Ōban), which remained in circulation up to the 19th century, are exceptional. Emperor Mutsuhito abolished the feudal system in 1868 and abandoned Japan's policy of isolation. He also radically reformed the monetary system in 1871, introducing the decimal system (1 yen = 100 sen) and instructing that coins be minted on the European model.

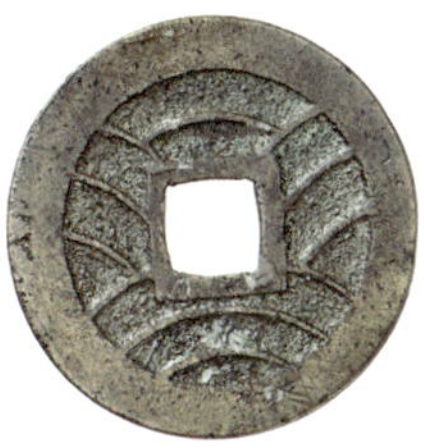

49

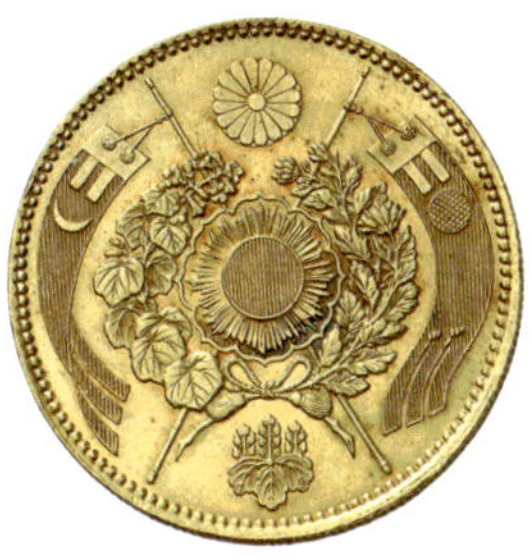

50

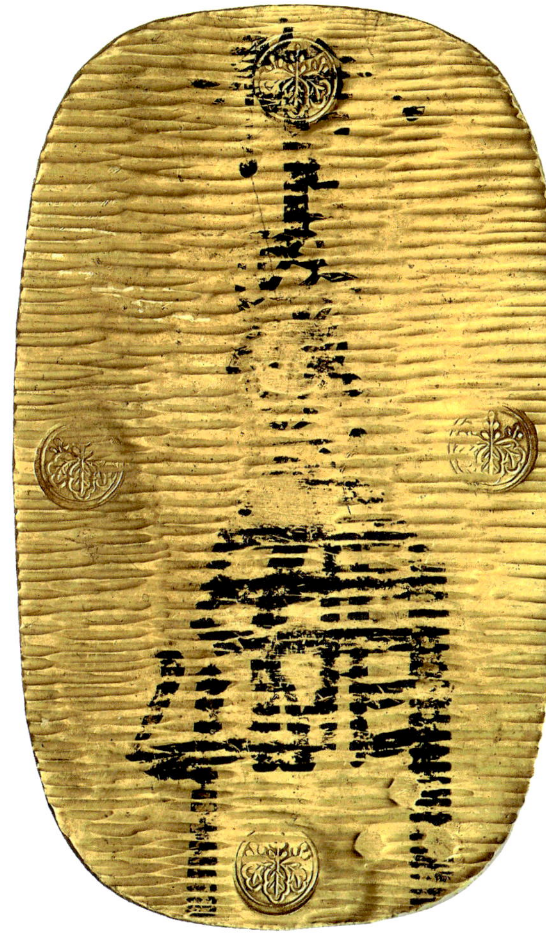

51

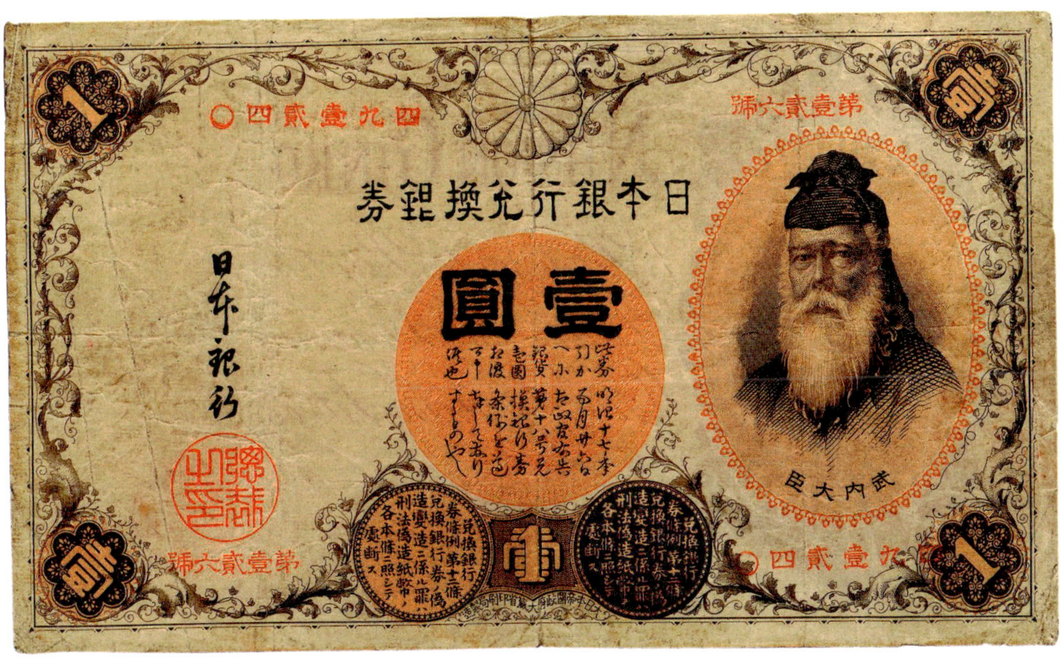

52

49 **TSŪHŌ,** 1768 – 1788

50 **20 YEN,** 1870

51 **ŌBAN,** 1725 – 1743 (SCALE 1:0.8)

52 **1 YEN,** 1889

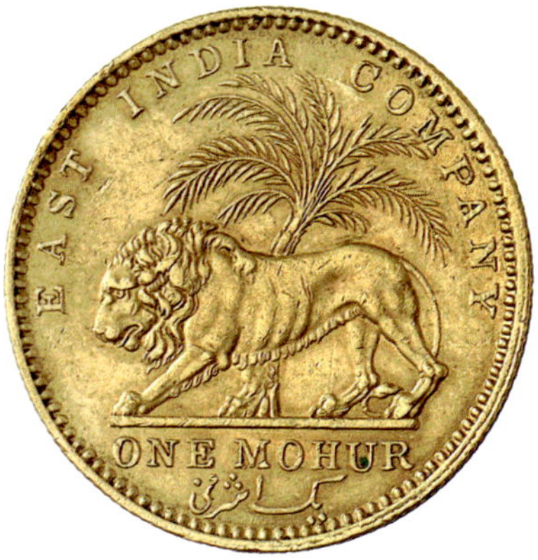

53

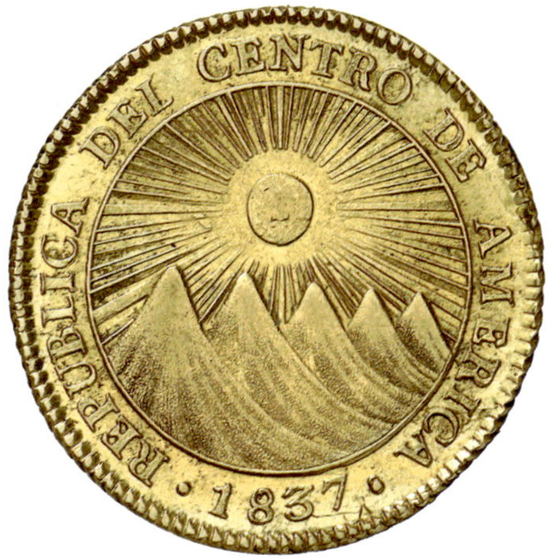

57

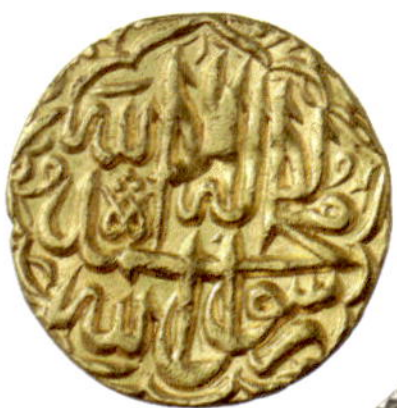

54

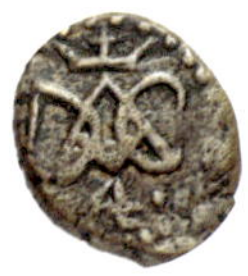

55

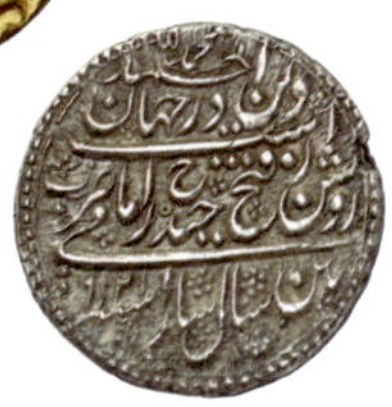

56

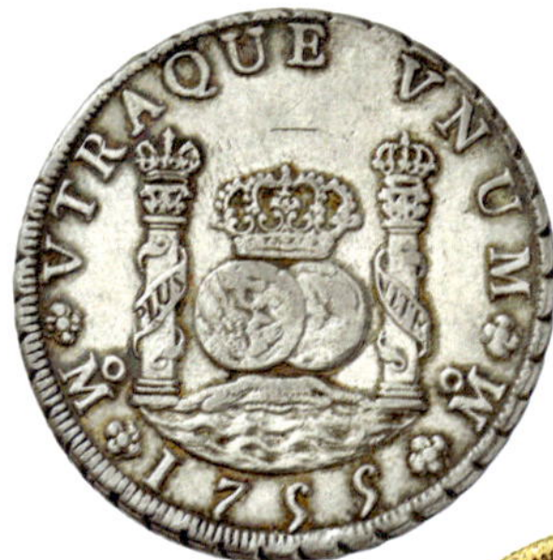

58

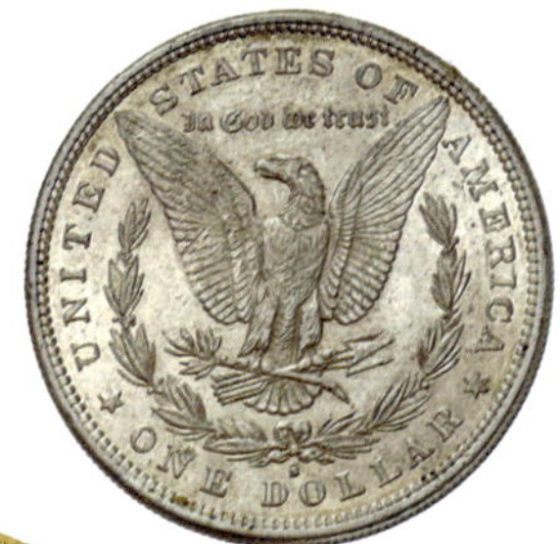

59

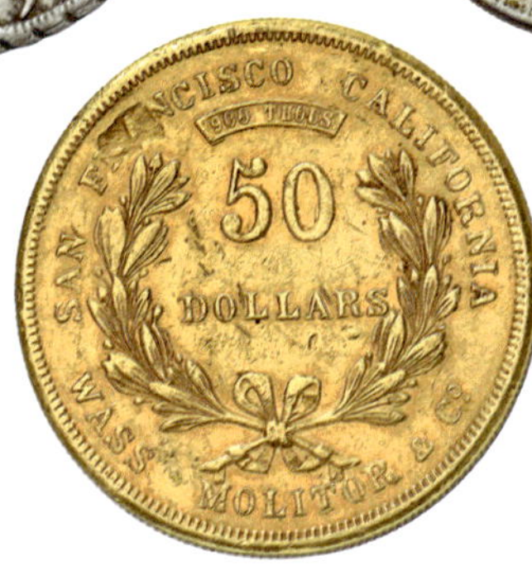

60

INDIA

The British East India Company (EIC) began to expand throughout the Indian subcontinent in the 17th century. A wide variety of gold and silver coins were used in India, issued by native rulers and European colonial powers. The British colonial rulers reformed the coin system in 1835 in order to harmonise it. They introduced modern coin minting and gave the coins a western design. In 1858, the British parliament called an end to the EIC's rule over large parts of India and transferred its rights – including the right to mint coins – to the Crown.

53 **EAST INDIA COMPANY, MOHUR,** 1841 (SCALE 2:1)

54 **MUHAMMAD AKBAR, MOHUR,** 1568/1569

55 **DANISH INDIA, 4 KAS,** 1730–1746

56 **KINGDOM OF MYSORE, RUPEE,** 1787

THE NEW WORLD

Colonialisation brought coins to the Americas. In 1535, the Spanish already began to mint coins in present-day Mexico. The Spanish 8-real coins played an important role in the New World, as the English did not allow their colonies to mint coins of any kind. Beginning late in the 18th century, the United States of America minted dollar coins which matched the 8-real coins in fineness, weight and size. The gold rush enveloped the USA in the 19th century; at that time, private entrepreneurs began minting gold dollar coins.

57 **REPUBLIC OF CENTRAL AMERICA, 4 ESCUDOS,** 1837 (SCALE 2:1)

58 **MEXICO, 8 REALES,** 1755

59 **USA, DOLLAR,** 1880

60 **50 DOLLARS,** 1855, MINTED FROM THE PROCEEDS OF THE CALIFORNIA GOLD RUSH

THE ROAD TO THE DEUTSCHE MARK

The German states continued their path towards a monetary union in the 19th century. In the Dresden Coinage Convention of 1838, most German states established fixed exchange rates between the north German thaler and the south German gulden and decided to mint a unified currency. This "union coin" had a nominal value of 2 thalers or 3½ gulden. It was commonly known as the "champagne thaler" as, in those days, a bottle of champagne cost 2 thalers. The Vienna Coinage Treaty of 1857 went one step further by making the Prussian thaler the common currency for the whole of Germany and Austria. After the German Reich was founded in 1871, the government introduced the Mark as the new currency for Germany.

61 **PRINCIPALITY OF WALDECK AND PYRMONT, DOUBLE THALER,** 1842 (SCALE 2:1)

62 **FRANKFURT, DOUBLE UNION THALER,** 1862

63 **KINGDOM OF SAXONY, SIEGESTHALER,** 1871

64 **GERMAN REICH, 1 MARK,** 1896

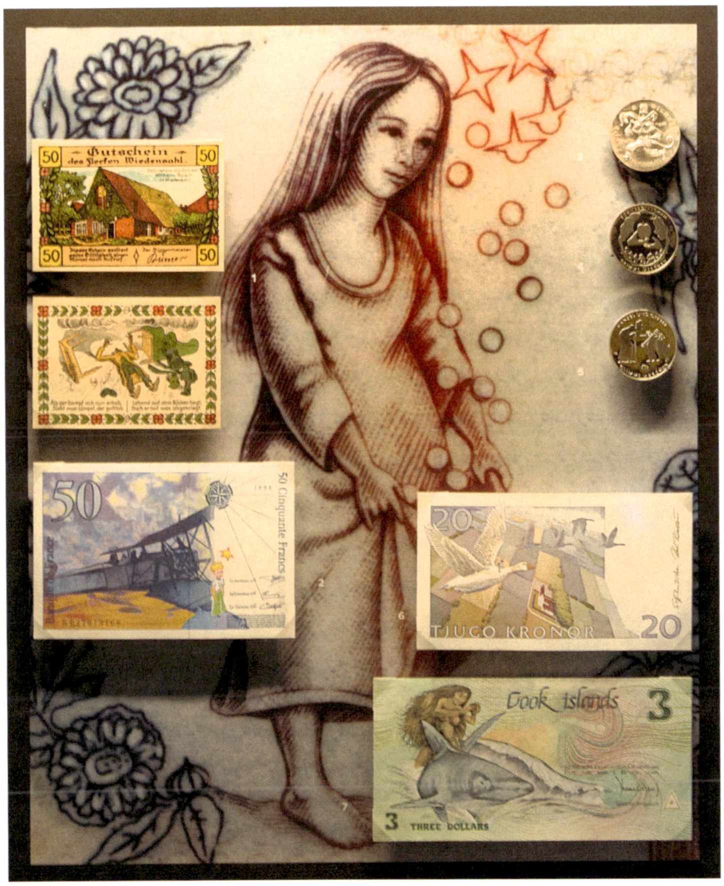

ONCE UPON A TIME ...

BANKNOTES AND COINS WITH MOTIFS OF GRIMMS' FAIRY TALES AND SOUTH-PACIFIC LEGENDS, WITH MAX AND MORITZ OF WILHELM BUSCH, THE LITTLE PRINCE OF SAINT-EXUPÉRY OR SELMA LAGERLÖFS NILS HOLGERSSON.

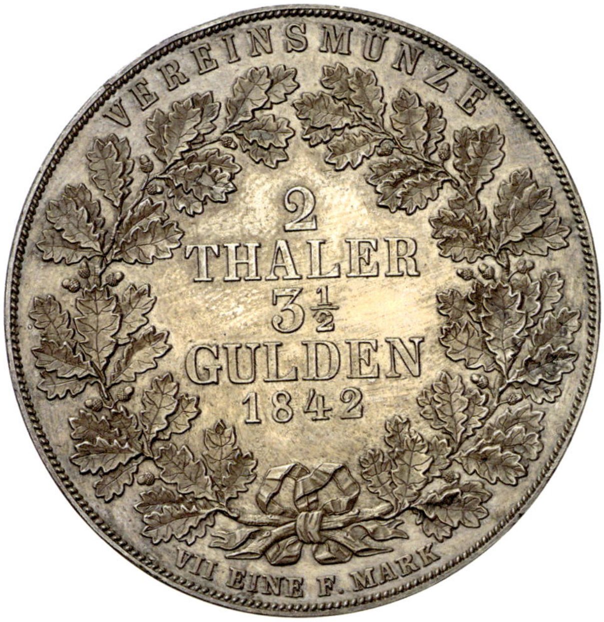

61

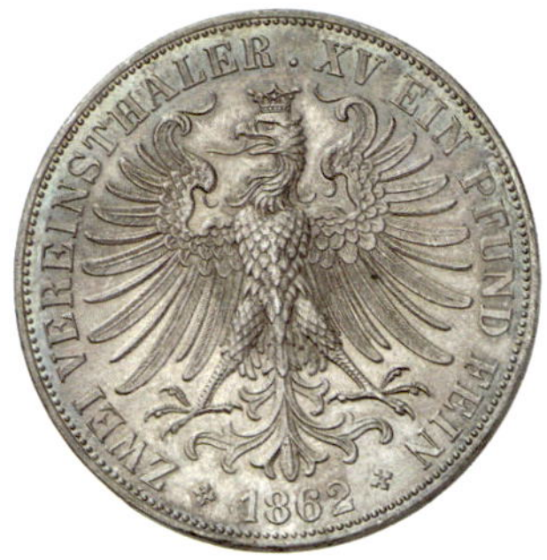

62

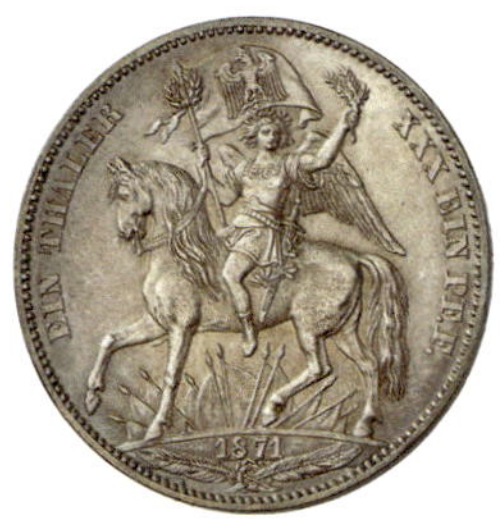

63

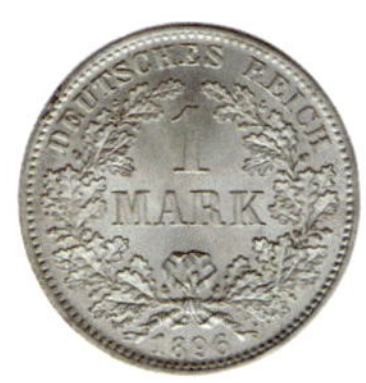

64

NOTE-WORTHY RECORDS

Banknotes are more than just a means of payment – they are calling cards that represent a country's history and culture. Some banknotes stand out simply because they are so unique.

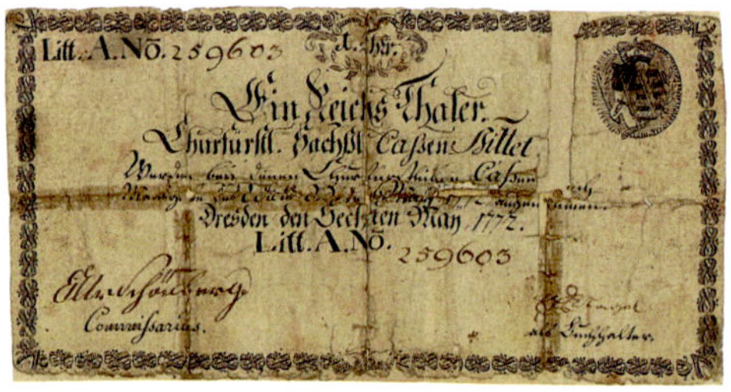

65

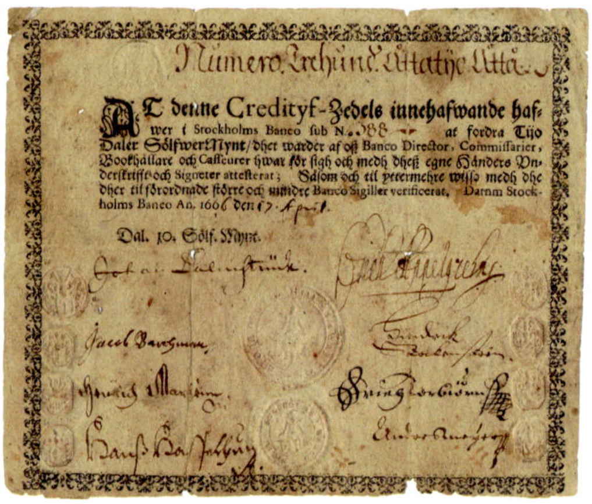

66

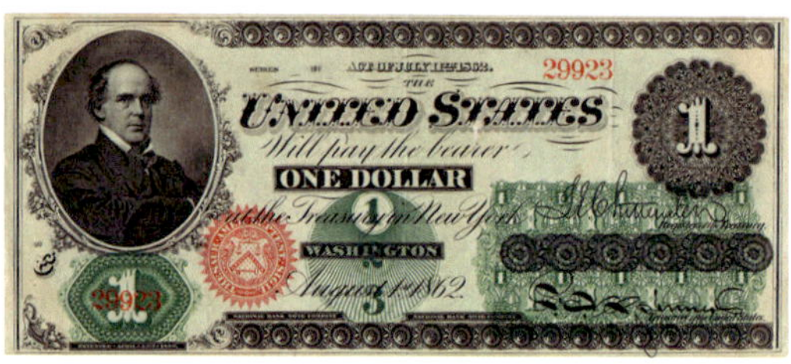

67

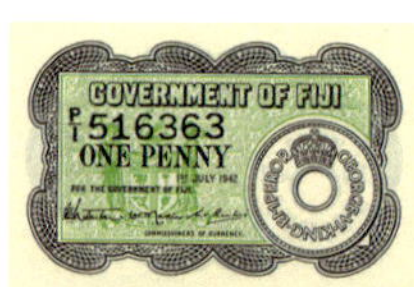

68

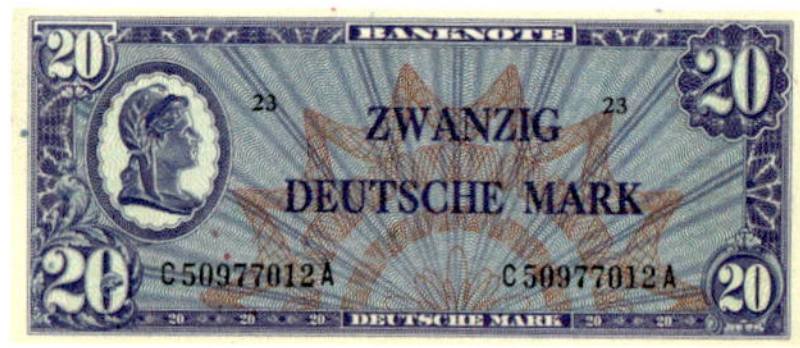

69

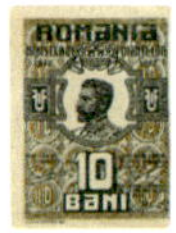

70

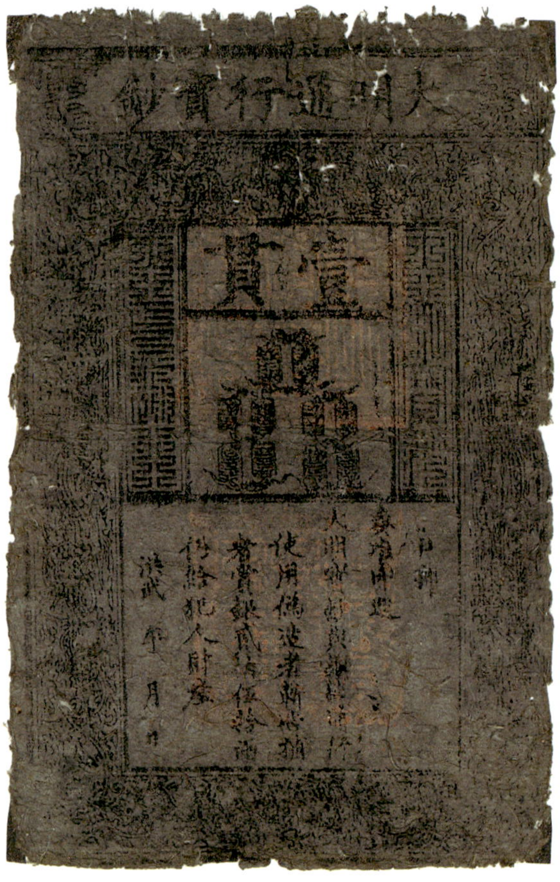

71

65
THE OLDEST GERMAN BANKNOTE
Saxony, 1 reichstaler, 1772

66
EUROPE'S OLDEST BANKNOTE
Sweden, 10 dalers, 1666

67
THE LONGEST-LIVED BANKNOTE
USA, 1 dollar, 1862, still valid

68
THE BANKNOTE WITH THE LOWEST FACE VALUE
Fiji, 1 penny, 1942

69
THE SHORTEST-LIVED BANKNOTE
Germany, 20 DM, 20 June 1948, only valid until August 1949

70
THE WORLD'S SMALLEST BANKNOTE
Romania, 10 bani, 1917, size: 32 x 43 mm

71
THE WORLD'S OLDEST BANKNOTE
China, 1 kuan, 1368–1399

72
THE WOMAN MOST OFTEN PORTRAYED IN BANKNOTES
Seychelles, 50 rupees, 1973, with the image of Queen Elizabeth II of Great Britain

73
THE ONLY GERMAN BANKNOTE TO DEPICT A RULER
German East Africa, 100 rupees, 1905, with the image of Kaiser Wilhelm II

74
THE EUROPEAN BANKNOTE WITH THE LONGEST SERIES OF DIGITS
Yugoslavia, 500,000,000,000 dinar, 1993

75
THE GERMAN BANKNOTE WITH THE HIGHEST FACE VALUE
German Reich, 100 trillion Mark, 1924

76
THE WORLD'S FIRST COMMEMORATIVE BANKNOTE
Nicaragua, 1 peso, 1894, commemorating the 402nd anniversary of the discovery of America

77
THE BANKNOTE WITH THE MOST LANGUAGES
USSR, 25 rouble, 1947, value given in 16 languages

78
THE FIRST MODERN POLYMER BANKNOTE
Australia, 10 dollars, 1988

79
THE MOST FAMOUS FORGERY
German Reich, 10-pounds counterfeit, 1942–1945

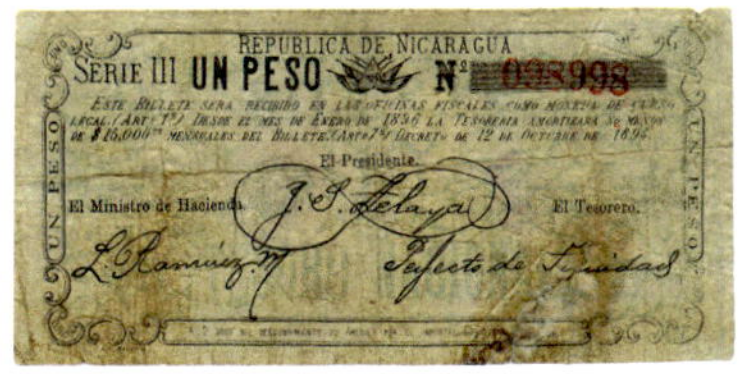

76

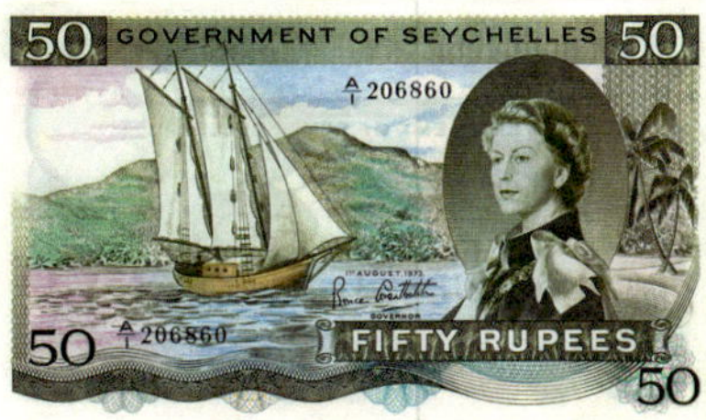

72

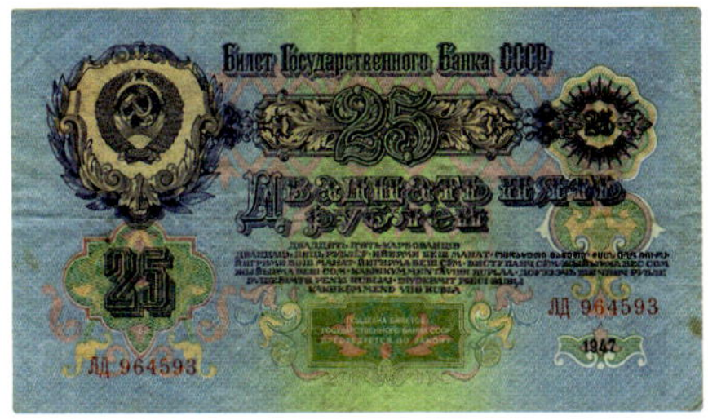
77

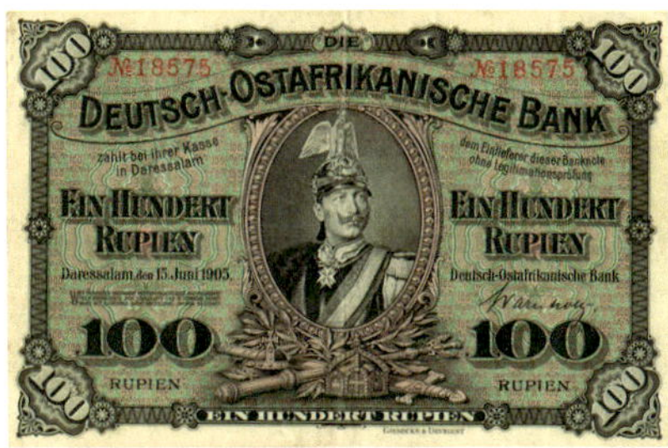

73

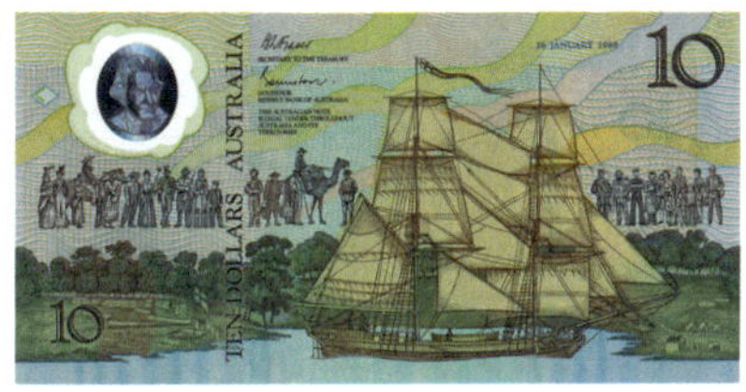

78

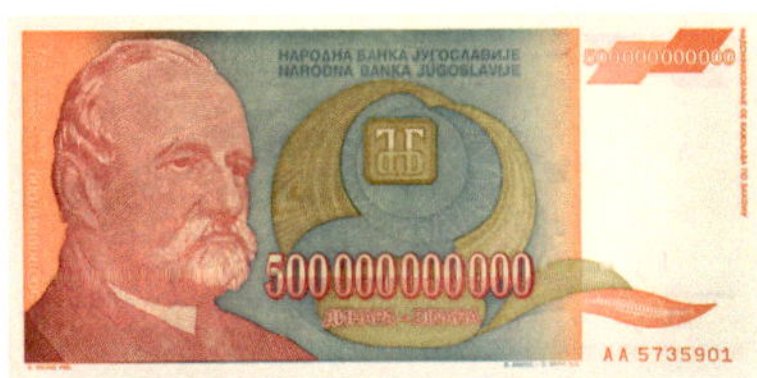

74

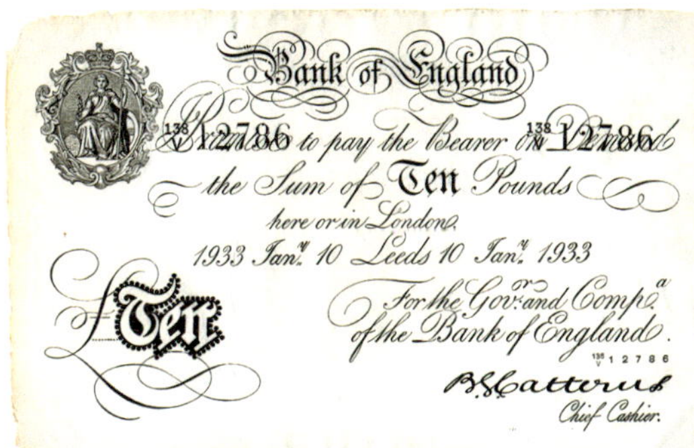

79

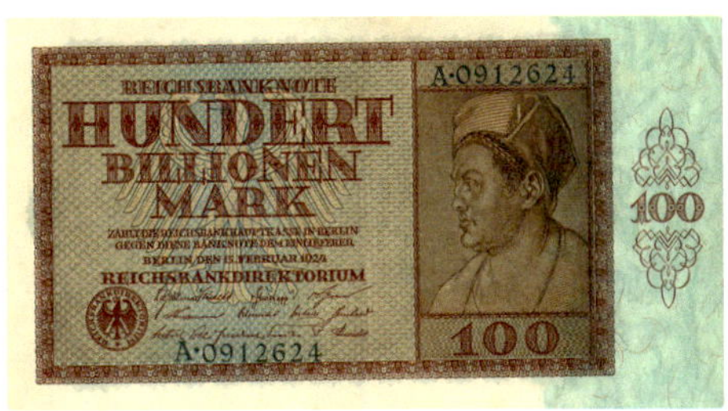

75

MONEY IS AS MONEY DOES

In many parts of the world, coins long ago became established as a means of payment. In some cultures, however, plants, minerals, animals or metal objects were exchanged and used as a measure of value. For example, mussels, snails, salt, tea bricks or cocoa beans served as currency, as well as feathers, small axes or certain stones. Some of these were still in use as late as the 20th century. Such objects were often used not only as a means of payment but also as jewellery, cult objects or prestigious items.

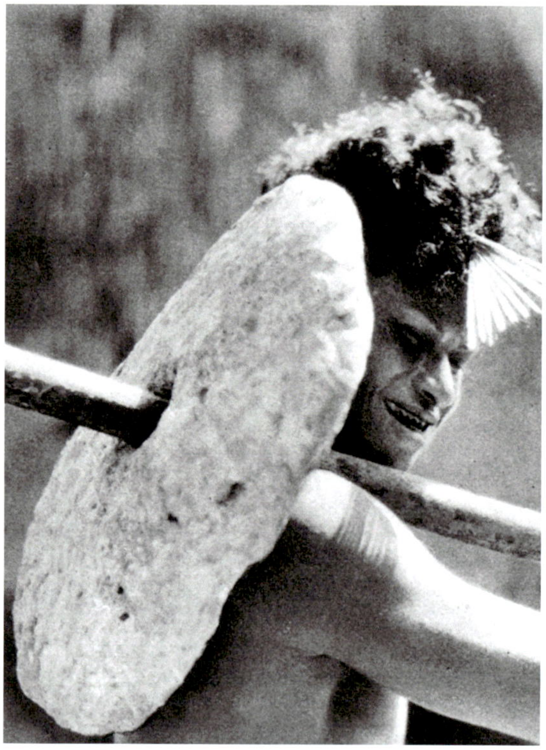

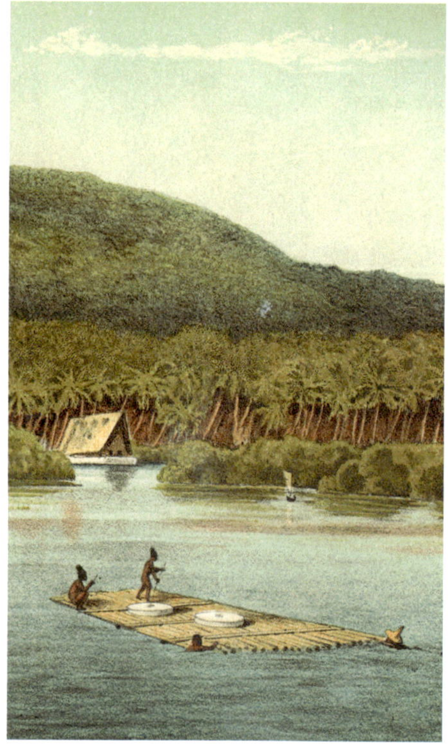

80 **RAI (STONE MONEY),** 69 KG

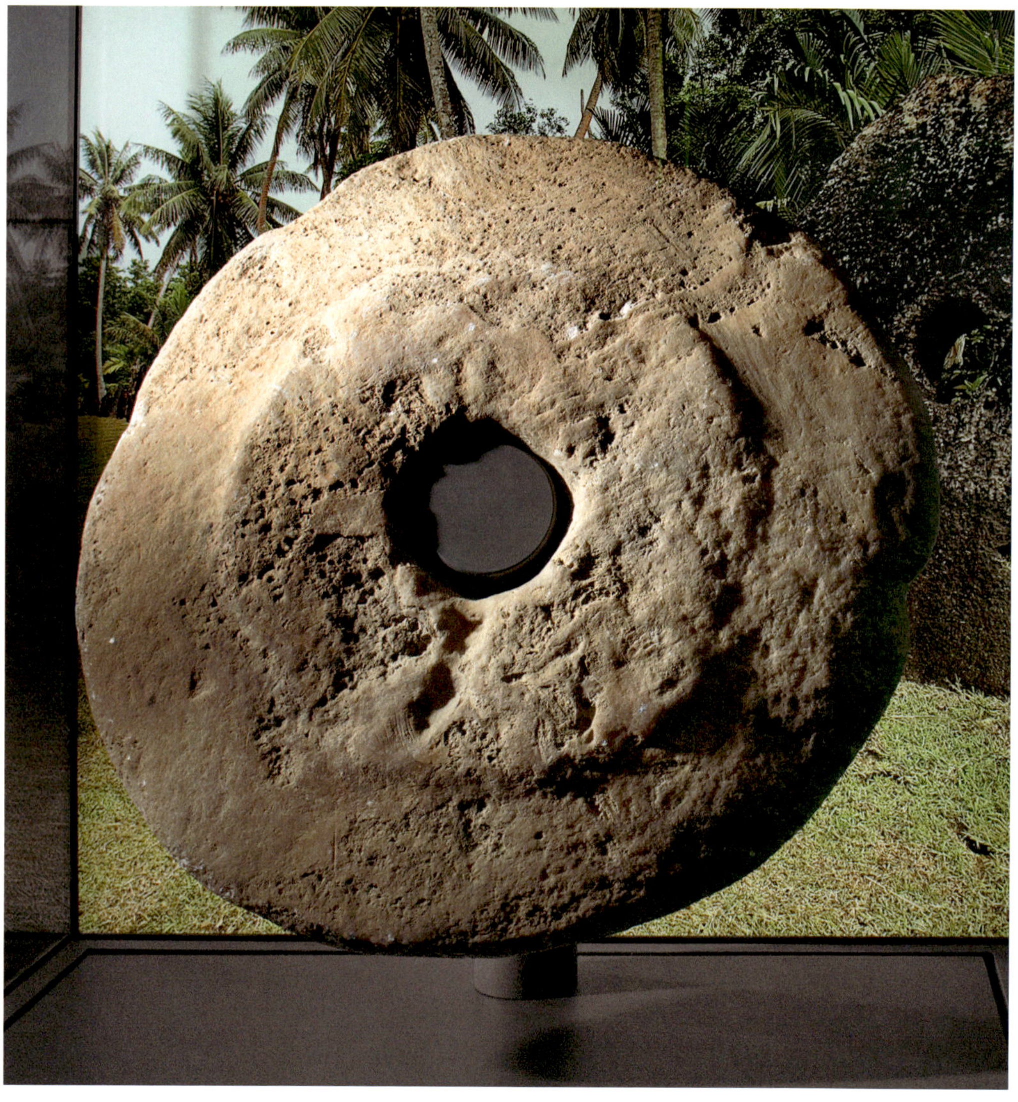

WORLD'S LARGEST CURRENCY

The stone money of the South Pacific island of Yap was probably already in use more than 1,500 years ago. Aragonite does not occur naturally on Yap. The stones, up to four metres in size, were transported on rafts from Palau, 400 km away.

COWRIE SNAILS, ASIA, OCEANIA, AFRICA, UNTIL MID-20TH C

Cowries were the global currency among the traditional media of payment. They are found in the Indian Pacific Ocean. Already used 3,000 years ago as currency in China, Arabic traders brought them to Africa in the 7th century AD.

MARKET VALUE OF COWRIES IN SUDAN IN 1850:
8 COWRIES = 1 EGG
1,000 COWRIES = 1 SHEEP
6,000–7,000 COWRIES = 1 OX

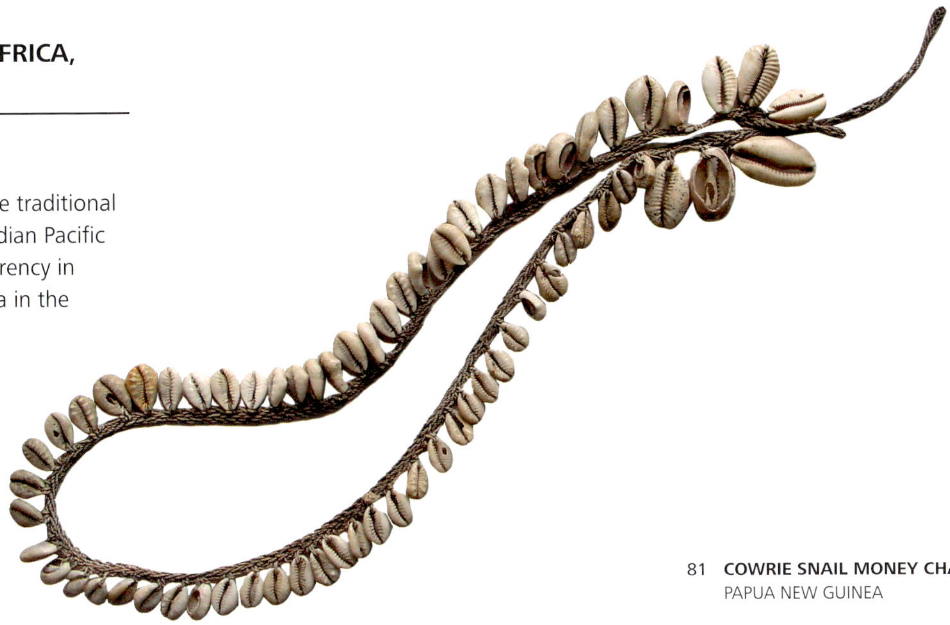

81 **COWRIE SNAIL MONEY CHAIN**
PAPUA NEW GUINEA

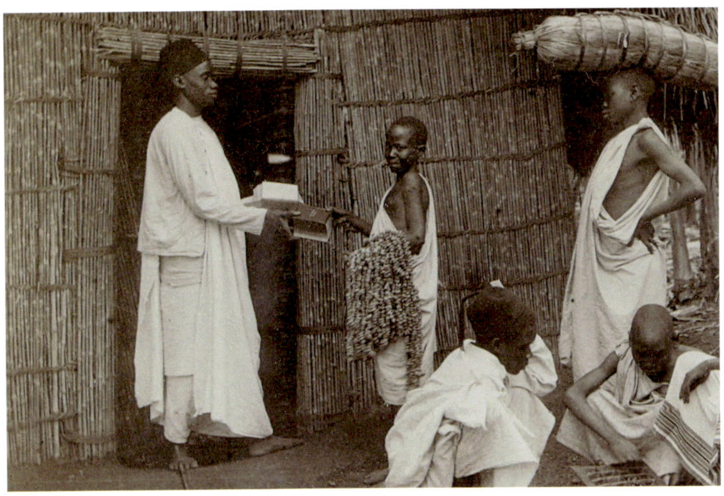

A UGANDAN BOY BUYS A BIBLE WITH COWRIES
(CA 1900).

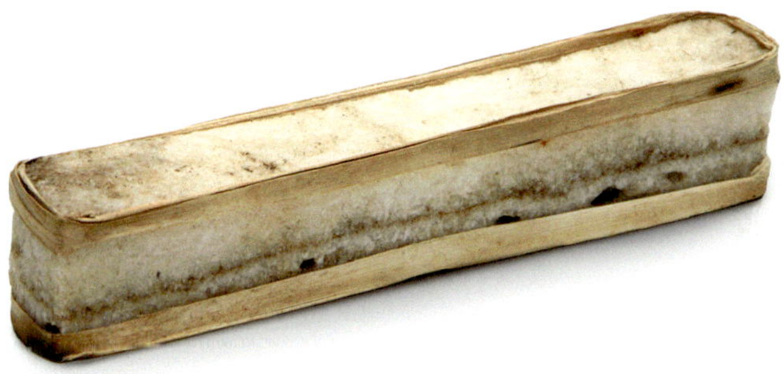

82 **BAR OF SALT AS CURRENCY**

COCOA BEANS, CENTRAL AMERICA, UNTIL END 19TH C

The Mayans used cocoa beans as currency, expressing the value of all kinds of items in terms of cocoa beans. The beans were so valuable that people even forged them, reproducing them out of clay or drilling into them and filling the husk with soil.

BARS OF SALT (AMOLI) AS CURRENCY, ETHIOPIA, UNTIL CA 1940

Salt is a vital good and sought-after commodity. In some parts of the world, salt served as a medium of payment into the 20th century. The value of the Ethiopian salt bars grew with their distance from the salt breaks.

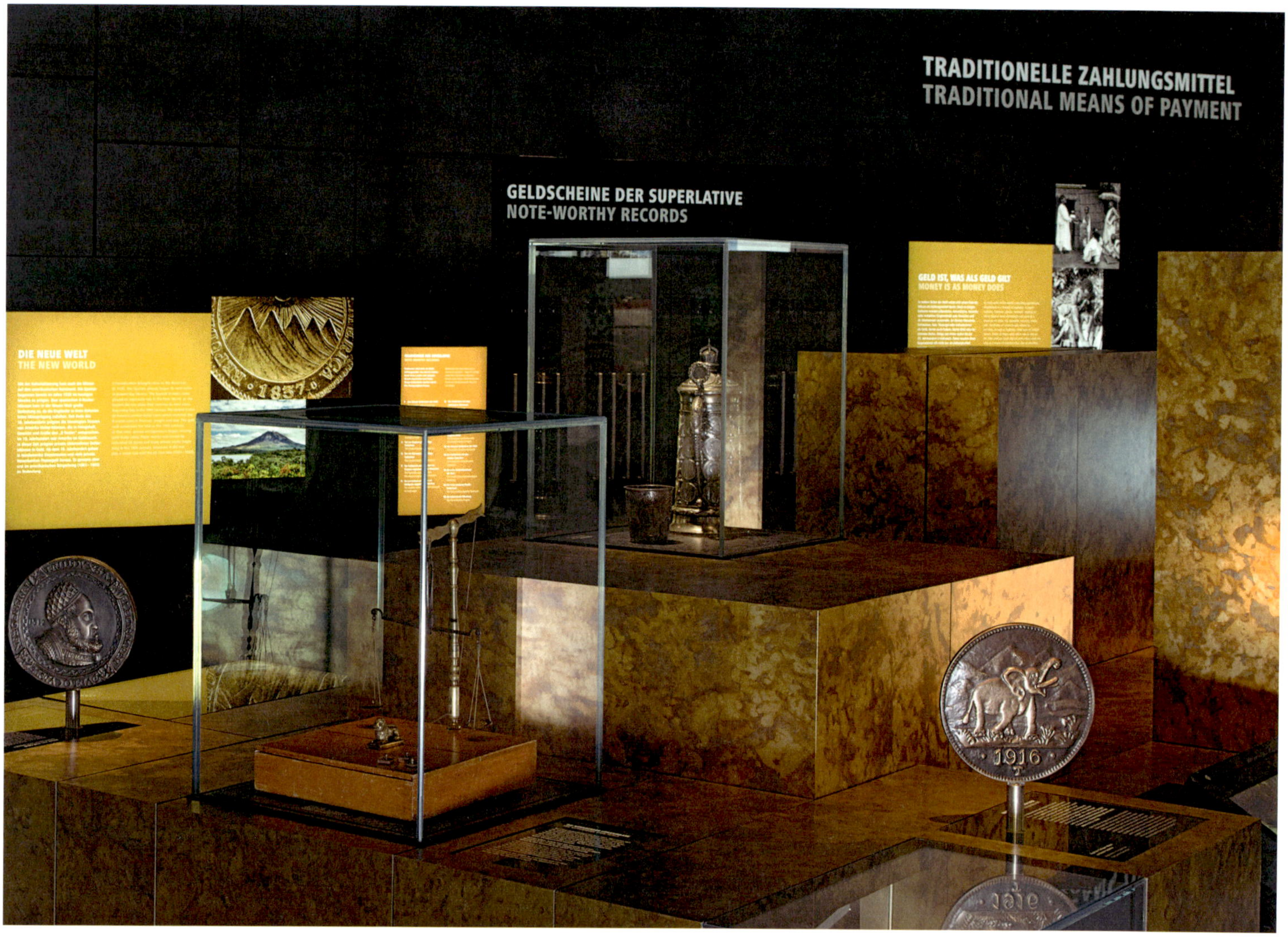
TRADITIONELLE ZAHLUNGSMITTEL
TRADITIONAL MEANS OF PAYMENT
GELDSCHEINE DER SUPERLATIVE
NOTE-WORTHY RECORDS
DIE NEUE WELT
THE NEW WORLD
1837
1916

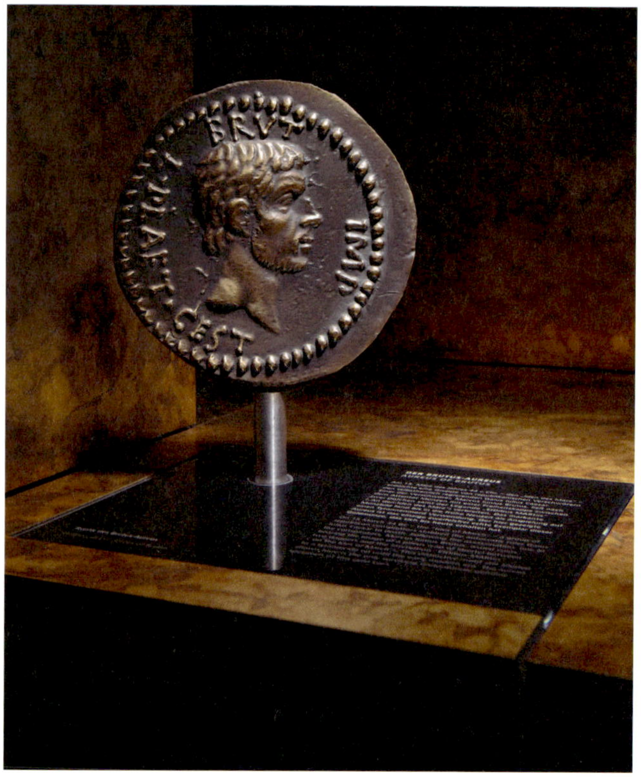
BRVT
IMP

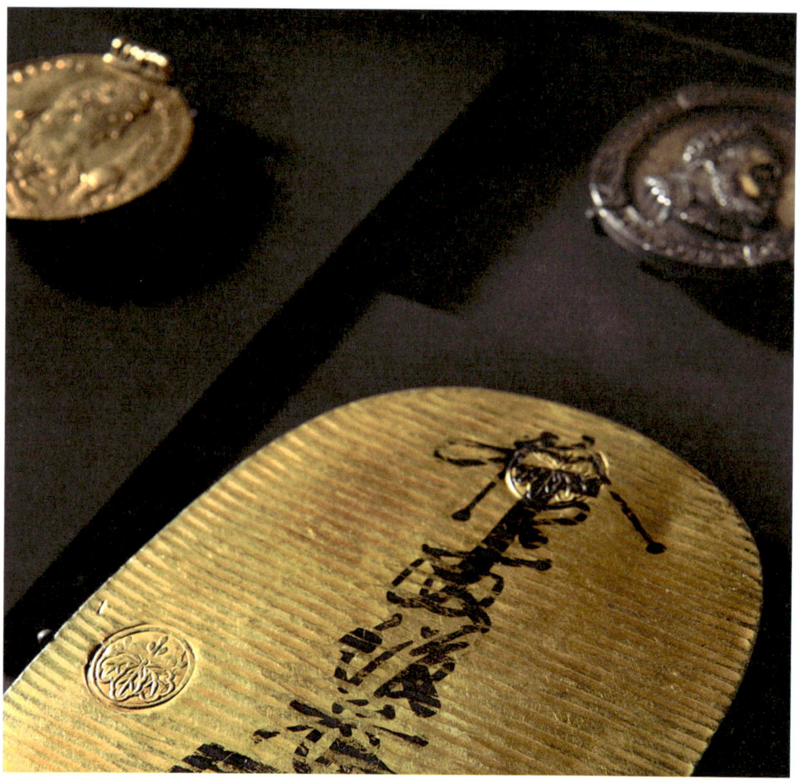

AUREUS OF BRUTUS

On 15 March 44 BC – the "Ides of March" – a group of republican conspirators stabbed the autocratic ruler Gaius Julius Caesar to death. Following the assassination, one of the conspirators, Marcus Junius Brutus, issued coins bearing the image of a pileus (cap of liberty) between two daggers and the inscription "*EID MAR*" (Eidibus Martiis – "on the Ides of March"). This distinctive motif was still used until the early modern era as an allusion to tyrannicide. The aureus shown in the Money Museum is the only surviving specimen of this gold coin which is definitely genuine.

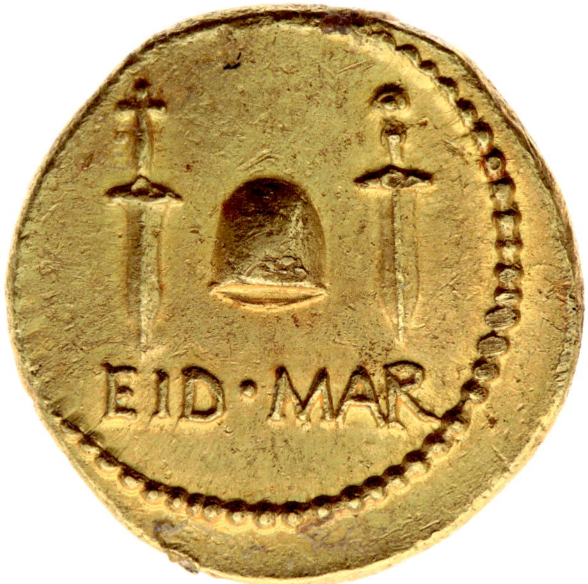

83
AUREUS OF BRUTUS
43/42 BC
(SCALE 4:1)

LORENZO DI PIERFRANCESCO DE' MEDICI MEDAL, 1537

The powerful Medici successfully established a hereditary duchy in Florence and did away with the Republic. Alessandro de' Medici ruled as Duke of Florence from 1531. Lorenzo di Pierfrancesco de' Medici, a distant relative, murdered him in 1537. He cited a love of liberty and the desire to preserve the Republic to justify his deed. It was probably motivated more by envy and hate, however, as Alessandro had passed him over in favour of Cosimo de' Medici as successor.

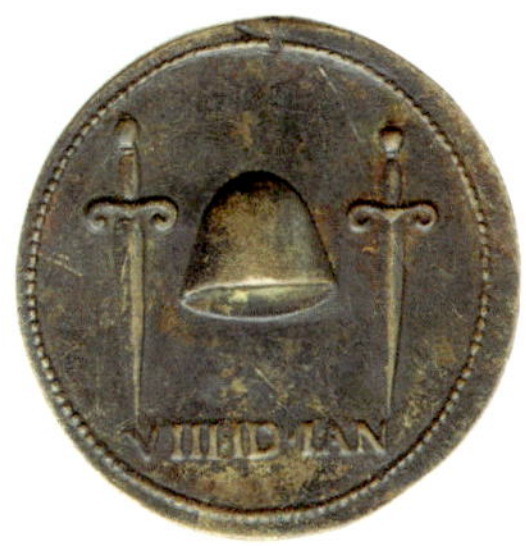

84
LORENZO DI PIERFRANCESCO DE' MEDICI, MEDALLION
1537

HEINRICH II, KING OF FRANCE MEDAL, 1552

In the mid-16th century, the German imperial princes felt threatened by the Catholic claim to power of Emperor Charles V. The princely opposition sought help from King Henry II of France; in 1552 the Treaty of Chambord was concluded between them, in which Henry pledged his support. On this medal, probably minted to mark this occasion, Henry was depicted as a guarantor of liberty.

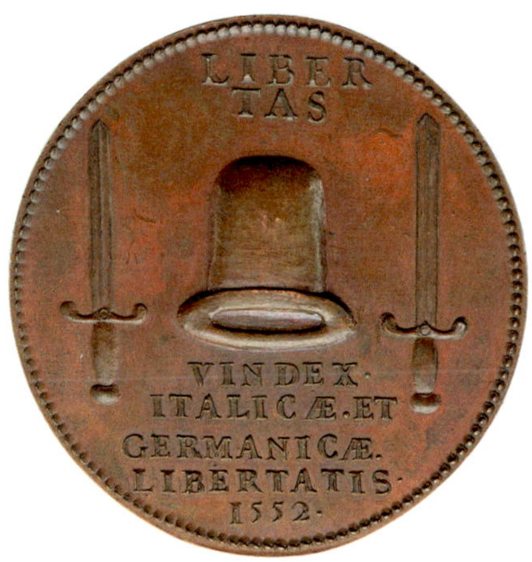

85
HENRY II, MEDAILLON
1552

WHEN IN NEED, GOLD WILL DO

Over the history of money, times of siege and emergency have brought forth some unique coins. When no other metal was available, objects made of gold were often melted down. The tyrant Lachares, for example, took the temple treasure at the Acropolis of Athens. During the Siege of Vienna in 1529, the defenders minted "klippen" by melting down church treasures: these square coins were easier to produce than the common round ones. Another example is the 15-rupees piece produced in German East Africa during World War I, which many consider to be the most beautiful German coin ever minted.

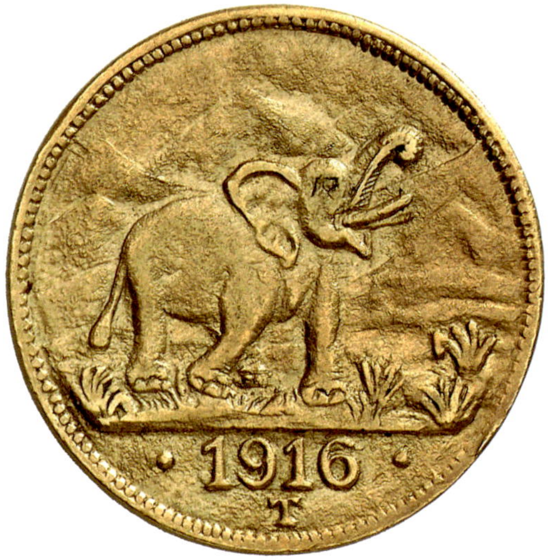

86
GERMAN EAST AFRICA, 15 RUPEES, 1916
(SCALE 3:1)

THE BIRD OF PARADISE

Until as recently as the 20th century, dried birds of paradise skins served as currency on the Pacific island of New Guinea, though only for important ceremonies such as weddings. These songbirds, with their colourful feathers, are also a popular motif for coins and banknotes. When, in 1894, the German New Guinea Company obtained the right to mint coins for the then-German protectorate, it chose the bird of paradise as the motif. Today, the bird of paradise is found on all of Papua New Guinea's currency.

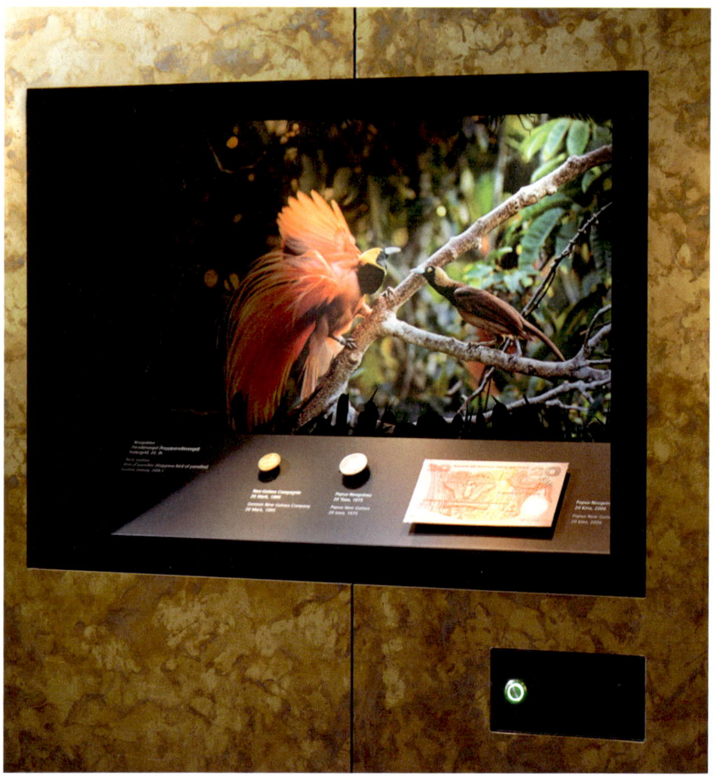

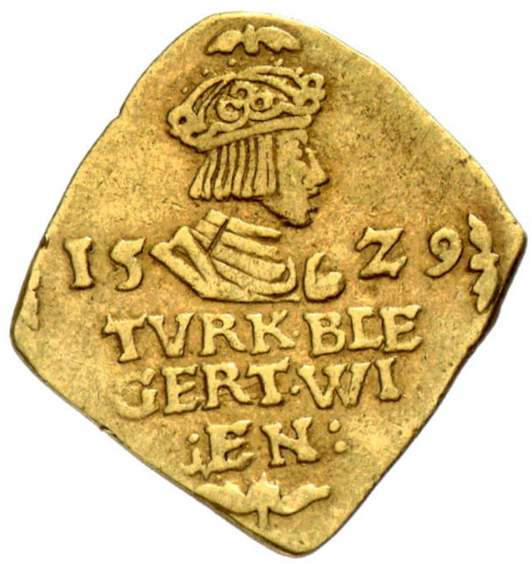

87
DUCAT (KLIPPE), 1529
(SCALE 3:1)

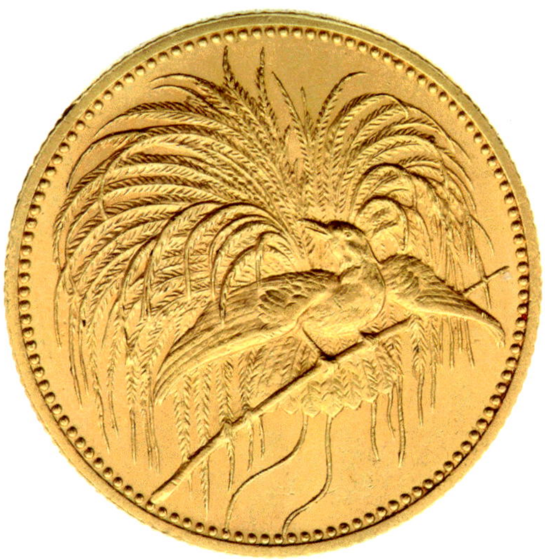

88
GERMAN NEW GUINEA, 20 MARK, 1895
(SCALE 3:1)

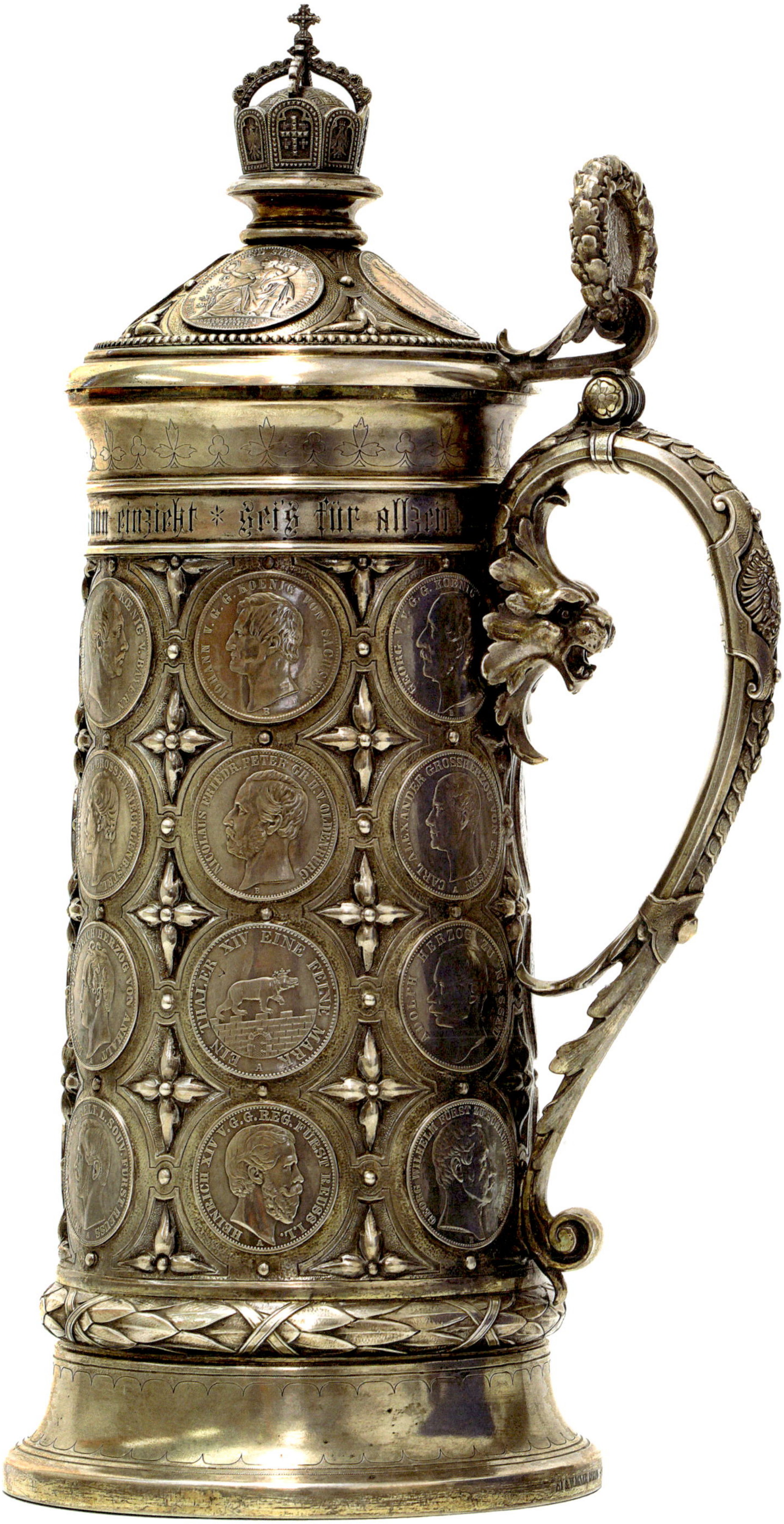

HERE'S TO THE GERMAN REICH !

The custom of decorating drinking vessels with coins has been around in Germany since the 16th century. This tankard commemorates the foundation of the German Reich in 1871 and the introduction of the Mark as its currency. The 33 thaler coins come from the individual German states and from Austria. The 1-Mark coin worked into the lid's thumb piece symbolises the inception of the new currency area. Altogether, the coins had a value of exactly 100 Mark.

89 **COIN-DECORATED TANKARD**, 1873

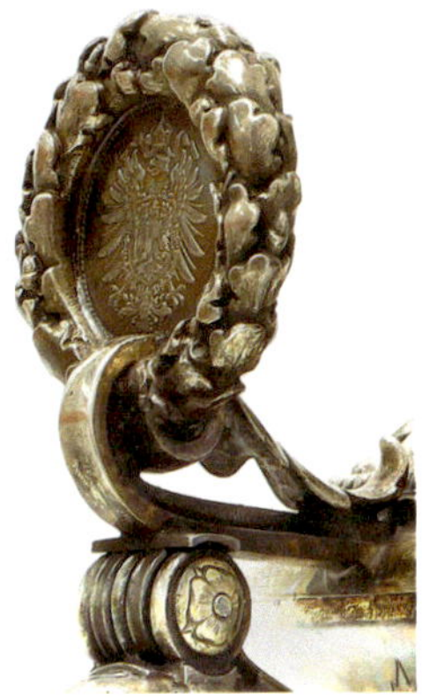

THE THUMB REST IS USED TO LIFT THE LID WITH YOUR THUMB. THE SILVERSMITHS WORKED A 1-MARK COIN, THE NEW CURRENCY IN THE GERMAN REICH, INTO THIS PROMINENT PART OF THE LID. THE NEW CURRENCY SYMBOLISES THE NEW AND STANDS IN SHARP CONTRAST TO THE 33 THALER COINS THAT REPRESENT THE PAST.

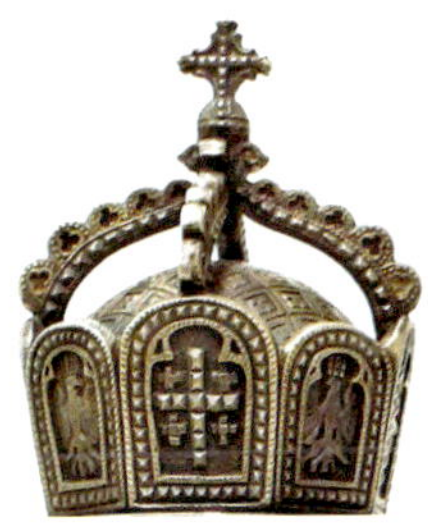

ON TOP OF THE LID IS A CROWN, THE DESIGN OF WHICH IS CLOSELY MODELLED ON THE CROWN OF THE NEW EMPIRE. THIS CROWN WAS NEVER ACTUALLY MADE AND EXISTED ONLY AS A MODEL, BUT WAS STILL PRESENT IN THE EMPIRE'S POLITICAL IMAGERY.

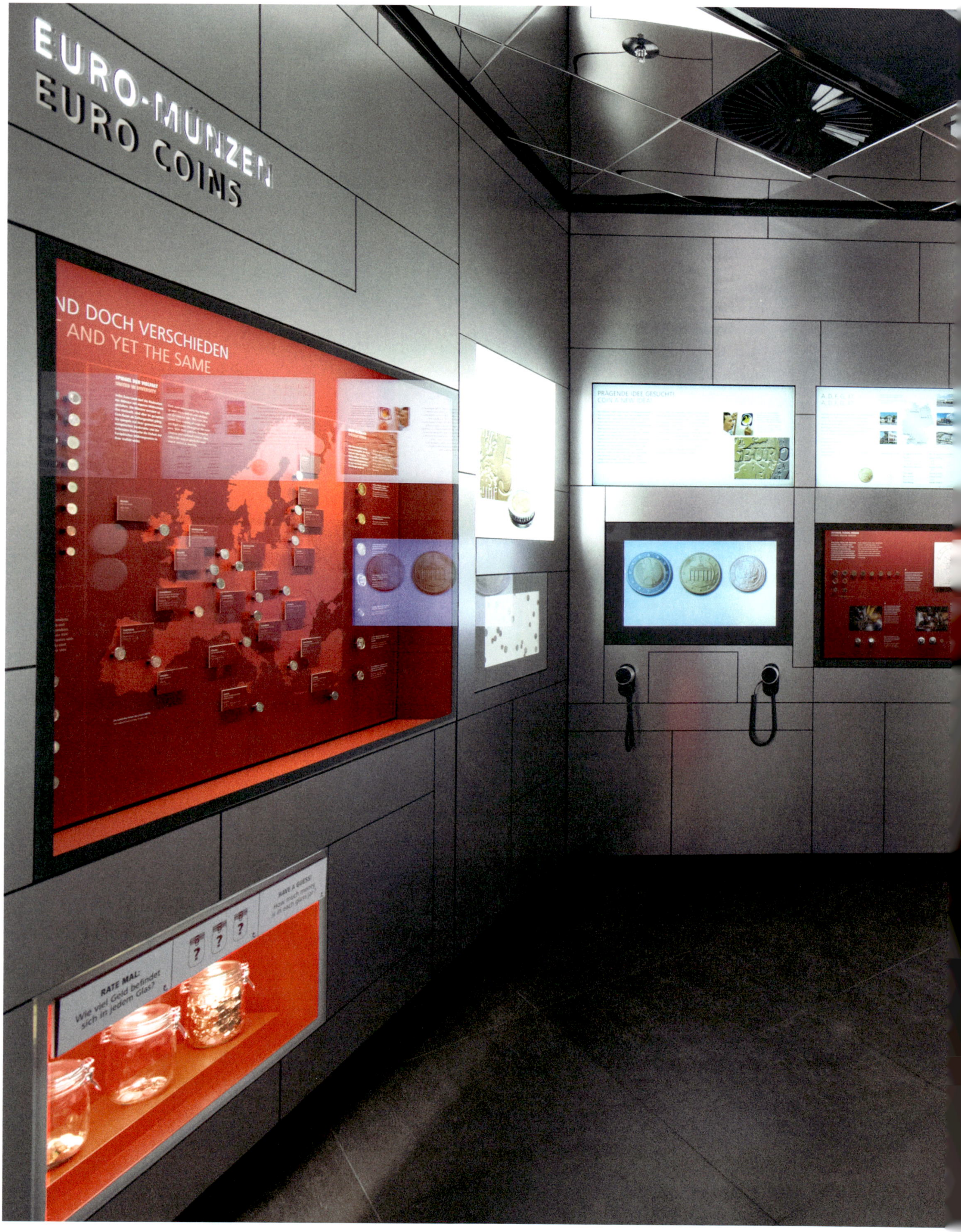
EURO-MÜNZEN
EURO COINS
ND DOCH VERSCHIEDEN
AND YET THE SAME
RATE MAL:
Wie viel Geld befindet sich in jedem Glas?
HAVE A GUESS!

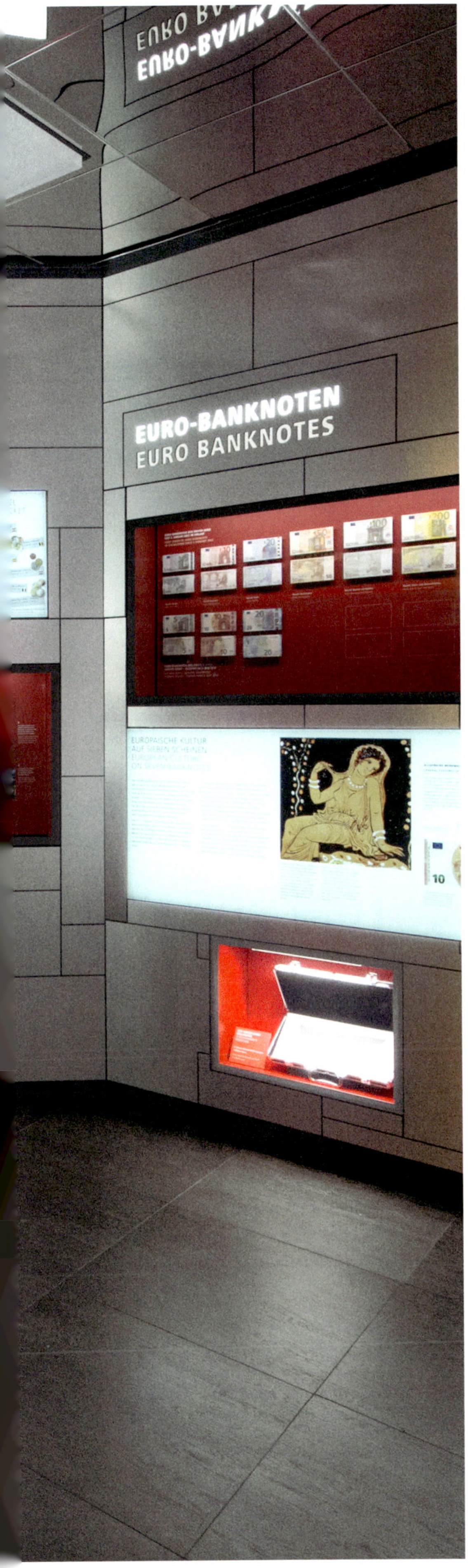

VAULT

The steel-panelled vault is a modern treasure chamber of knowledge surrounding euro cash; the single currency has been circulating as cash in many European countries since 2002.

Text panels, exhibits, films and media stations illustrate euro cash from many angles: visitors can see, for instance, the various draft designs of euro coins and notes, as well as the two current series of banknotes and the coins issued by every euro-area country. The visitor will also be shown the individual stages in the manufacturing process at mints and printing works.

In Germany, coins are minted by the Federal Ministry of Finance, whereas the Deutsche Bundesbank holds the monopoly over the issuing of banknotes. The Bundesbank's tasks in supplying and processing cash are manifold: it not only circulates new currency through the conduit of commercial banks, but also regularly inspects circulating banknotes and coins, destroys and replaces mutilated currency and weeds out counterfeits.

THE SAME AND YET DIFFERENT

UNITED IN DIVERSITY

As of 1 January 2002, more than 300 million people in Europe have been using the euro as their means of payment. The obverse sides of the eight euro coins are the same in all euro-area countries: images of the European continent and the twelve stars of the European flag. Each euro-area country has the right to mint euros with its own design on the reverse side. The coins thus reveal their country of origin but are legal tender throughout the euro area. With their common European obverse and national reverse, they reflect the way in which the euro area is united in diversity.

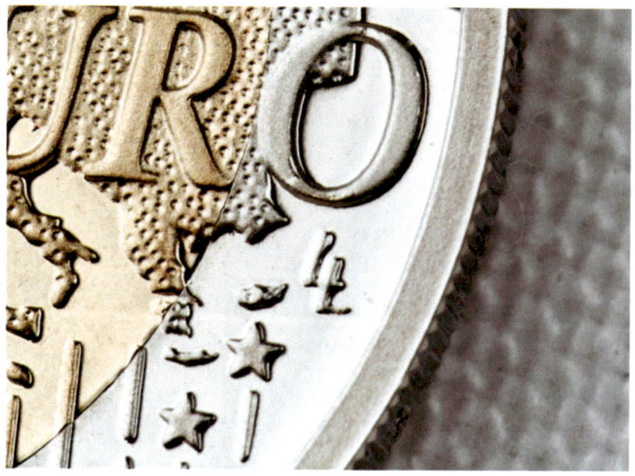

LUC LUYCX OF THE ROYAL BELGIAN MINT IS THE DESIGNER OF THE EUROPEAN SIDE OF THE EURO COINS. HIS INITIALS "LL" APPEAR ON EVERY COIN.

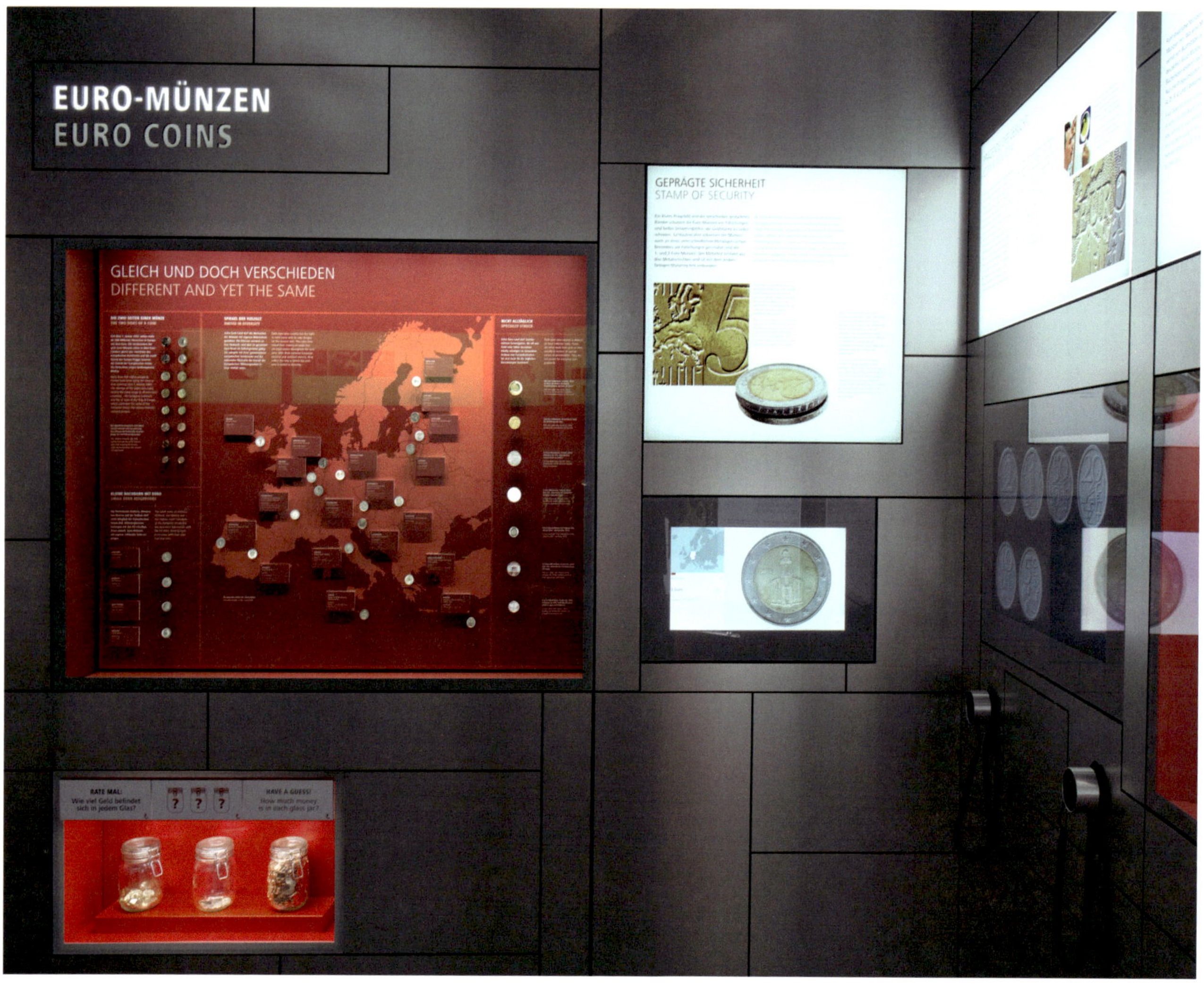

DRAWN, MILLED, MINTED

Steel, copper, nickel, zinc, aluminium and tin – in differing alloys – are the raw materials that comprise euro coins. Transforming them into the shiny coins in our purses and wallets is an arduous process that fuses design, craftsmanship and state-of-the-art technology. First, an artist needs to come up with a coin design. Then, the designers sculpt a scaled-up plaster model of both sides of the coin. A laser scans the model and transfers it to the computer. A computer-aided machine mills the design, in its actual size, into a block of steel. This produces the master dies, from which several copies are subsequently made. The master dies are impressed on a steel body under high pressure. This is how the working dies are created. In the coining press, both sides of the coin are minted at the same time from the blanks.

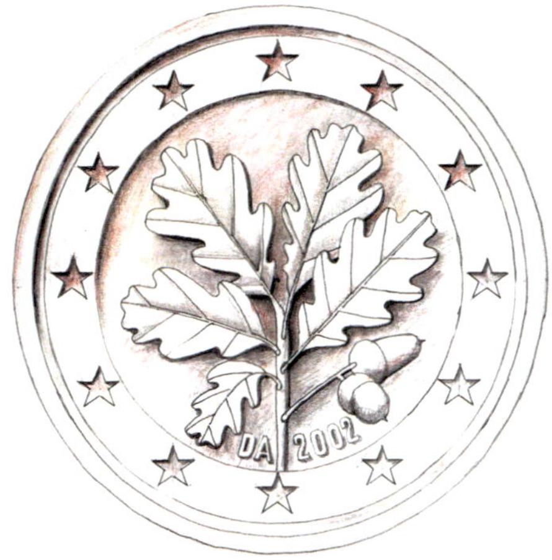

90 DRAFT DESIGN OF THE GERMAN REVERSE OF THE 1-CENT COIN BY ROLF LEDERBOGEN

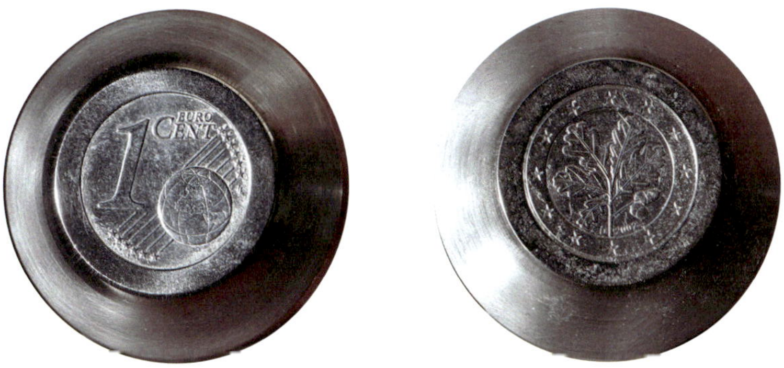

91 MASTER DIES FROM THE PICTURE SIDE OF THE 1-CENT COIN. THE DESIGNS ARE JUST AS VISIBLE ON THE MASTER DIES AS ON THE FUTURE COINS.

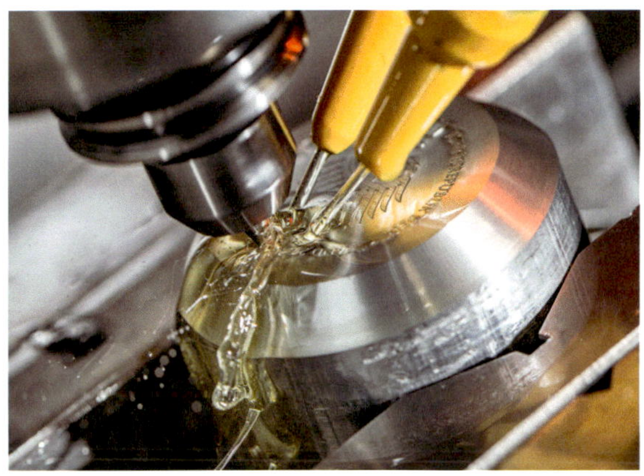

DIE MILLING

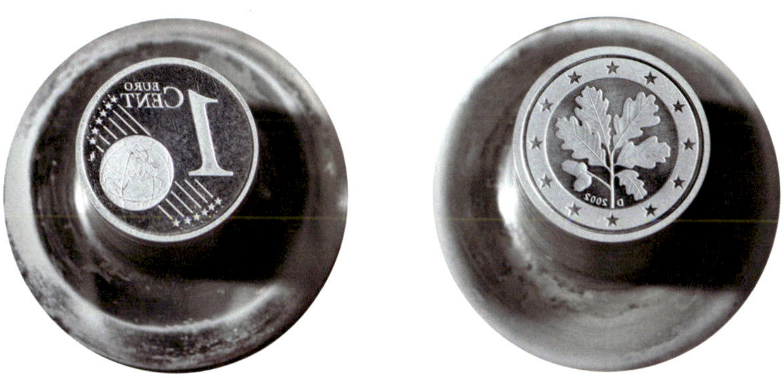

92 LOWER DIE/STAMPING DIE (MATRIX) FOR THE 1-CENT COIN. ON THE STAMPING DIES, IMAGES AND LETTERING ARE BACK TO FRONT AND RECESSED SO THAT THEY APPEAR CORRECTLY ON THE COIN LATER.

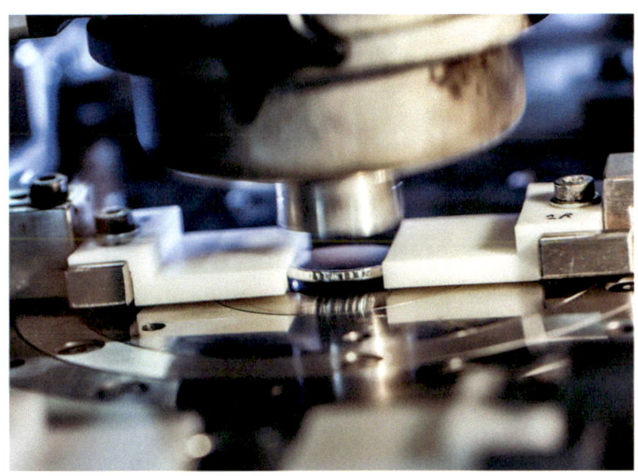

COIN-MINTING MACHINE

EUROPEAN CULTURE ON SEVEN BANKNOTES

The seven banknotes are identical throughout the euro area and show architectural elements from different periods of Europe's cultural history. The ECB began introducing the second series of euro banknotes in 2013. New elements are the improved security features, a bolder colour scheme and an additional motif. Europa, a figure from Greek mythology, appears in the watermark and the hologram, which is why the new series is called the Europa series.

93 **STAMPING DIE (PATRIX) WITH THE HEAD OF EUROPA AS A WATERMARK MOTIF.**

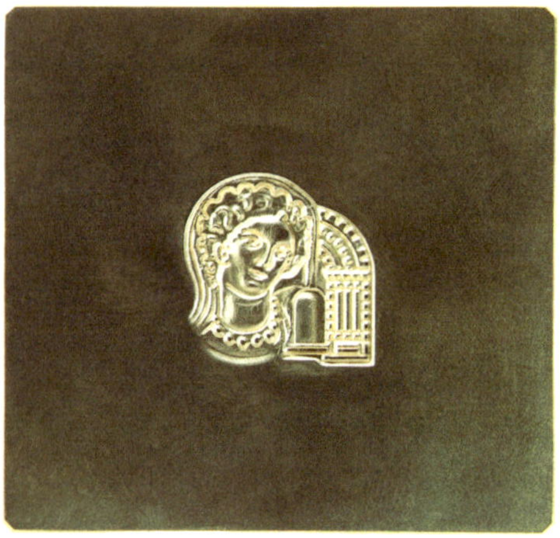

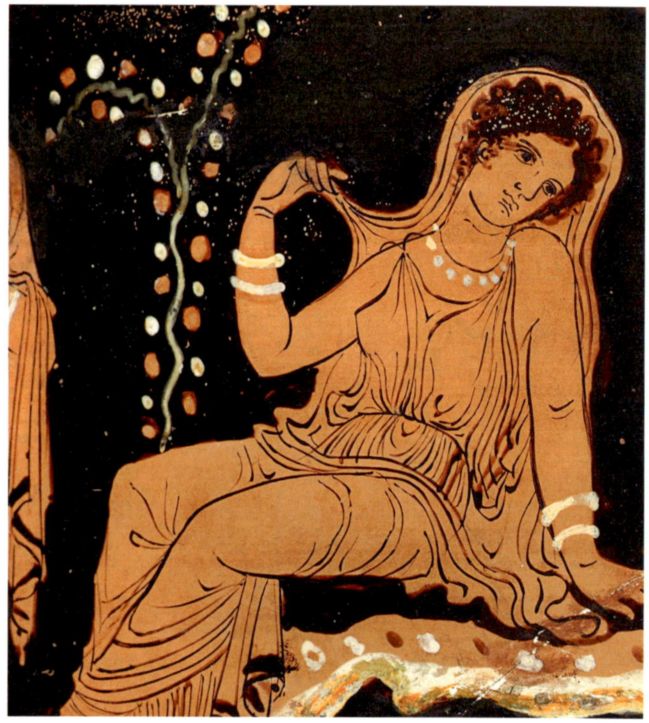

EUROPA IS A PHOENICIAN PRINCESS FROM GREEK MYTHOLOGY WITH WHOM THE FATHER OF THE GODS, ZEUS, FELL IN LOVE. EUROPA WAS PLAYING BY THE SEASIDE ONE DAY WHEN ZEUS TRANSFORMED HIMSELF INTO A BULL AND CARRIED HER AWAY ON HIS BACK ACROSS THE SEA TO CRETE. EUROPA'S ABDUCTION HAS OFTEN FOUND ITS WAY INTO LITERATURE AND ART. OUR CONTINENT IS NAMED AFTER HER.

DESIGNERS GO HEAD TO HEAD

In February 1996, the European Monetary Institute (EMI), the predecessor to the European Central Bank, launched a competition with very stringent conditions to design the first euro banknotes. Ten months later, the EMI Council declared Robert Kalina from Austria the winner. His design comprising windows, gates and bridges presented a convincing vision of a united Europe with a shared history and a common future. In 2006, Reinhold Gerstetter won the competition to design the second series of euro banknotes. His idea to use the portrait of Europa as an additional image gave the series its name "Europa series".

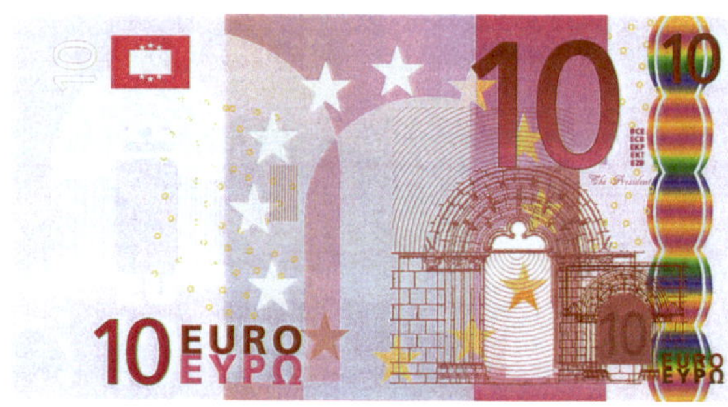

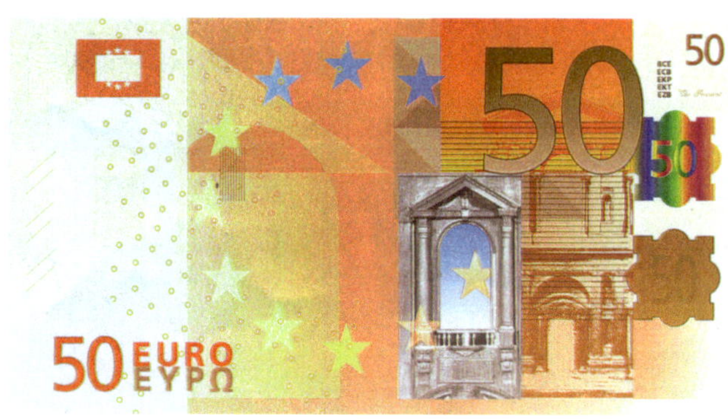

THE WINNING COMPETITION DESIGN BY ROBERT KALINA. THE DESIGN UNDERWENT NUMEROUS REVISIONS BEFORE THE FIRST EURO BANKNOTES WERE PRINTED.

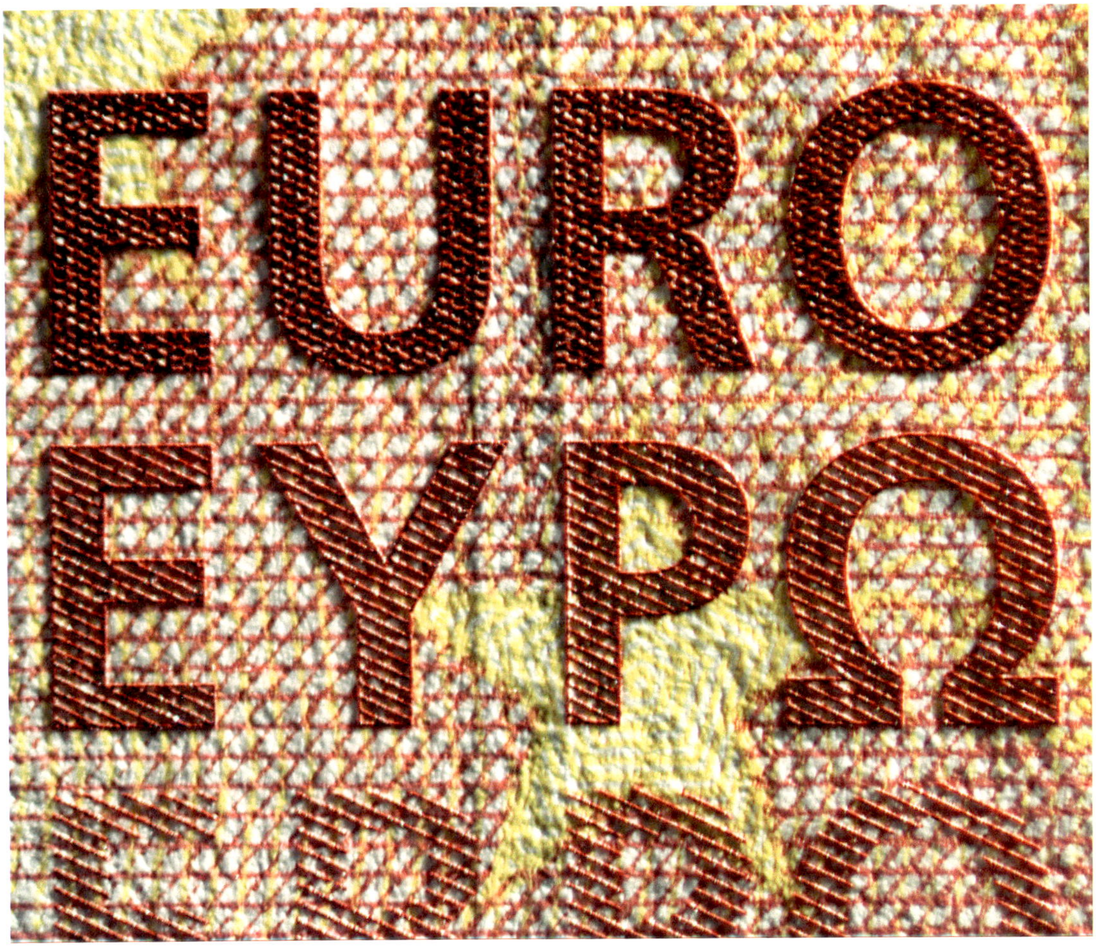

THE RAISED PRINT ON BANKNOTES COMES FROM INTAGLIO PRINTING. INK IS TRANSFERRED UNDER HIGH PRESSURE FROM THE INDENTATIONS ENGRAVED ON THE PRINTING PLATE ON TO THE BANKNOTE PAPER. ON THE FRONT OF THE BANKNOTE, YOU CAN RUN YOUR FINGERS OVER THE IMAGE, THE VALUE NUMERAL, THE WORD EURO AND THE ABBREVIATIONS FOR THE ECB.

ONE STEP AHEAD OF COUNTERFEITERS

Banknotes have more secrets than you might think. They have many visible and invisible security features to make it harder for counterfeiters to forge them. Producing banknotes is an incredibly intricate process and uses state-of-the-art technology. Counterfeit protection begins with the paper that banknotes are printed on. The paper used for euro banknotes is made of a special type of cotton and contains unique features. High-security printing works use a number of processes such as offset and intaglio printing as well as special inks. The rest is a secret …

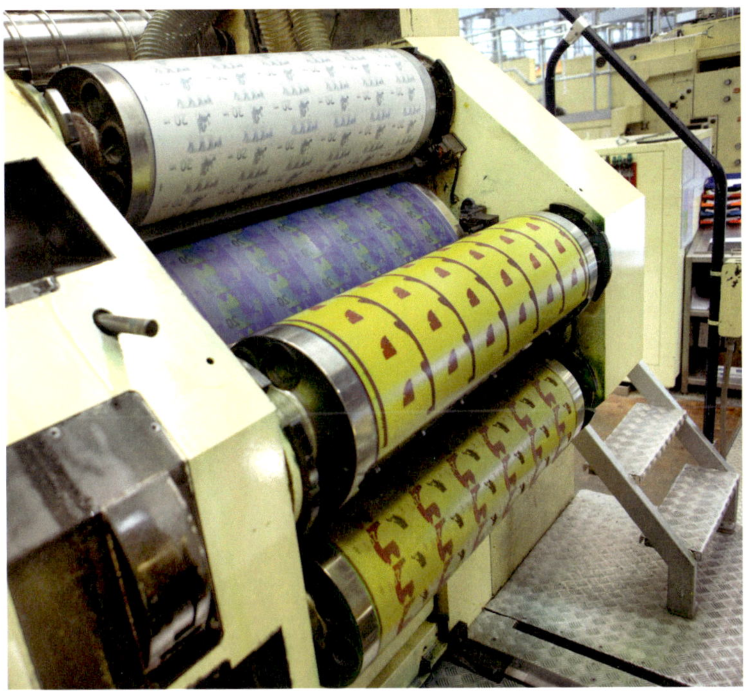

IN SIMULTANEOUS DRY OFFSET PRINTING, LETTER PRESS AND OFFSET PRINTING PLATES TRANSFER INK TO PAPER VIA A RUBBER SHEET. MOTIFS FROM EIGHT PLATES IN UP TO 16 COLOURS ARE PRINTED ON BANKNOTES SIMULTANEOUSLY.

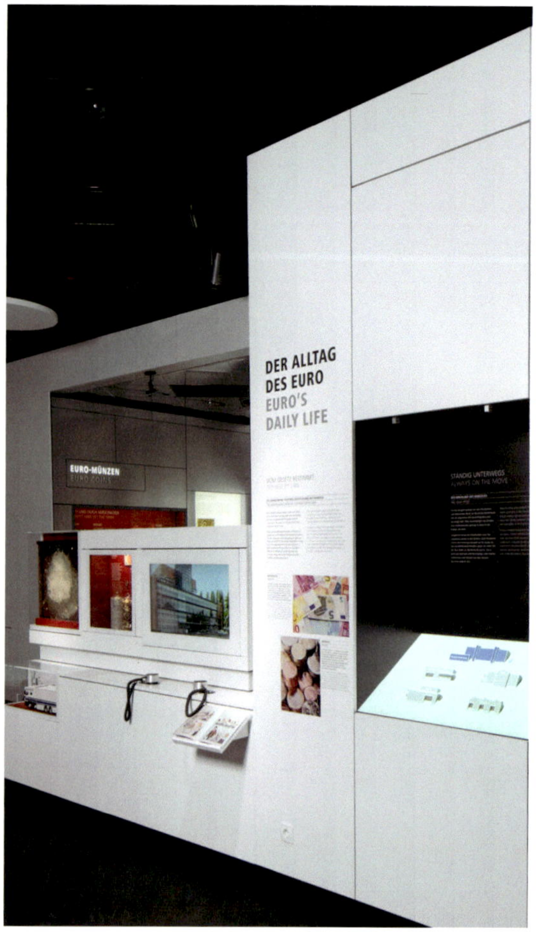

DEFINED BY LAW

THE BUNDESBANK PROVIDES GERMANY WITH CASH

Only government-authorised bodies have the right to issue euro banknotes and coins, the legal tender in the euro area. Everyone must accept them to settle a financial obligation. The European Central Bank together with the national central banks decides each year how much fresh cash needs to be produced to make sure there is enough cash in circulation. In Germany, the Deutsche Bundesbank brings cash into circulation via commercial banks.

COINAGE

It has always been the sole prerogative of the ruler of a country to mint coins. This centuries-old tradition has prevailed to the present day, so the government of each euro-area country is responsible for minting coins. This is known as the "coinage prerogative". In Germany, the Federal Ministry of Finance arranges for euro coins to be minted.

MONOPOLY

In the euro area, only the European Central Bank and the national central banks have the right to print banknotes and bring them into circulation. In other words, they have a monopoly on banknotes. In Germany, only the Deutsche Bundesbank has the right to issue banknotes. Pieces of printed paper only become legal tender when the Bundesbank issues them to the commercial banks.

ALWAYS ON THE MOVE

THE CASH CYCLE

New currency goes straight from the printing works and mints to the Deutsche Bundesbank, which supplies commercial banks with the cash they need. Bank customers then withdraw the cash either at the counter or from ATMs. In turn, retailers bring their cash takings back to the banks. Private individuals also pay surplus cash into their bank accounts. The commercial banks keep only part of this cash. The rest is returned to the Bundesbank, which checks it and removes damaged or counterfeit banknotes and coins from circulation, thus completing the cycle.

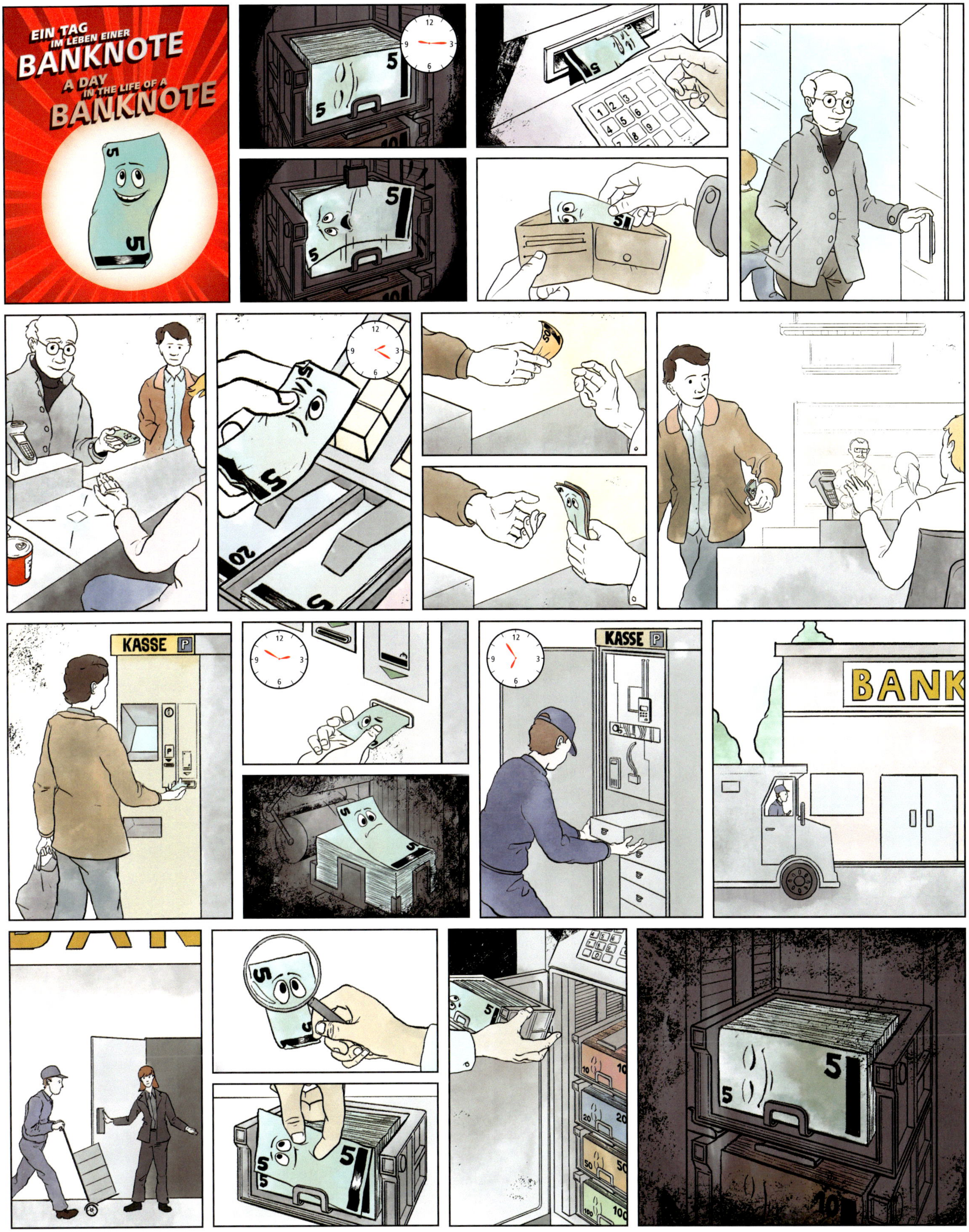
EIN TAG IM LEBEN EINER BANKNOTE
A DAY IN THE LIFE OF A BANKNOTE
KASSE P
KASSE P
BANK

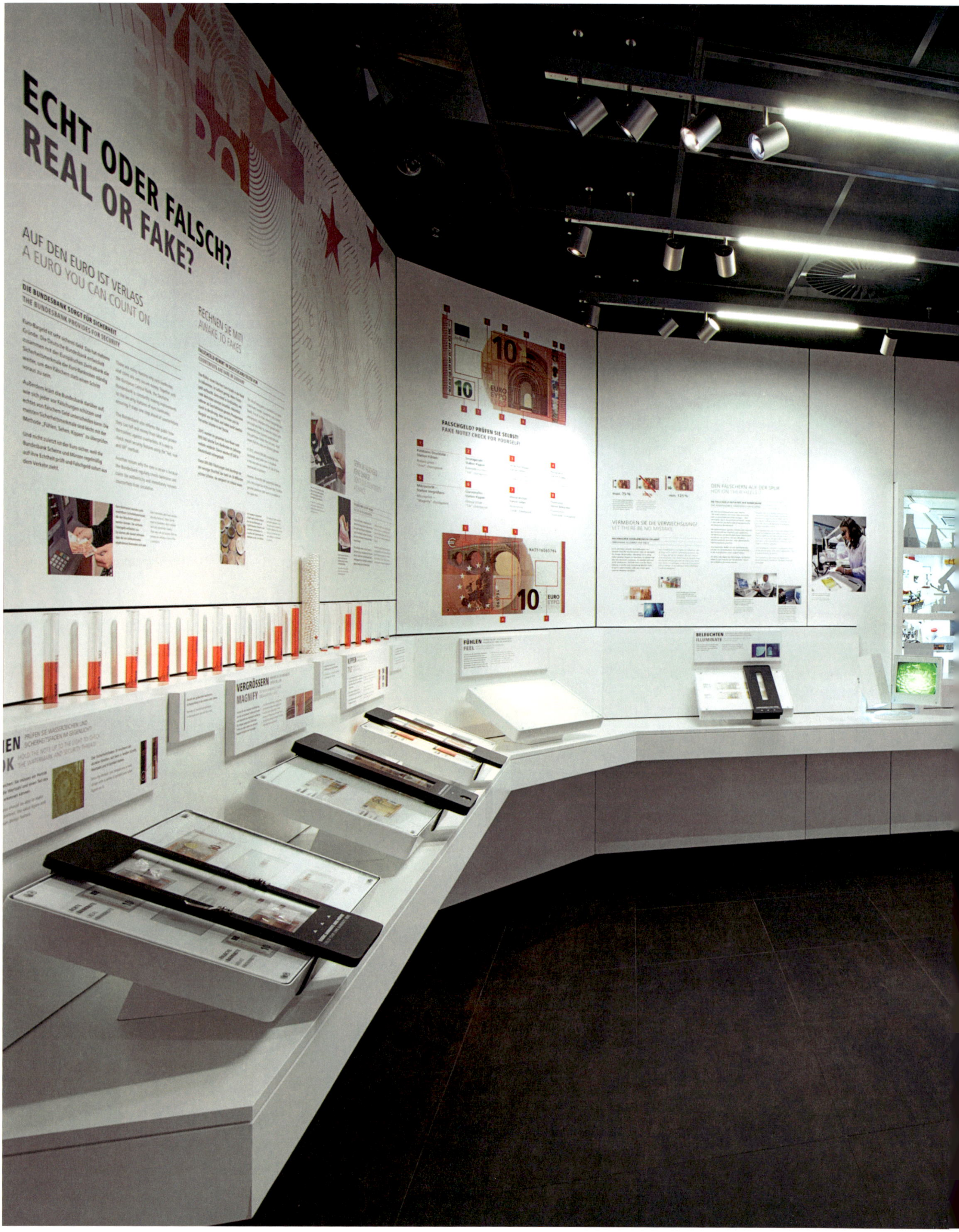
ECHT ODER FALSCH?
REAL OR FAKE?
AUF DEN EURO IST VERLASS
A EURO YOU CAN COUNT ON
DIE BUNDESBANK SORGT FÜR SICHERHEIT
THE BUNDESBANK PROVIDES FOR SECURITY
RECHNEN SIE MIT
AWAKE TO FAKES
FALSCHGELD? PRÜFEN SIE SELBST!
FAKE NOTE? CHECK FOR YOURSELF!
VERMEIDEN SIE DIE VERWECHSLUNG!
VERGRÖSSERN
MAGNIFY
FÜHLEN
FEEL
BELEUCHTEN
ILLUMINATE

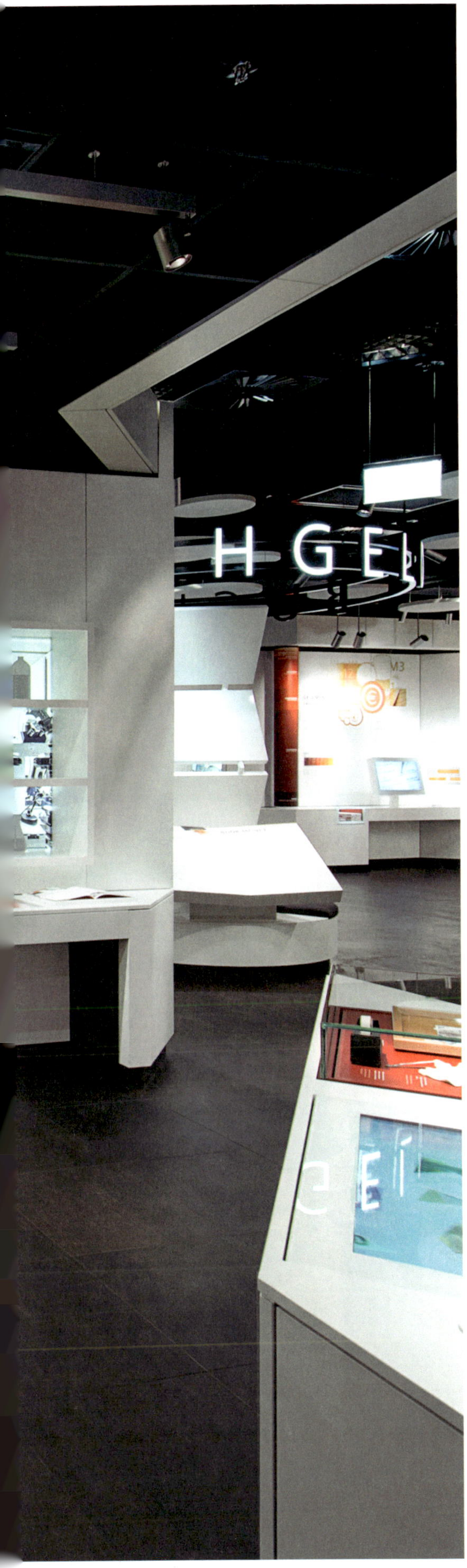

LABORATORY

The Deutsche Bundesbank is constantly improving the euro banknotes' security features, regularly inspects notes and coins for authenticity and detains counterfeits immediately. At the laboratories of its National Analysis Centre, it classifies counterfeits and enters them into a Europe-wide database.

Even in the Money Museum's laboratory, where visitors can try things out for themselves, everything revolves around the following question: real or fake? It is very easy to detect counterfeits using the "feel, look, tilt" method: at various activity stations, visitors can inspect banknotes held against a light, highly magnified, tilted and under ultraviolet light to detect individual security features and can touch the relief-like surface of the banknotes. A microscope is used to detect counterfeit coins.

How much counterfeit money is in circulation in Germany and the rest of the euro area? What are the most frequently forged banknotes and coins, and what do you do if you find yourself holding a fake euro banknote? Answers to practical questions surrounding counterfeit money make up the informative background of the laboratory.

A EURO YOU CAN COUNT ON

THE BUNDESBANK PROVIDES FOR SECURITY

There are many reasons why euro banknotes and coins are very secure money. Together with the European Central Bank, the Deutsche Bundesbank is constantly making improvements to the security features of euro banknotes, ensuring it stays one step ahead of counterfeiters. The Bundesbank also informs the public how they can tell real money from fakes and protect themselves against counterfeits. It is easy to check most security features using the "feel, look and tilt" method. Another reason why the euro is secure is because the Bundesbank regularly checks banknotes and coins for authenticity and immediately removes counterfeits from circulation.

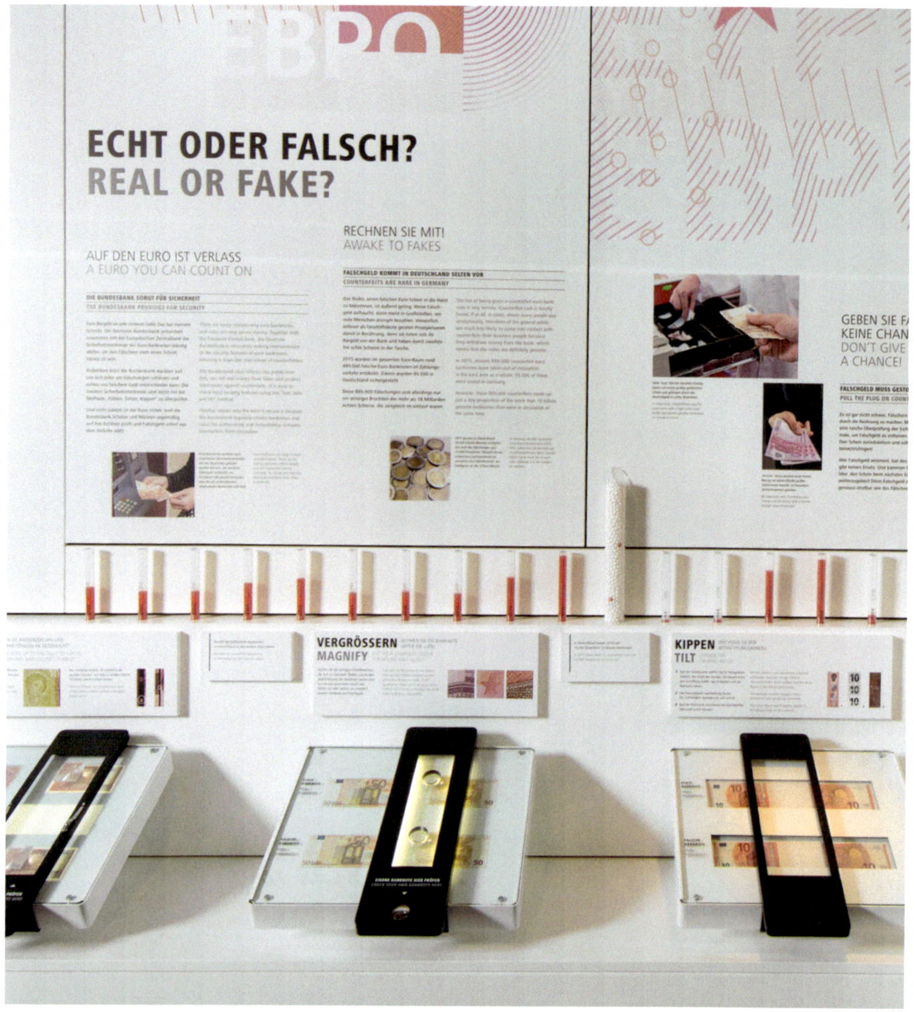

AWAKE TO FAKES

COUNTERFEITS ARE RARE IN GERMANY

The risk of being given a counterfeit euro banknote is very remote. Counterfeit cash is mostly found, if at all, in cities, where many people pay anonymously. Members of the general public are much less likely to come into contact with counterfeits than business people because they withdraw money from the bank, which means that the notes are definitely genuine. In 2015, around 899,000 counterfeit euro banknotes were taken out of circulation in the euro area as a whole. 95,500 of these were seized in Germany. However, these 899,000 counterfeits made up just a tiny proportion of the more than 18 billion genuine banknotes that were in circulation at the same time.

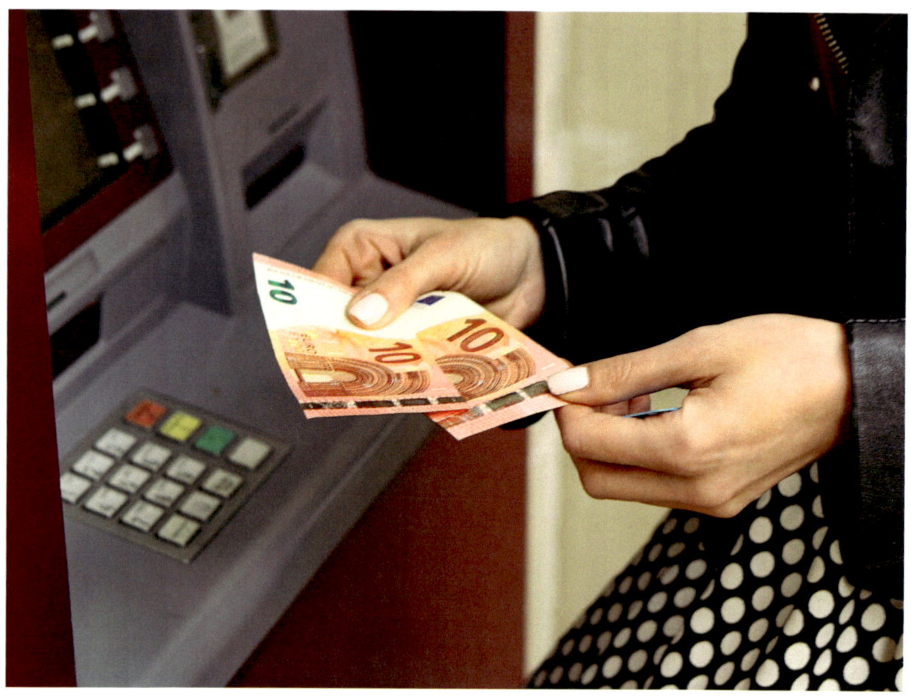

EURO BANKNOTES ALSO HAVE INVISIBLE SECURITY FEATURES. THESE CAN BE READ BY MACHINES, WHICH RELIABLY SORT OUT COUNTERFEIT MONEY.

FAKE NOTE? CHECK FOR YOURSELF!

1 FÜHLBARES DRUCKBILD
RAISED PRINT

2 SMARAGDZAHL
EMERALD NUMBER

3 SICHERHEITSFADEN
SECURITY THREAD

4 HOLOGRAMM
HOLOGRAM

5 MIKROSCHRIFT
MICROPRINT

6 GLANZSTREIFEN
GLOSSY STRIPE

7 WASSERZEICHEN
WATERMARK

8 FLUORESZENZ
FLUORESCENCE

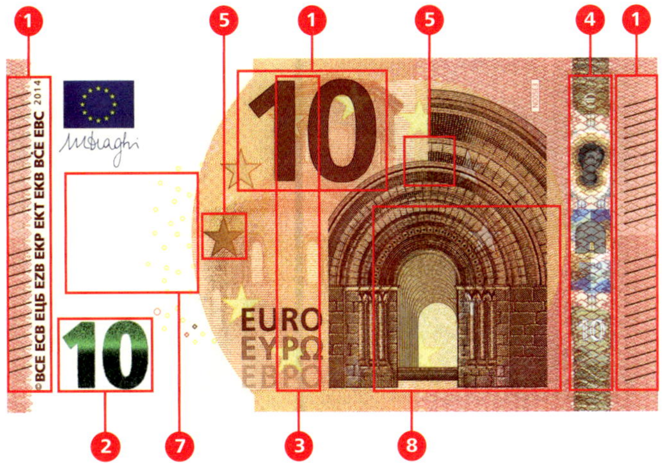

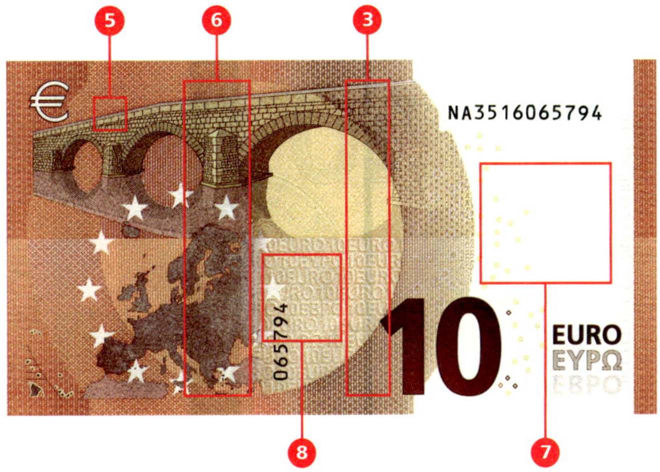

DON'T GIVE COUNTERFEITS A CHANCE!

PULL THE PLUG
ON COUNTERFEITING

Spoiling a counterfeiter's plans is child's play, really. Usually, a quick check of a banknote's security features is enough to uncover a fake. Then, all you need to do is reject the note and immediately call the police. Anyone who accepts counterfeit money loses out: reimbursements are out of the question. And don't even think about just passing it on to someone else at the shops – it is just as much a crime to distribute counterfeit money as it is to produce it!

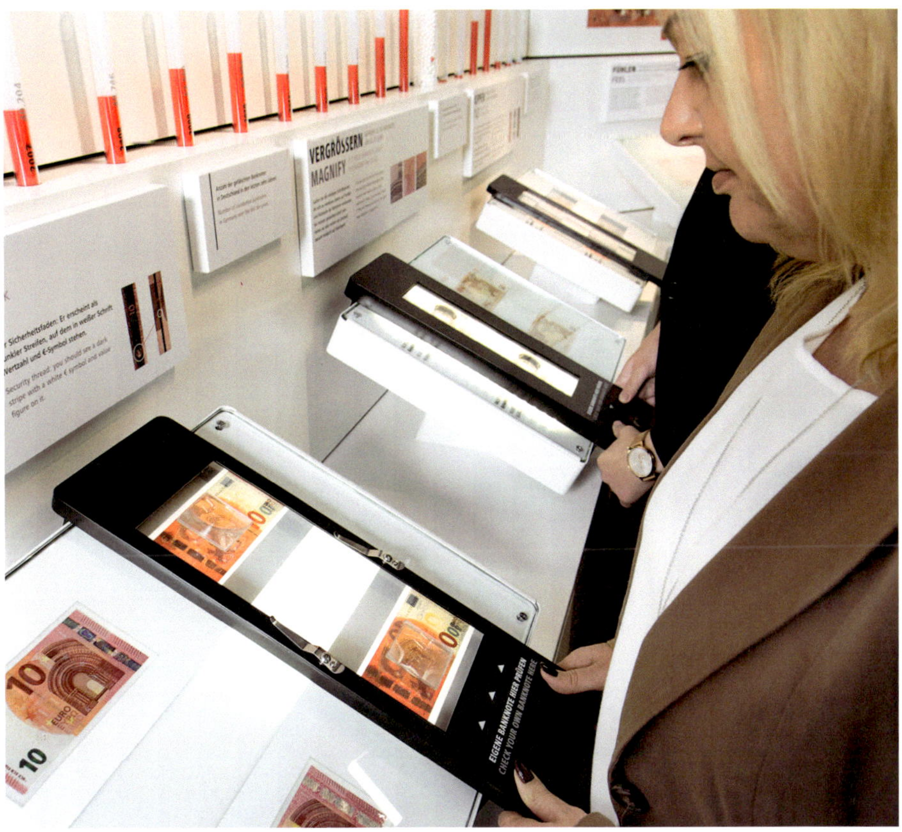

HOT ON THEIR HEELS

THE BUNDESBANK'S COUNTERFEIT DETECTIVES

Whether 300-euro fantasy notes or forged 100-dollar notes, fivers without a reverse or professional printed counterfeits – all the counterfeit money detected in Germany ends up in the labs of the Deutsche Bundesbank's National Analysis Centre. With investigative skill, the experts decipher the forger's thumbprint and compare the forgery's features with counterfeits already known to them. That way, they can assign notes originating from the same counterfeiting workshop to the same counterfeit category. Their findings are inputted in a database which all the central banks and police authorities in the European Union can access. The counterfeits are stored as evidence in the Bundesbank's vaults for 20 years and then destroyed.

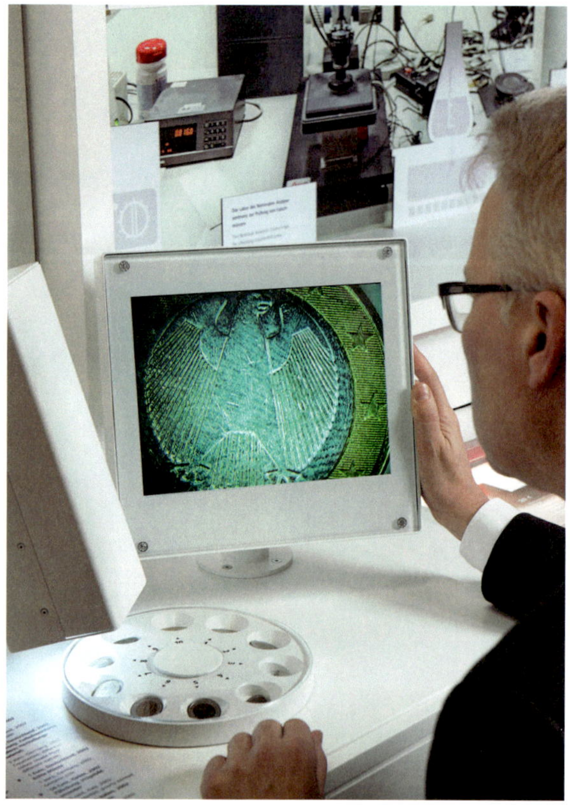

DISTINGUISHING GENUINE FROM COUNTERFEIT COINS IN THE MONEY MUSEUM WITH THE AID OF A MICROSCOPE

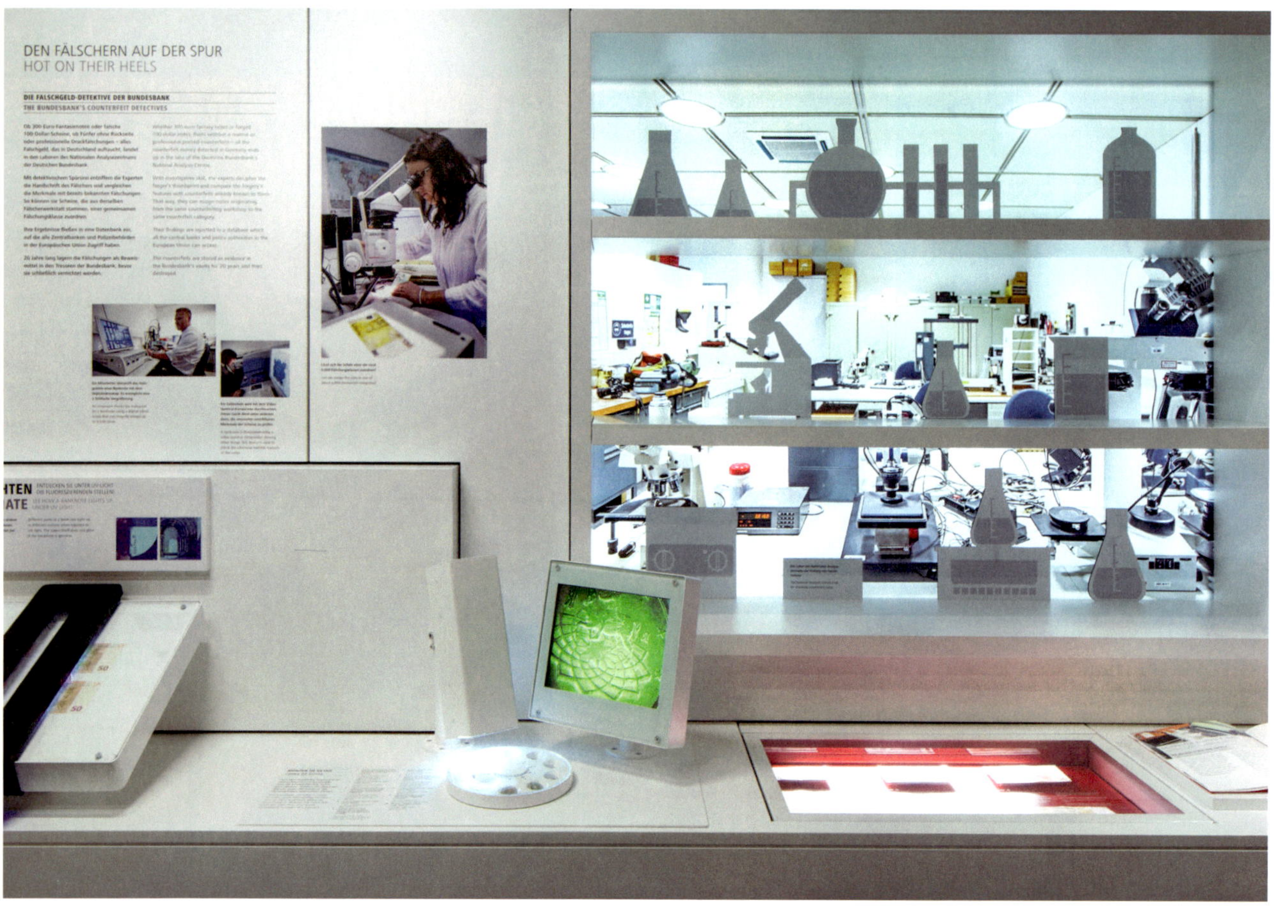

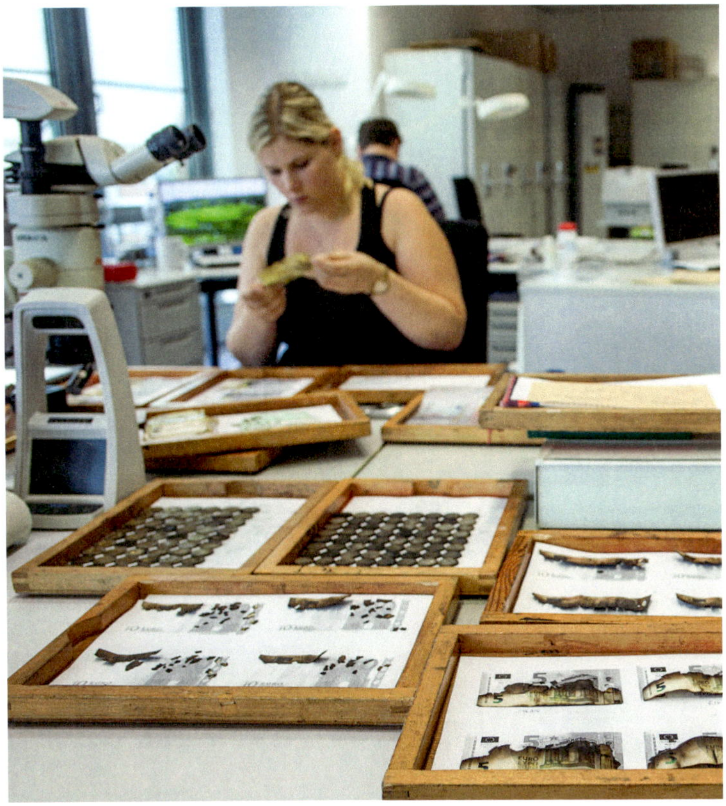

BURNT, BITTEN, RIPPED, ROTTEN

THE BUNDESBANK REPLACES DAMAGED MONEY

The dog chewed up your 50-euro note, an envelope full of cash landed in the shredder, mice used your banknotes to pad out their nest, or your buried treasure started decaying in the garden? On average, 30 million euro worth of cash is badly damaged or mutilated each year. If this accidentally happens to your money, the Deutsche Bundesbank's National Analysis Centre in Mainz can help. It is often painstaking work trying to piece the remains back together, but if the team in Mainz manages to reconstruct more than half of the banknote, you'll get a freshly printed banknote as a replacement. As a rule, damaged coins and mutilated Deutsche Mark notes can also be exchanged. However, anyone found to have intentionally damaged money will go away empty-handed.

AROUND 100,000 DAMAGED BANKNOTES END UP IN THE MONEY PUZZLERS' LAB EACH MONTH.

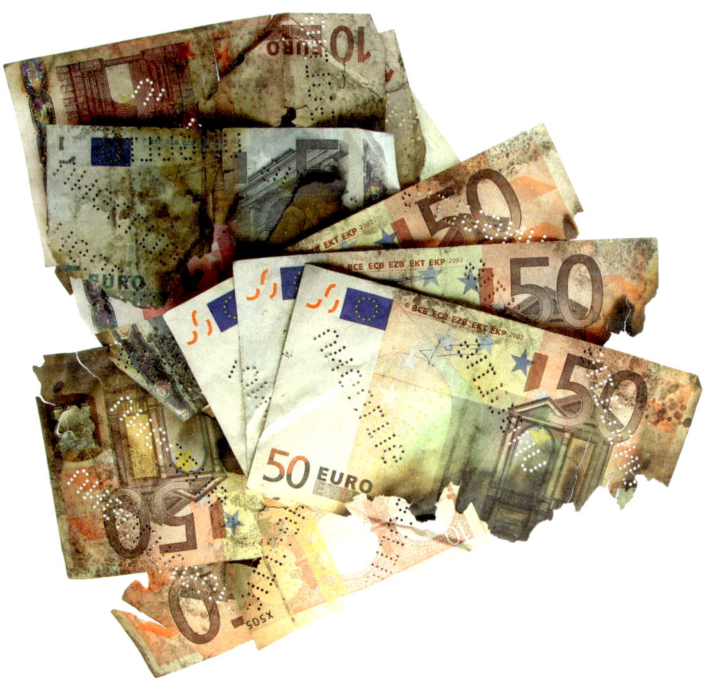

94 O CHRISTMAS TREE: MANY BANKNOTES END UP IN MAINZ AFTER CHRISTMAS. WHEN TREES CATCH ALIGHT, CASH GIFTS TEND TO BURN JUST AS BRIGHT.

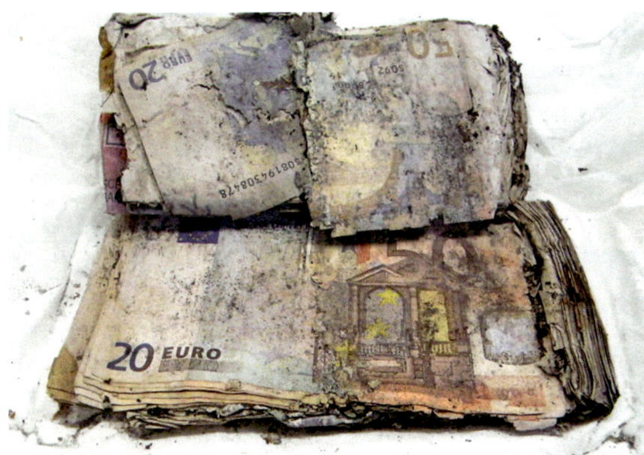

THE ANALYSIS CENTRE ALSO STEPS IN WHEN NATURAL DISASTERS SUCH AS FLOODS STRIKE. THESE ARE BANKNOTES FROM AN ATM FILLED WITH DIRTY WATER.

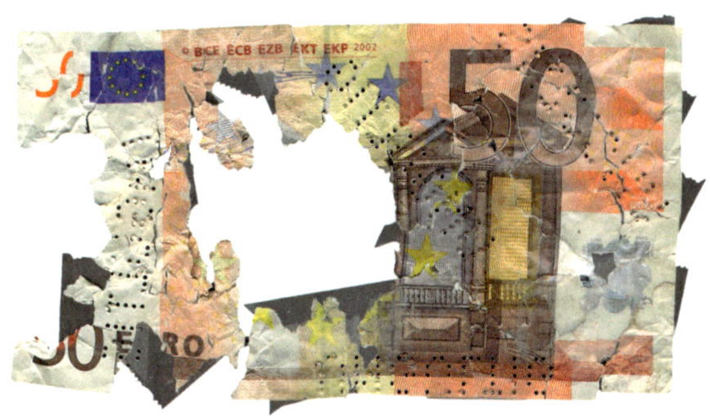

95 ALL CHEWED UP: A PARROT MADE A MEAL OF THIS BANKNOTE.

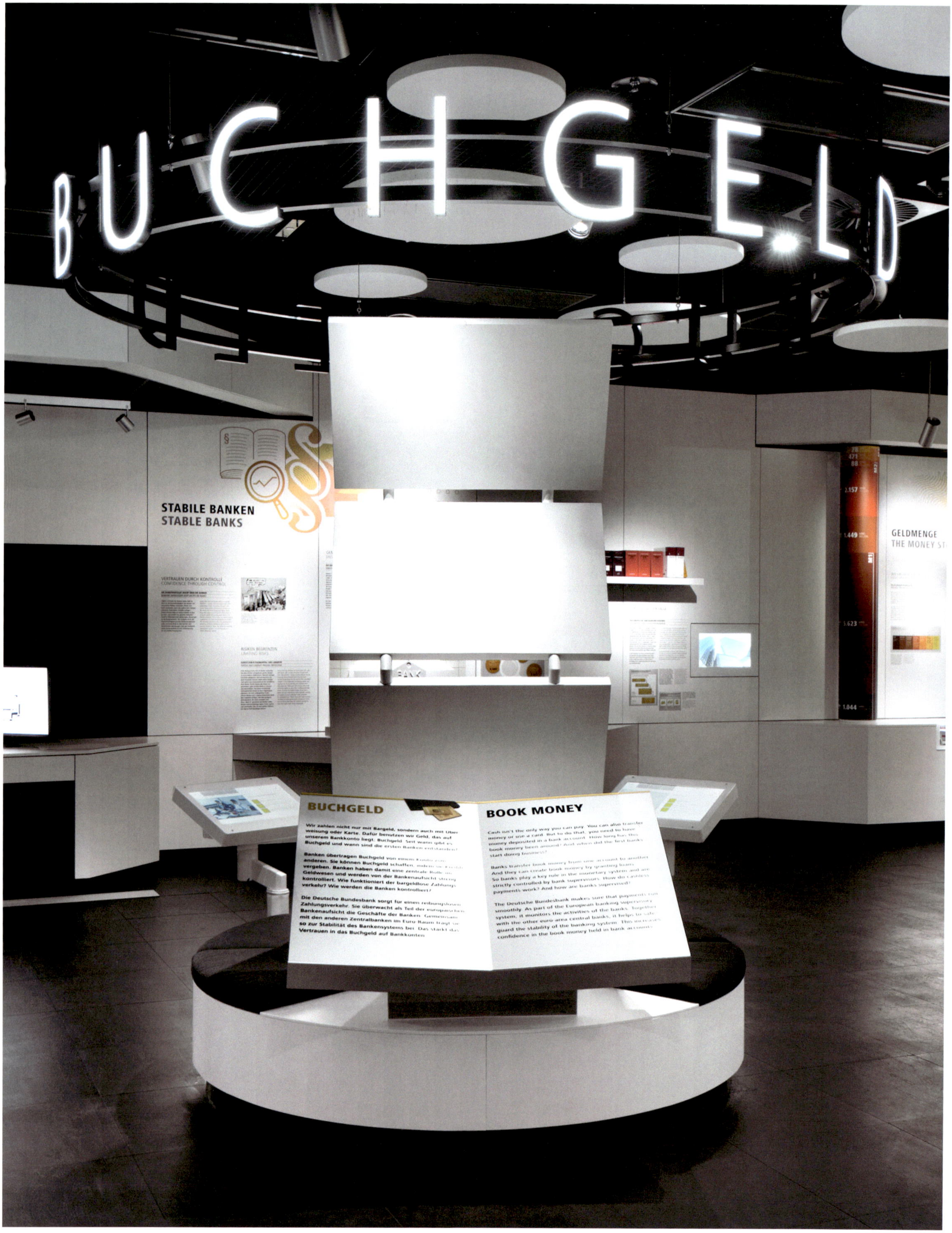
BUCHGELD
STABILE BANKEN
STABLE BANKS
BUCHGELD
BOOK MONEY

CASH ISN'T THE ONLY WAY YOU CAN PAY. YOU CAN ALSO TRANSFER MONEY OR USE A CARD. BUT TO DO THAT, YOU NEED TO HAVE MONEY DEPOSITED IN A BANK ACCOUNT. HOW LONG HAS THIS BOOK MONEY BEEN AROUND? AND WHEN DID THE FIRST BANKS START DOING BUSINESS?

BANKS TRANSFER BOOK MONEY FROM ONE ACCOUNT TO ANOTHER. AND THEY CAN CREATE BOOK MONEY BY GRANTING LOANS. SO BANKS PLAY A KEY ROLE IN THE MONETARY SYSTEM AND ARE STRICTLY CONTROLLED BY BANK SUPERVISORS. HOW DO CASHLESS PAYMENTS WORK? AND HOW ARE BANKS SUPERVISED?

THE DEUTSCHE BUNDESBANK MAKES SURE THAT PAYMENTS RUN SMOOTHLY. AS PART OF THE EUROPEAN BANKING SUPERVISORY SYSTEM, IT MONITORS THE ACTIVITIES OF THE BANKS. TOGETHER WITH THE OTHER EURO-AREA CENTRAL BANKS, IT HELPS TO SAFE – GUARD THE STABILITY OF THE BANKING SYSTEM. THIS INCREASES CONFIDENCE IN THE BOOK MONEY HELD IN BANK ACCOUNTS.

BOOK MONEY

"TRANSFERS INSTEAD OF PAYING IN CASH"

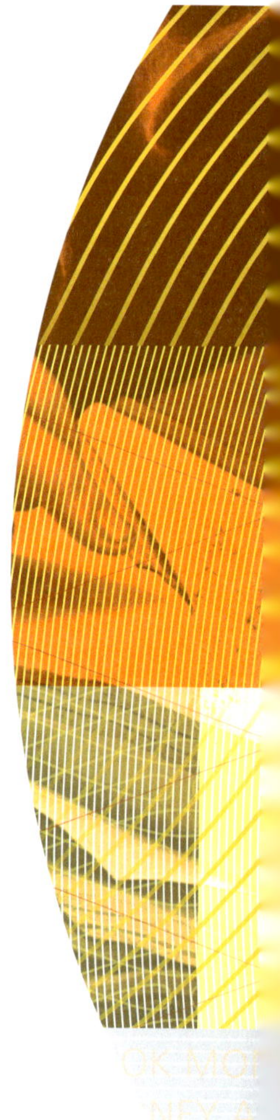

A LOOK BACK THROUGH HISTORY

Book money and cashless payments are not an invention of the computer age but have developed in Europe since the Middle Ages: merchants in northern Italy began to write down their customers' credits and debts by hand in account ledgers, issued bills of exchange and enabled payments to be made by merely booking payments from one account to another.

The first banks were formed in Italy in the High Middle Ages. Our journey through time will follow the evolution of banking up to and into the 19th century before then turning to selected banking crises from history. The example of King Edward III, whose default in the 14th century already drove his creditors into ruin, will show that banking crises are not a preserve of the modern era. However, it wasn't until the 20th century that governments began to think in earnest about crisis prevention measures such as banking supervision.

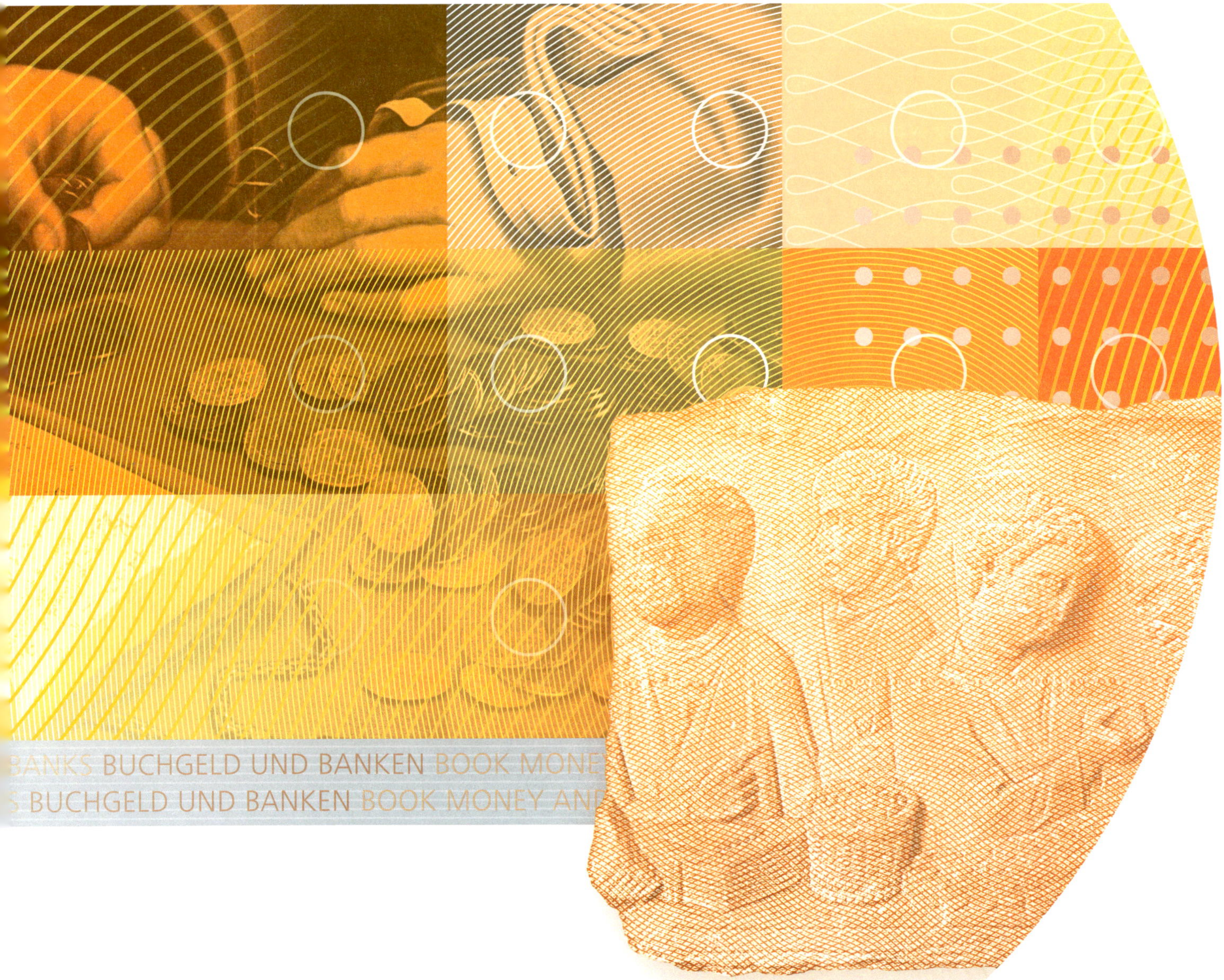
BANKS BUCHGELD UND BANKEN BOOK MONE
S BUCHGELD UND BANKEN BOOK MONEY AN

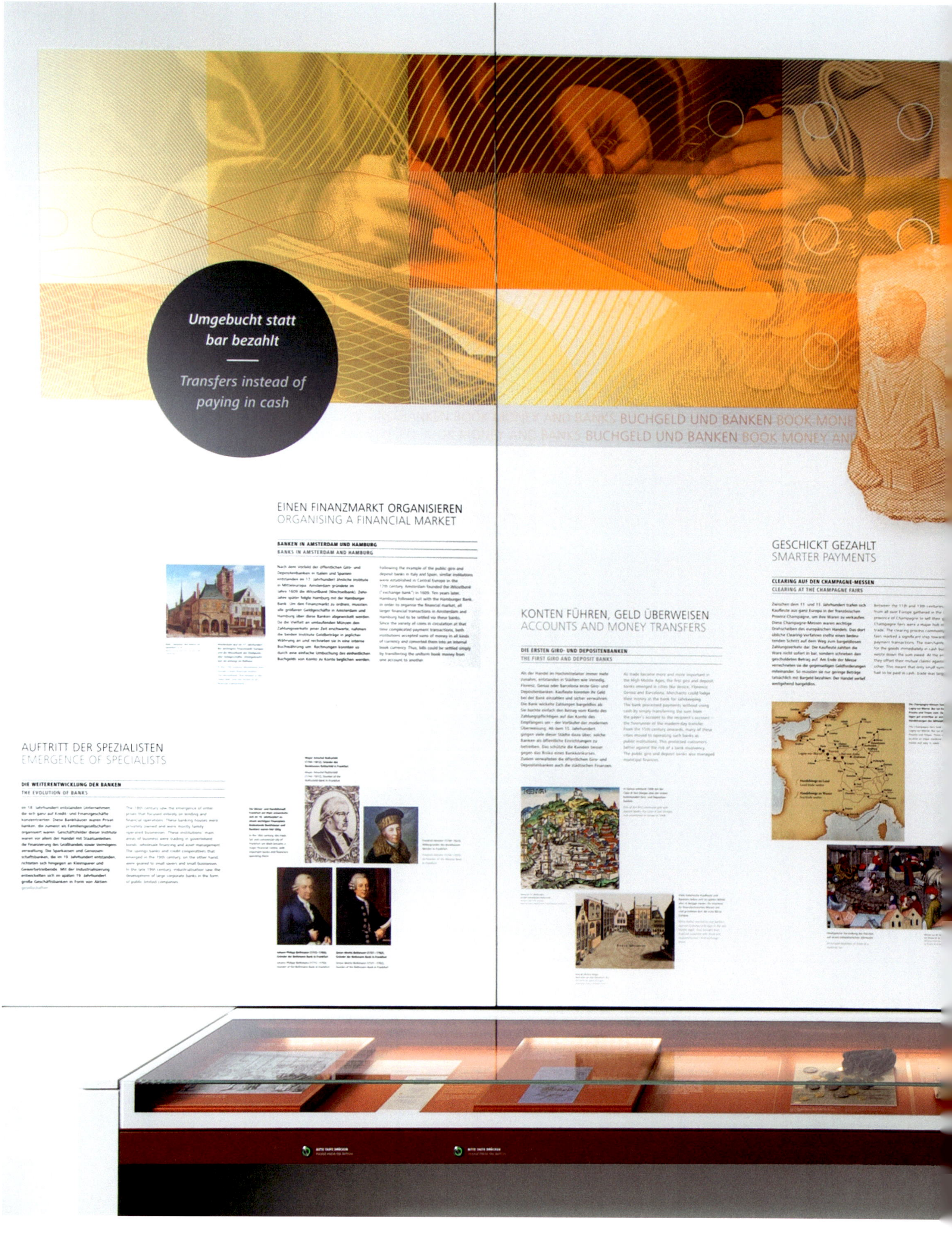
Umgebucht statt bar bezahlt
Transfers instead of paying in cash
BUCHGELD UND BANKEN BOOK MONEY
BUCHGELD UND BANKEN BOOK MONEY
EINEN FINANZMARKT ORGANISIEREN
ORGANISING A FINANCIAL MARKET
BANKEN IN AMSTERDAM UND HAMBURG
BANKS IN AMSTERDAM AND HAMBURG
GESCHICKT GEZAHLT
SMARTER PAYMENTS
CLEARING AUF DEN CHAMPAGNE-MESSEN
CLEARING AT THE CHAMPAGNE FAIRS
KONTEN FÜHREN, GELD ÜBERWEISEN
ACCOUNTS AND MONEY TRANSFERS
DIE ERSTEN GIRO- UND DEPOSITENBANKEN
THE FIRST GIRO AND DEPOSIT BANKS
AUFTRITT DER SPEZIALISTEN
EMERGENCE OF SPECIALISTS
DIE WEITERENTWICKLUNG DER BANKEN
THE EVOLUTION OF BANKS

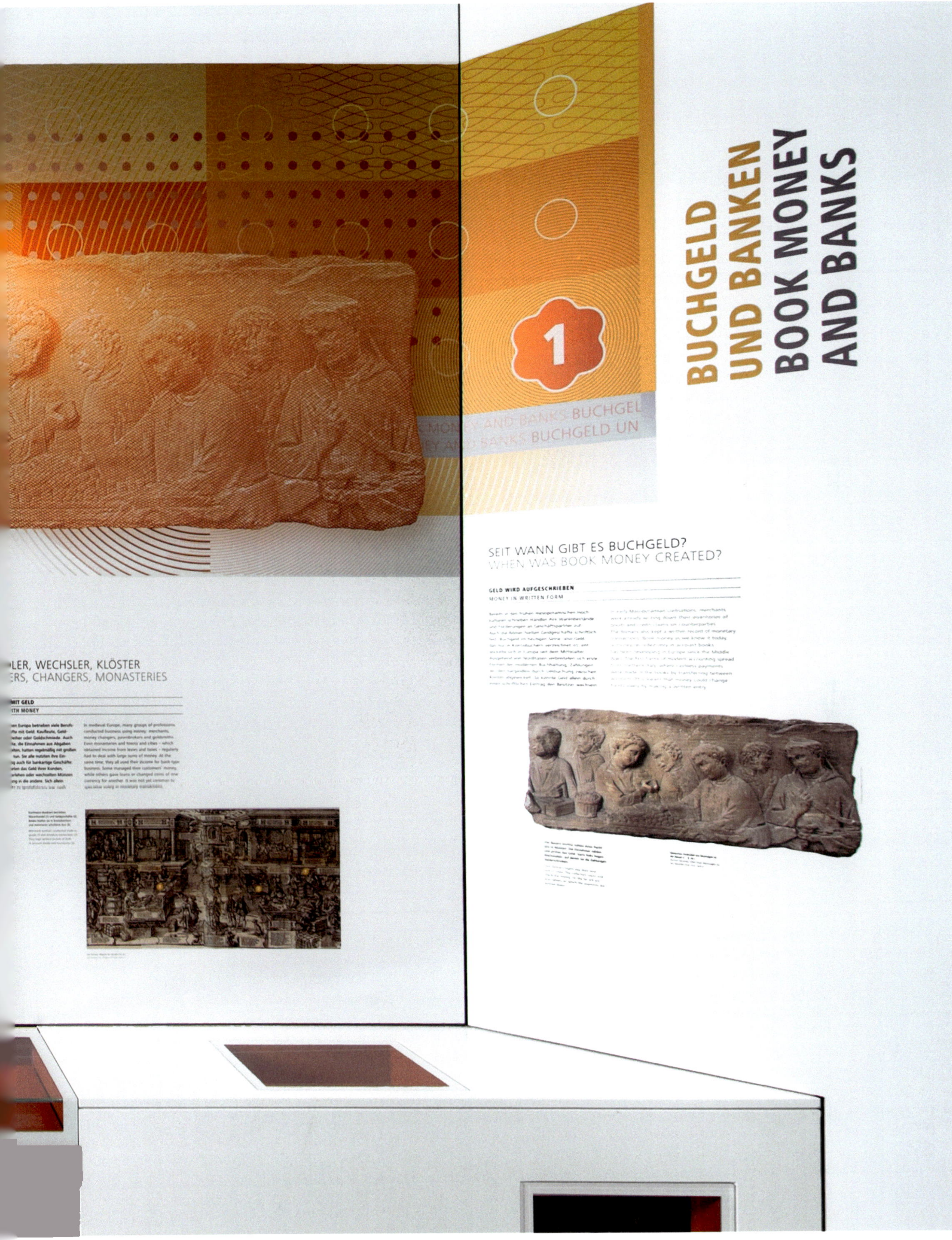
1
BUCHGELD
UND BANKEN
BOOK MONEY
AND BANKS
SEIT WANN GIBT ES BUCHGELD?
WHEN WAS BOOK MONEY CREATED?
GELD WIRD AUFGESCHRIEBEN
MONEY IN WRITTEN FORM
LER, WECHSLER, KLÖSTER
ERS, CHANGERS, MONASTERIES

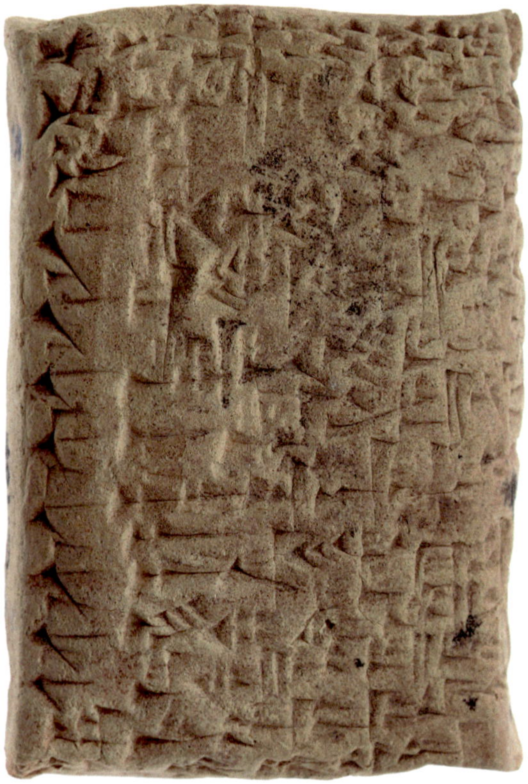

96 **MESOPOTAMIA, CUNEIFORM TABLET,** 1799 BC

WHEN WAS BOOK MONEY CREATED?

MONEY IN WRITTEN FORM

In early Mesopotamian civilisations, merchants were already writing down their inventories of goods and credit claims on counterparties. The Romans also kept a written record of monetary transactions. Book money as we know it today, ie money recorded only in account books, has been developing in Europe since the Middle Ages. The first forms of modern accounting spread from northern Italy, where cashless payments were made in the books by transferring between accounts. This meant that money could change hands solely by making a written entry.

SMARTER PAYMENTS

CLEARING AT THE CHAMPAGNE FAIRS

Between the 11th and 13th centuries, merchants from all over Europe gathered in the French province of Champagne to sell their goods. These Champagne fairs were a major hub of European trade. The clearing process commonly used at the fairs marked a significant step towards cashless payment transactions. The merchants did not pay for the goods immediately in cash but instead wrote down the sum owed. At the end of the fair, they offset their mutual claims against each other. This meant that only small sums actually had to be paid in cash: trade was largely cash-free.

ARCHETYPAL DEPICTION OF TRADE AT A MEDIEVAL FAIR

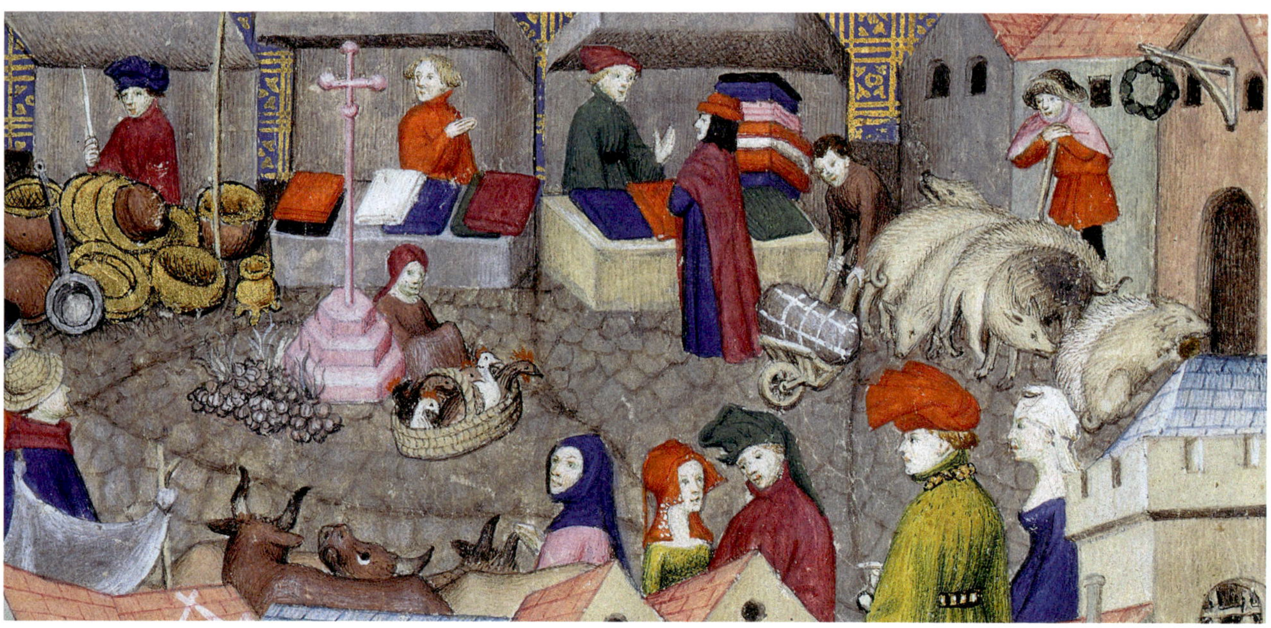

ACCOUNTS AND MONEY TRANSFERS

THE FIRST GIRO AND DEPOSIT BANKS

As trade became more and more important in the High Middle Ages, the first giro and deposit banks emerged in cities like Venice, Florence, Genoa and Barcelona. Merchants could lodge their money at the bank for safekeeping. The bank processed payments without using cash by simply transferring the sum from the payer's account to the recipient's account – the forerunner of the modern-day transfer.

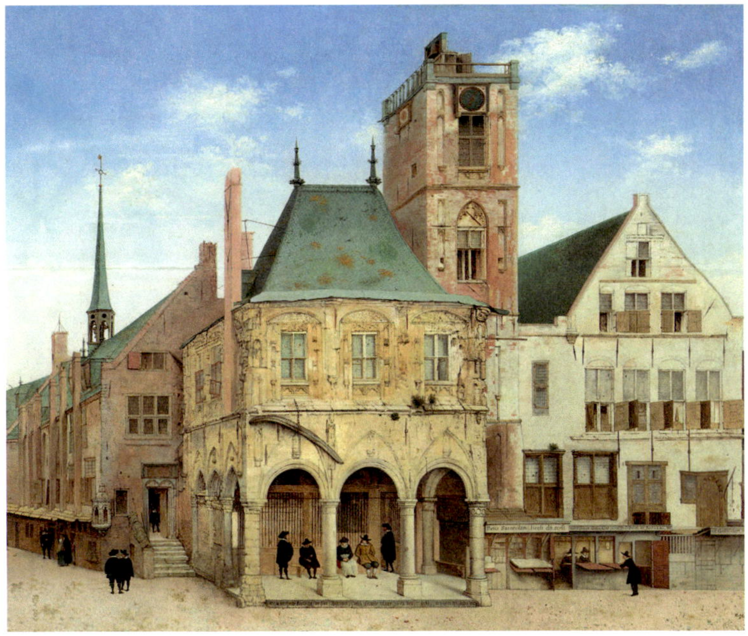

IN THE 17TH CENTURY, AMSTERDAM WAS EUROPE'S MAIN FINANCIAL MARKET, AND THE WISSELBANK WAS THE CENTRE OF ALL FINANCIAL TRANSACTIONS.

A PIONEERING INVENTION: THE BILL OF EXCHANGE

In the Middle Ages, Italian merchants developed the bill of exchange – a security with a written payment order. This allowed large sums of money to be moved over long distances. This was easier and safer than transporting heavy coinage.

WHY IS A BANK CALLED A "BANK" ?

TOWNS AND CITIES OFTEN USED TO HAVE THEIR OWN COINS. IF YOU TRAVELLED, YOU FIRST HAD TO EXCHANGE YOUR MONEY BEFORE PAYING FOR ANYTHING. THE MONEY CHANGERS IN ITALY WORKED OUTSIDE AT A LARGE WOODEN TABLE. IN ITALIAN, THIS TABLE WAS CALLED BANCO. THAT IS WHY TO THIS DAY WE CALL THE PLACE WHERE WE CARRY OUT OUR MONEY TRANSACTIONS A "BANK".

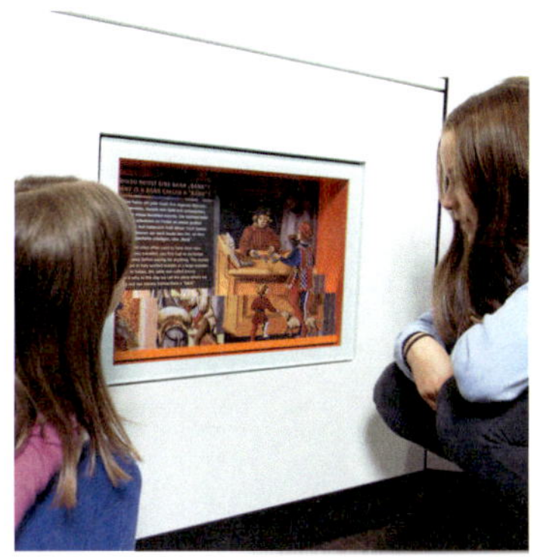

97 **BILL OF EXCHANGE FOR 150 GULDEN,** 1833

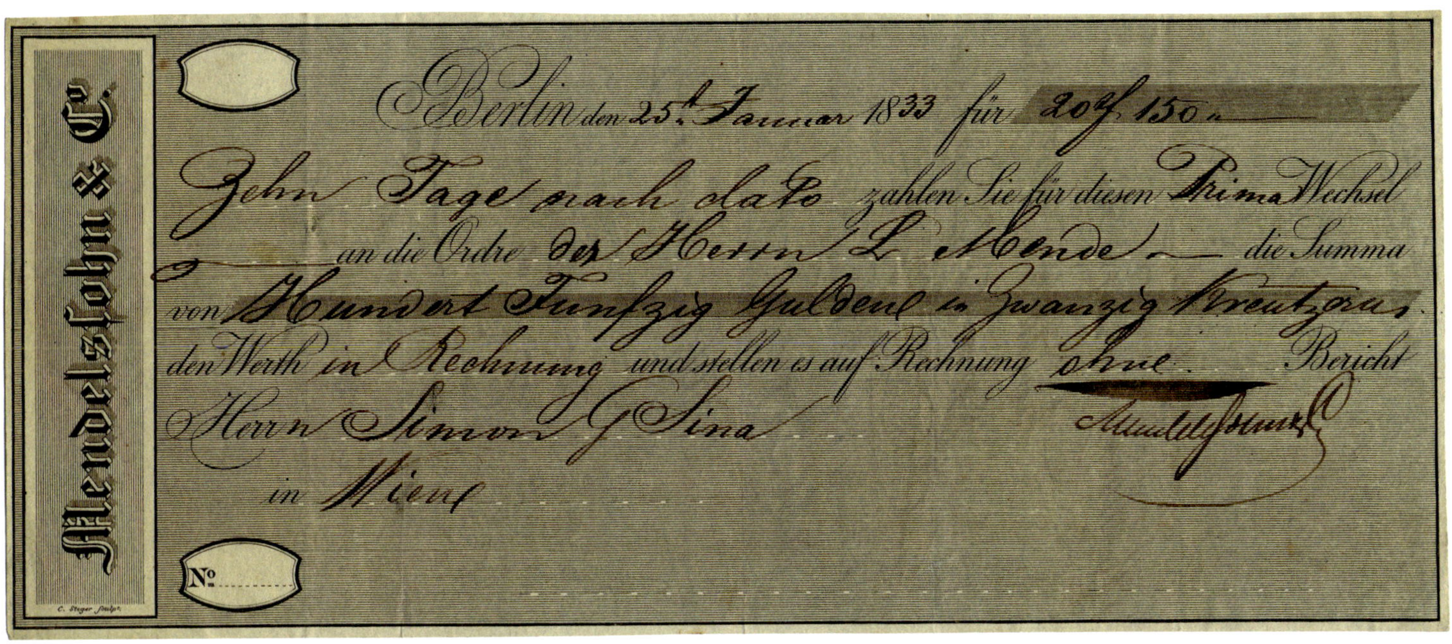

Mendelssohn & Co.

Berlin den 25t Januar 1833 für 20 f 150.—

Zehn Tage nach dato zahlen Sie für diesen Prima Wechsel an die Ordre des Herrn L. Mende — die Summa von Hundert Funfzig Gulden in Zwanzig Kreutzern den Werth in Rechnung und stellen es auf Rechnung ohne Bericht

Herrn Simon G. Sina in Wien

Mendelssohn & Co.

No.

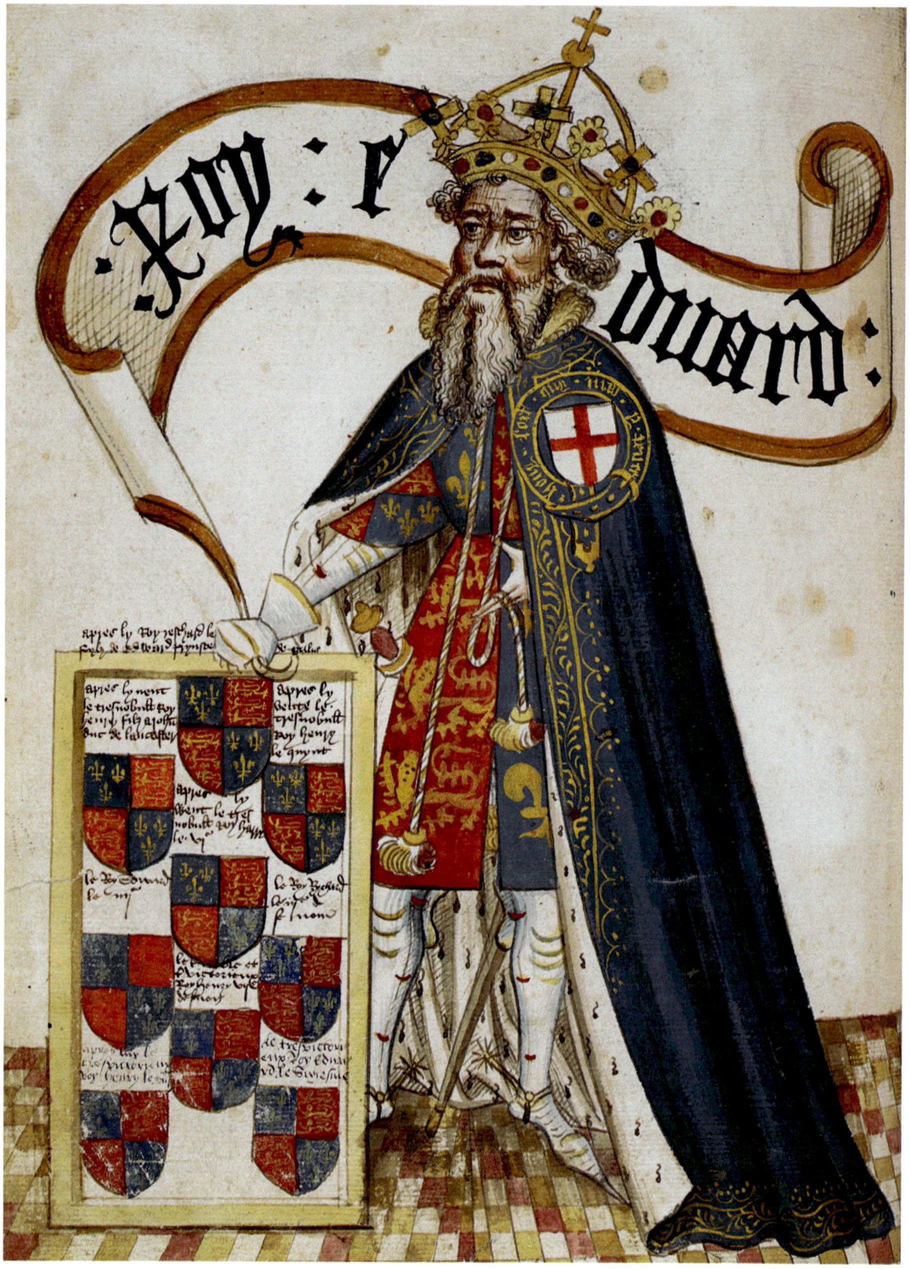

FLORENTINES IN CRISIS

KING EDWARD'S
SOVEREIGN BANKRUPTCY

For merchant bankers in the Middle Ages, lending money was a lucrative but risky business. Leading mercantile families in Florence, including the Bardi and Peruzzi families, granted sizeable loans to King Edward III of England (1312–1377) to fund his wars, particularly the Hundred Years' War against France he started in 1337. However, in 1343, he stopped making his repayments, driving many of his creditors into ruin. His successor, Richard II (1367–1400), later cleared part of the debt.

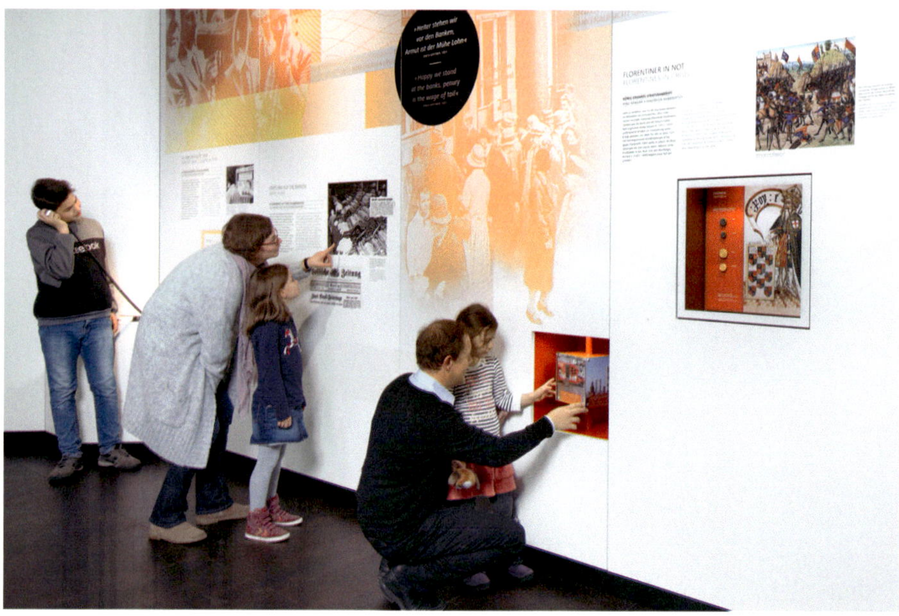

"HAPPY WE STAND AT THE BANKS, PENURY IS THE WAGE OF TOIL."

ERICH KÄSTNER, 1931

BANK RUNS

1931 BANKING CRISIS LEADS TO BANK SUPERVISION

The global economic crisis that broke out in 1929 triggered a serious banking crisis in Germany. The Darmstädter und Nationalbank, a leading big bank, got into payment difficulties owing to loan defaults. On 13 July 1931 it ran out of cash and its counters remained closed. The news spread like wildfire and customers of other banks, too, now feared for their savings. In panic, they stormed the banks to rescue their money. Although the Reich government and Reichsbank were able to prevent the uncontrolled collapse of the institutions, the economic crisis intensified. As a result of this crisis, the government introduced banking supervision.

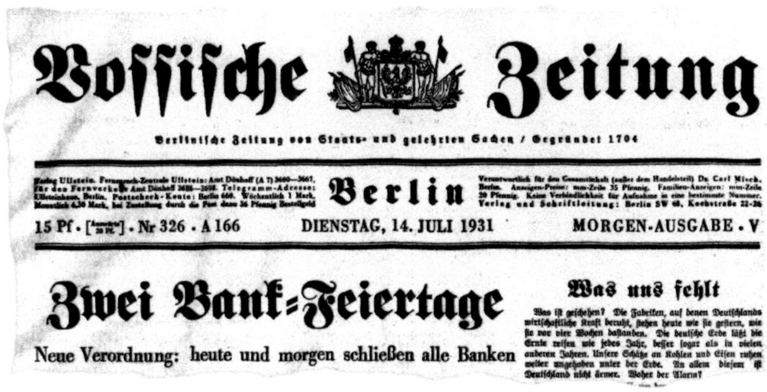

Vossische Zeitung

Berliner Zeitung von Staats- und gelehrten Sachen / Gegründet 1704

Berlin

15 Pf. · Nr 326 · A 166 DIENSTAG, 14. JULI 1931 MORGEN-AUSGABE · V

Zwei Bank-Feiertage

Neue Verordnung: heute und morgen schließen alle Banken

Was uns fehlt

THE REICH GOVERNMENT ORDERED THE CLOSURE OF ALL BANKS ON 14 AND 15 JULY 1931 TO HALT THE RUNS ON BANKS AND PREVENT OTHER BANKS FROM COLLAPSING.

HERSTATT BANK COLLAPSE IN 1974

FROM BANK FAILURE TO DEPOSIT PROTECTION

I D Herstatt, a privately owned bank in Cologne, collapsed on 26 June 1974. Unlucky speculation on the foreign exchange market had caused the bank to flounder. Because restructuring failed, the bank was closed by the banking authorities. All accounts were blocked. Customers, worried about their money, demonstrated in front of the bank's head office in Cologne. At the time, it was the biggest bank collapse to have hit Germany and prompted the creation of the Federal Association of German Banks' voluntary deposit guarantee fund in 1976. This guarantee now protects the customer funds of all affiliated credit institutions in the event of insolvency.

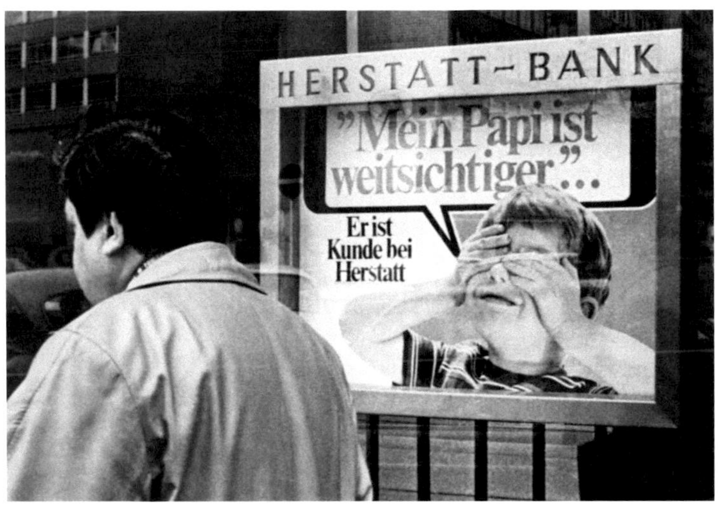

THIS ADVERTISEMENT FROM THE EARLY 1970S READS: MY DAD, A HERSTATT CUSTOMER, HAS MORE FORESIGHT. IN RETROSPECT, THIS SLOGAN MUST HAVE SEEMED LIKE A BAD JOKE TO MANY CUSTOMERS WHO WERE SCARED OF LOSING EVERYTHING. HOWEVER, IN THE END, CUSTOMERS GOT AROUND 82 % OF THEIR DEPOSITS BACK.

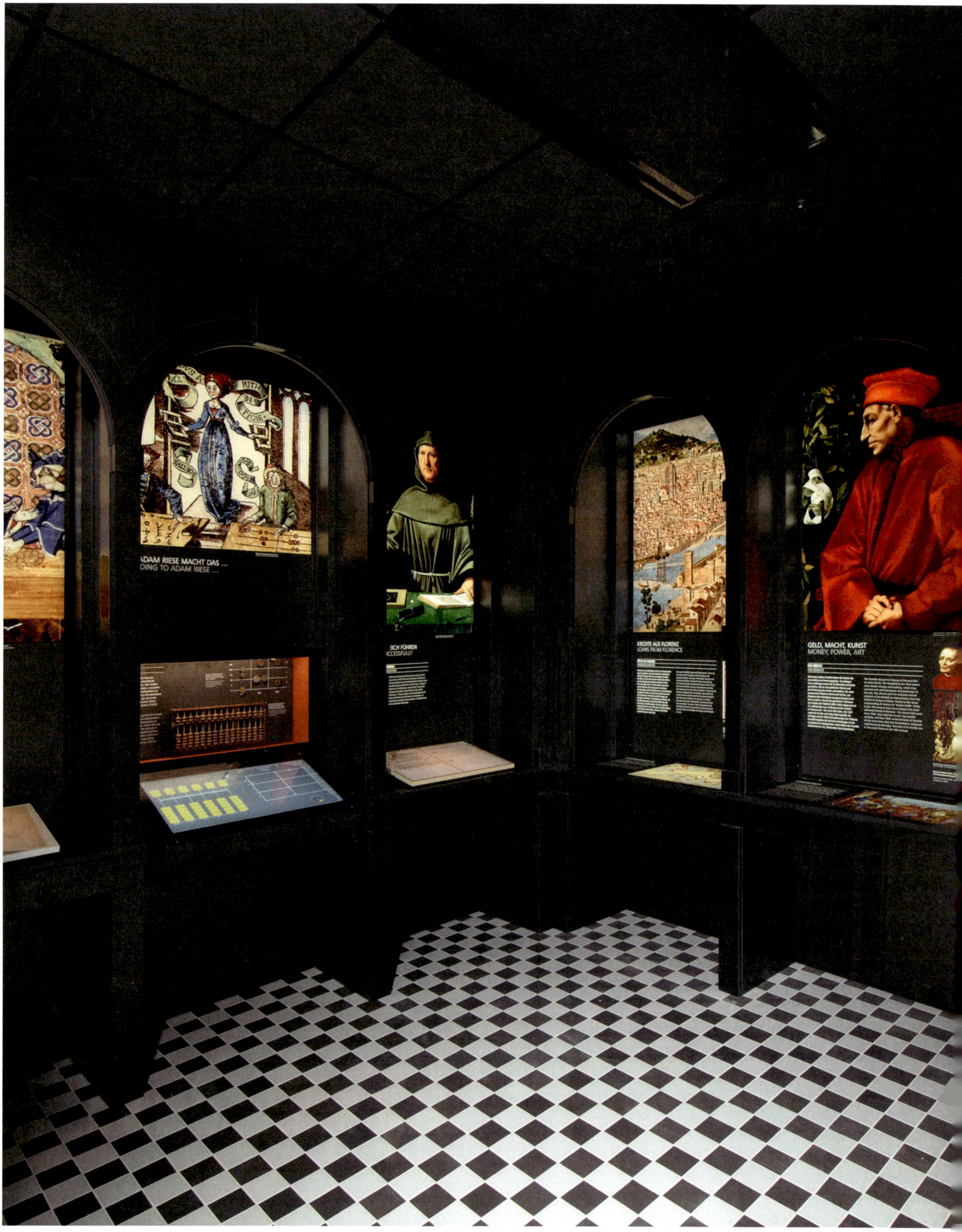
ADAM RIESE MACHT DAS ...
KREDITE AUS FLORENZ
LOANS FROM FLORENCE
GELD, MACHT, KUNST
MONEY, POWER, ART

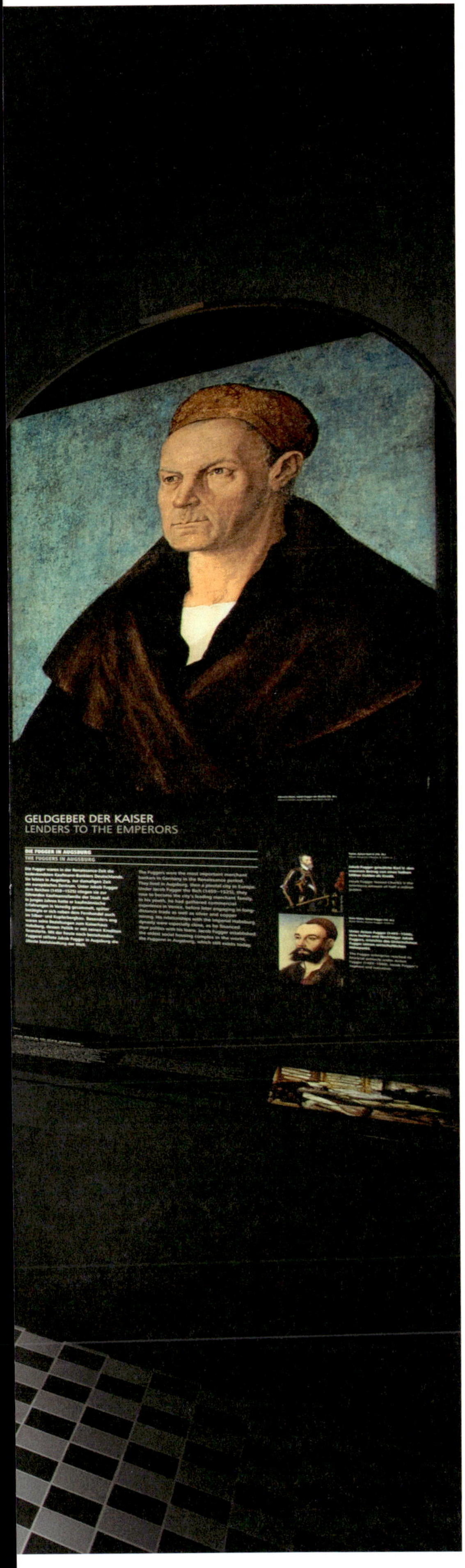

THE LANGUAGE OF MONEY

The Renaissance cabinet "The language of money", with the powerful imagery of its rounded arches, will take the visitor back in time to the beginnings of modern banking in Italy, where the world was in transition from the Middle Ages to the early modern period, in which Venice, Genoa and Florence were the most important economic hubs. Italian merchants were spinning their webs of trade far beyond their continent's frontiers. Having made themselves wealthy, they increasingly began to engage in banking business and thus gain influence. Powerful Florentine merchant-bankers, such as the Bardi, Peruzzi or Medici families, lent money to popes and monarchs all over Europe. This is why much of the vocabulary from the financial industry comes from Italian.

At the same time, Italian mathematicians were revolutionising the merchants' world. For centuries, the latter had been using the abacus or counting stones on lines. Soon, Fibonacci popularised the Indo-Arabic system of numerals, and Luca Pacioli the techniques of double-entry bookkeeping, throughout Europe.

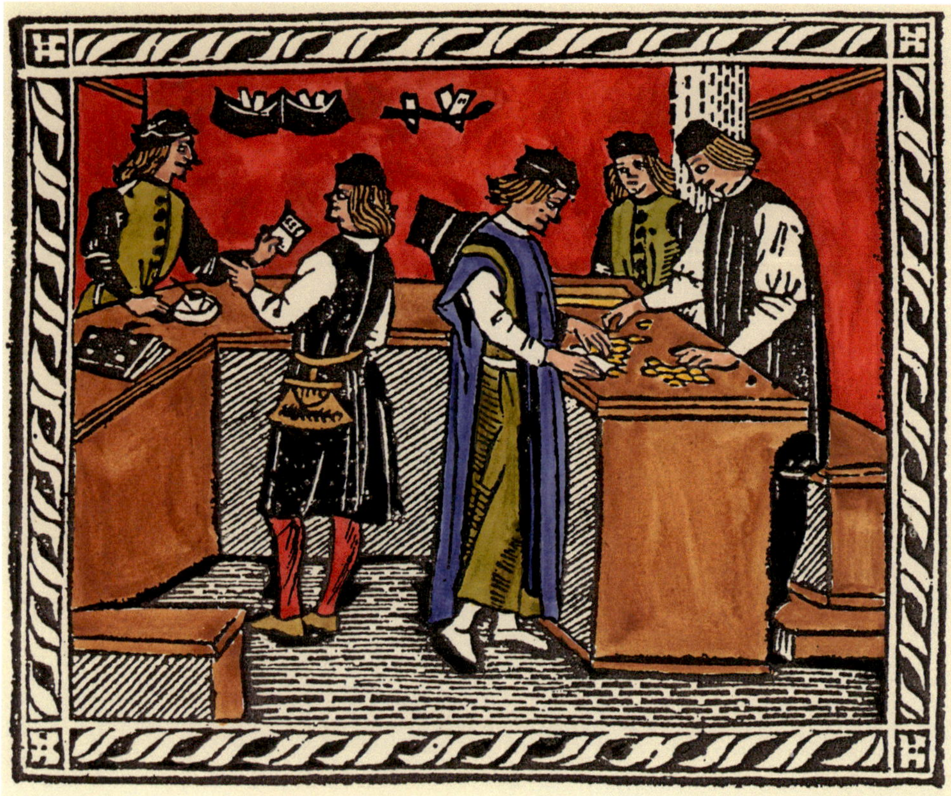

MONETARY TRANSACTIONS IN A FLORENTINE BANK

VENICE & CO.

MERCHANTS SET UP MERCHANT BANKS

The origins of modern banking can be found in medieval Italy with Venice, Genoa and Florence the most important economic centres of the time. Merchants reaped abundant profits from the export of high-quality goods produced in these cities and long-distance trade with luxury products such as silk and spices. They began to conduct banking business with the money they earned. Through a vast network of trade routes and branches, these merchant bankers extended their influence across Europe.

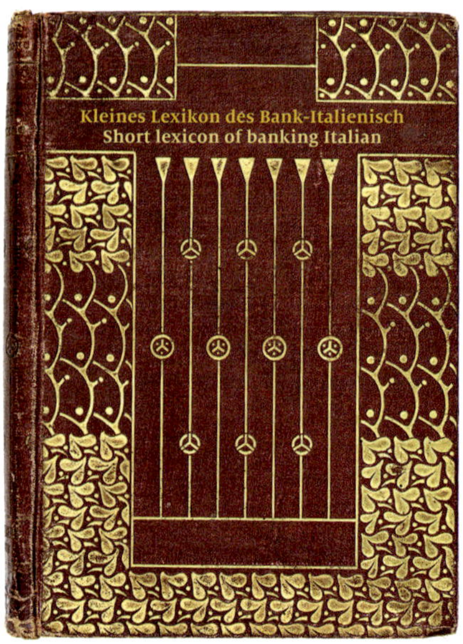

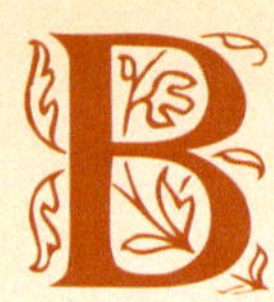

bancarotta

BANKROTT
BANKRUPT

wörtlich „zerbrochener Tisch" – zahlungsunfähigen Geldwechslern wurde ihr Arbeitstisch zerstört, um eine Fortsetzung des Geschäfts unmöglich zu machen.

literally, "broken bench" – insolvent money-changers' benches were broken in order to make it impossible for them to continue their business.

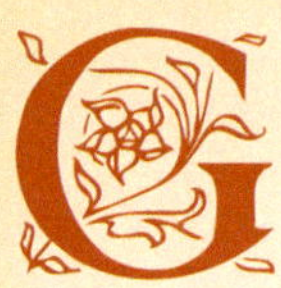

giro

GIRO
GIRO

wörtlich „Weg, Runde" – bezieht sich auf den bargeldlosen Zahlungsverkehr, in dem das Giral- oder Buchgeld auf den Bankkonten zirkuliert, gewissermaßen die Runde macht.

literally, "circle, round" – payment transfers in which book money circulates on bank accounts.

FROM AGIO TO VALUTA

THE FINANCIAL WORLD SPEAKS ITALIAN

The key role played by Italian merchants in the medieval monetary system has persisted to the present day. Many specialist financial terms have Italian origins. The word "bank", for example, comes from the Italian banco, originally referring to the bank or counter on which the money changer conducted his business.

ACCORDING TO ADAM RIESE …

COUNTING WITH MONEY

The Hindu-Arabic numeral system arrived in Europe in the 12th century, making written mathematics simpler. The most important mathematician of the Middle Ages, Leonardo da Pisa, better known as Fibonacci, played a key role in the spread of its use. However, it was German mathematician Adam Riese who introduced German craftsmen and merchants to the concept of calculating with numerals in his book *Rechenung auff den Linihen und Federn* (1522).

DOING BUSINESS SUCCESSFULLY

THE REVOLUTION OF DOUBLE-ENTRY BOOKKEEPING

Italian merchants had long been using it. But it was only in 1494 that the Franciscan monk and mathematician Luca Pacioli described double-entry bookkeeping in detail for the first time. His book *Summa de Arithmetica, Geometria, Proportioni et Proportionalita* introduced it to the whole of Europe. Today, double-entry bookkeeping still forms the basis for all business enterprises, as it precisely records all transactions, enabling them to be directed effectively.

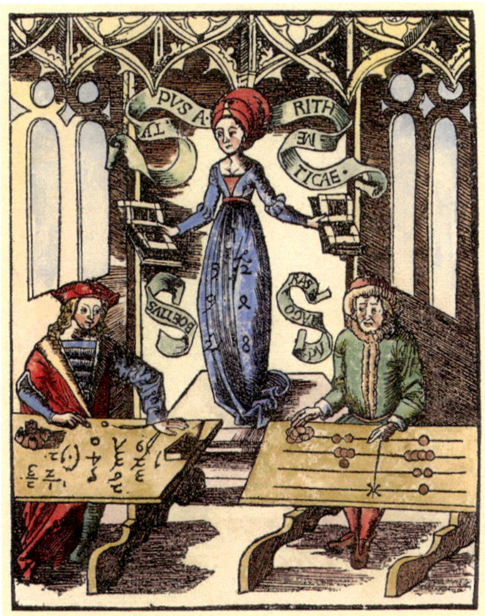

ALLEGORY OF ARITHMETIC

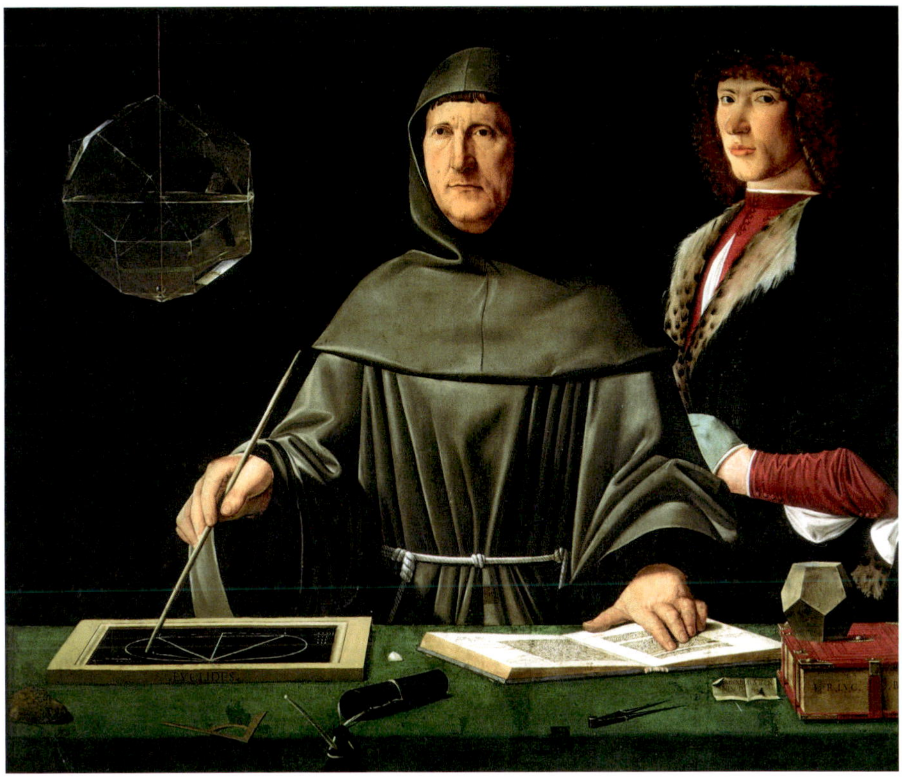

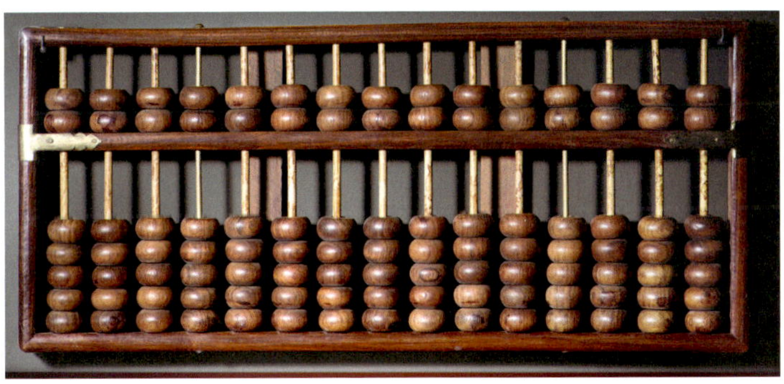

98 SINCE ANCIENT TIMES, NEARLY EVERY CULTURE HAS USED AN ABACUS AS A COUNTING TOOL. THIS CHINESE ABACUS (FROM CA 1900) WAS USED HORIZONTALLY.

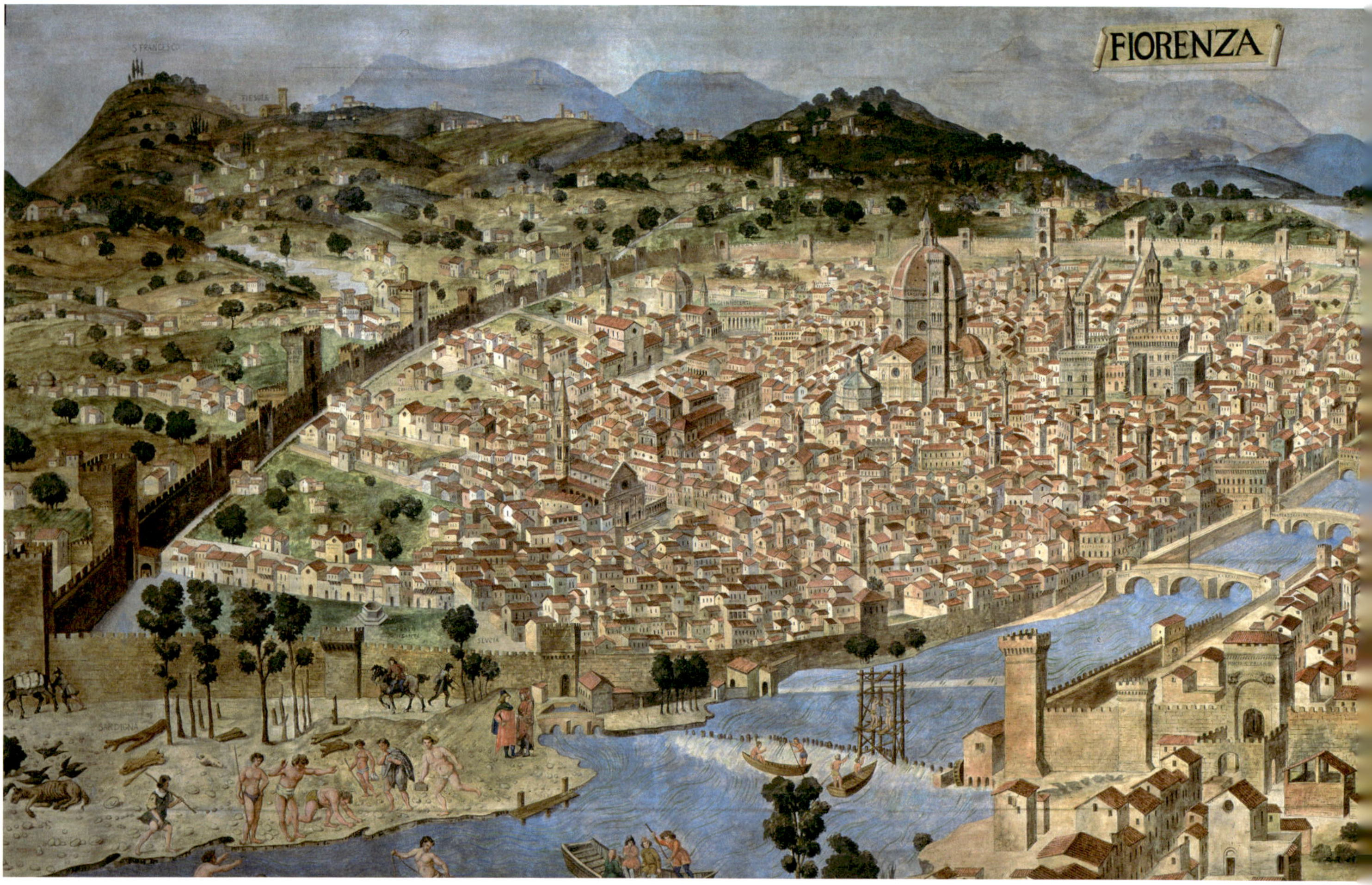

LOANS FROM FLORENCE

POWERFUL FAMILIES

During the Middle Ages and Renaissance, Florence was one of the largest and financially most important cities in Europe. The Bardi, Peruzzi and Acciaiuoli families that lived there were among the most powerful merchant bankers of their time. From the mid-13th century, their branch networks had spread across the entire continent. They moved money and goods all over Europe, granted loans to the Church and financed the luxurious lifestyles and the wars of kings and princes. In return, they gained trade monopolies and control over the monarchs' revenues.

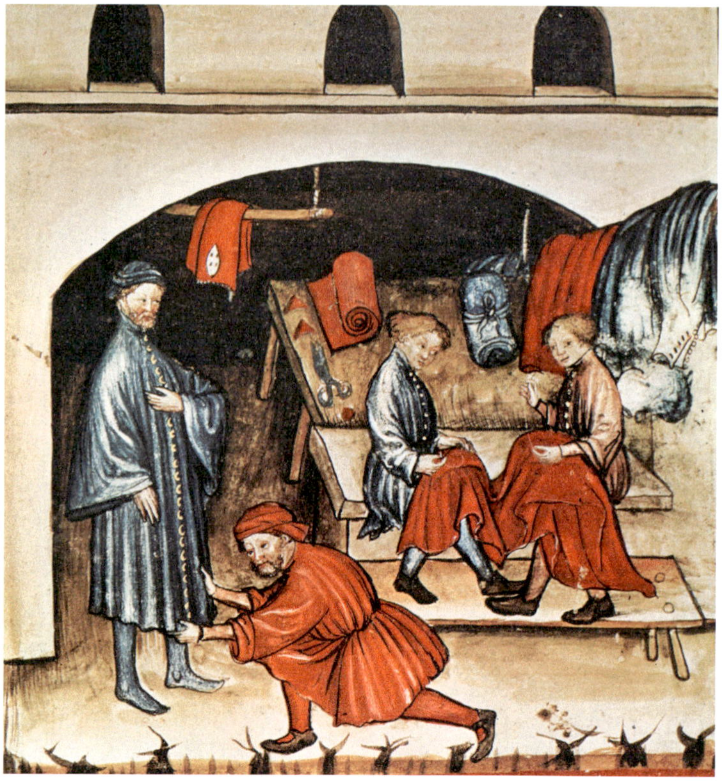

MERCHANT BANKERS OFTEN OWED THEIR FORTUNES TO TRADE IN CLOTH PRODUCED IN FLORENCE.

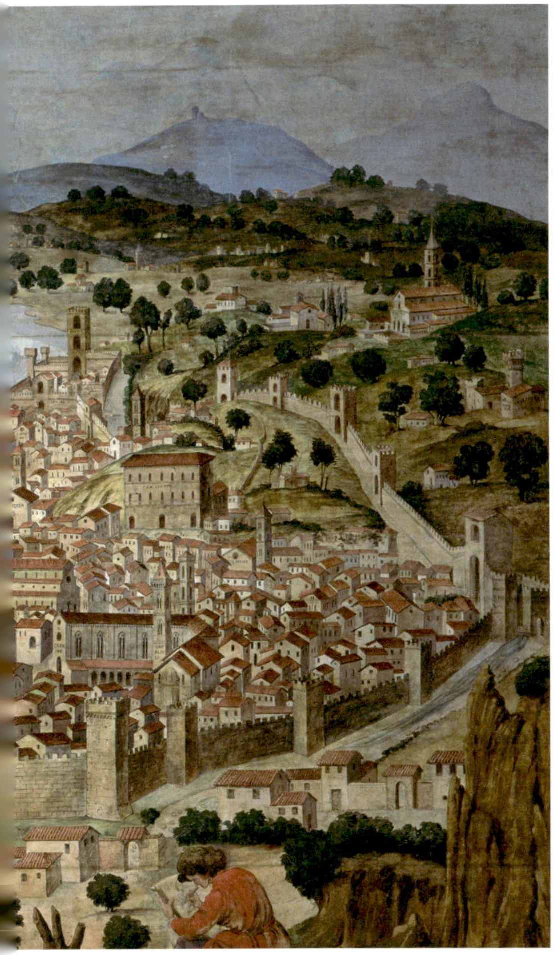

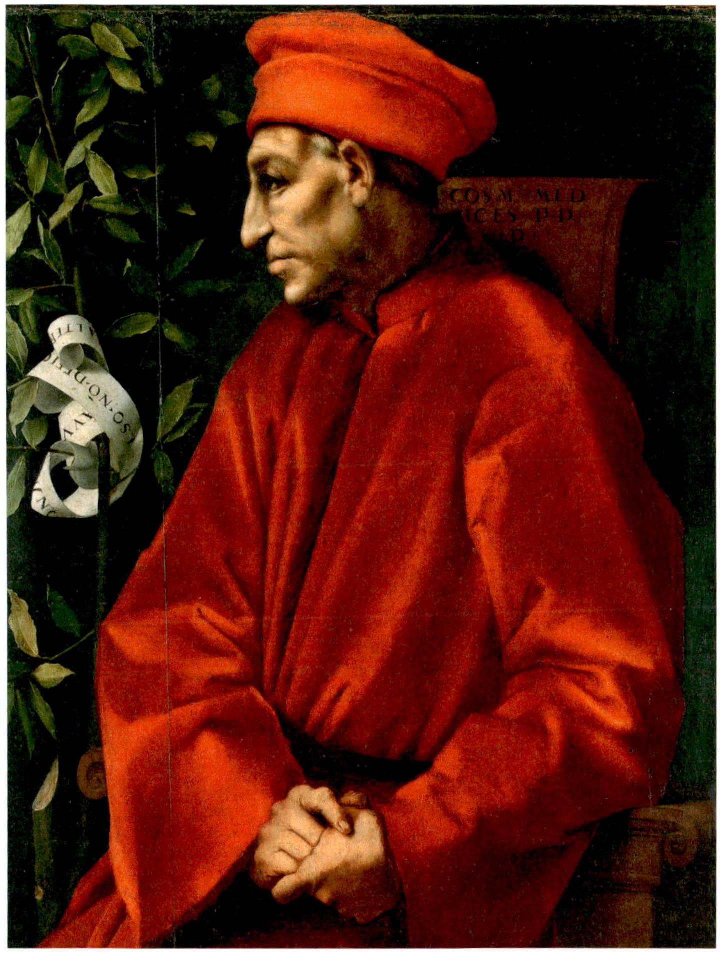

COSIMO DE' MEDICI

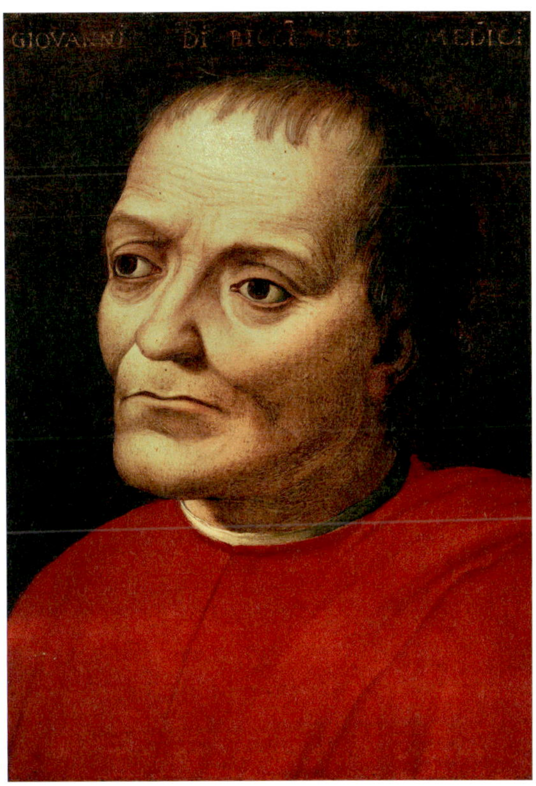

MONEY, POWER, ART

THE MEDICIS

The Medicis shaped the history of Florence like no other family. The foundations for their ascent were textile trading and banking, which they married with political power and patronage of the arts. The Church used the extensive branch network of the Medicis to channel levies from the faithful of Europe to Rome. Thanks to the clever manoeuvring of Cosimo de' Medici (1389–1464), in the 15th century they rose to become the most influential family in Florence – for around 300 years. From 1531, they ruled the former city republic as dukes, and from 1569, as Grand Dukes of Tuscany. At the same time, they tied themselves to European royal houses by marriage. Two sons of the family rose to the papal throne in the 16th century.

GIOVANNI DI BICCI DE' MEDICI (1360–1429) FOUNDED THE BANCO MEDICI IN 1397.

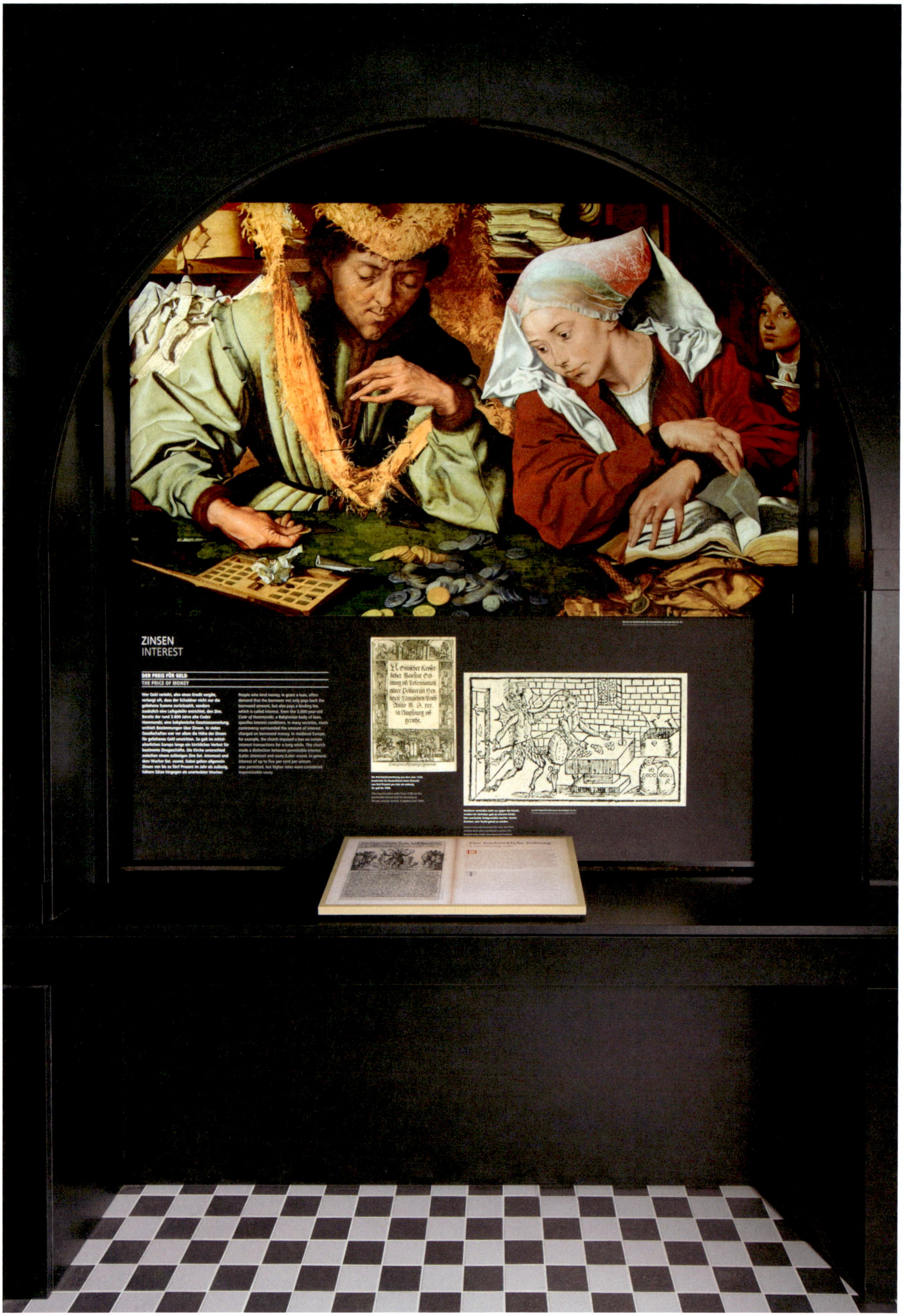
ZINSEN
INTEREST
DER PREIS FÜR GELD
THE PRICE OF MONEY

LENDERS TO THE EMPERORS

THE FUGGERS IN AUGSBURG

The Fuggers were the most important merchant bankers in Germany in the Renaissance period. They lived in Augsburg, a pivotal city in Europe at that time. Under Jacob Fugger the Rich (1459–1525), they rose to become the city's leading merchant family. In his youth, he had gathered commercial experience in Venice, before later engaging in long-distance trade as well as in silver and copper mining. His relationships with the imperial Habsburg dynasty were especially close, as he financed their politics with his loans.

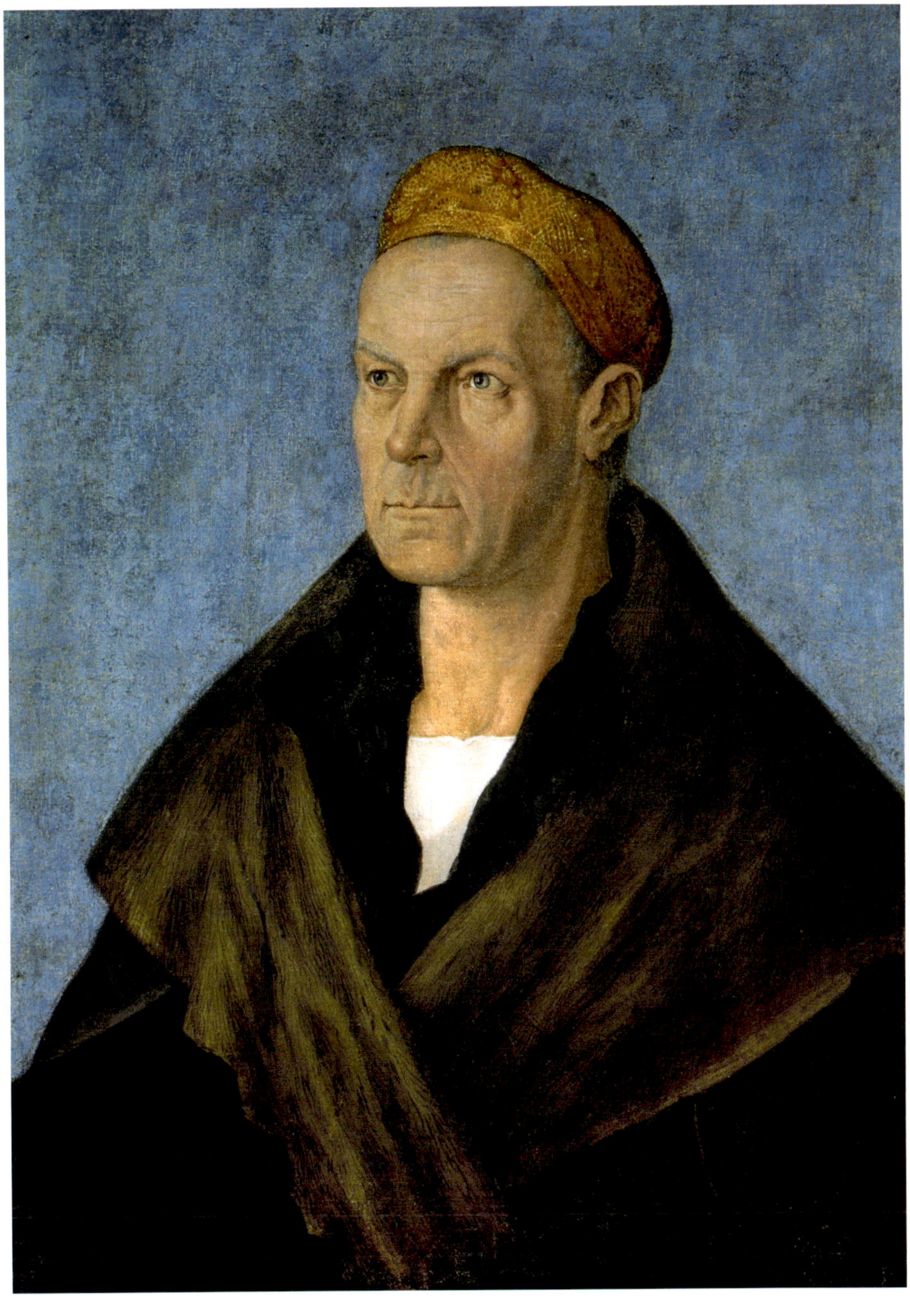

INTEREST

THE PRICE OF MONEY

People who lend money, ie grant a loan, often demand that the borrower not only pays back the borrowed amount, but also pays a lending fee, which is called interest. Even the 3,800-year-old Code of Hammurabi, a Babylonian body of laws, specifies interest conditions. In many societies, much controversy surrounded the amount of interest charged on borrowed money. In medieval Europe, for example, the Church imposed a ban on certain interest transactions for a long while. The Church made a distinction between permissible interest (Latin: interesse) and usury (Latin: usura). In general, interest of up to five per cent per annum was permitted, but higher rates were considered impermissible usury.

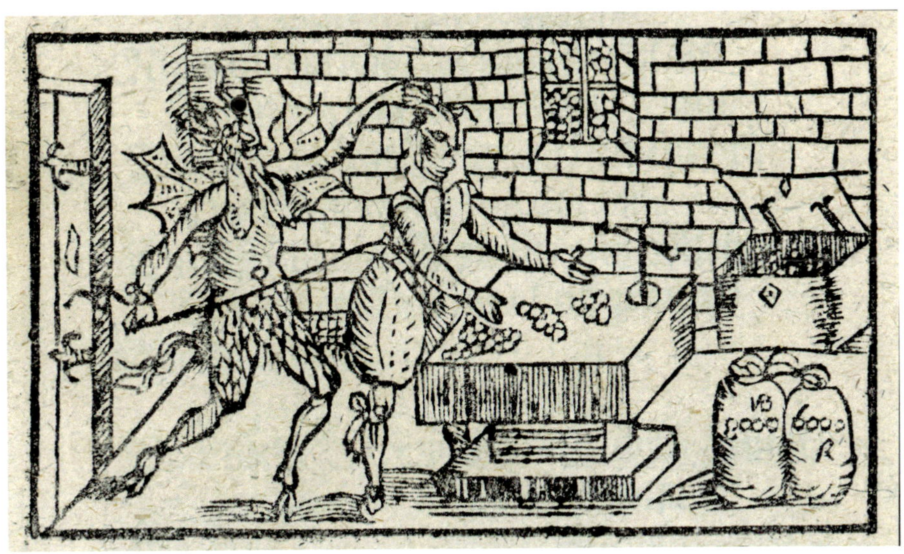

USERERS NOT ONLY BREACHED THE LAW, BUT THEIR ACTIONS WERE ALSO CONSIDERED A SERIOUS SIN. ANYONE WHO MADE UNAUTHORISED MONETARY TRANSACTIONS HAD TO FEAR BEING TAKEN BY THE DEVIL.

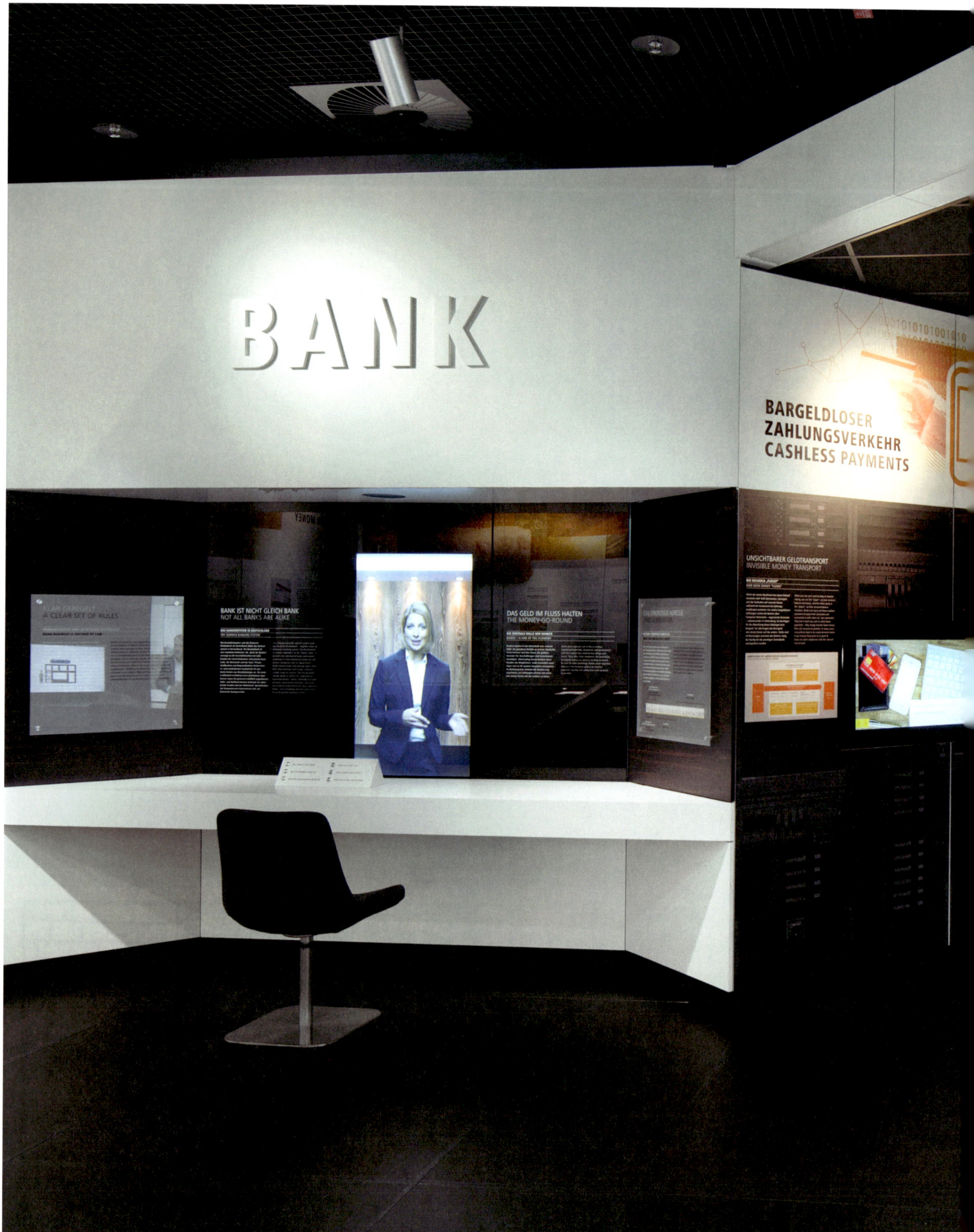
BANK
BARGELDLOSER
ZAHLUNGSVERKEHR
CASHLESS PAYMENTS
BANK IST NICHT GLEICH BANK
NOT ALL BANKS ARE ALIKE
DAS GELD IM FLUSS HALTEN
THE MONEY-GO-ROUND
UNSICHTBARER GELDTRANSPORT
INVISIBLE MONEY TRANSPORT
A CLEAR SET OF RULES

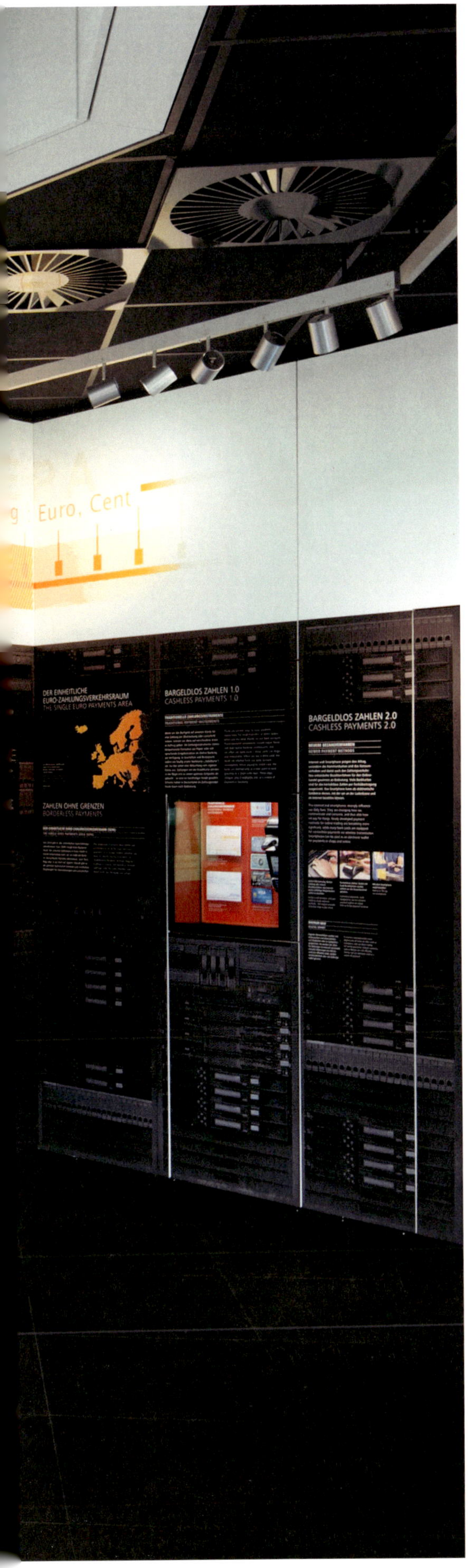

BANK BRANCH

Book money is the foundation for cashless payments and is nowadays much more important for the economy than cash.

At the bank branch, a virtual clerk will greet visitors and explain to them the services that banks offer and their pivotal role in economic activities. A look behind the scenes of cashless payments shows the complex processes triggered by a card payment or transfer and how book money travels through banks' giro networks to "flow" from one account to another. The Deutsche Bundesbank ensures that these processes are secure and smooth.

At a multimedia advisory station, visitors will find out how banks, just by booking a credit, are able to create new money, and will learn about the limits to their creation of book money. Visitors can also explore banks interactively and unearth the particular risks inherent in banking business. Banking supervisors monitor banks' governance and risk management in order to avert crises. The Single Supervisory Mechanism, which supervises euro-area banks and is based at the European Central Bank, has been in existence since 2014; the Deutsche Bundesbank is also a member of this set-up.

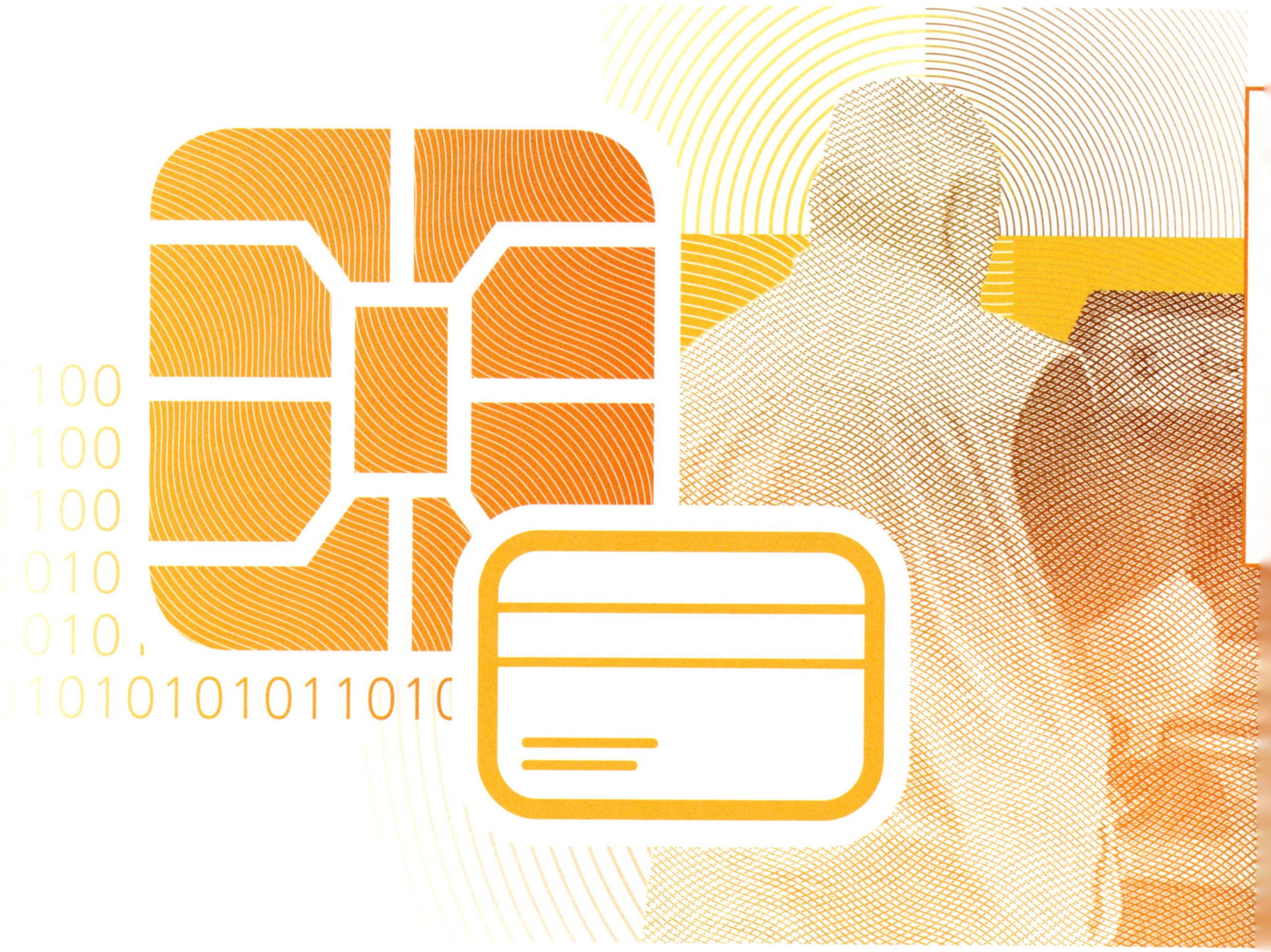

JUST NUMBERS?

BOOK MONEY – YOUR CREDIT BALANCE

Important though banknotes and coins may be in everyday life, it's safer and more convenient to pay the rent or make large purchases by credit transfer or card. The money you use for such payments is the book money deposited in your bank account. You can't touch book money because it's no more than a set of data in the bank's computer systems. The term book money refers to the early days of banking when money changers noted their customers' credit balances manually in their ledgers. This immaterial money is the basis of cashless payment systems and plays the leading role in today's business world. In the euro area there is about eight times more book money than cash.

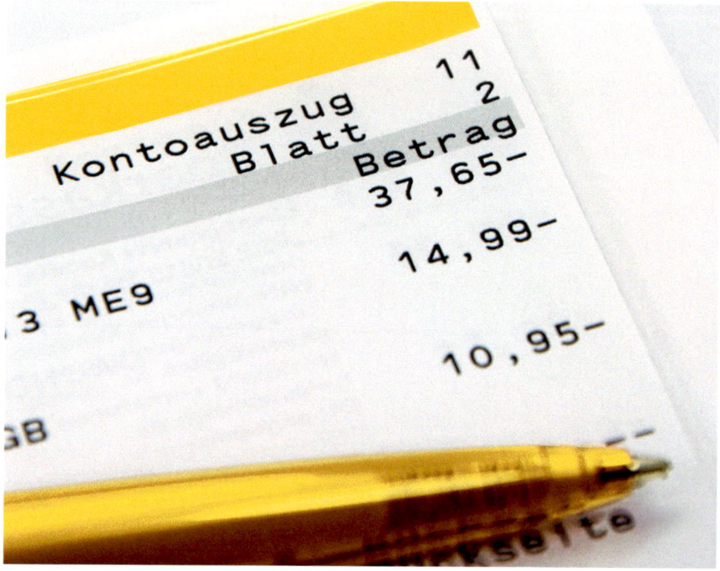

KEEPING TABS: ACCOUNT STATEMENTS LIST CREDIT AND DEBIT ENTRIES, AND THE ACCOUNT BALANCE SHOWS YOU HOW MUCH BOOK MONEY IS CURRENTLY IN YOUR ACCOUNT. BOOK MONEY MOVES FROM ONE ACCOUNT TO ANOTHER, WHICH IS WHY IT IS SOMETIMES CALLED "GIRO MONEY" (ITALIAN GIRO = CIRCLE OR ROUND).

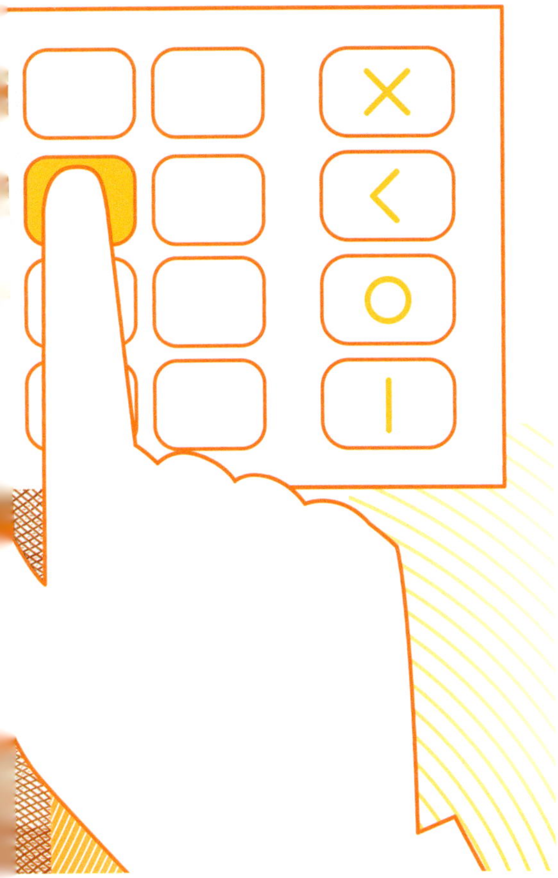

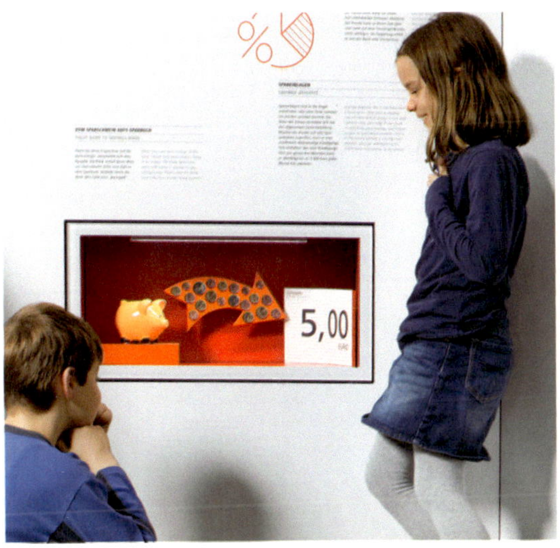

PIGGY BANK TO SAVINGS BOOK

WHEN YOU TAKE YOUR SAVINGS TO THE BANK, WATCH HOW YOUR MONEY CHANGES ITS SHAPE. THE BANK TAKES YOUR COINS AND WRITES A NUMBER IN YOUR SAVINGS BOOK. THAT'S WHY THE BANK NOW CALLS YOUR MONEY "BOOK MONEY".

HOW QUICKLY DO YOU NEED YOUR MONEY?

THREE TYPES OF BOOK MONEY

Credit balances on bank accounts are also called deposits. There are three types of deposits, depending on how quickly you need your money.

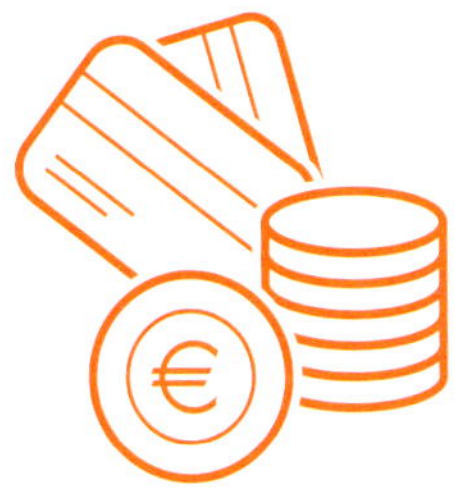

SIGHT DEPOSITS

Credit balances are mainly used for payments. These sight deposits, as they are known, can be withdrawn immediately, without notice, in cash, or be used for credit transfers or bank card purchases. Sight deposits earn little or no interest.

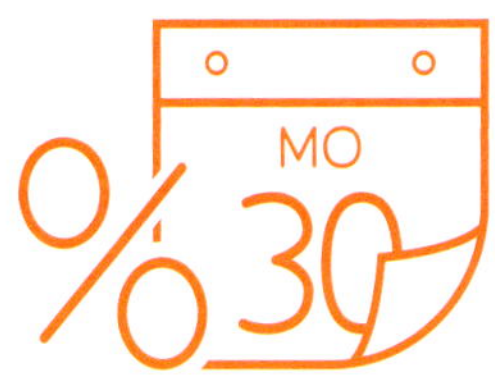

TIME DEPOSITS

Time deposits are credit balances that are left with the bank for a fixed period of time. You cannot withdraw this money during this period, but it does earn interest.

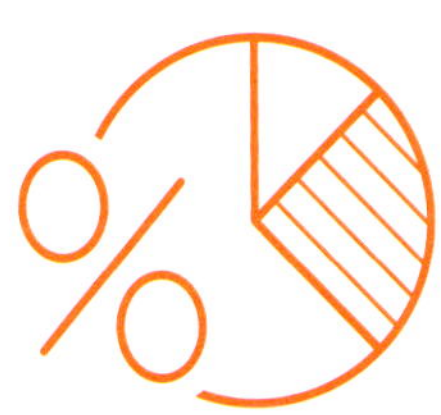

SAVINGS DEPOSITS

Savings deposits don't normally have a fixed term. They earn a variable rate of interest that moves in line with interest rates generally. If you want to withdraw your savings, you'll have to give at least three months' notice. If the notice period is exactly three months, you can withdraw up to 2,000 euro each month at no charge.

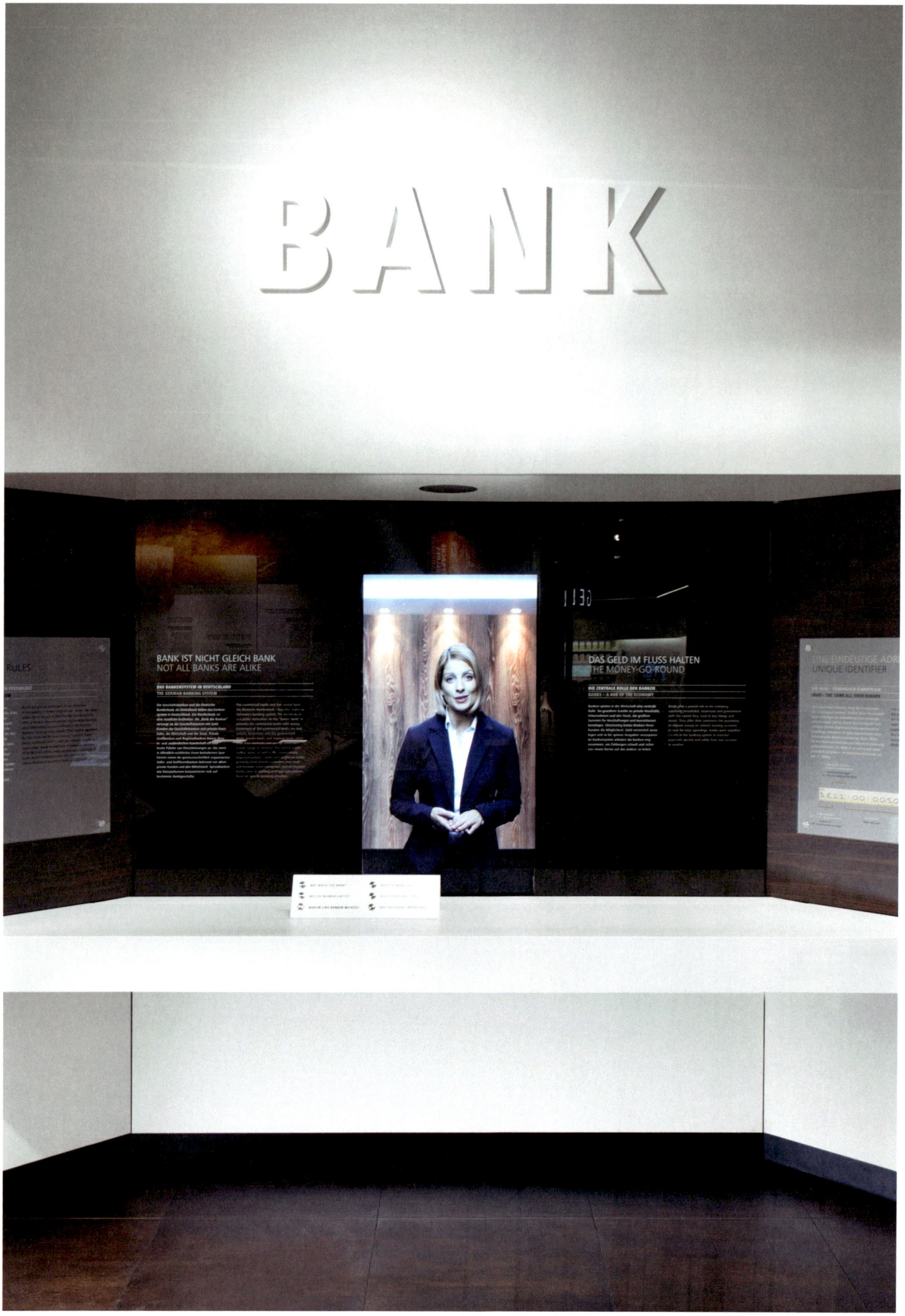
BANK
BANK IST NICHT GLEICH BANK
NOT ALL BANKS ARE ALIKE
DAS GELD IM FLUSS HALTEN
THE MONEY-GO-ROUND
UNIQUE IDENTIFIER

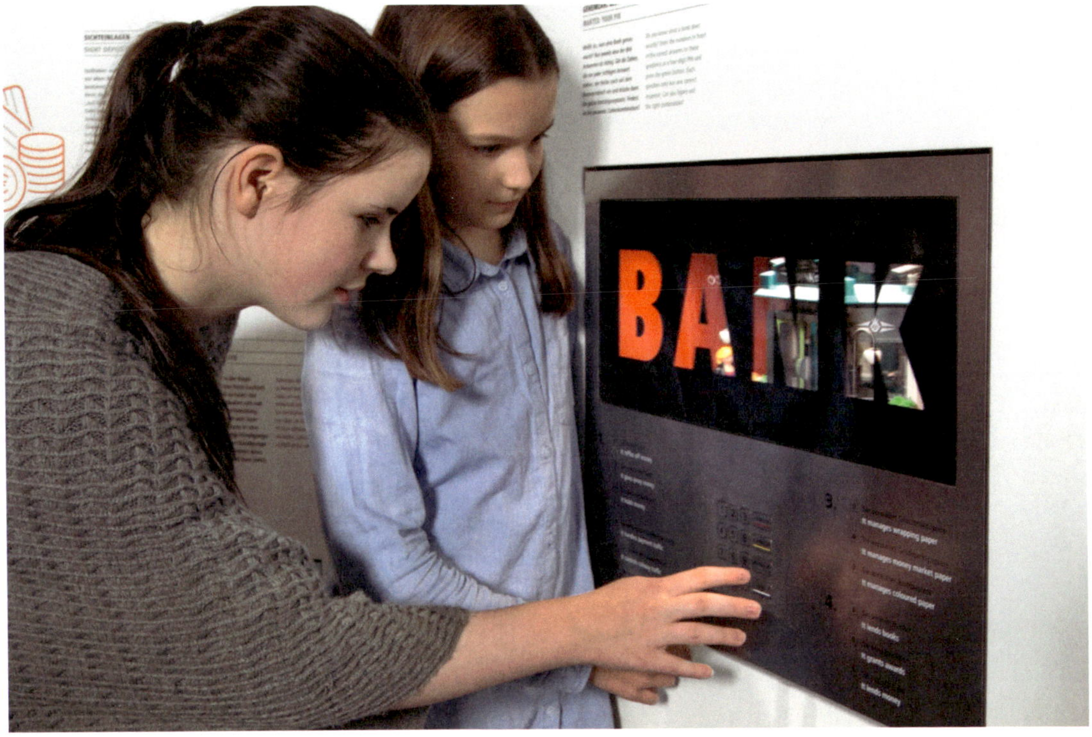

WANTED: YOUR PIN

A CLEAR SET OF RULES

BANK BUSINESS IS DEFINED BY LAW

Banks are just as much part of our daily lives as the bakery or flower shop on the corner. But what makes them unique is that the law clearly defines what a bank is. Anyone conducting banking business on a commercial basis as defined in the German Banking Act is running a bank. They require approval for this from the German Federal Financial Supervisory Authority (BaFin) and are subject to special supervision. Banking business includes acceptance of funds from others (deposit business), granting of loans (credit business) and safe custody and administration of securities (safe custody business).

NOT ALL BANKS ARE ALIKE

THE GERMAN BANKING SYSTEM

The commercial banks and the central bank – the Deutsche Bundesbank – together make up Germany's banking system. The Bundesbank is a public institution. As the "banks' bank" it provides the commercial banks with money. Customers of the commercial banks are individuals, businesses and the government. Major private banks and regional banks often offer their domestic and foreign customers a wide range of services. The mostly public savings banks as well as the cooperatively organised people's banks and Raiffeisen banks primarily serve private customers and small and medium-sized enterprises. Special-purpose banks, such as building and loan associations, focus on specific banking activities.

THE MONEY-GO-ROUND

BANKS – A HUB OF THE ECONOMY

Banks play a pivotal role in the economy, supplying households, businesses and government with the capital they need to buy things and invest. They offer their customers the possibility to deposit money on interest bearing accounts to save for later spendings. Banks work together closely in the banking system to transfer payments quickly and safely from one account to another.

HOW CASHLESS PAYMENTS WORK

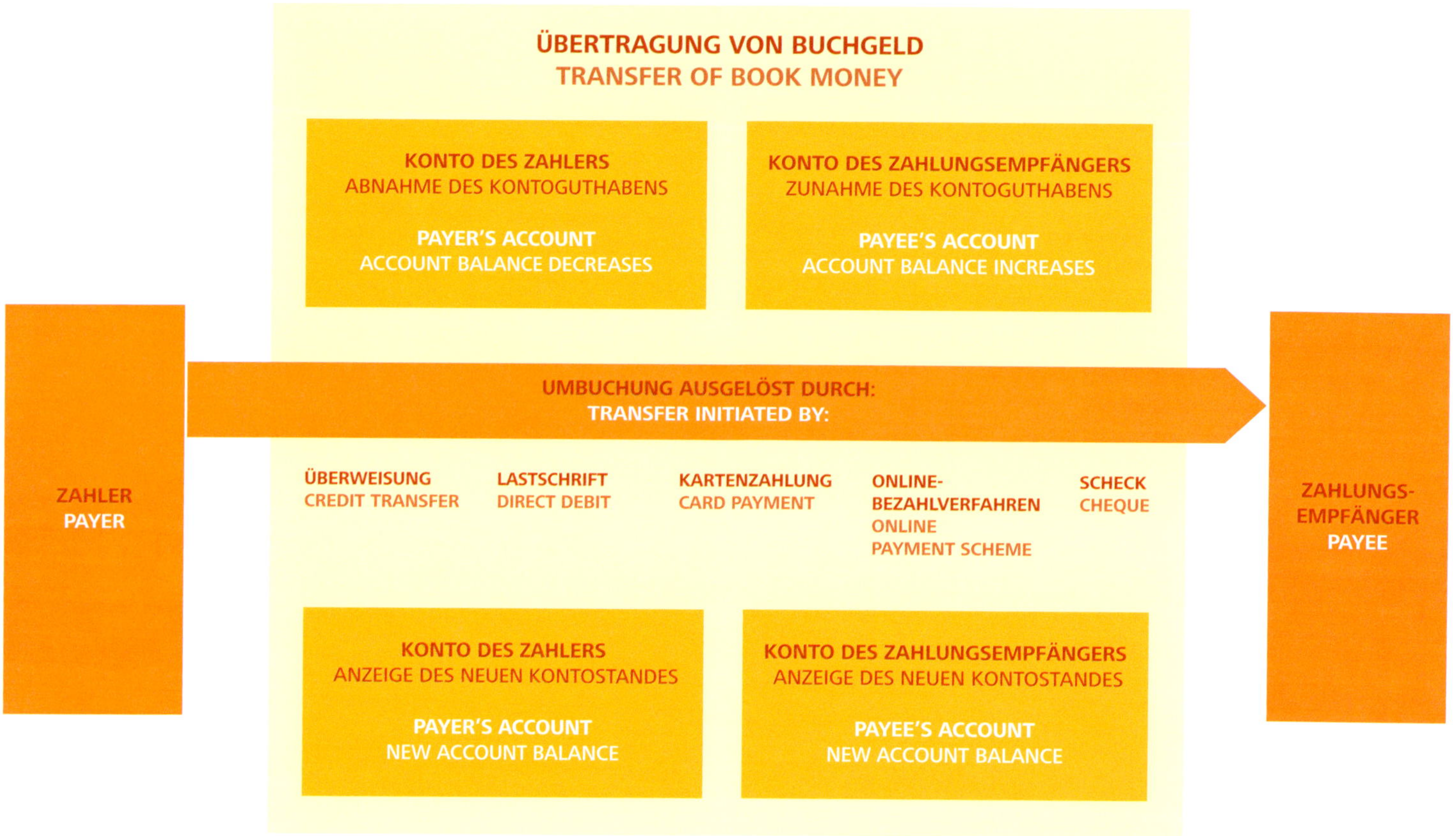

INVISIBLE MONEY TRANSPORT

HOW BOOK MONEY "FLOWS"

When you use your card to shop or transfer money, you are the "payer", so your account balance decreases, and the other party is the "payee", so their account balance increases. Banks can carry out these cashless payments because their computers are connected to each other via "giro networks". They don't need any cash to settle these payments–they simply transfer book money from one account to another. In many cases, transactions have to be made between banks to get money from point A to point B; these are often conducted with the relevant central bank.

ACCOUNT TO ACCOUNT

CLEARING UND SETTLEMENT

The first stage of the money transfer process is called "clearing". In this stage, banks transmit payment instructions electronically and clarify all the information necessary for the payments to take place. The next stage is "settlement": the payments are booked to the appropriate accounts and the book money "flows" from one account to the other. Each day, banks process millions of payments for their customers. Amongst themselves, however, banks do not settle each transaction individually, just their net totals.

BORDERLESS PAYMENTS

THE SINGLE EURO PAYMENTS AREA (SEPA)

The Single Euro Payments Area (SEPA) was established in 2014. For non-cash euro payments, it no longer matters whether you want to transfer money from Berlin to neighbouring Potsdam, to Paris, Riga or a village in Cyprus: the technical formats and legal rules for credit transfers and direct debits are the same everywhere.

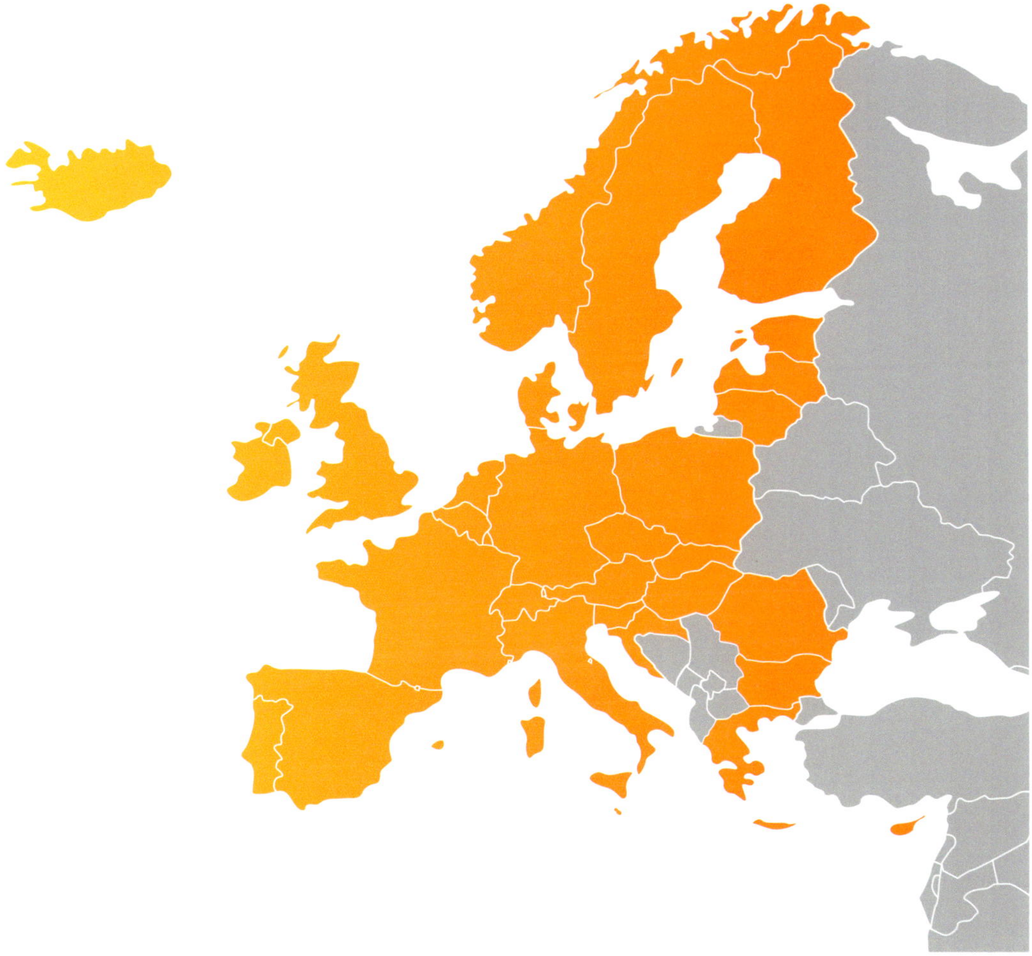

SEPA MEMBERS: ALL EU MEMBER STATES PLUS ICELAND, LIECHTENSTEIN, MONACO, NORWAY, SAN MARINO AND SWITZERLAND (AS OF 2016).

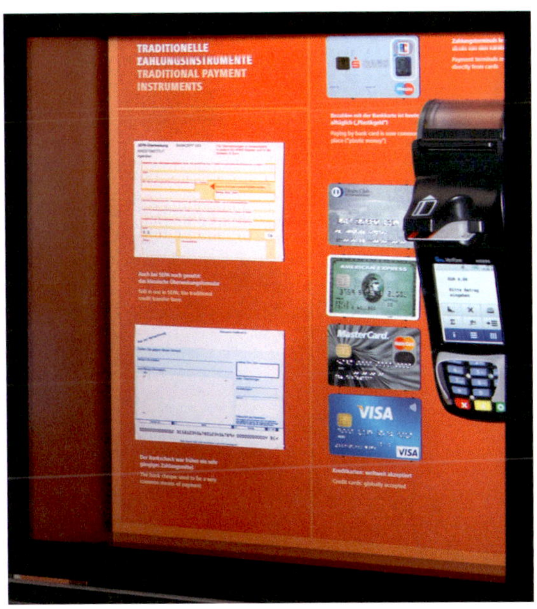

CASHLESS PAYMENTS 1.0

TRADITIONAL PAYMENT INSTRUMENTS

There are various ways to issue payment instructions for credit transfers or direct debits, which use the book money on our bank accounts. These payment instruments include paper forms and their online banking counterparts, and we often use bank cards ("debit cards") in shops and restaurants. When we use a debit card, the funds are debited from our bank account immediately. When paying by credit card, the funds are debited only at a later point in time–granting us a short-term loan. These days, cheques play a negligible role as a means of payment in Germany.

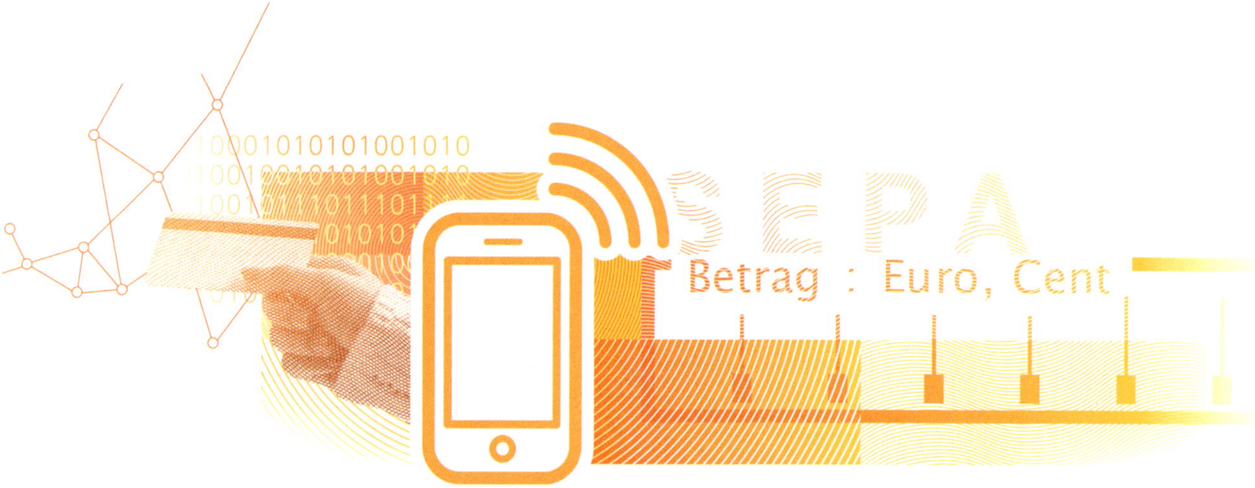

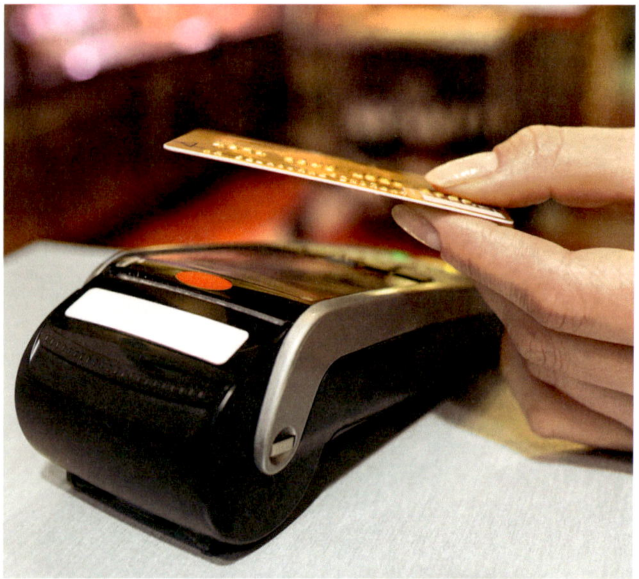

CASHLESS PAYMENTS 2.0

NEWER PAYMENT METHODS

The internet and smartphones strongly influence our daily lives. They are changing how we communicate and consume, and thus also how we pay for things. Newly developed payment methods for online trading are becoming more significant, while many bank cards are equipped for contactless payments via wireless transmission. Smartphones can be used as an electronic wallet for payments in shops and online.

WITH THE CONTACTLESS TECHNOLOGY KNOWN AS NEAR FIELD COMMUNICATION (NFC), CARD PAYMENTS CAN INCREASINGLY BE MADE ON THE GO. IF THE TERMINAL IS FITTED WITH THE SAME TECHNOLOGY, YOU CAN SIMPLY HOLD YOUR CARD AGAINST THE TERMINAL TO MAKE YOUR PAYMENT. FOR PAYMENTS UP TO A VALUE OF €25, THERE IS NO NEED TO EVEN ENTER YOUR PIN.

DIGITAL WALLETS IN SMARTPHONES WITH NFC FUNCTIONALITY OR QR CODE SUPPORT GO ONE STEP FURTHER. THE IDEA HERE IS THAT A SUITABLY EQUIPPED MOBILE PHONE CAN BE USED TO MAKE PAYMENTS AT THE COUNTER, SIMILARLY TO A PLASTIC CARD.

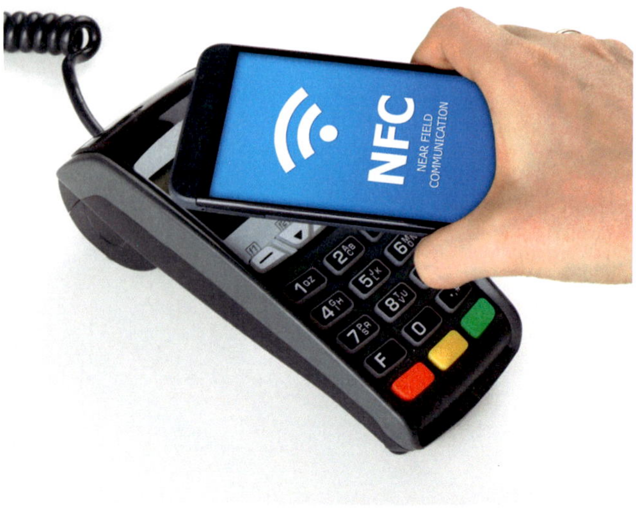

DIGITAL MONEY

Consumers and businesses store digital units of value on chip car ds or computers, and use them mainly for online payments. Virtual currencies such as Bitcoin are not officially money, but are variously used as a means of payment.

IS IT REALLY YOU?

KEEPING PAYMENTS SAFE

When you pay online or by card or smartphone, security won't be far from your mind. Banks and payment service providers need to check that the person making a payment is authorised to do so. They use various methods based on the criteria of "knowledge" (eg password or PIN), "possession" (eg card or mobile phone) and "biometrics" (eg fingerprint); these methods work best in combination.

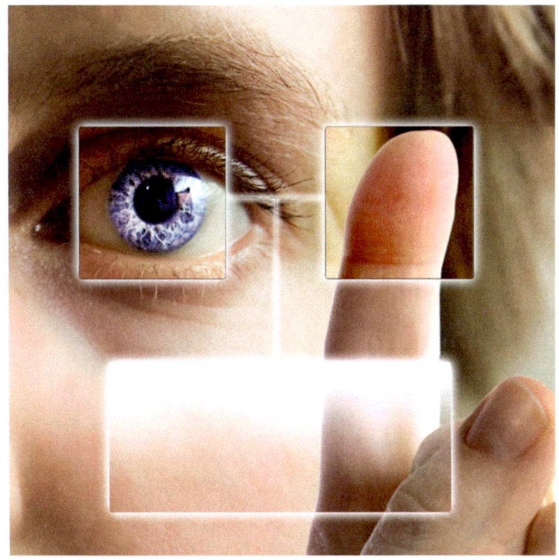

IRIS RECOGNITION AND FINGERPRINTS ARE METHODS OF BIOMETRIC IDENTIFICATION THAT USE UNIQUE PHYSICAL TRAITS TO CLEARLY ESTABLISH A PERSON'S IDENTITY.

OPERATE, SECURE, OVERSEE

THE BUNDESBANK'S ROLE IN PAYMENTS

The Deutsche Bundesbank provides for the smooth operation of payments. It oversees the security of payment systems and makes fast and reliable payment platforms available. The Bundesbank's payment systems complement as well as connect the commercial banks' giro networks. Together with the central banks of Italy and France, the Bundesbank operates Europe's central payment system, TARGET2, which allows banks to transfer large sums to one another within a matter of seconds.

A PEEK INSIDE THE DEUTSCHE BUNDESBANK'S TARGET2 ROOM

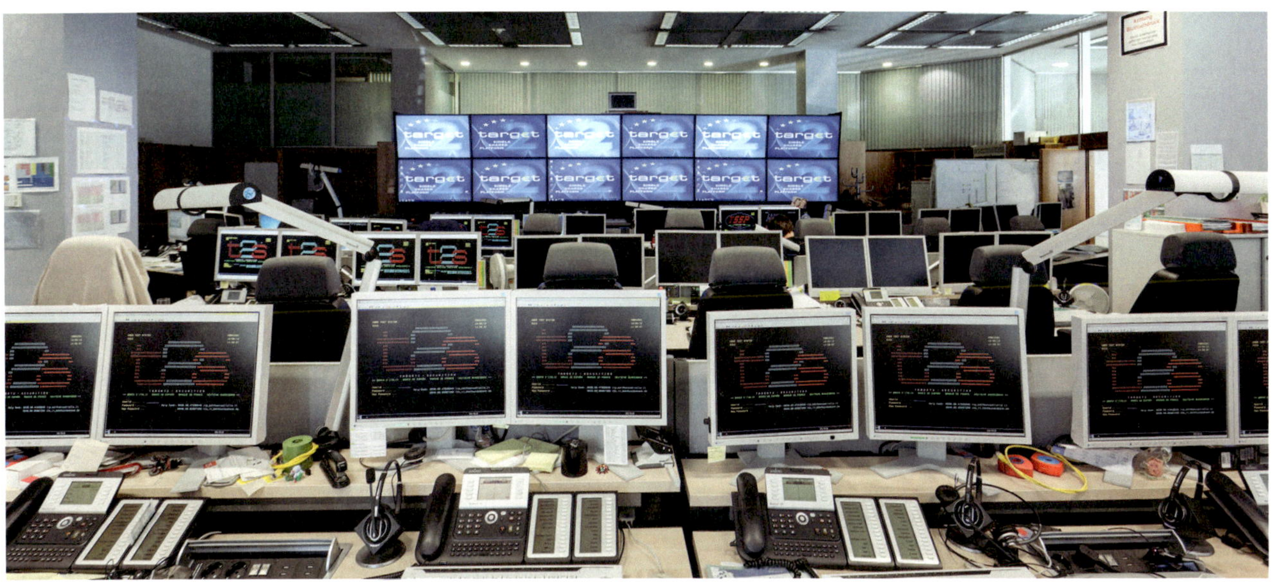

WHERE DOES MONEY COME FROM?

BOOK MONEY CREATION AND ITS LIMITATIONS

When a bank grants a loan, it credits the amount to the customer's account as a sight deposit. If it purchases a building or a security from the customer, the proceeds of the sale are also credited to the customer's account. In both situations, the bank has created money by making credit entries – money that was not there previously.

Many people think the bank can only lend the money that it has received previously from other customers in the form of savings deposits. But that's not the case. For the bank creates new money by granting loans.

Banks cannot just create an unlimited amount of money. It is in their own interest to restrict the amount of book money they create, as this always involves risks and costs.

If the customer doesn't pay back the loan, the bank is left sitting on the debt and makes a loss. This risk is the most important reason why banks are cautious when creating book money through lending.

Aside from this, the banks are monitored by banking and financial supervision. If a bank runs too many risks, it not only jeopardises its owners' capital, but its customers' deposits as well.

Monetary policy also keeps a close eye on how much book money the banks create. If it's too much – or too little – it can jeopardise the primary objective of monetary policy – price stability.

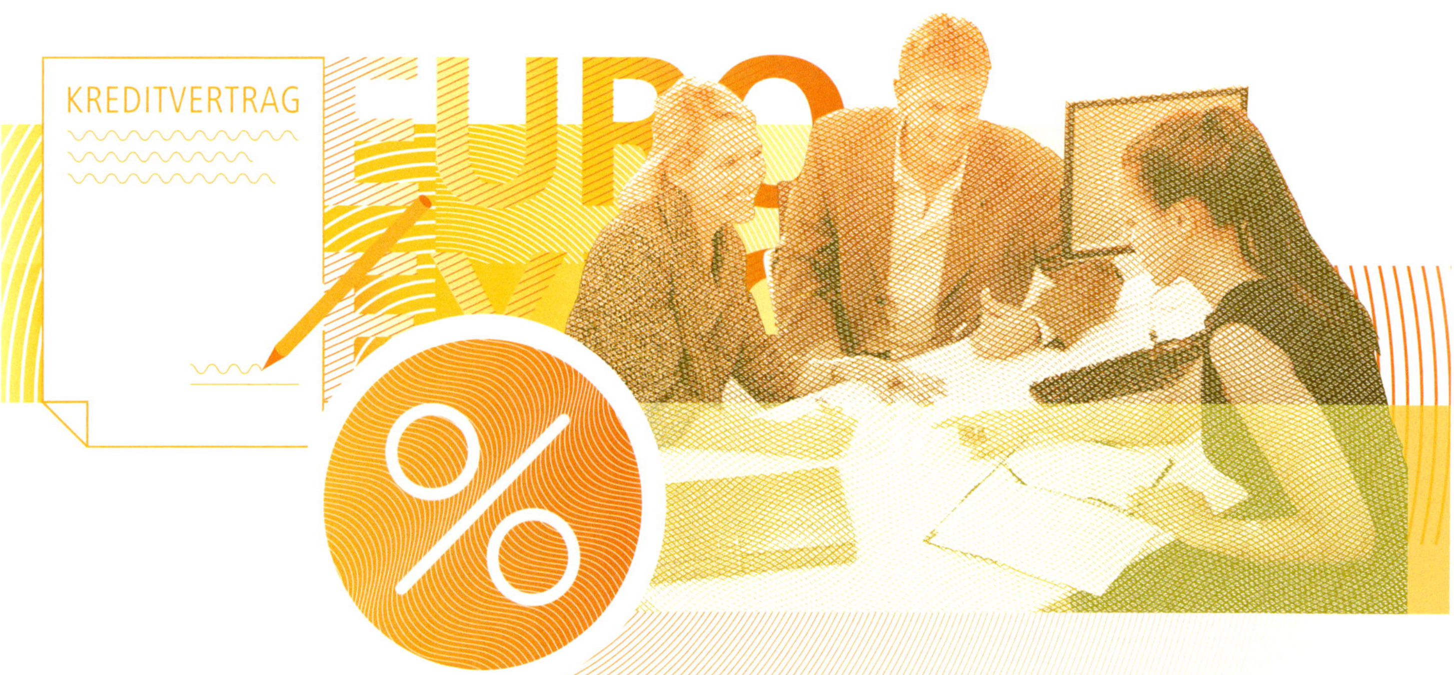

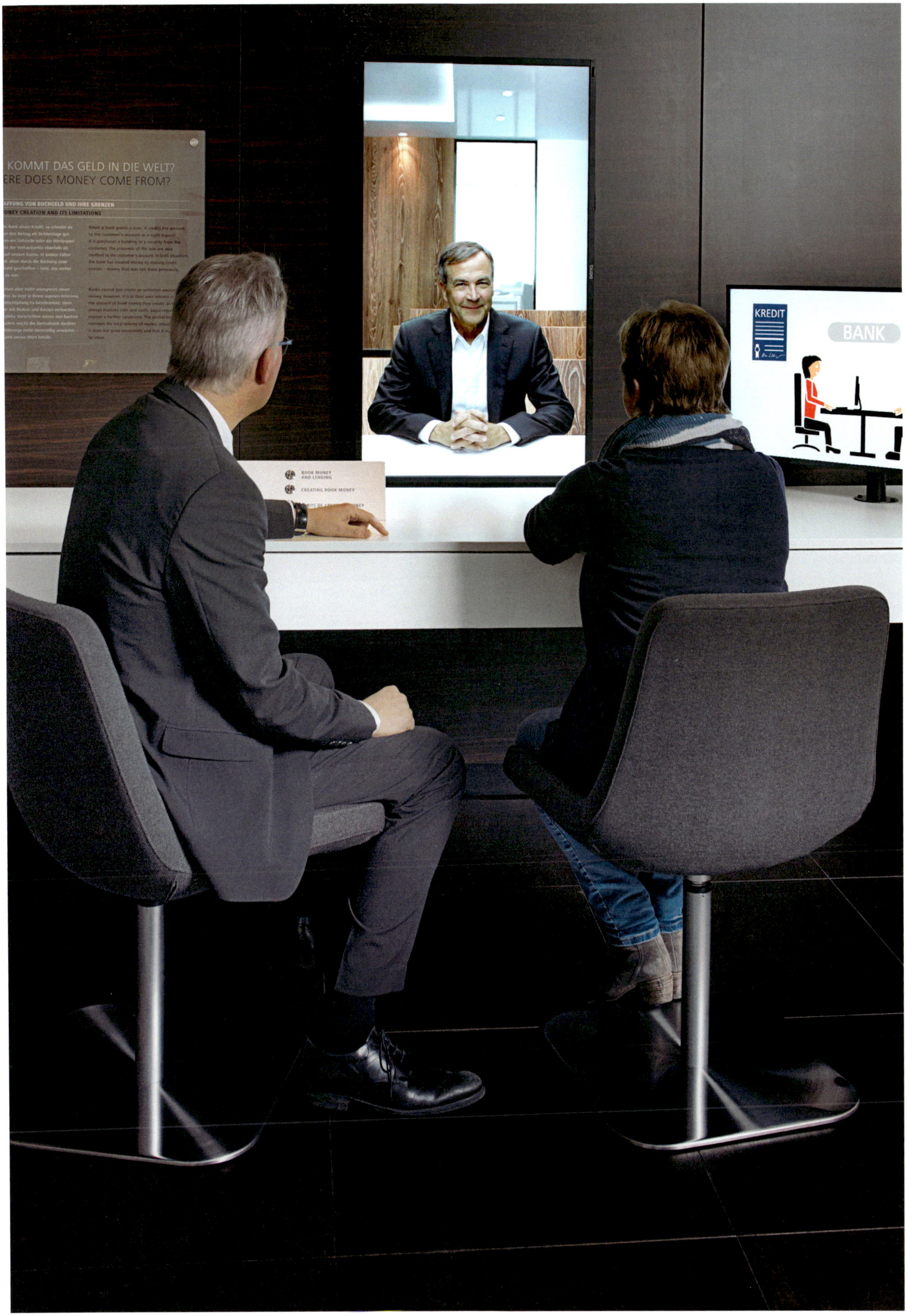
KOMMT DAS GELD IN DIE WELT?
DOES MONEY COME FROM?
BOOK MONEY AND LENDING
CREATING BOOK MONEY
KREDIT
BANK

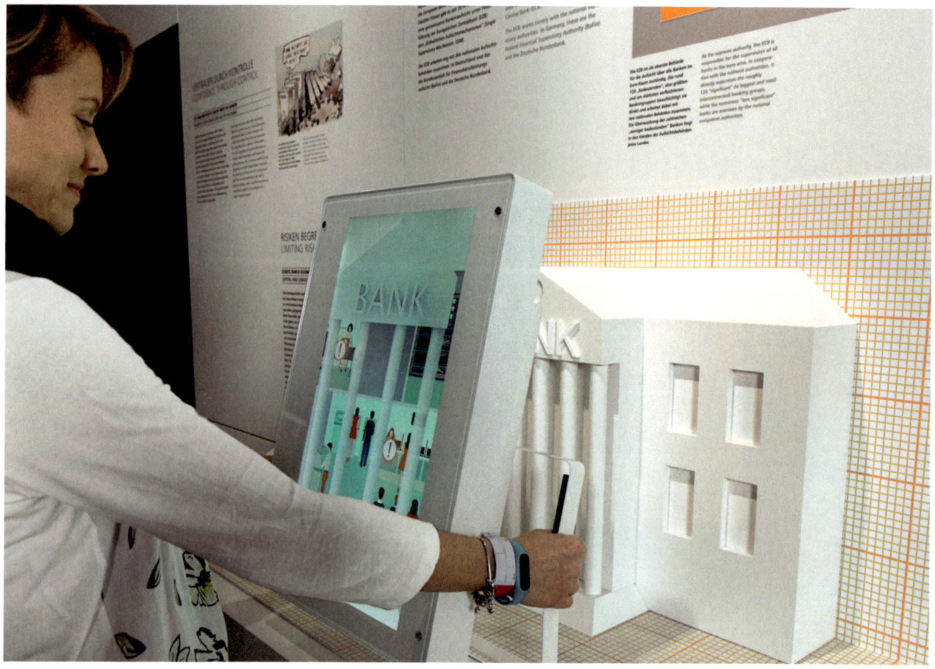

CONFIDENCE THROUGH CONTROL

BANKING SUPERVISORS KEEP AN EYE ON BANKS

Every day, we trust banks with our money. However, certain risks are associated with operating a bank. If a bank collapses, this could have serious financial consequences for every one of its customers. Other banks may also experience financial difficulties as a result, which ultimately could impact the whole economy. This is why we need banking supervisors. It is their responsibility to monitor the business activities and risk management practices of each individual bank and to prevent banking crises. An effective banking supervisory system is a prerequisite of a stable financial system.

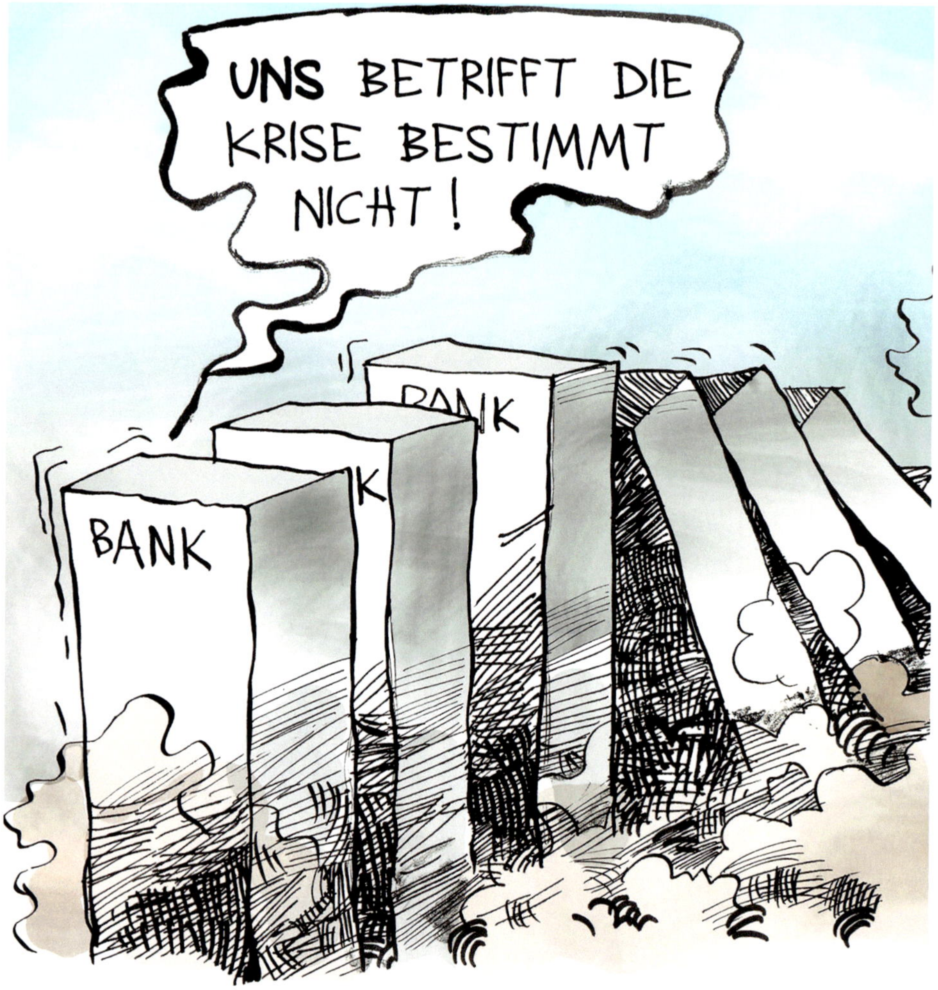

THE INTERCONNECTEDNESS OF BANKS HARBOURS THE RISK OF DOMINO EFFECTS: IF ONE BANK COLLAPSES, IT MAY DRAG OTHERS DOWN WITH IT. IT IS THE BANKING SUPERVISORS' JOB TO PREVENT CHAIN REACTIONS. THE SPEECH BUBBLE SAYS: "THIS CRISIS WILL CERTAINLY NOT AFFECT US!"

ENSURING STABILITY TOGETHER

EUROPEAN BANKING SUPERVISION

Given that banks often operate internationally, banking supervision should not stop at the borders of each individual country. All banks, regardless of their location, should be overseen in accordance with uniform rules. The European Banking Authority (EBA) was established in 2011 with the aim of harmonising supervisory standards and practices in Europe. Furthermore, the Single Supervisory Mechanism (SSM) was set up for the euro area in 2014 under the direction of the European Central Bank (ECB). The ECB works closely with the national supervisory authorities. In Germany, these are the Federal Financial Supervisory Authority (BaFin) and the Deutsche Bundesbank.

JUST IN CASE

THE EUROPEAN SINGLE RESOLUTION MECHANISM

The Single Resolution Mechanism (SRM) exists to ensure that difficulties encountered by an internationally active bank based in the euro area do not endanger the stability of the financial system. The SRM governs the recovery and orderly resolution of banks in the euro area. If it is not possible for a bank to be restructured, it will be wound down – with the systemically important parts being retained, where possible. In Germany, the Financial Market Stabilisation Agency (FMSA) is responsible for resolving nationally active banks.

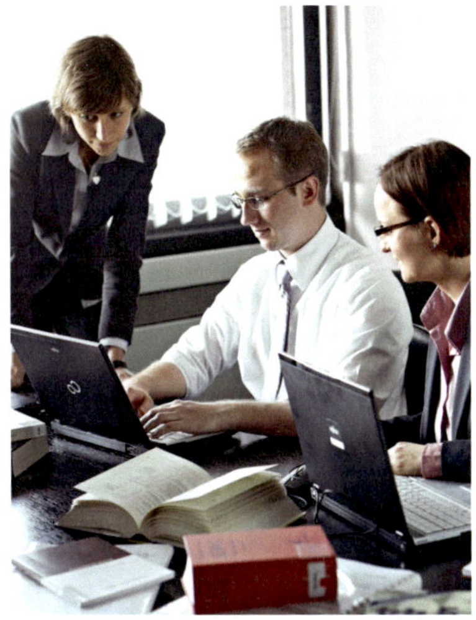

BANKING SUPERVISORS DO NOT RELY SOLELY ON REPORTS AND NOTIFICATIONS PROVIDED BY BANKS, BUT ALSO CONDUCT INSPECTIONS ON SITE. THIS GIVES THEM DIRECT INSIGHT INTO THE BANKS' OPERATIONS.

RESPONSIBILITIES WITHIN THE SINGLE SUPERVISORY MECHANISM (SSM)

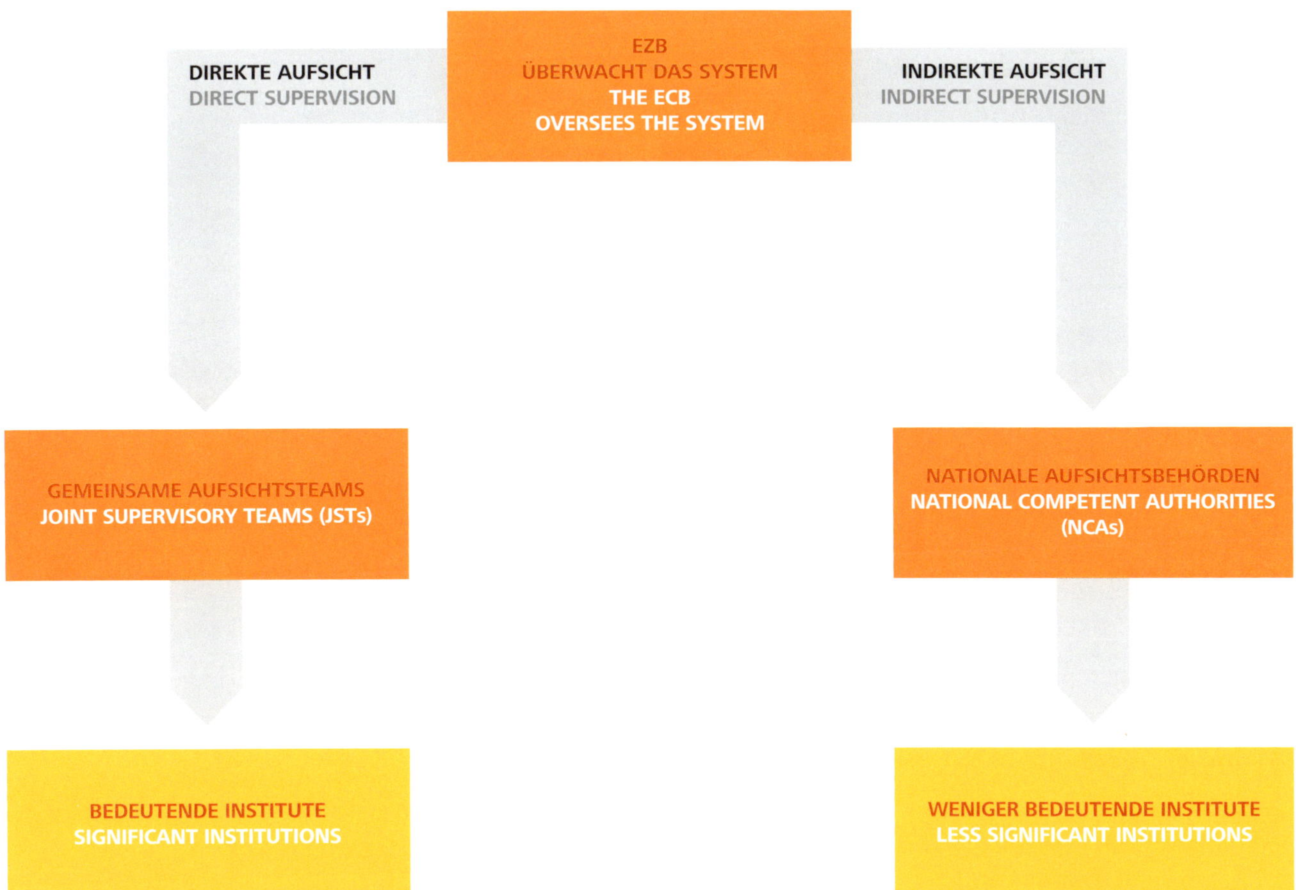

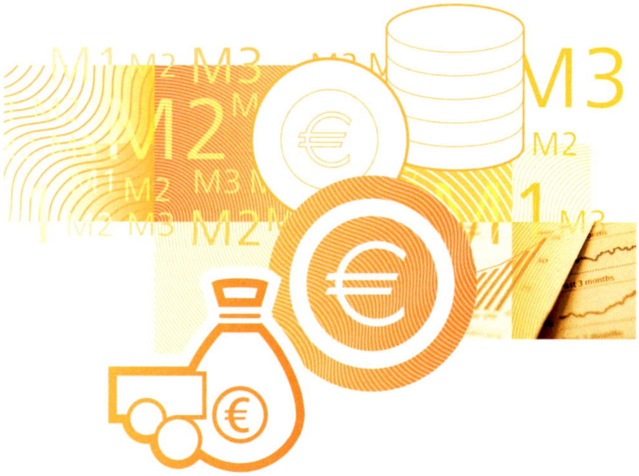

HOW MUCH MONEY EXISTS?

EURO-AREA MONETARY AGGREGATES

To find out how much money exists, you first of all need to clarify what you actually mean by "money". Euro-area central banks define it as all money belonging to "non -banks", ie to individuals, enterprises and the public sector. Banks' credit balances do not count as money under this definition. Money can serve as a means of payment and a store of value and can be quickly converted from one function to another. For this reason, euroarea central banks define three separate monetary aggregates based on how quickly the money is available to the bank customer. These are called M1, M2 and M3. The letter "M" comes from the English word "money".

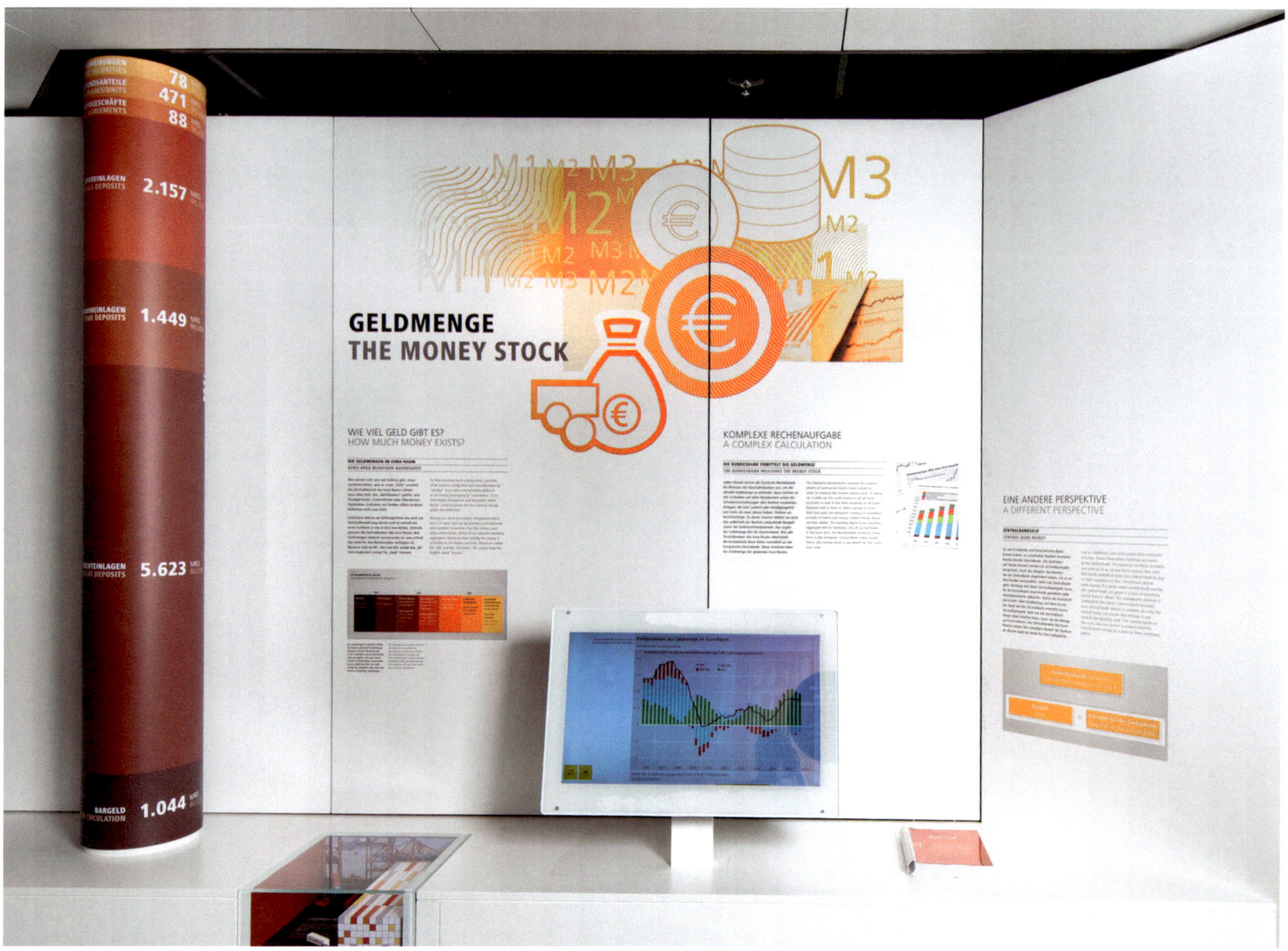

THE MONETARY AGGREGATES M1, M2 AND M3

M1		M2		M3		
BARGELD **CURRENCY IN CIRCULATION**	**SICHTEINLAGEN** **SIGHT DEPOSITS**	**TERMINEINLAGEN** MIT LAUFZEIT BIS ZU ZWEI JAHREN **TIME DEPOSITS** WITH AN AGREED MATURITY UP TO 2 YEARS	**SPAREINLAGEN** MIT KÜNDIGUNGS-FRIST BIS ZU 3 MONATEN **SAVINGS DEPOSITS** REDEEMABLE AT A PERIOD OF NOTICE UP TO 3 MONTHS	**REPOGESCHÄFTE** REPURCHASE AGREEMENTS	**GELDMARKT-FONDSANTEILE** **MONEY MARKET FUND (MMF) SHARES/UNITS**	**BANKSCHULD-VERSCHREIBUNGEN** MIT LAUFZEIT BIS ZU ZWEI JAHREN **BANK DEBT SECURITIES** WITH A MATURITY UP TO 2 YEARS

M1 = Bargeld + Sichteinlagen; M2 = M1 + Termineinlagen + Spareinlagen; M3 = M2 + Repogeschäfte + Geldmarktfondsanteile + Bankschuldverschreibungen

A DIFFERENT PERSPECTIVE

CENTRAL BANK MONEY

Just as individuals and enterprises have accounts at banks, banks themselves maintain accounts at the central bank. The balances on these accounts are referred to as central bank money. The cash that banks withdraw from the central bank to pay to their customers is also considered central bank money. If a bank needs central bank money, the central bank can grant it a loan or purchase assets from it. When the subsequent amount is credited to the bank's central bank account, new central bank money is created. As only the central bank can create this money, it can control the quantity well. The central banks in the euro area use banks' constant need for central bank money as a lever in their monetary policy.

ZENTRALBANKGELD (GELDBASIS)
CENTRAL BANK MONEY (BASE MONEY)

=

BARGELD
CASH

+

EINLAGEN BEI DER ZENTRALBANK
DEPOSITS AT THE CENTRAL BANK

ALL OUR CASH IN ONE PLACE

IMAGINE IF WE WERE TO COLLECT THE ENTIRE STOCK OF EURO CASH AND LOAD IT ONTO A SHIP IN 50-EURO BANKNOTES. IT WOULD FILL UP 338 HUGE CONTAINERS COMPLETELY.

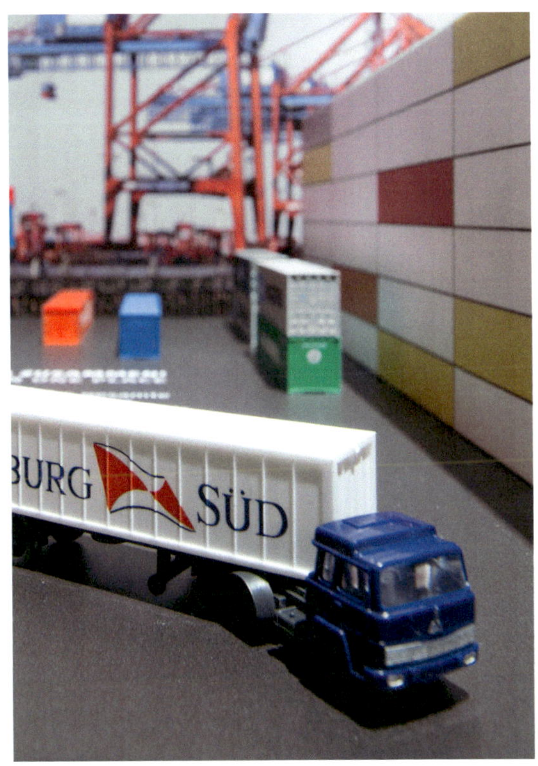

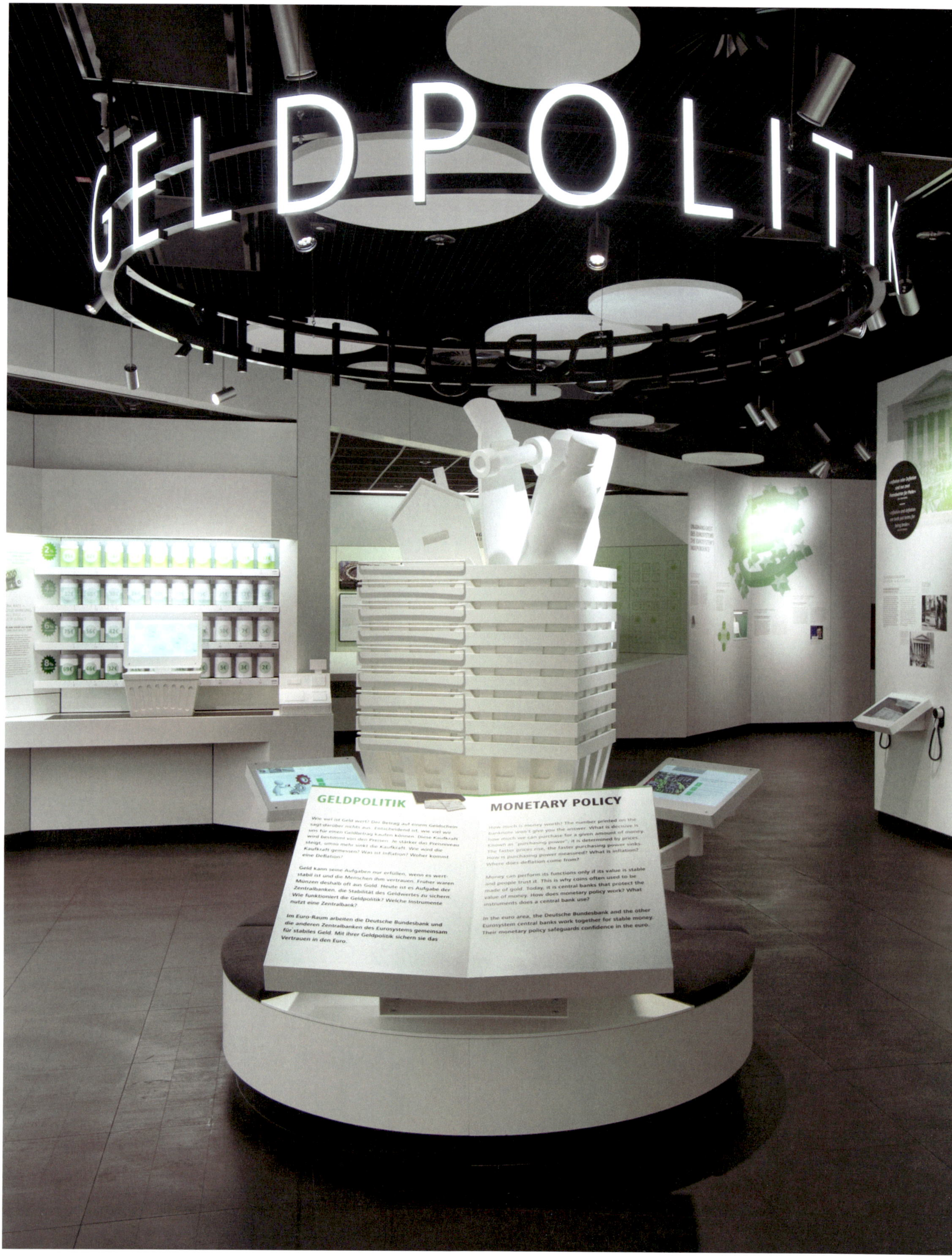
GELDPOLITIK
GELDPOLITIK
Wie viel ist Geld wert? Der Betrag auf einem Geldschein sagt darüber nichts aus. Entscheidend ist, wie viel wir uns für einen Geldbetrag kaufen können. Diese Kaufkraft wird bestimmt von den Preisen. Je stärker das Preisniveau steigt, umso mehr sinkt die Kaufkraft. Wie wird die Kaufkraft gemessen? Was ist Inflation? Woher kommt eine Deflation?
Geld kann seine Aufgaben nur erfüllen, wenn es wertstabil ist und die Menschen ihm vertrauen. Früher waren Münzen deshalb oft aus Gold. Heute ist es Aufgabe der Zentralbanken, die Stabilität des Geldwertes zu sichern. Wie funktioniert die Geldpolitik? Welche Instrumente nutzt eine Zentralbank?
Im Euro-Raum arbeiten die Deutsche Bundesbank und die anderen Zentralbanken des Eurosystems gemeinsam für stabiles Geld. Mit ihrer Geldpolitik sichern sie das Vertrauen in den Euro.
MONETARY POLICY
How much is money worth? The number printed on the banknote won't give you the answer. What is decisive is how much we can purchase for a given amount of money. Known as "purchasing power", it is determined by prices. The faster prices rise, the faster purchasing power sinks. How is purchasing power measured? What is inflation? Where does deflation come from?
Money can perform its functions only if its value is stable and people trust it. This is why coins often used to be made of gold. Today, it is central banks that protect the value of money. How does monetary policy work? What instruments does a central bank use?
In the euro area, the Deutsche Bundesbank and the other Eurosystem central banks work together for stable money. Their monetary policy safeguards confidence in the euro.

HOW MUCH IS MONEY WORTH? THE NUMBER PRINTED ON THE BANKNOTE WON'T GIVE YOU THE ANSWER. WHAT IS DECISIVE IS HOW MUCH WE CAN PURCHASE FOR A GIVEN AMOUNT OF MONEY. KNOWN AS "PURCHASING POWER", IT IS DETERMINED BY PRICES. THE FASTER PRICES RISE, THE FASTER PURCHASING POWER SINKS. HOW IS PURCHASING POWER MEASURED? WHAT IS INFLATION? WHERE DOES DEFLATION COME FROM?

MONEY CAN PERFORM ITS FUNCTIONS ONLY IF ITS VALUE IS STABLE AND PEOPLE TRUST IT. THIS IS WHY COINS OFTEN USED TO BE MADE OF GOLD. TODAY, IT IS CENTRAL BANKS THAT PROTECT THE VALUE OF MONEY. HOW DOES MONETARY POLICY WORK? WHAT INSTRUMENTS DOES A CENTRAL BANK USE?

IN THE EURO AREA, THE DEUTSCHE BUNDESBANK AND THE OTHER EUROSYSTEM CENTRAL BANKS WORK TOGETHER FOR STABLE MONEY. THEIR MONETARY POLICY SAFEGUARDS CONFIDENCE IN THE EURO.

MONETARY POLICY

"NO, MONEY IS A SYMBOL!"

A LOOK BACK THROUGH HISTORY

In the early days, whenever people thought about money, the questions were quite basic: What is money? What makes it valuable? Who determines the value of money?

For centuries, coins made of precious metal formed the foundation of money. Many rulers arbitrarily reduced their coins' weight and purity in order to make a profit for themselves. This rattled monetary stability and often ended up stoking inflation – as was impressively shown by the example of the Kipper- und Wipperzeit (literally, the era of "tipping the scales").

The history of money is marked by numerous periods of devastating inflation and deflation. They destabilised monetary systems, wrecked economies and unleashed severe crises. The paramount monetary policy task of many central banks is to ensure the value of money. It wasn't until the 20th century that central banks evolved into "guardians of the currency" and their political independence was legally enshrined.

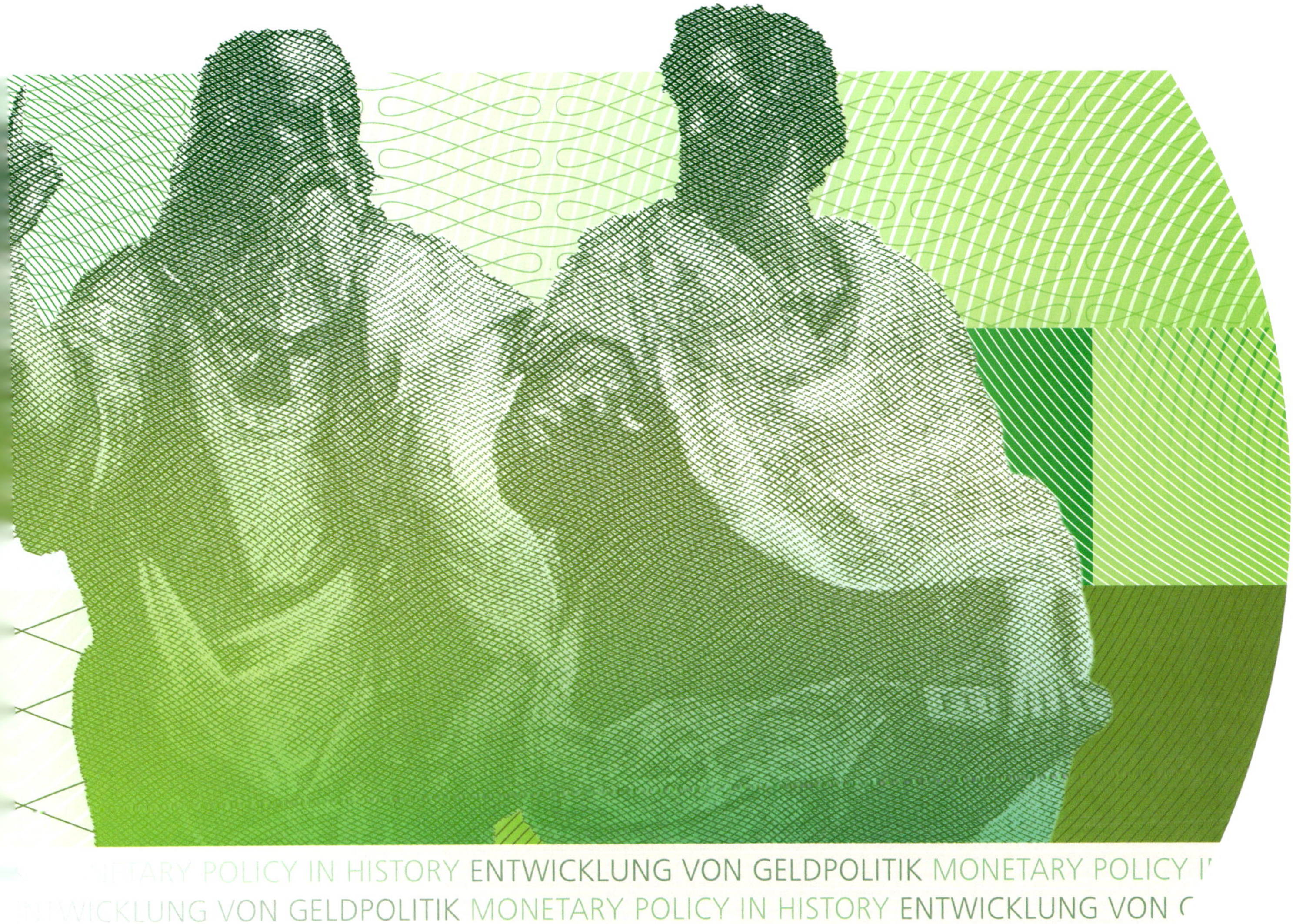

"I SAY MONEY IS A COMMODITY!"

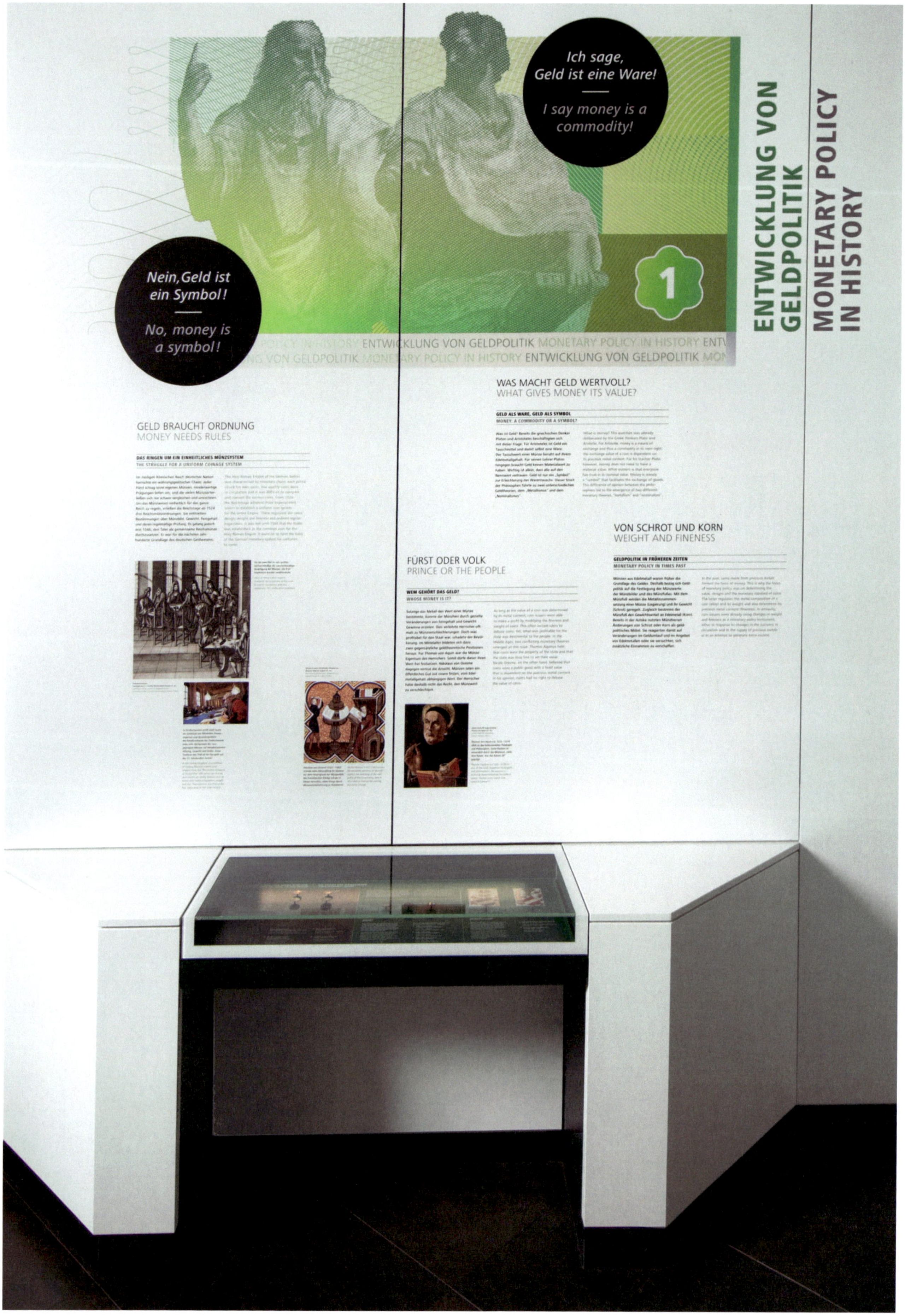
Ich sage, Geld ist eine Ware!
I say money is a commodity!
Nein, Geld ist ein Symbol!
No, money is a symbol!
1
ENTWICKLUNG VON GELDPOLITIK
MONETARY POLICY IN HISTORY
WAS MACHT GELD WERTVOLL?
WHAT GIVES MONEY ITS VALUE?
GELD BRAUCHT ORDNUNG
MONEY NEEDS RULES
VON SCHROT UND KORN
WEIGHT AND FINENESS
FÜRST ODER VOLK
PRINCE OR THE PEOPLE

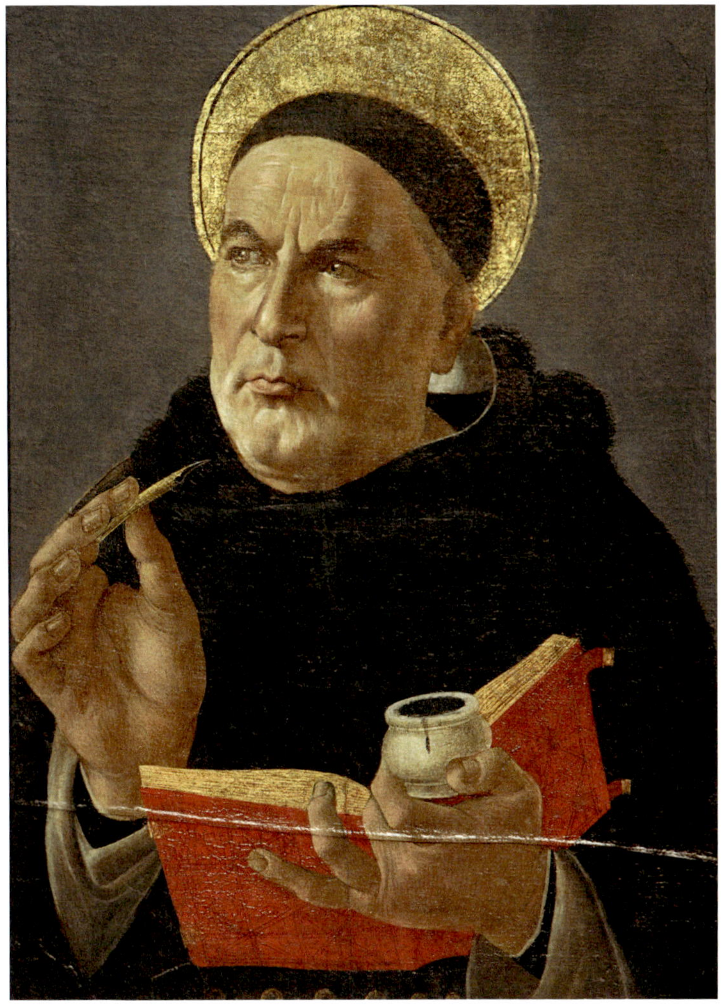

THOMAS AQUINAS (CA 1225–1274) IS ONE OF THE MOST IMPORTANT THEOLOGIANS AND PHILOSOPHERS. HIS POSITION IS PRIMARILY CHARACTERISED BY THE BIBLICAL WORDS "RENDER UNTO CAESAR THAT WHICH IS CAESAR'S".

WHAT GIVES MONEY ITS VALUE?

MONEY: A COMMODITY OR A SYMBOL?

What is money? This question was already deliberated by the Greek thinkers Plato and Aristotle. For Aristotle, money is a means of exchange and thus a commodity in its own right: the exchange value of a coin is dependent on its precious metal content. For his teacher Plato, however, money does not need to have a material value. What matters is that everyone has trust in its nominal value. Money is merely a "symbol" that facilitates the exchange of goods. This difference of opinion between the philosophers led to the emergence of two different monetary theories, "metallism" and "nominalism".

PRINCE OR THE PEOPLE

WHOSE MONEY IS IT?

As long as the value of a coin was determined by its metal content, coin issuers were able to make a profit by modifying the fineness and weight of coins. This often incited rulers to debase coins. Yet, what was profitable for the state was detrimental to the people. In the Middle Ages, two conflicting monetary theories emerged on this issue. Thomas Aquinas held that coins were the property of the state and that the state was thus free to set their value. Nicole Oresme, on the other hand, believed that coins were a public good with a fixed value that is dependent on the precious metal content. In his opinion, rulers had no right to debase the value of coins.

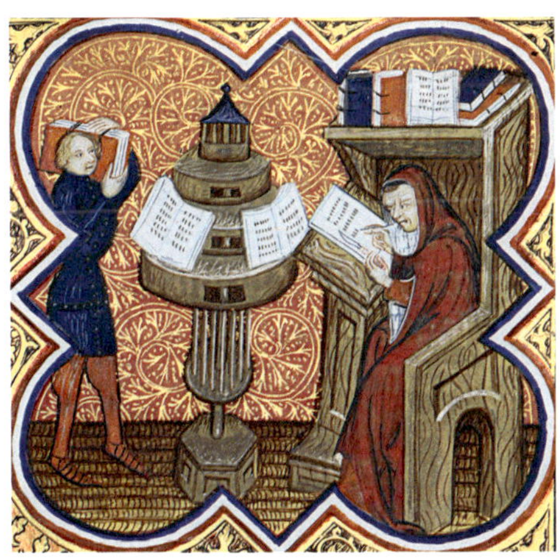

NICOLE ORESME (1322–1382) WROTE HIS SCHOLASTIC DOCTRINE *DE MONETA* AGAINST THE BACKDROP OF THE COIN POLICY OF THE FRENCH KING JOHN II, WHO TRIED TO FINANCE HIS WARS BY DEBASING COINAGE.

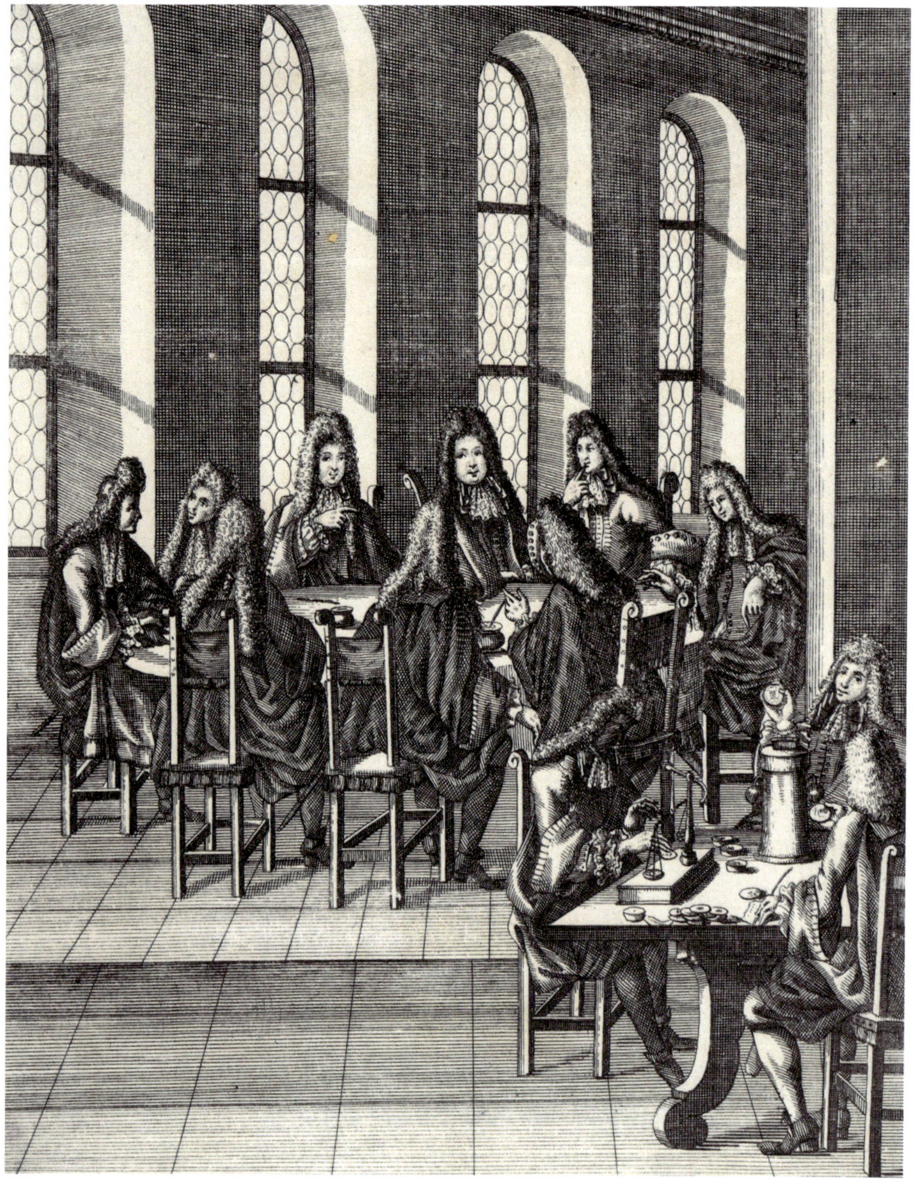

MONEY NEEDS RULES

THE STRUGGLE FOR A UNIFORM COINAGE SYSTEM

The Holy Roman Empire of the German Nation was characterised by monetary chaos: each prince struck his own coins, low-quality coins were in circulation and it was difficult to compare and convert the various coins. From 1524, the Reichstage adopted three imperial mint orders to establish a uniform coin system for the entire Empire. These regulated the coins' design, weight and fineness and ordered regular inspections. It was not until 1566 that the thaler was established as the common coin for the Holy Roman Empire. It went on to form the basis of the German monetary system for centuries to come.

COIN POLICY DELIBERATIONS BY ENVOYS AT A COMMITTEE OF COIN EXPERTS

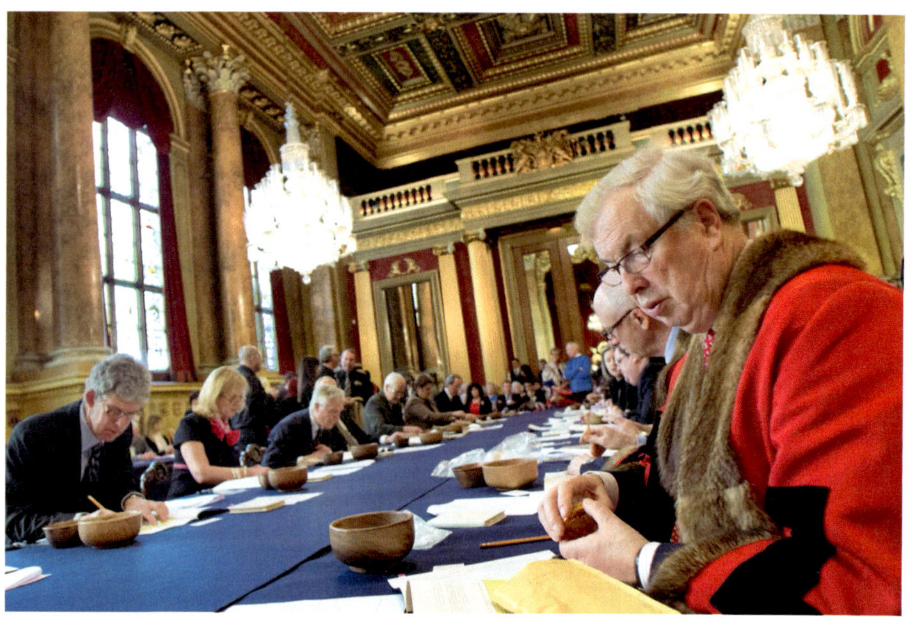

IN THE UNITED KINGDOM, A COMMITTEE OF LEADING FINANCIAL EXPERTS AND ASSAYERS FROM THE "WORSHIPFUL COMPANY OF GOLDSMITHS" STILL CARRIES OUT ANNUAL SPOT CHECKS ON NEWLY MINTED COINS TO ASSESS THEIR METAL COMPOSITION, WEIGHT AND SIZE. THIS TRADITION, THE TRIAL OF THE PYX, DATES BACK TO THE 12TH CENTURY.

"NICE ON THE OUTSIDE, UGLY ON THE INSIDE ..." – COIN ISSUERS' TRICKS

99 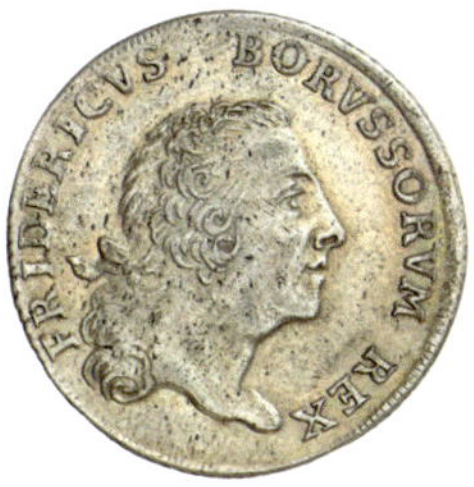

100 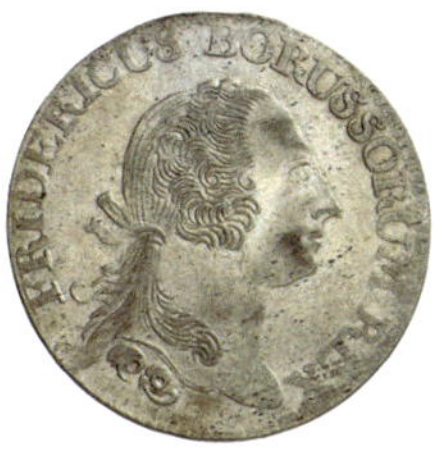

101 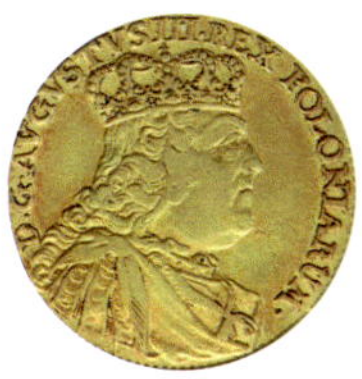

102 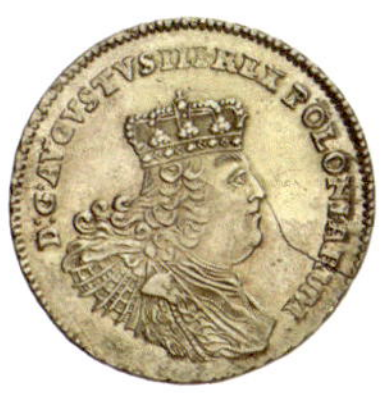

During the Seven Years' War, the fineness of Prussian coins was reduced with the explicit approval of Prussian King Frederick II. This allowed him to produce more coins from the same quantity of metal. Furthermore, he allowed foreign coins, such as the Saxony August d'or, to be restruck below par in the occupied territories using dies that had been seized. The overall cost of the war amounted to around 140 million thalers – Frederick II was able to finance 30 million of this amount through profits made from debasing coins.

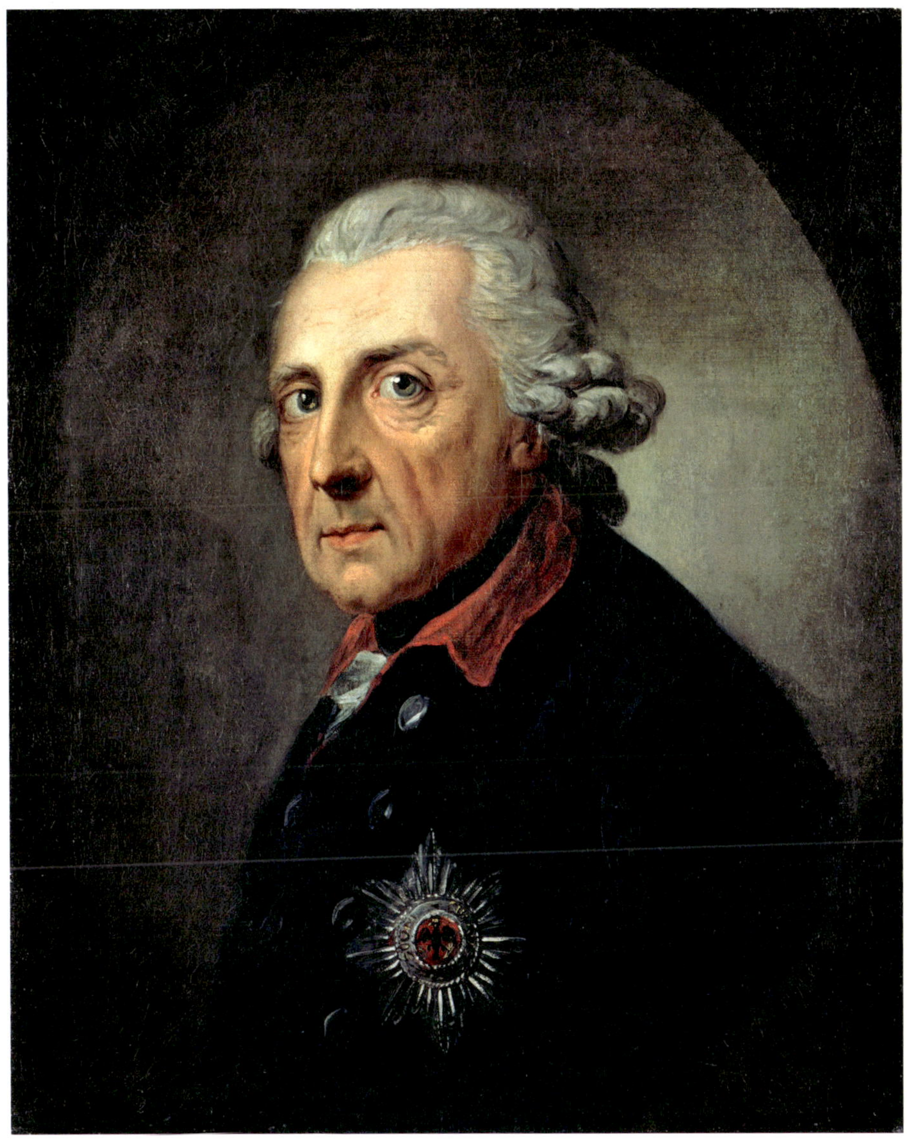

99 **8 GUTE GROSCHEN**
REGULAR COIN

100 **8 GUTE GROSCHEN**
MINTED WITH A 41% REDUCED SILVER CONTENT

101 **AUGUST D'OR**
REGULAR COIN

102 **NEW AUGUST D'OR**
WAR MONEY BY FREDRICK II

"INFLATION AND DEFLATION ARE BOTH JUST TERMS FOR BEING BROKE."

CARL FÜRSTENBERG

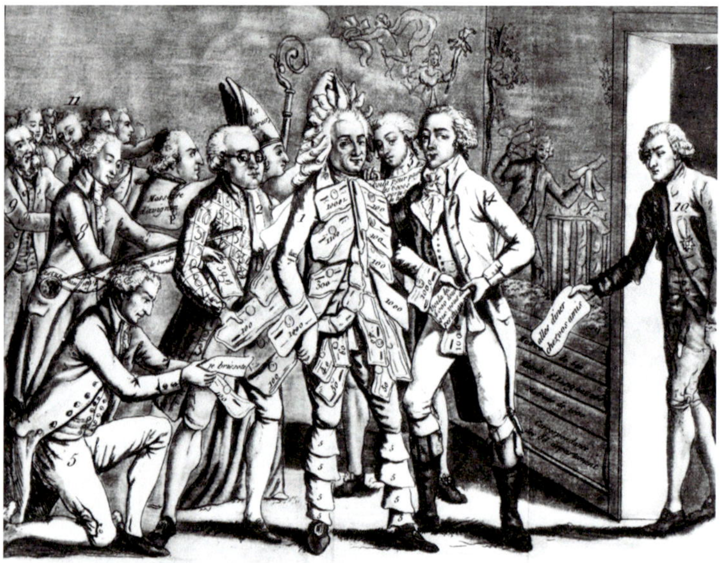

FRANCE EXPERIENCED HYPERINFLATION IN THE WAKE OF THE FRENCH REVOLUTIONARY WARS: THE PAPER MONEY ISSUED FROM 1789, KNOWN AS ASSIGNATS, BECAME WORTHLESS IN JUST A FEW YEARS.

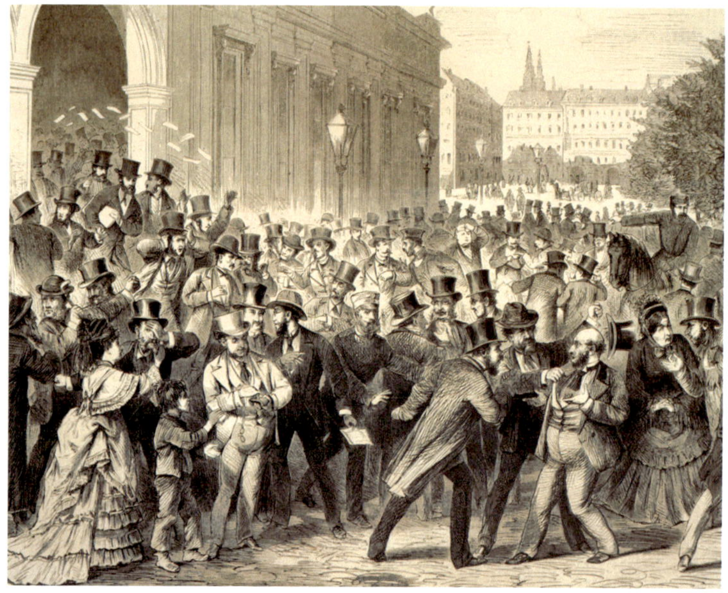

THE CRASH OF THE VIENNA STOCK EXCHANGE ON 9 MAY 1873 WAS THE PRECURSOR TO A LONG PHASE OF FALLING PRICES AND WEAK ECONOMIC GROWTH.

THREAT TO PROSPERITY

INFLATION AND DEFLATION

Ever since ancient times, there have been periods in which prices have surged and the value of money has fallen. Such inflation was often triggered by wars, political crises or poor monetary or economic policy. High inflation often goes hand in hand with a rise in unemployment and general economic upheaval. But periods of deflation, which are characterised by prices falling persistently across the board, are also fraught with economic danger because price drops cripple economic activity. Inflation and deflation are detrimental to a society's prosperity.

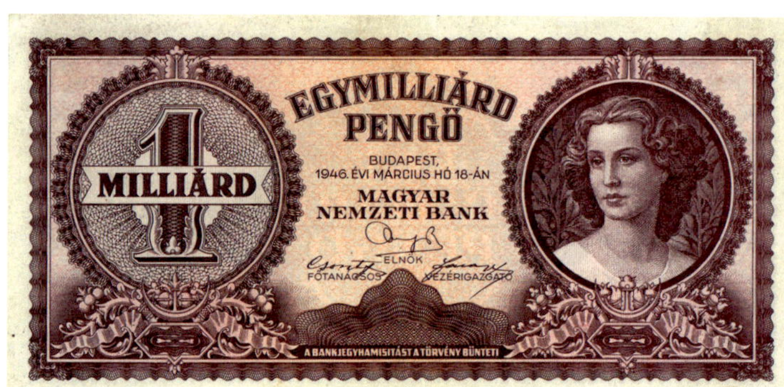

SHORTLY AFTER WORLD WAR II, THE INFLATION RATE IN HUNGARY ROSE TO OVER 200 PER CENT PER DAY.

TIPPER AND SEE-SAW

EUROPE'S FIRST PERIOD OF RUNAWAY INFLATION

The Tipper and see-saw time (1618–1624) was one of the worst monetary crises of the early modern age and affected large swaths of Central Europe. In order to finance the Thirty Years' War, many princes debased their currencies by reducing coins' silver content. A growing number of inferior coins flooded into circulation, resulting in price rises and reducing the population's purchasing power. It was only when the princes started receiving the debased money in taxes and customs fees and felt the effects of their currencies' depreciation that the debased coins were discredited, withdrawn and recoined, returning the monetary system to an even keel.

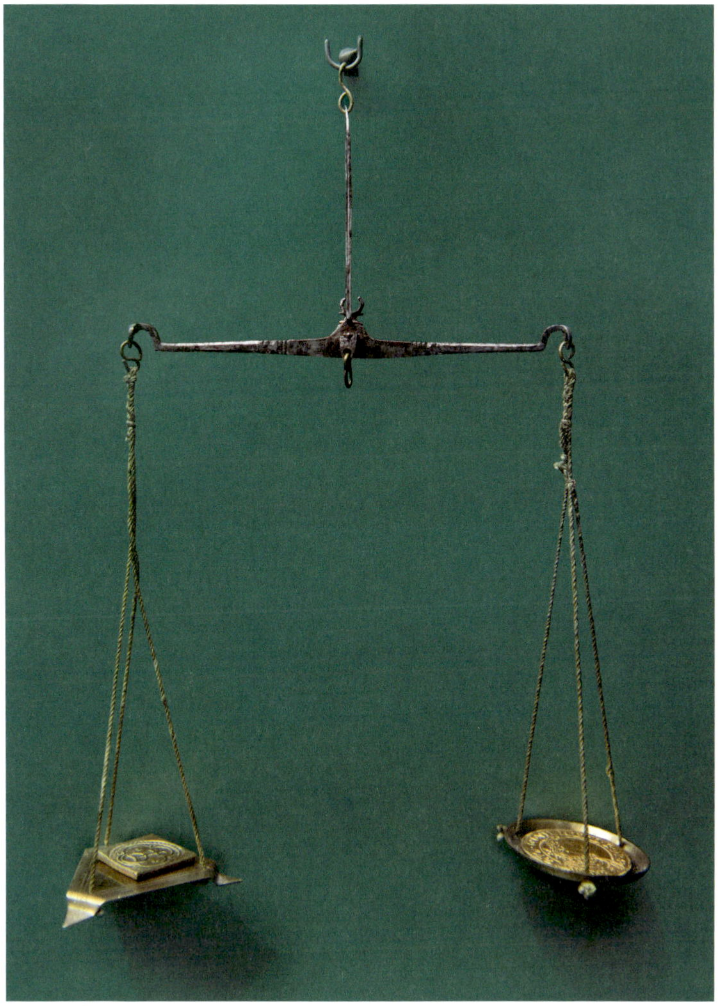

103 **COIN SCALE**
CA 1620

BUYERS SCOURED THE COUNTRY FOR SILVER COINS. THE TERM "TIPPER AND SEE-SAW" (FROM THE GERMAN KIPPER UND WIPPER) IS DERIVED FROM THEIR MODUS OPERANDI. A COIN WAS PLACED ON A SCALE CALLED A WIPPE ("SEE-SAW") BY A KIPPER ("TIPPER"). THE WIPPE TIPPED IF THE COIN WAS HEAVIER AND THUS OF FULL VALUE. SUCH COINS WERE THEN USED AS THE RAW MATERIAL FOR DEBASED COINS.

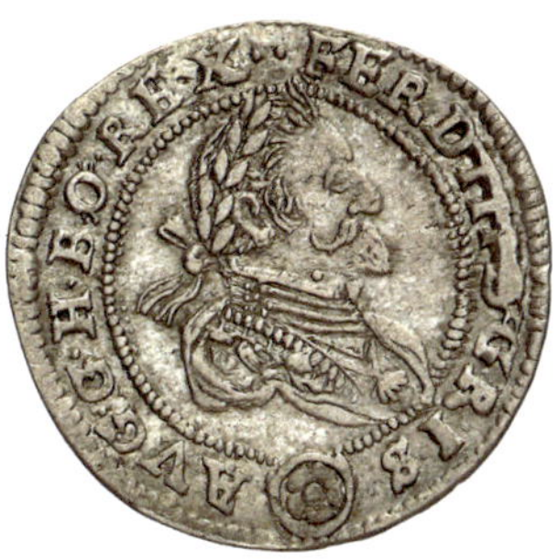

104 **GROSCHEN**
REGULAR COIN, 1626
(SCALE 2:1)

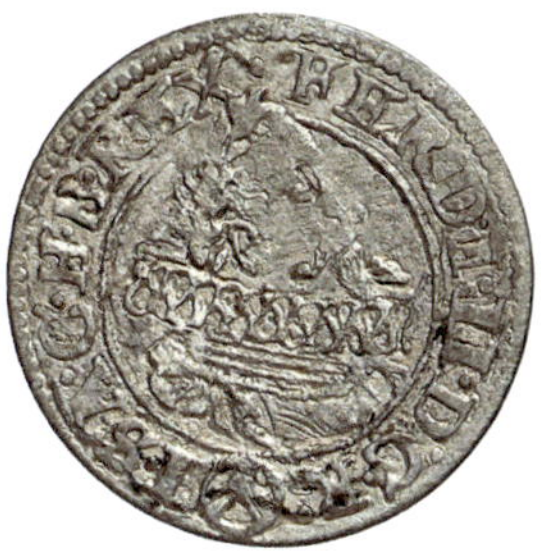

105 **GROSCHEN**
DEBASED COIN, 1623
(SCALE 2:1)

COIN ISSUERS MELTED DOWN THE SILVER COINS AND MIXED THEM WITH COPPER TO PRODUCE INFERIOR COINS. IN THE END, THEY WERE MADE ALMOST ENTIRELY OF COPPER AND WERE RECOGNISABLE AS DEBASED COINS EVEN TO THE NAKED EYE.

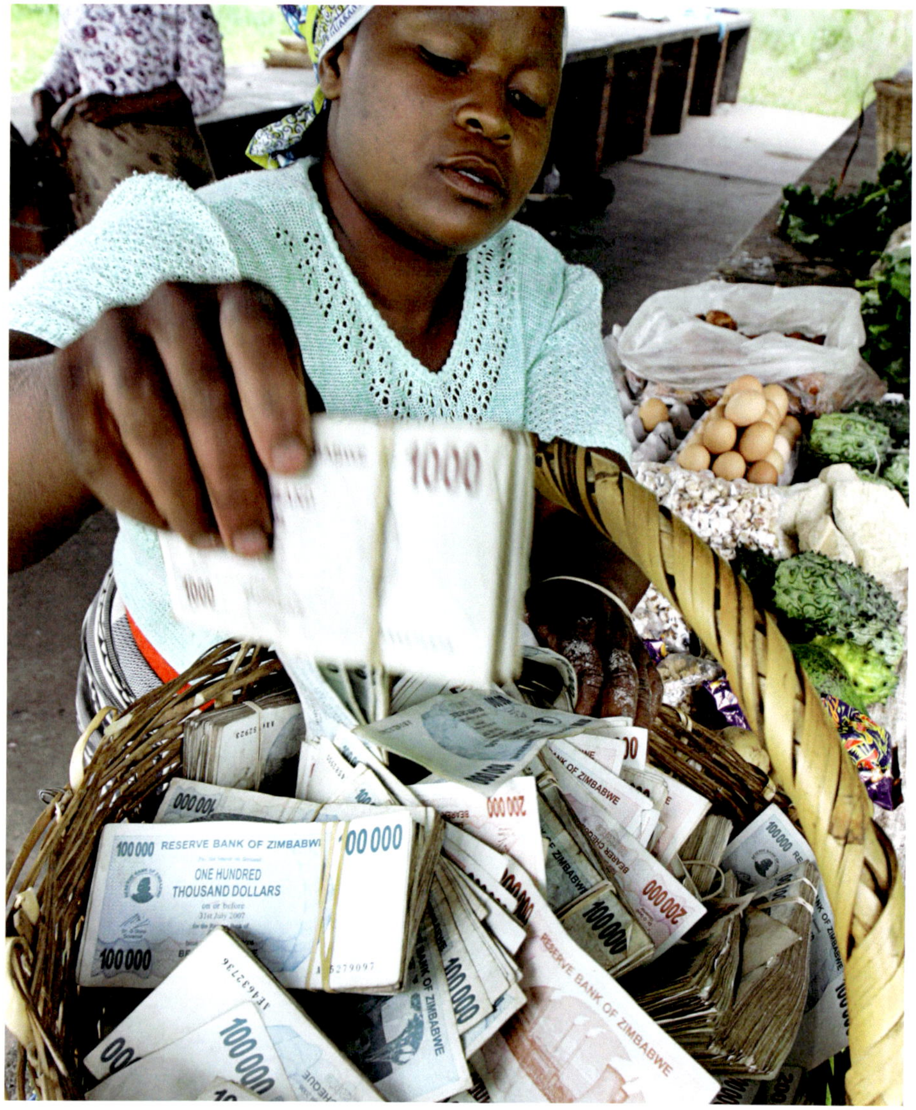

THE FIRST HYPERINFLATION IN THE THIRD MILLENIUM

Hyperinflation is defined as inflation that exceeds 50 per cent per month. In November 2008, Zimbabwe's inflation rate topped 79 billion per cent, with prices doubling every 24.7 hours. The government printed banknotes in larger and larger denominations before being forced to abandon the Zimbabwean dollar in February 2009. The government permitted the use of foreign currencies, the most significant of these being the US dollar and the South African rand.

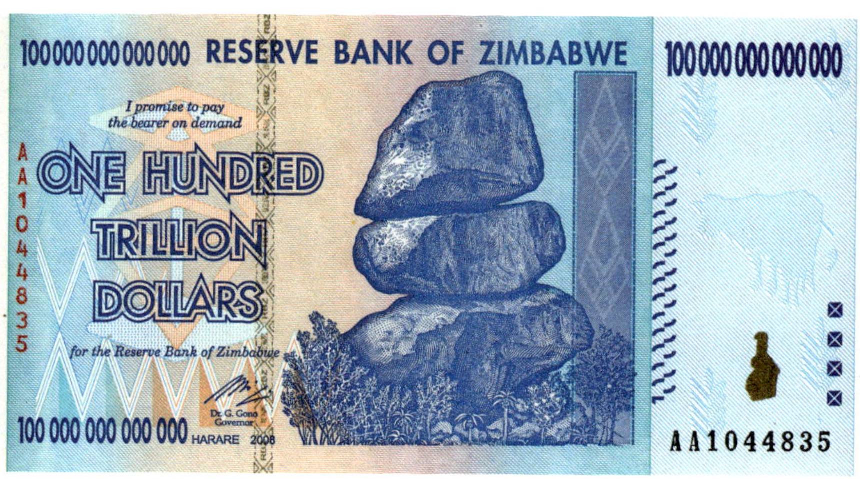

106 **100 TRILLION ZIMBABWEAN DOLLARS,** 2009

ON THURSDAY, 24 OCTOBER 1929 ("BLACK THURSDAY") PRICES PLUMMETED ON THE NEW YORK STOCK EXCHANGE. ON THE FOLLOWING DAY, ON "BLACK FRIDAY", THE NEWS TRIGGERED LOSSES IN EUROPE, TOO.

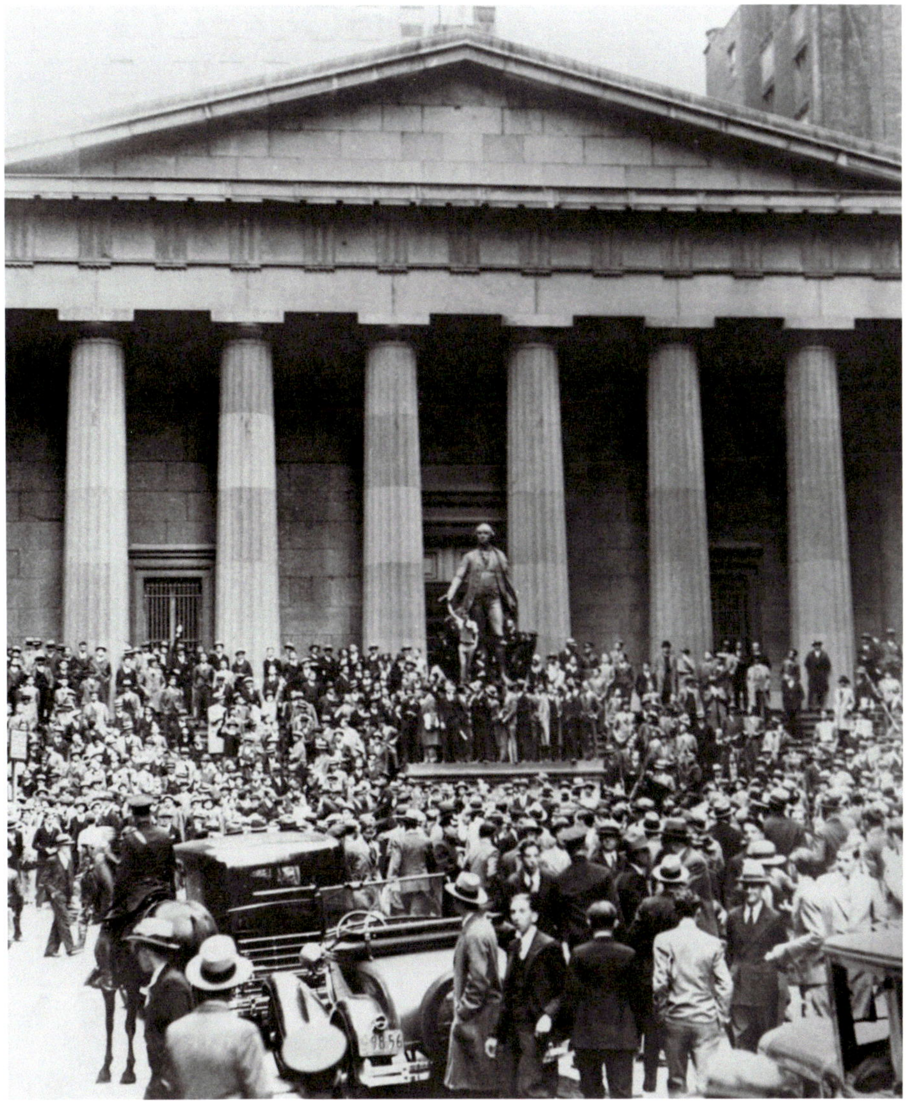

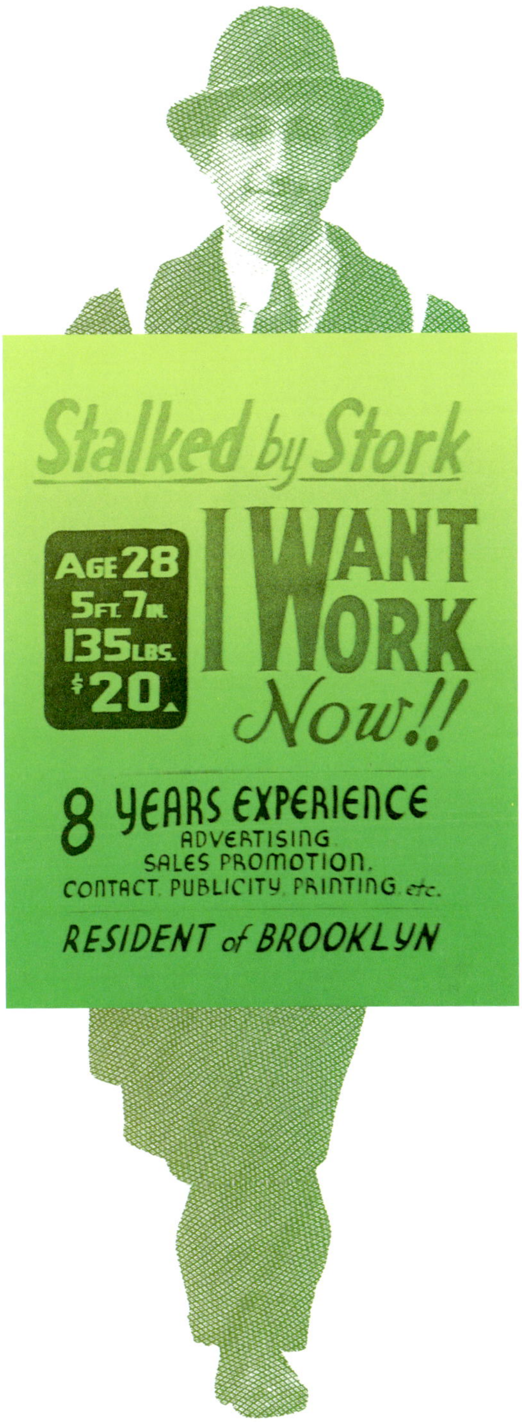

DEFLATION – A VICIOUS CIRCLE

THE GREAT DEPRESSION IN THE USA

The crash on the New York Stock Exchange on Wall Street in October 1929 triggered an economic crisis. As demand for their products shrank, firms lowered their prices, cut back production and laid off employees. Despite this, the Fed continued to pursue a restrictive monetary policy. The money supply in the USA plunged 31 per cent between 1929 and 1933, leading to a deflationary spiral: the general price level fell by one-third, while economic output declined by 30 per cent. At the same time, the unemployment rate went up from 3.2 per cent to 24.9 per cent. The Great Depression in the USA triggered a worldwide economic crisis which also hit Germany hard.

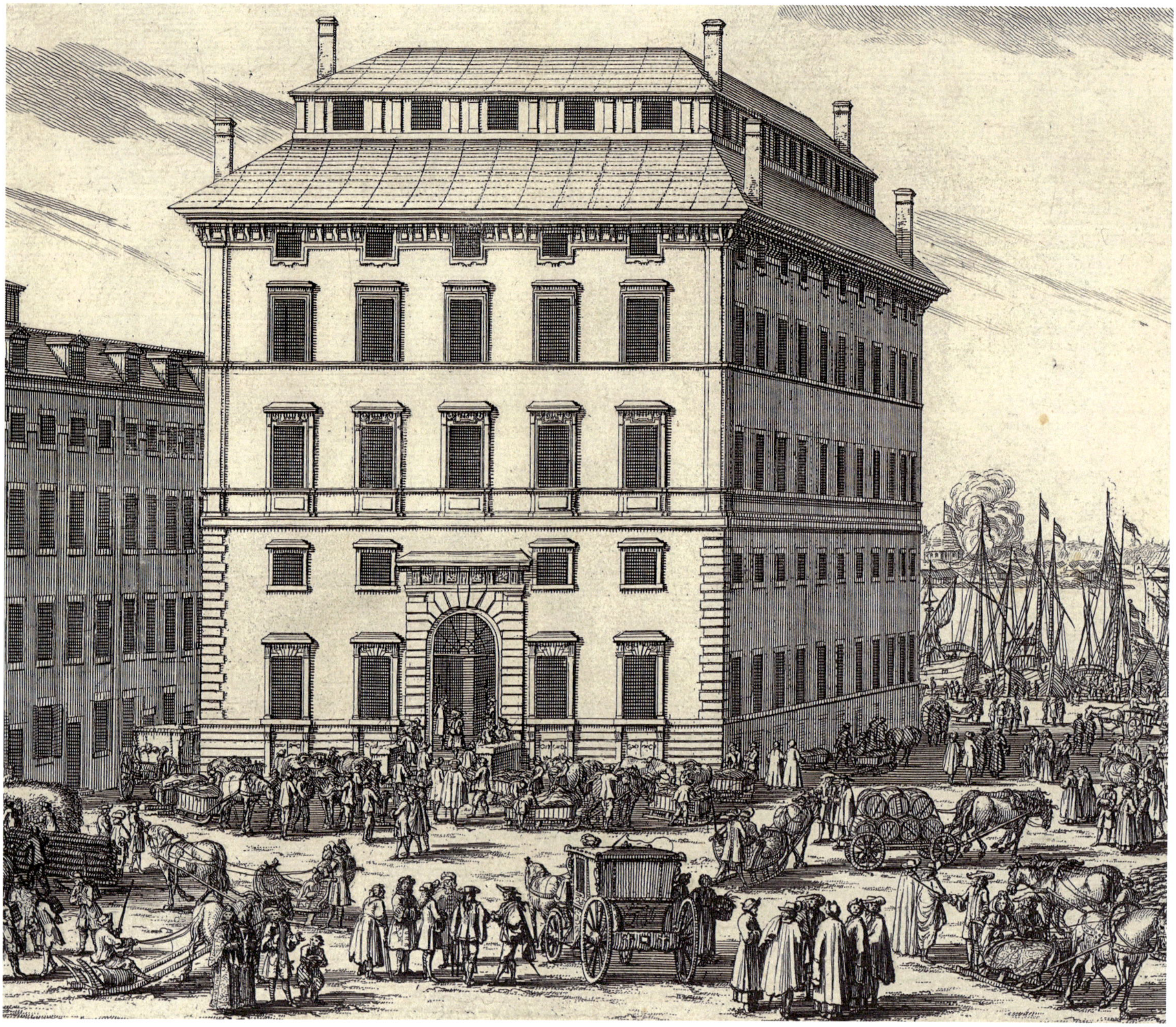

SVERIGES RIKSBANK DATES BACK TO 1668, WHICH MAKES IT THE WORLD'S OLDEST CENTRAL BANK. ITS ORIGINAL ROLE WAS TO FINANCE THE OPERATIONS OF SWEDISH GOVERNMENT.

RECENT INSTITUTIONS

THE ORIGINS OF CENTRAL BANKS

Money has been around for centuries, but central banks – today's "guardians of the currency" – are comparatively recent institutions. Sveriges Riksbank, dating back to 1668, is the oldest central bank in the world. The Bank of England was founded soon after in 1694. Banco Nacional de San Carlos, the forerunner of Banco de España, was created in 1782, followed by the Banque de France in 1800. Most European countries set up their central banks in the 19th century, like Germany's Reichsbank in 1876. The first central bank in Asia was founded in Japan in 1882, but it was not until the 20th century that most countries in the world established central banks. Often, the present-day national central banks originally had other aims and tasks.

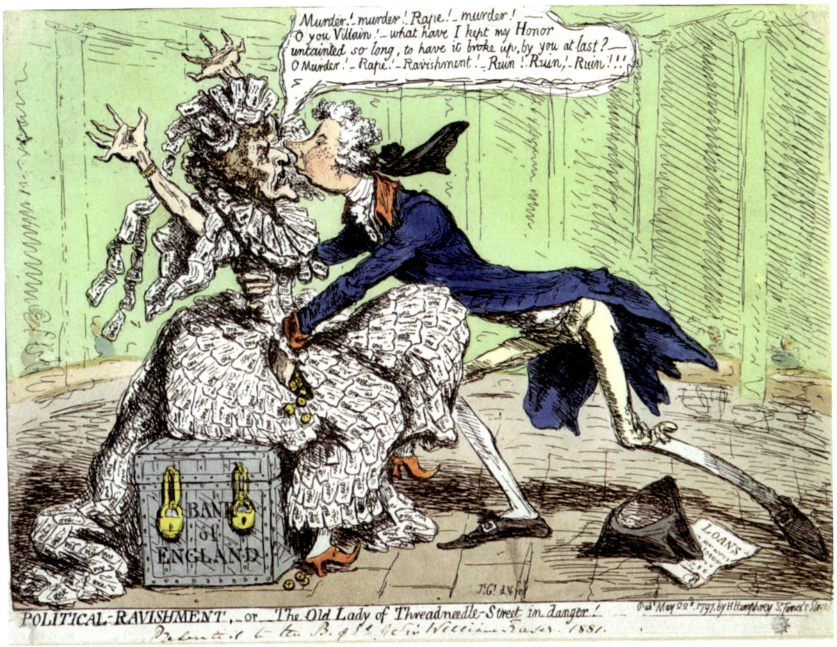

THE ORIGINAL PURPOSE OF THE BANK OF ENGLAND WAS TO FINANCE THE ENGLISH GOVERNMENT. ONLY LATER DID IT BECOME THE CENTRAL BANK.

GUARDIANS OF THE CURRENCY

THE TASKS OF A CENTRAL BANK

From the 18th century, the increasing use of banknotes and cashless payments began to change the monetary and financial system. Banks were now able to grant loans without having to maintain an equivalent amount in stocks of coins or precious metals. Governments set up their own central banks and gave them the sole right (monopoly) to issue banknotes. The proceeds from this, along with central bank loans to government, helped to finance public tasks. However, crises were repeatedly triggered by printing too much new money. In the 20th century, many countries therefore made their central banks independent from government. These were tasked with pursuing a monetary policy with the prime objective of safeguarding price stability.

FED AS A MODEL

INDEPENDENT CENTRAL BANKS

The Federal Reserve System (Fed), the central banking system of the USA, was established in 1913. In its monetary policy, the Fed is independent of instructions from the government. After World War II, the West German banking system was modelled on the Fed with a decentralised structure and independence from German government bodies. This independence is enshrined in the 1957 Bundesbank Act. The Deutsche Bundesbank was thus able to pursue a monetary policy that focused on the price stability of the Deutsche Mark. This stability policy played a part in the long-lasting upswing in the German economy. In the second half of the 20th century, more and more national governments gave independence to their central banks.

GREENBACK

Before the Federal Reserve System regulated the issuance of paper money centrally, many different banknotes were in circulation in the USA. When the USA's Federal Reserve System (Fed) was established, banknotes assumed their definitive form: first issued by the Fed in 1914, the US dollar's appearance has changed very little up to the present day.

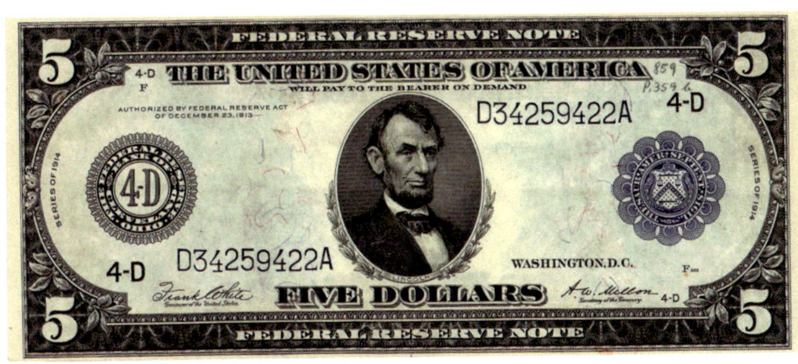

107 **5 DOLLARS**
1914

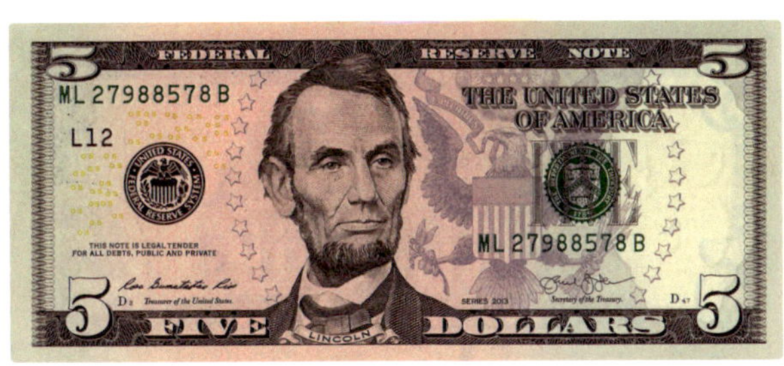

108 **5 DOLLARS**
2013

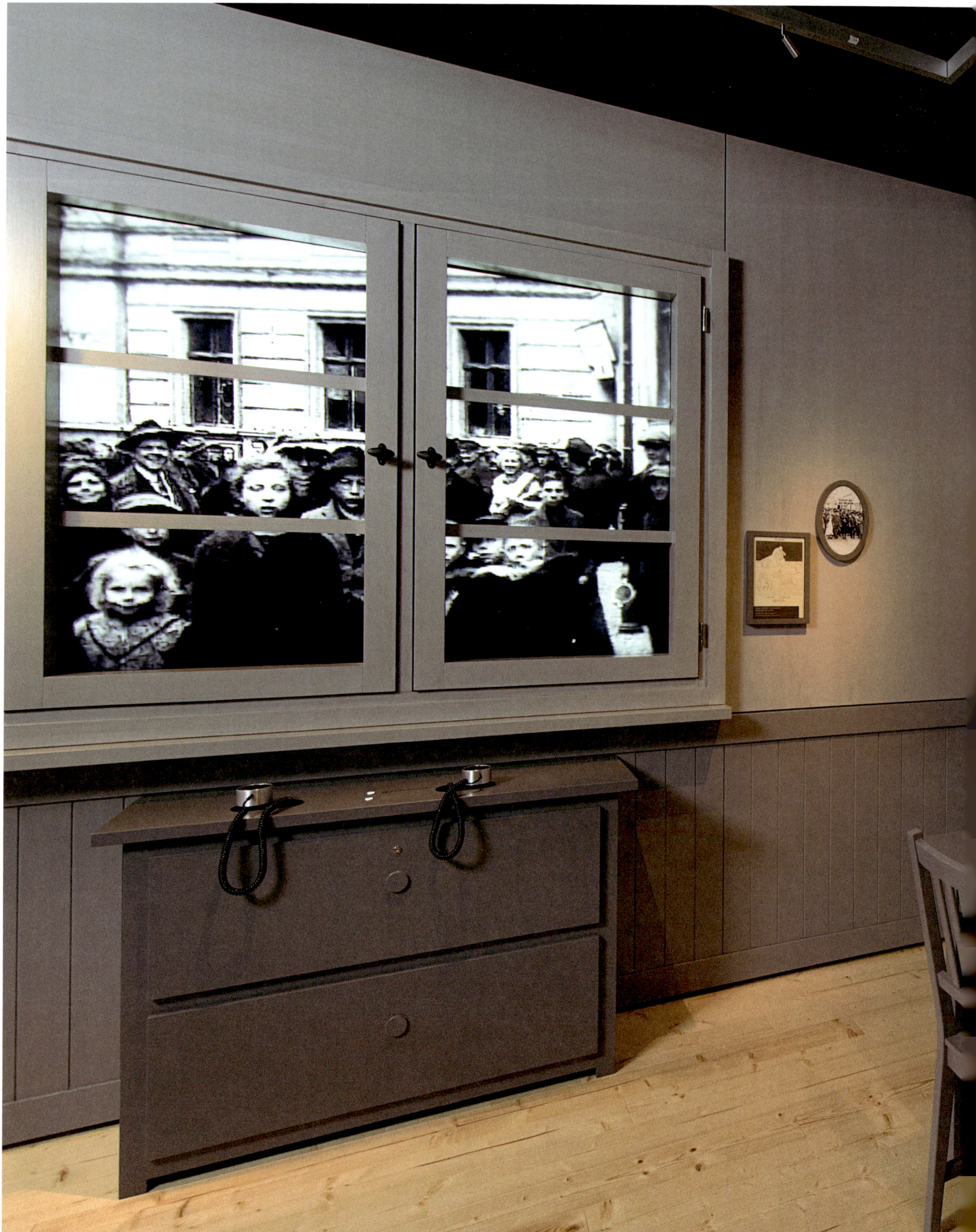

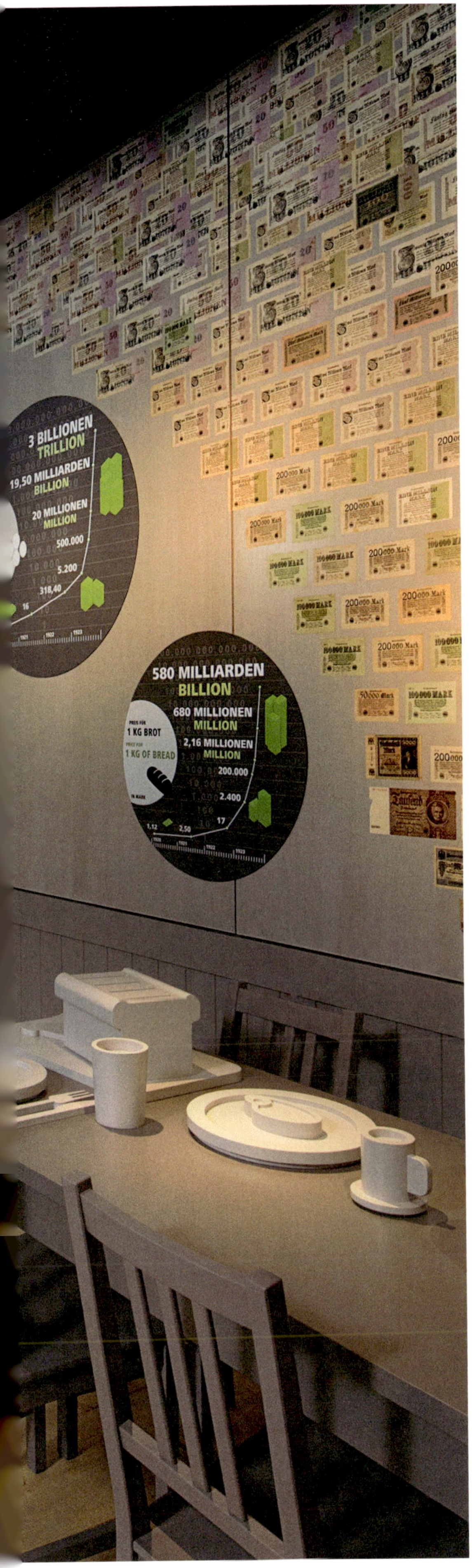

INFLATION IN 1923

Let us go back in time to the year 1923: the visitor enters a stylised worker's dwelling. Framed black-and-white photographs document everyday life in Germany in this period. D-Mark notes denominated in the millions are pasted on the wall. A large window opens out to the streets as they looked back then:

historic footage shows the bleakness of German cities as prices were skyrocketing every day and the population was becoming impoverished. Despite churning out ever-increasing quantities of banknotes at ever-higher denominations, the Reichsbank was unable to keep up with demand. Cities, local governments and firms began issuing emergency money (Notgeld). More and more money was in circulation, and its value was dropping by the day – at the height of the period of hyperinflation, ten eggs were selling for 3 trillion Mark.

A wood stove is crackling in a corner of the room as a reminder that frustrated people had resorted to using the worthless paper money as heating fuel. On 20 November 1923, the Rentenmark was introduced as part of a currency reform, putting a stop to inflation.

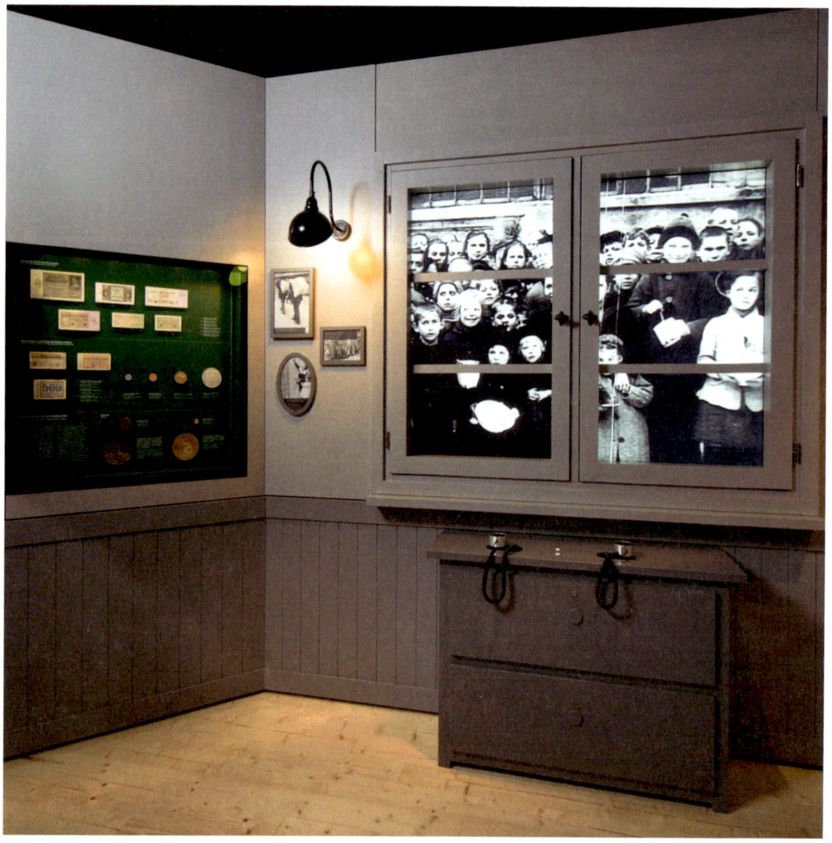

THE MARK BECOMES WORTHLESS

INFLATION IN 1923

In World War I, the German government instructed the Reichsbank to grant it limitless loans, nabling it to finance about one-third of the war's cost by printing money. Banknotes in circulation consequently rose from 2.6 billion to 22.2 billion Mark between 1914 and 1918, causing the Mark to lose value and prices to increase. After the war, the Weimar Republic continued this borrowing policy, financing about three-quarters of state expenditure by selling debt to the Reichsbank. The money supply continued to grow while the Mark lost its purchasing power. By mid-November 1923, at the peak of hyperinflation, the price of a loaf of bread had gone up to more than 230 billion Mark.

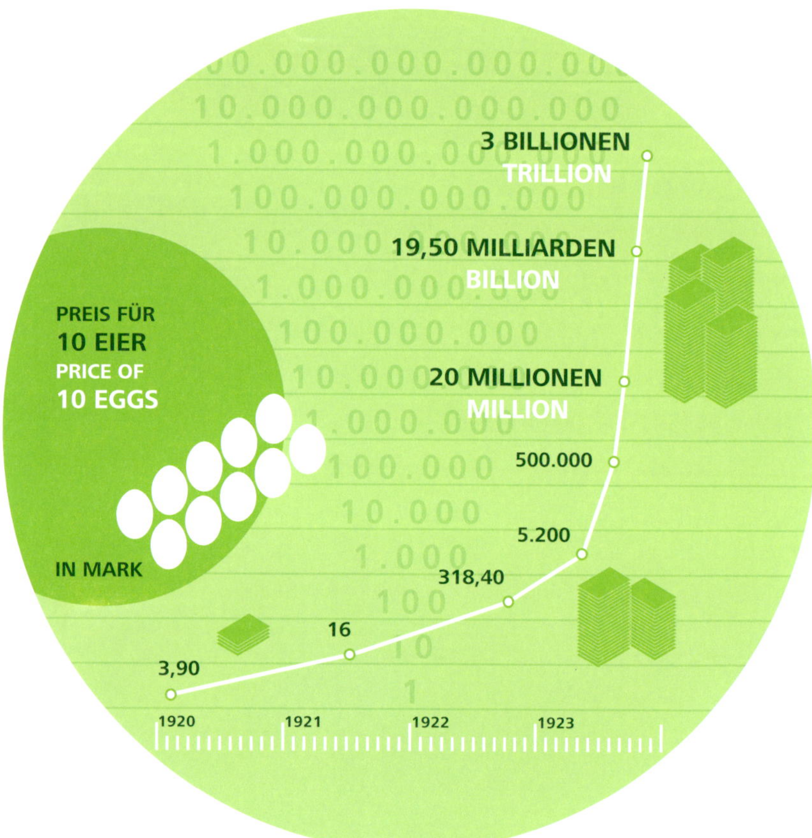

MONEY IN THE HYPERINFLATION ERA

During hyperinflation, prices rose faster than the Reichsbank could print new banknotes. As a result, cities, local governments and firms began producing Notgeld (emergency money) – sometimes with the Reichsbank's blessing, sometimes without. Coins were virtually irrelevant for payments and were minted only in exceptional cases and in very high denominations. On medals, the prevailing conditions were ridiculed. When hyperinflation ended in November 1923, 496 quintillion Reichsmark were circulating as banknotes and 727 quintillion Reichsmark as Notgeld banknotes.

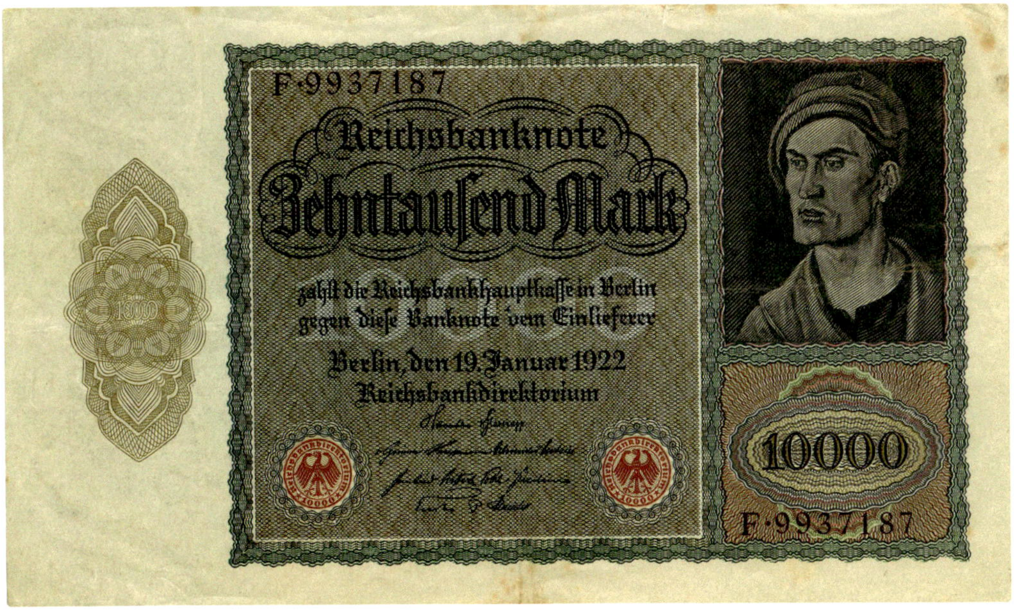

109

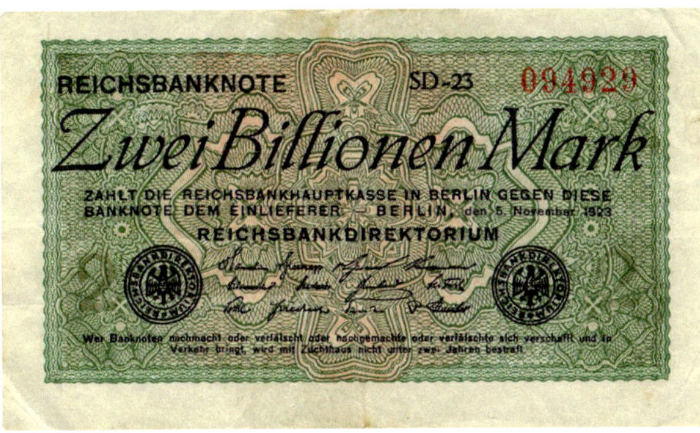

110

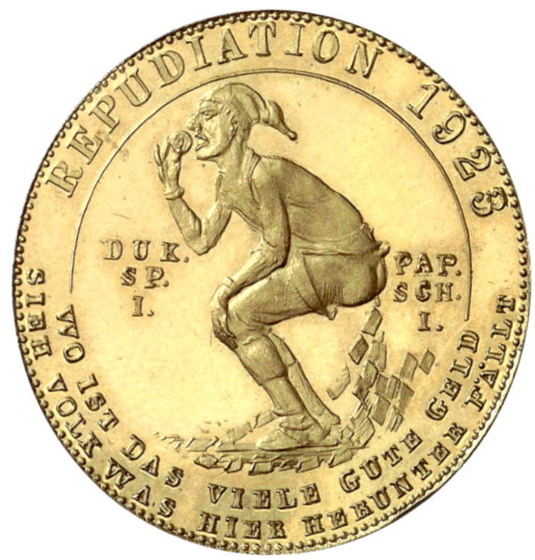

113

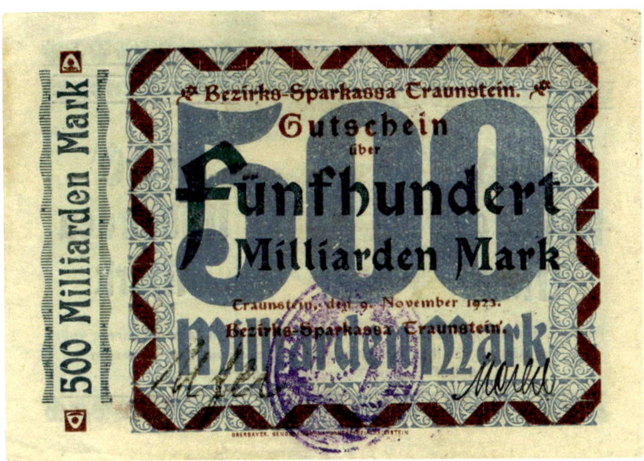

111

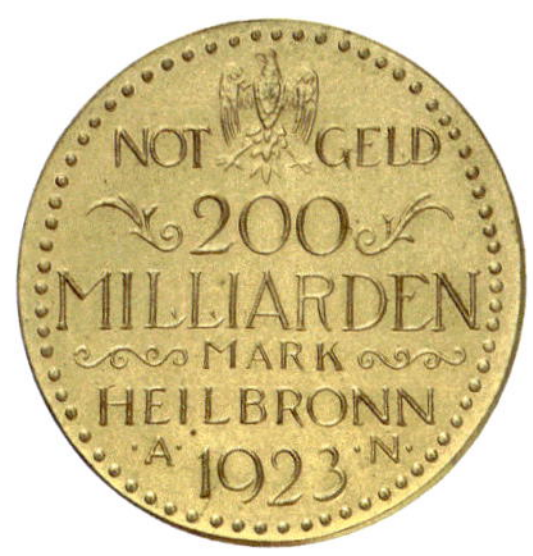

112

109 **REICHSBANK NOTE**
19 JANUARY 1922

110 **REICHSBANK NOTE**
5 NOVEMBER 1923

111 **INFLATION MONEY OF THE DISTRICT SAVINGS BANK TRAUNSTEIN,**
9 NOVEMBER 1923

112 **INFLATION MONEY OF THE CITY OF HEILBRONN**

113 **THIS SATIRICAL DUCAT FROM 1923 MOCKS THE WORTHLESSNESS OF THE PAPER MARK, SHOWING A MAN EATING GOLD COINS AND EXCRETING ENORMOUS AMOUNTS OF WORTHLESS PAPER MONEY.**

1,000,000,000,000 : 1

THE RENTENMARK MIRACLE

To stop inflation, the German government carried out a currency reform in November 1923. Rentenmark banknotes were issued by the Rentenbank, established specifically for this purpose. The value of these notes was backed by mortgages on land used for agriculture and business as well as by industrial bonds. The total volume was limited to 3.2 billion Rentenmark. As of 20 November 1923, people could exchange the inflated Mark for Rentenmark at a rate of one trillion to one. The Rentenmark was kept stable by a monetary policy which was strictly oriented to preserving the value of money as well as to fiscal consolidation. In the summer of 1924, the transition to the Reichsmark as legal tender completed the currency reform.

SOME EVEN USED THE WORTHLESS MARK BANKNOTES AS WALLPAPER OR AS FUEL, WHEREAS CHILDREN USED THEM TO MAKE THINGS WITH.

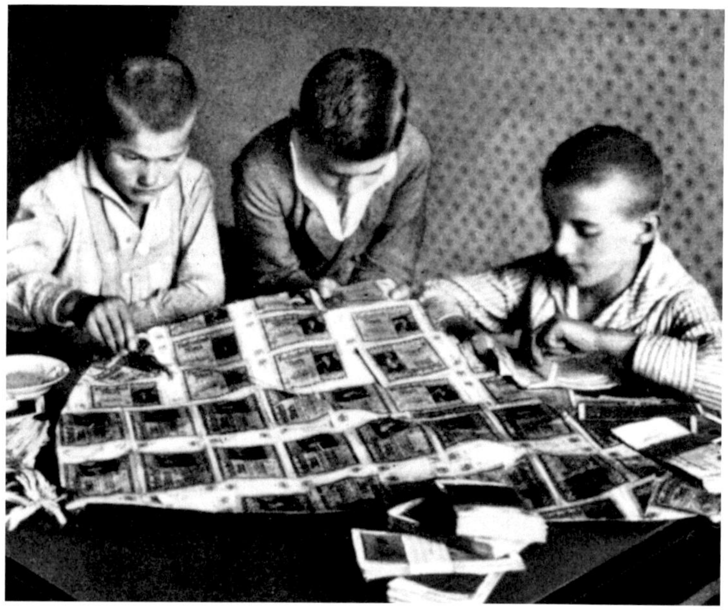

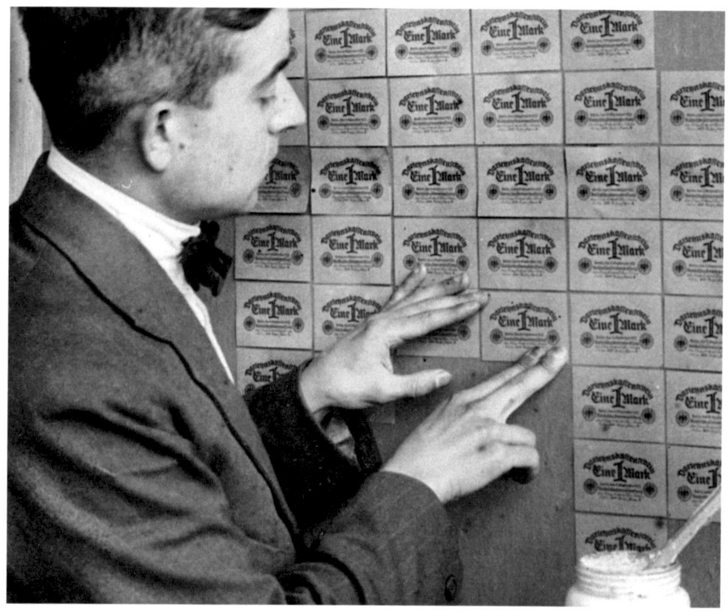

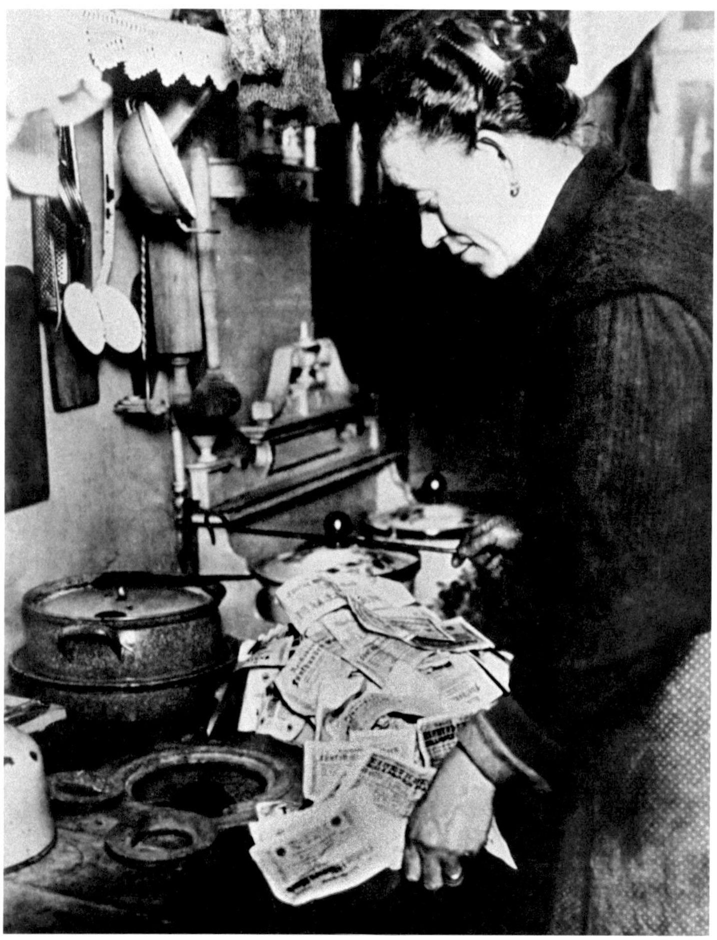

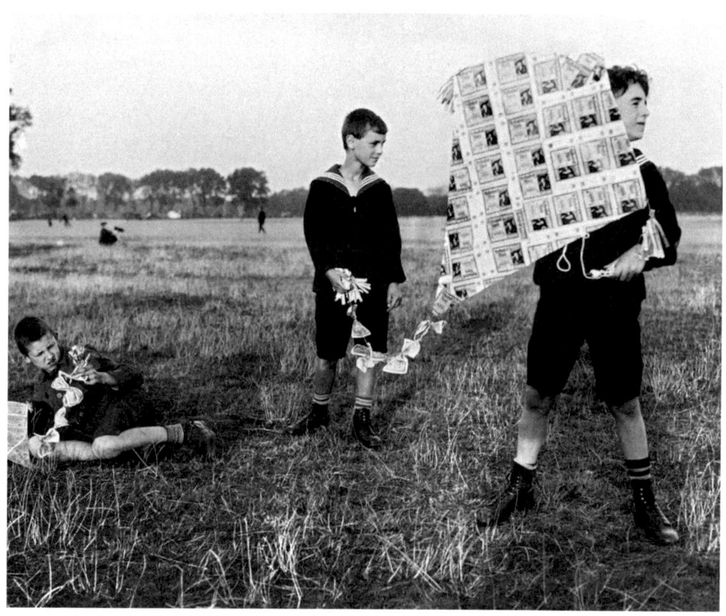

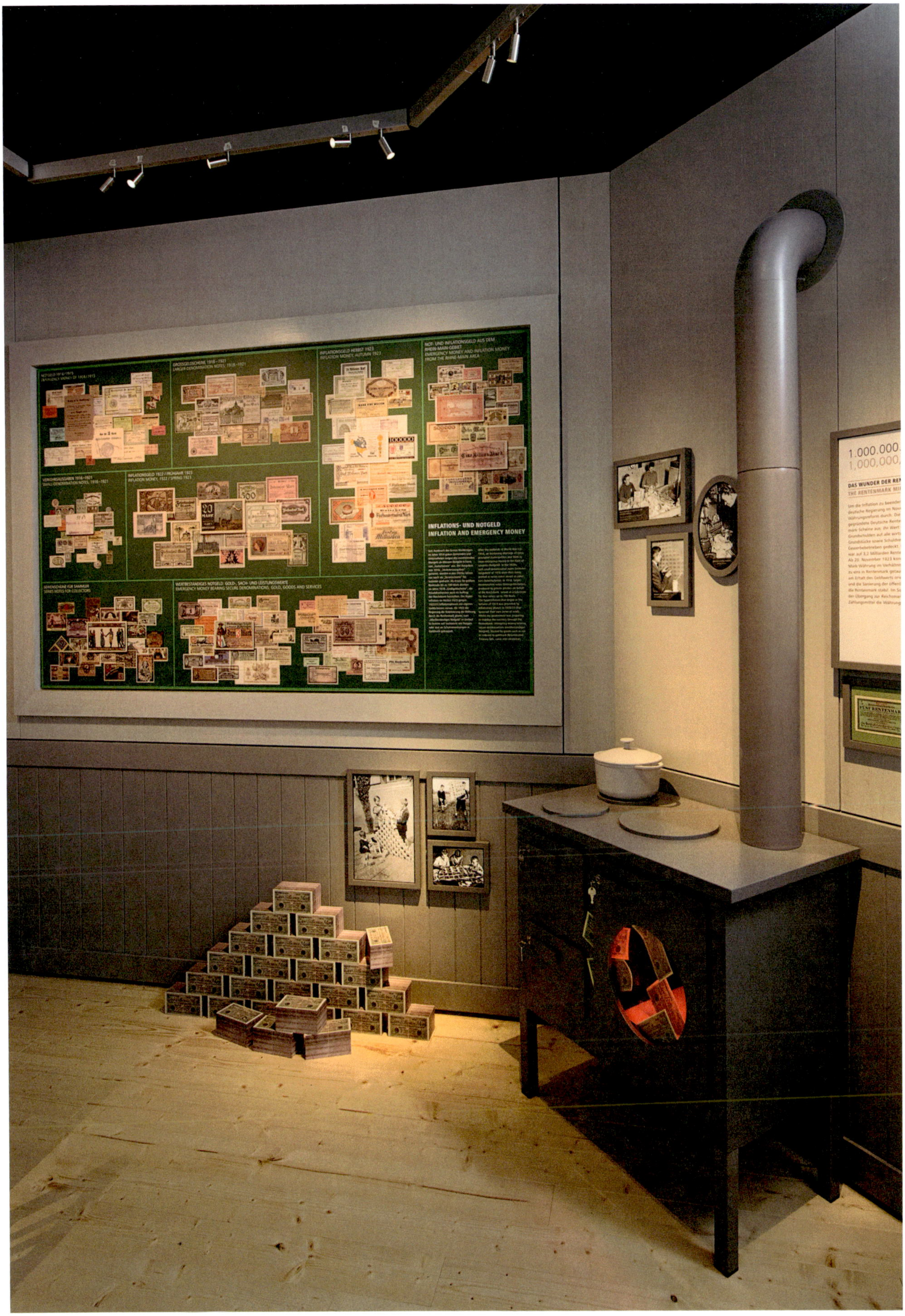
INFLATIONS- UND NOTGELD
INFLATION AND EMERGENCY MONEY

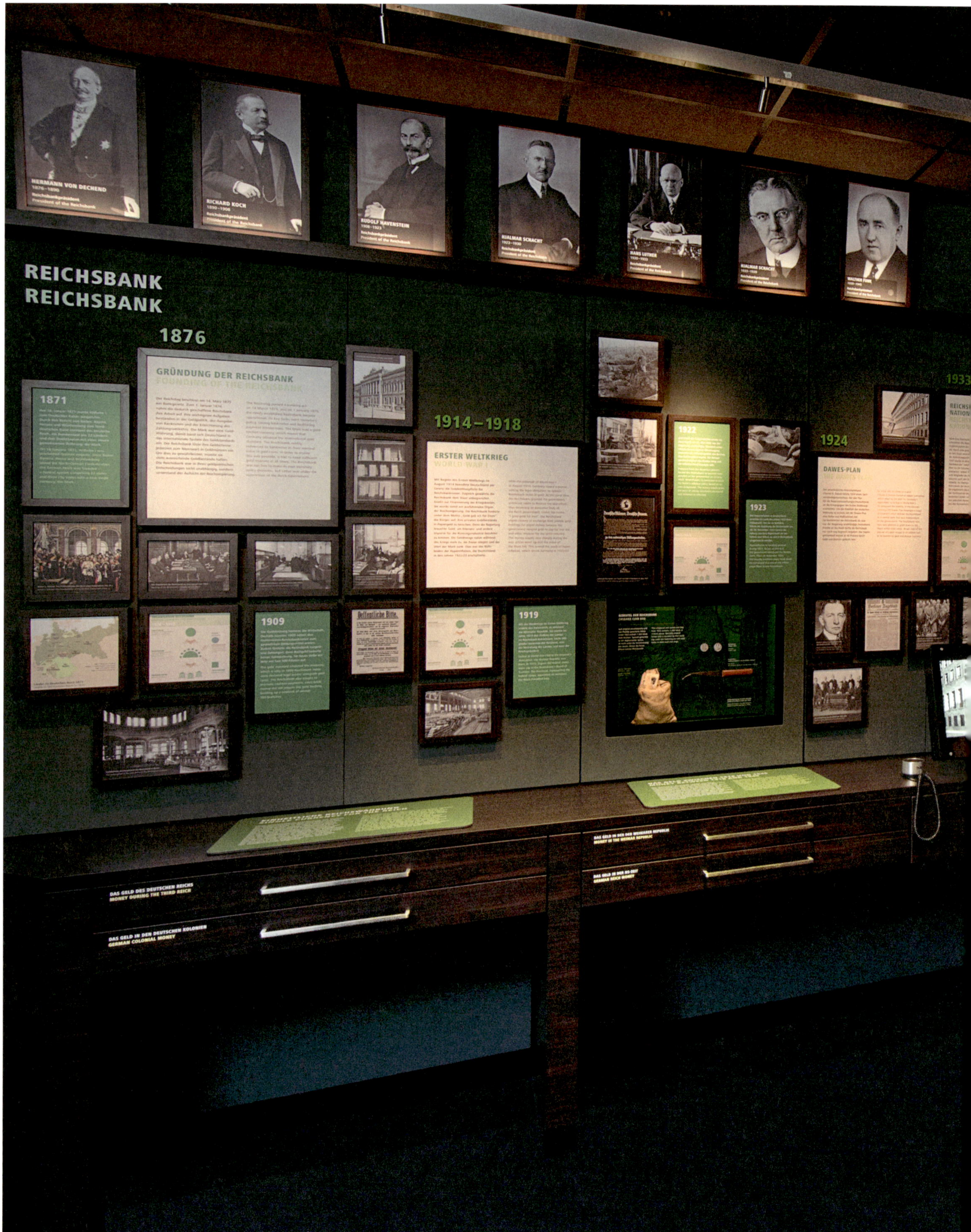
REICHSBANK
REICHSBANK
1876
GRÜNDUNG DER REICHSBANK
FOUNDING OF THE REICHSBANK
1871
1909
1914–1918
ERSTER WELTKRIEG
WORLD WAR I
1919
1922
1923
1924
DAWES-PLAN
1933

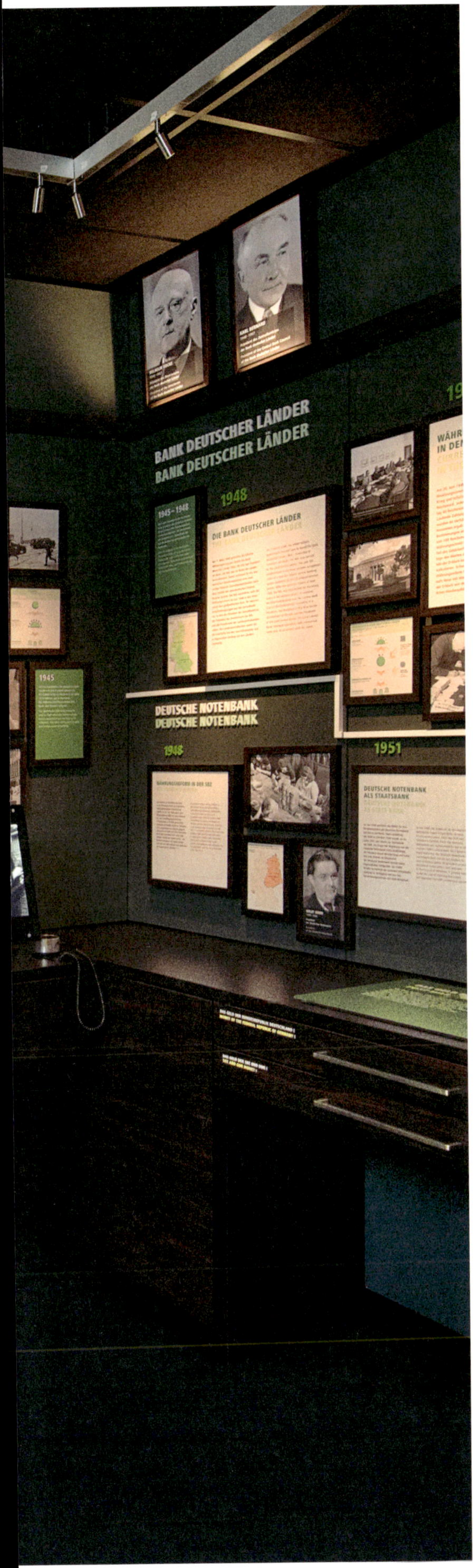

GERMAN CENTRAL BANK

The German central bank history cabinet looks like a 19th-century study and provides the visitor with a relaxing environment for reading, research and discovery.

Large-format portraits of all previous German central bank presidents form a sort of "hall of fame" overlooking the room. The walls are structured with notable dates from history. Within the context of contemporary history, framed texts, pictures, charts and rarities from the Deutsche Bundesbank's historic photo archive present a chronological history of the institution, beginning with the Reichsbank (founded in 1876) and running through the Bank deutscher Länder to the foundation in 1957 of the Deutsche Bundesbank, a member of the Eurosystem since 1999. German central bank history in the German Democratic Republic between 1948 and 1990 is covered in a separate section. At the same time, banknotes and coins in ten display drawers bear witness to the ups and downs of German monetary history.

The cabinet ends by returning to the present, as the Deutsche Bundesbank introduces itself, its current organisational structure and its tasks.

1871

On 18 January 1871, Wilhelm I was proclaimed German emperor. Once Baden, Bavaria, Hesse and Württemberg joined the North German Confederation, the German Reich was founded – a federal system comprising 22 states and three city states with a new single currency: the Mark.

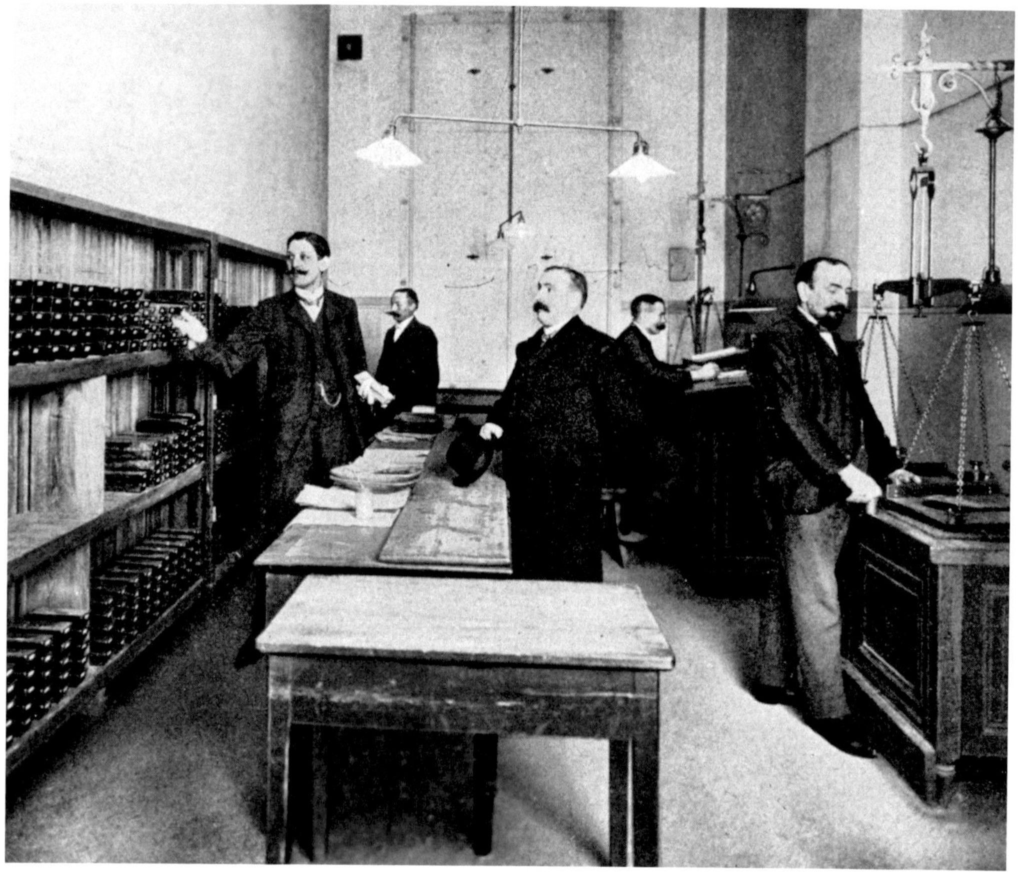

WEIGHING AND RECORDING GOLD BARS (CA 1900)

1876 FOUNDING OF THE REICHSBANK

The Reichstag passed a banking act on 14 March 1875, and on 1 January 1876, the newly established Reichsbank became operational. Its key tasks were monetary policy, issuing banknotes and facilitating payment transactions. The Mark was a gold-backed currency, which meant that Germany adopted the international gold standard. The Reichsbank readily redeemed its banknotes at their nominal value in gold coins. In order to ensure this was possible, it had to keep sufficient gold reserves at all times. The Reichsbank was not free to make its own monetary policy decisions, but rather was under the supervision of the Reich Government.

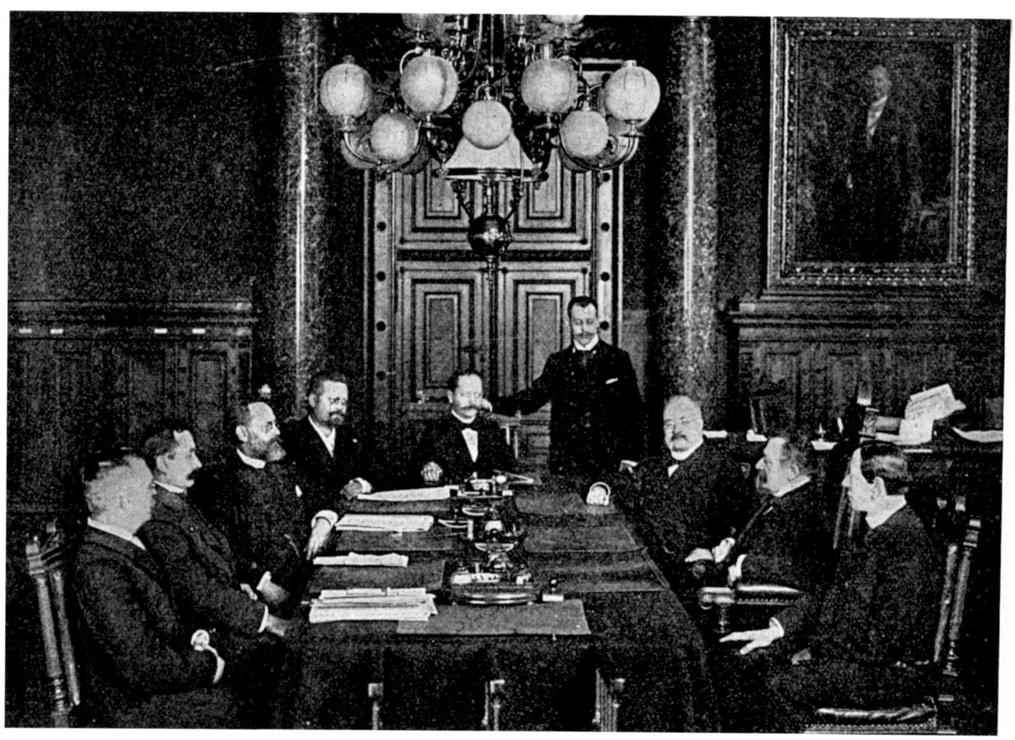

MEETING OF THE REICHSBANK'S DIRECTORATE (CA 1900)

SINGLE CURRENCY FOR THE REICH

For centuries, the diversity of currency systems and coins had hampered money flows in Germany. The German Reich put an end to that by establishing a single currency that was valid throughout its territory: the Mark. The Reichsbank issued its first banknotes in 1876. However, up to 1906 only 100-Mark and 1,000-Mark notes were printed.

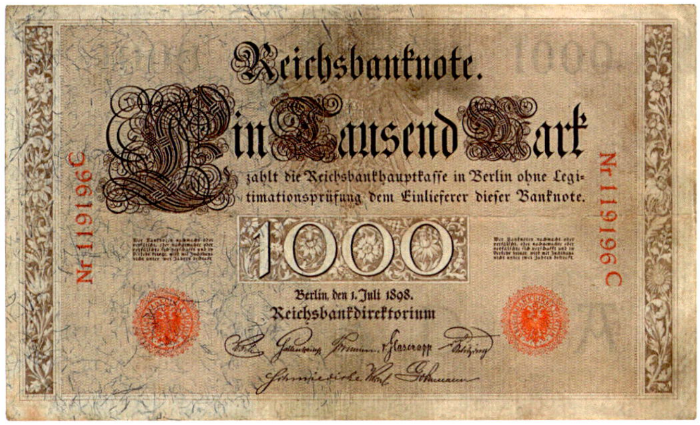

114 **1,000 MARK,** 1884

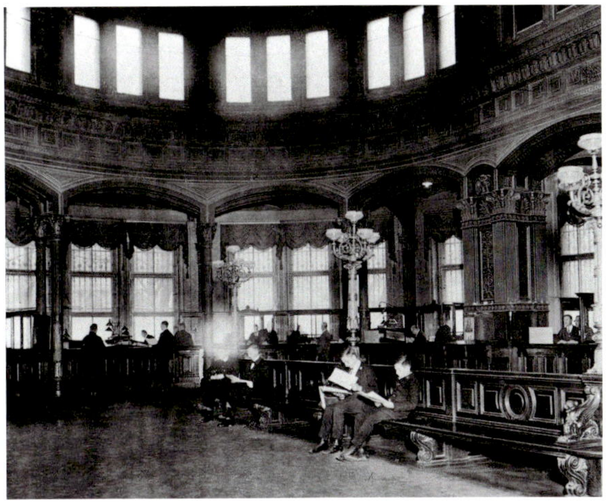

THE BANKING HALL IN THE CASH OFFICE OF THE REICHSBANK IN BERLIN

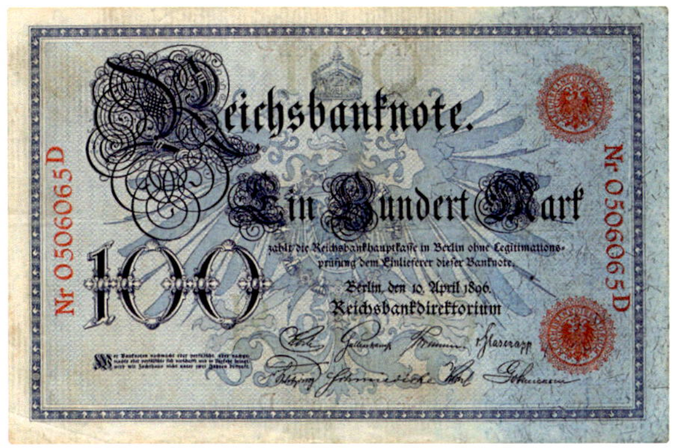

115 **100 MARK,** 1883

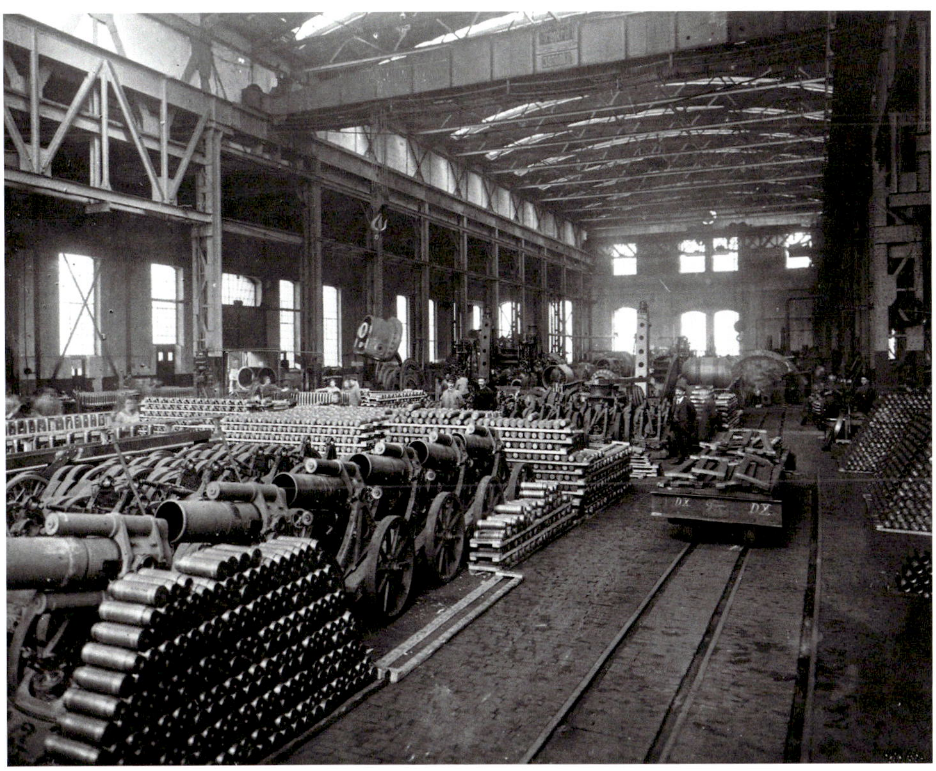

1914–1918 WORLD WAR I

With the outbreak of the World War I in August 1914, Germany issued a decree ending the legal obligation to redeem Reichsbank notes in gold. At the same time, the Reichsbank granted the government unlimited credit to finance the war effort, thus becoming an executive body of the Reich government. The money supply rose sharply during the war, prices went up and the value of the Mark fell. This sowed the seeds of hyperinflation, which shook Germany in 1922/1923.

MONEY IN THE WEIMAR REPUBLIC

During the First World War and in the Weimar Republic's early years, pre-war Mark banknotes were still in circulation. Inflation began to soar in summer 1922, sending prices sky-high. The Reichsbank printed more and more notes with higher and higher values. In November 1923, the government put an end to hyperinflation by introducing the Rentenmark. In 1924, the Reichsmark was brought into circulation alongside the Rentenmark at a one-to-one conversion rate.

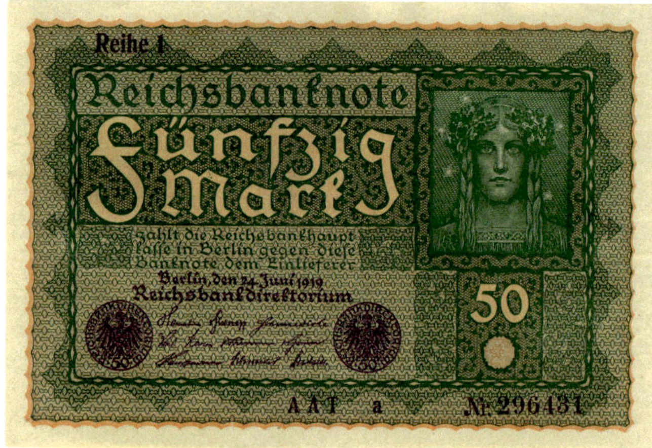

116

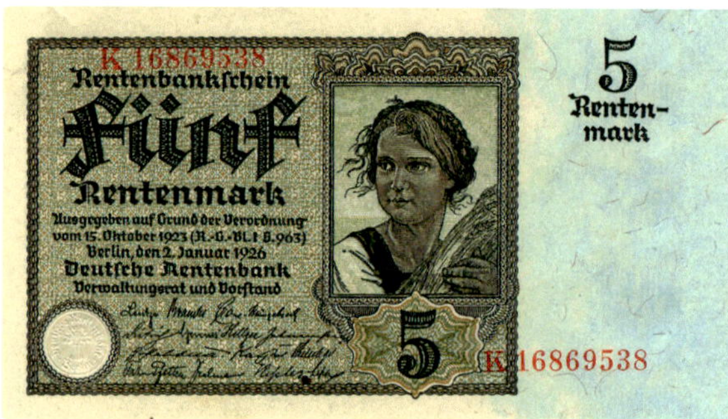

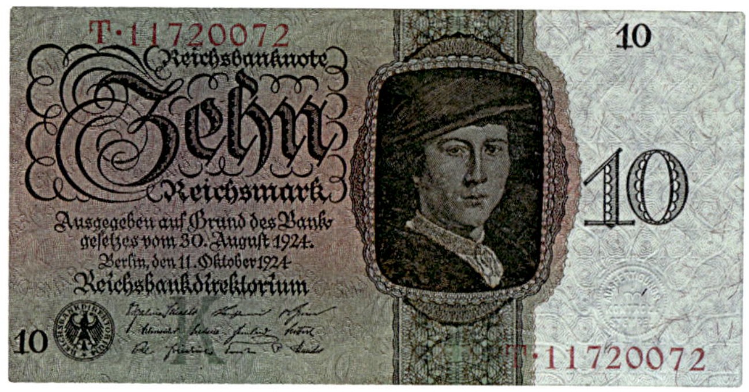

117 118

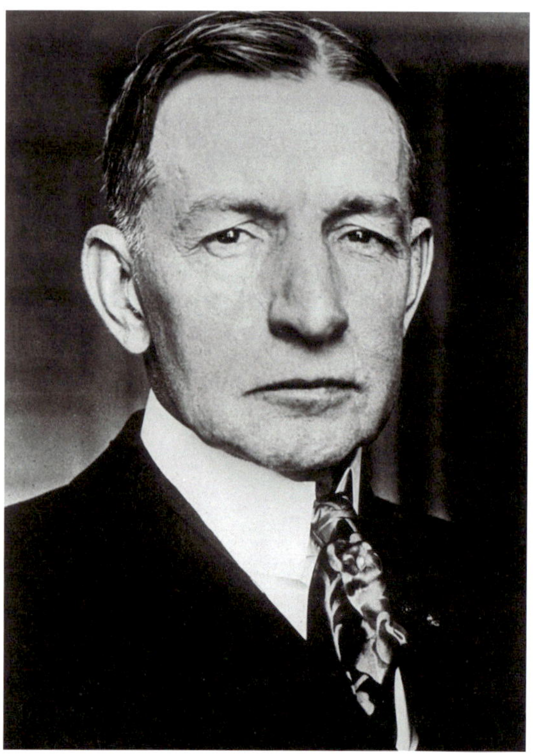

1922

Pressure from the victorious powers forced the Reichsbank to become independent of the government on 22 May 1922. Nevertheless, it still backed the Reich's inflation policy of its own accord.

1924 THE DAWES PLAN

In 1924, the US financial expert Charles G Dawes chaired an expert committee which drew up the plan for Germany's reparations to its foes in World War I. To safeguard the stability of the German currency, the Dawes Plan envisaged a range of measures which defined the Reichsbank as a central bank that was independent of the government. The Reichsbank was now only allowed to grant loans to the Reich within strict limits. Forty per cent of the volume of paper money in circulation had to be backed by gold and foreign currency.

119

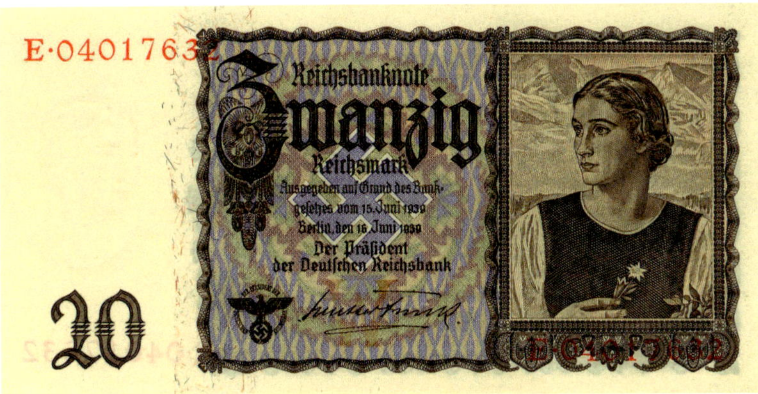

120

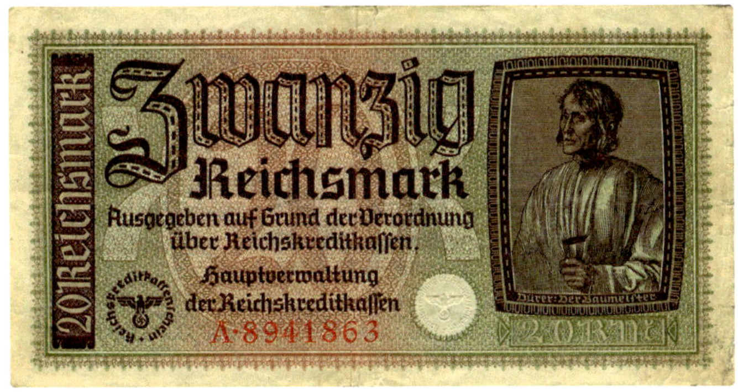

121

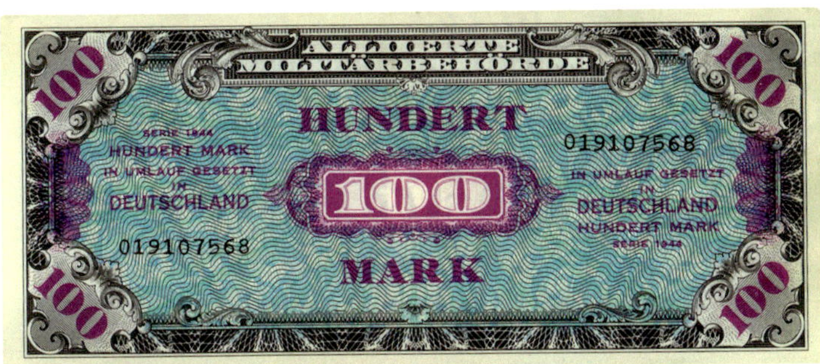

116 **50 MARK,** 1919

117 **5 RENTENMARK,** 1926

118 **10 REICHSMARK,** 1924

119 **20 REICHSMARK**, 1939

120 **REICH TREASURY OFFICE, 20 REICHSMARK**

121 **ALLIED MILITARY AUTHORITIES, 100 MARK,** 1944

1933–1945 REICHSBANK UNDER NATIONAL SOCIALISM

After the Nazis seized power in 1933, they gradually restricted the Reichsbank's independence. The Reichsbank secretly financed the rearmament policy of the Nazi regime. In 1937, it was ruled that the Reichsbank had to report directly to the "Führer and Reich Chancellor" Adolf Hitler. In 1939, Hitler dismissed six of the eight members of the Directorate of the Reichsbank – including the Reichsbank President, Schacht – for criticising the government's debt policy. During World War II, the Reichsbank financed the German war effort. It organised the unlawful confiscation of the gold reserves of countries occupied by Germany and was involved in looting Jewish assets and gold from the concentration camps.

NAZI MONEY

The Nazi regime retained the Reichsmark. During World War II, in some occupied countries, the authorities set up Reich treasury offices which brought Reich treasury notes into circulation as currency. The Allied military authorities began issuing scrip money (occupation money) in Germany in 1944, denominated in the Mark.

1945

The Reichsbank effectively ceased to exist in 1945 when the German armed forces capitulated and the Nazi state collapsed. The Allies confiscated its gold and foreign currency holdings.

1945–1948

After the collapse of the Reichsbank, the western Allies set up Land Central Banks in the states within their zones of occupation. These banks performed all central bank tasks, apart from producing and issuing banknotes.

1948 THE BANK DEUTSCHER LÄNDER

On 1 March 1948, the Allied military government enacted laws to found the Bank deutscher Länder (BdL). Domiciled in Frankfurt am Main, the BdL was owned by the Land Central Banks. This saw the establishment in the three western occupation zones of a two-tier federal central banking system modelled on the US Federal Reserve System. After the currency reform of June 1948, the BdL was responsible for monetary policy in the western zones.

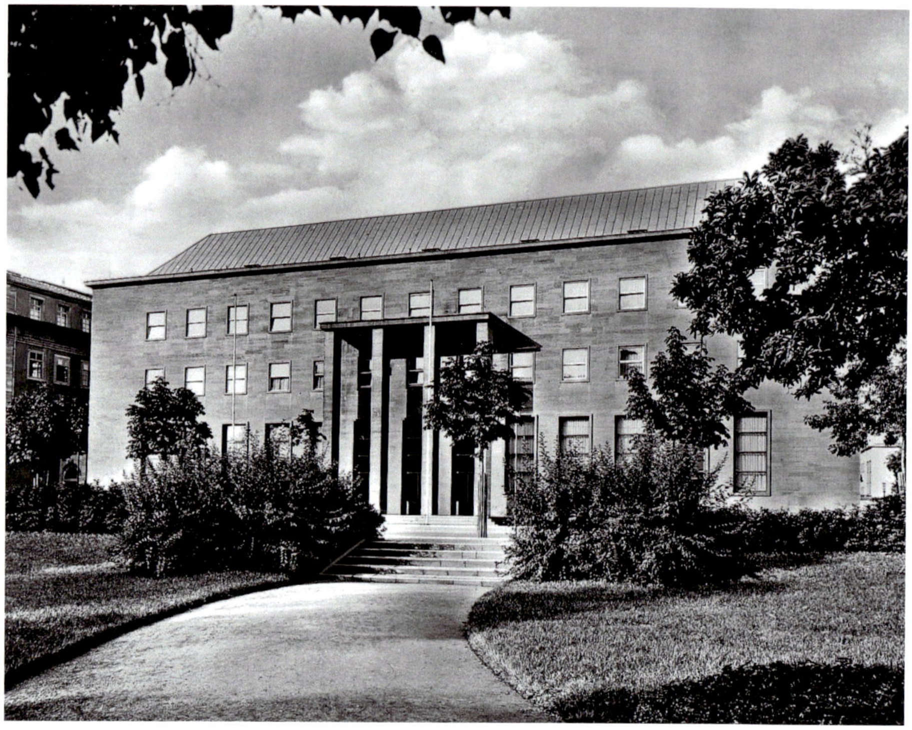

HEAD OFFICE OF THE BDL IN FRANKFURT (CA 1950)

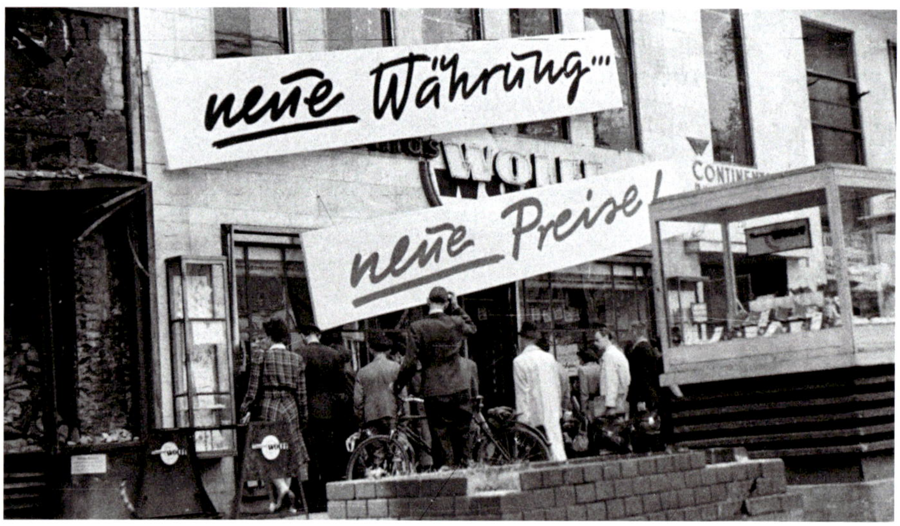

1948 CURRENCY REFORM IN THE WESTERN ZONES

On 20 June 1948, in the western occupation zones, the Deutsche Mark replaced the Reichsmark, which war and inflation had rendered worthless. On the first day after the currency reform, shop windows were already filled with goods again. The introduction of the Deutsche Mark was the beginning of West Germany's economic recovery.

MONEY ISSUED BY THE BANK DEUTSCHER LÄNDER

The Bank deutscher Länder was handed responsibility for issuing coins and banknotes in the western occupation zones almost as soon as it was founded in 1948, but initially had no influence on the design and manufacture of the banknotes. The first D-Mark banknotes were printed in the USA and shipped secretly to Germany using the code name Operation *Bird Dog*. They obviously have a certain resemblance to dollar notes.

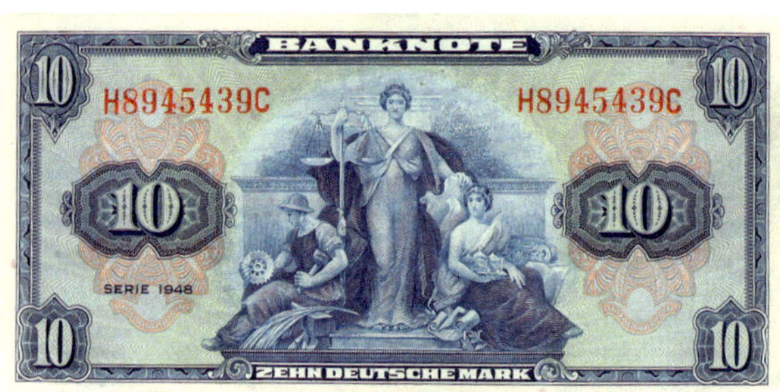

122 **10 DM,** 1948

127
DEUTSCHE NOTENBANK

1948 SOZ CURRENCY REFORM

In response to the currency reform in the western zones, the Soviet Military Administration in Germany (SMAD) also introduced a new currency in its occupation zone (SOZ) on 24 June 1948. 70 Reichsmark could be exchanged for 70 Mark on the conversion day. Due to printing problems there were no new banknotes to begin with; instead, adhesive coupons were stuck onto Reichsmark and Rentenmark notes. They were popularly known as "sticker marks".

1951 DEUTSCHE NOTENBANK AS STATE BANK

In July 1948, the SMAD set up the Deutsche Notenbank, based in East Berlin, to serve its occupation zone. After the GDR was founded in October 1949, the Deutsche Notenbank was transformed by law in 1951 into the GDR's central bank. As a government institution, the Deutsche Notenbank was not independent and did not conduct its own monetary policy. Its president enjoyed ministerial status with a seat and vote in the Council of Ministers. It granted loans under the central planning framework and operated the GDR's settlement system.

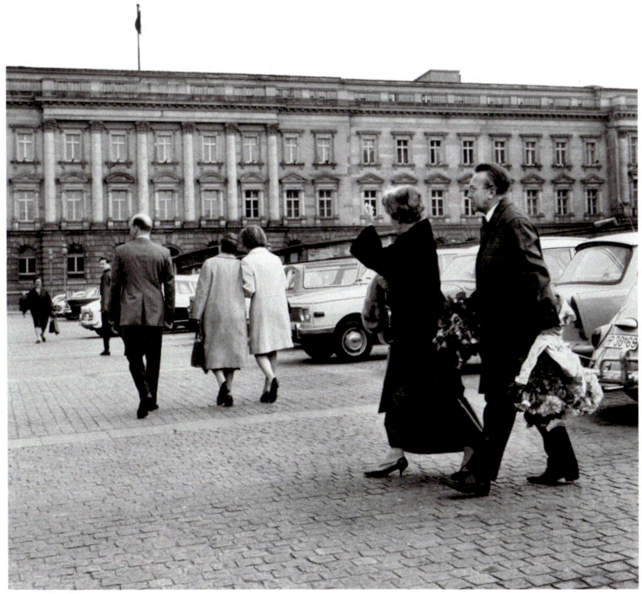

STAATSBANK DER DDR IN EAST BERLIN

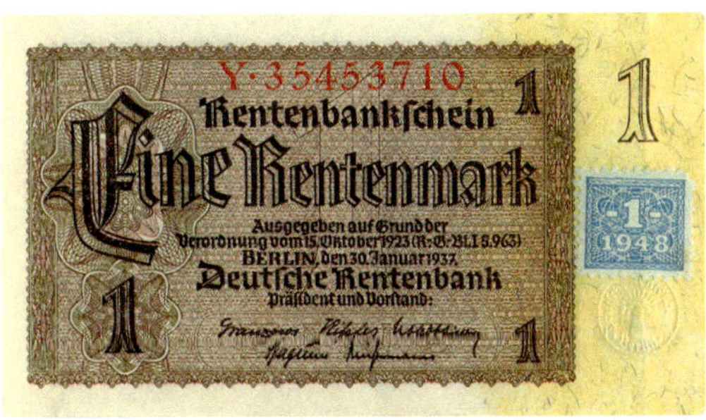

123

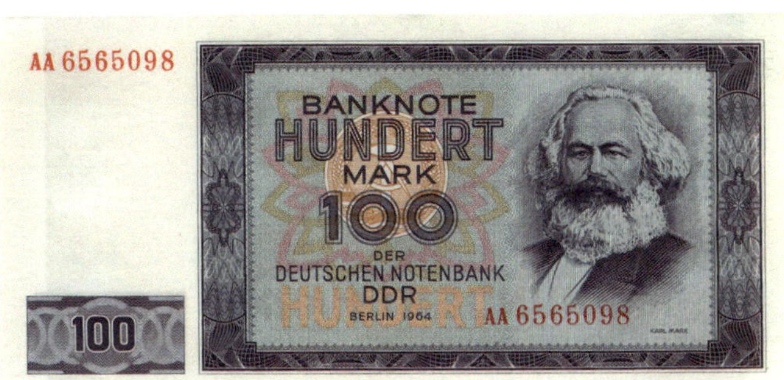

124

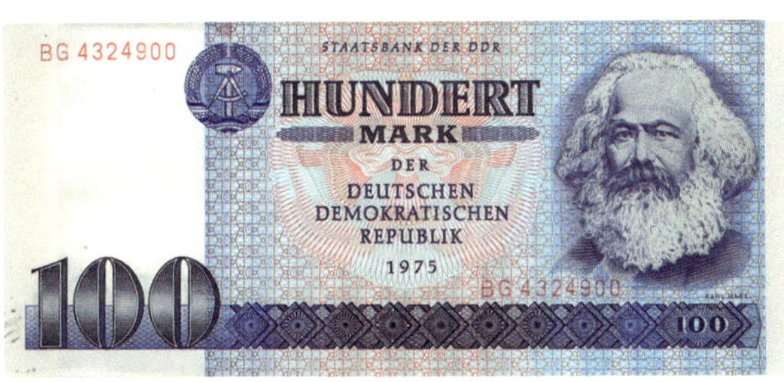

125

123 **COUPON MARK FROM THE SOV,** 1948

124 **100 MARK OF THE DEUTSCHE NOTENBANK,** 1964

125 **100 MARK OF THE GERMAN DEMOCRATIC REPUBLIC,** 1975

1964

The Deutsche Notenbank brought a new series of banknotes into circulation. The currency name was changed from "Deutsche Mark" to "Mark of the Deutsche Notenbank (MDN)".

1968

The Deutsche Notenbank was renamed Staatsbank der DDR in 1968. Henceforth, the currency was known as the "Mark of the German Democratic Republic".

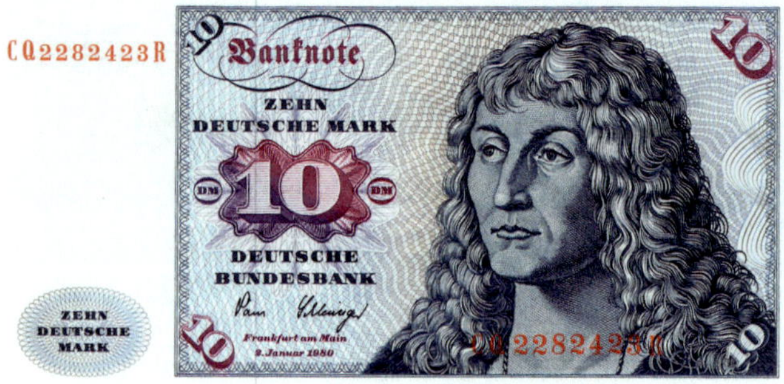

126 **10 DM,** 1989

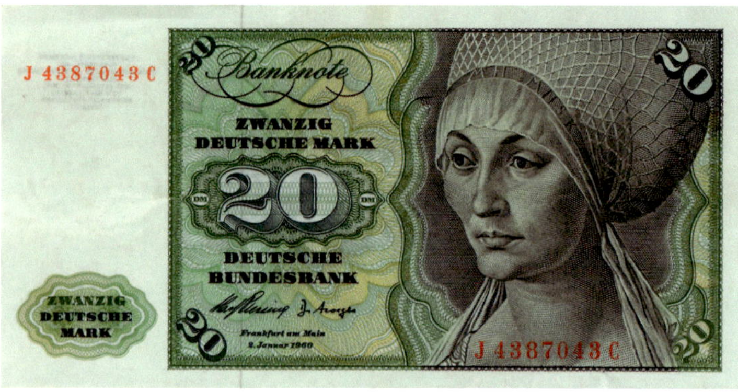

127 **20 DM,** 1991

1957 THE BUNDESBANK IS FOUNDED

The Bundesbank Act, under which the Deutsche Bundesbank was founded, came into effect on 1 August 1957. The Bank assumed all the tasks of the Bank deutscher Länder, notably that of safeguarding the currency's stability. It also regulated currency in circulation and the supply of cr edit to the economy. Its highest decision-making body was the Central Bank Council. Paragraph 12 of the Bundesbank Act stated that the Bundesbank must be independent of and not subject to instructions from the Federal Government in exercising its powers – a major prerequisite for the stability of the Deutsche Mark.

MONEY OF THE FEDERAL REPUBLIC OF GERMANY

When the Deutsche Bundesbank commenced its work in 1957, it developed a new banknote series. The first notes began circulating from 1961. Their design went unchanged for nearly 30 years.

1990 GERMAN MONETARY UNION

The Deutsche Mark became sole legal tender throughout Germany on 1 July 1990, ahead of political reunification on 3 October 1990. With German monetary union, the Bundesbank took over responsibility for monetary and exchange policy in the GDR, too. It set up branches and provided them with Deutsche Mark banknotes and coins. In the run-up to the currency changeover alone, the Bundesbank transported 440 million Deutsche Mark banknotes and 102 million Deutsche Mark coins to East Germany.

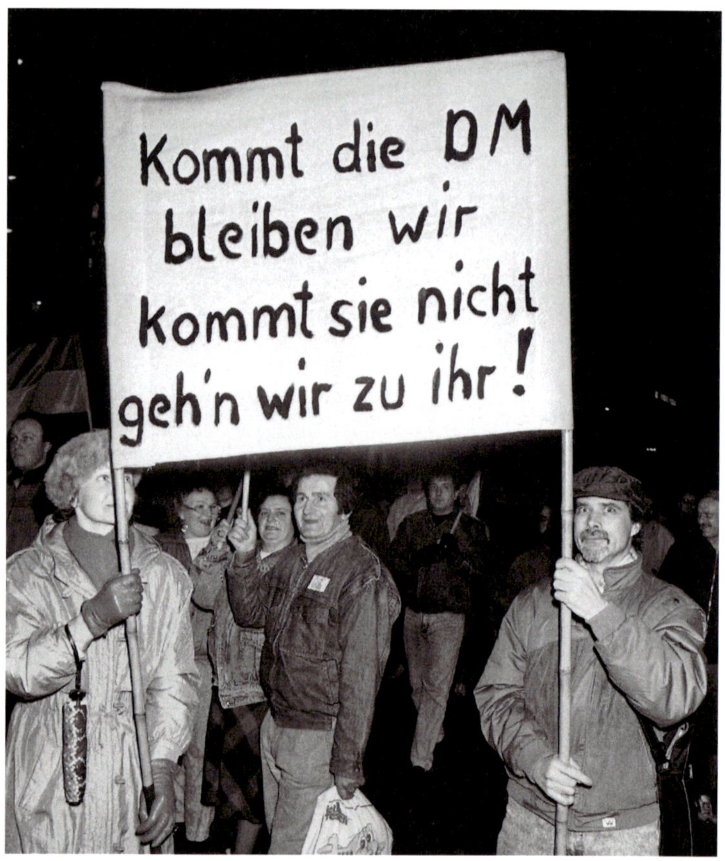

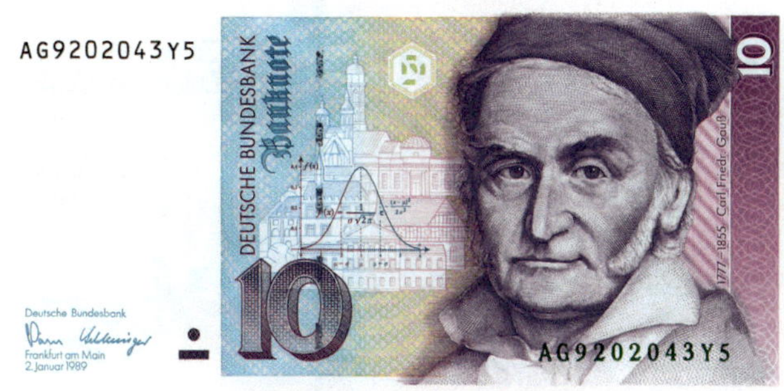

128 **10 DM,** 1989

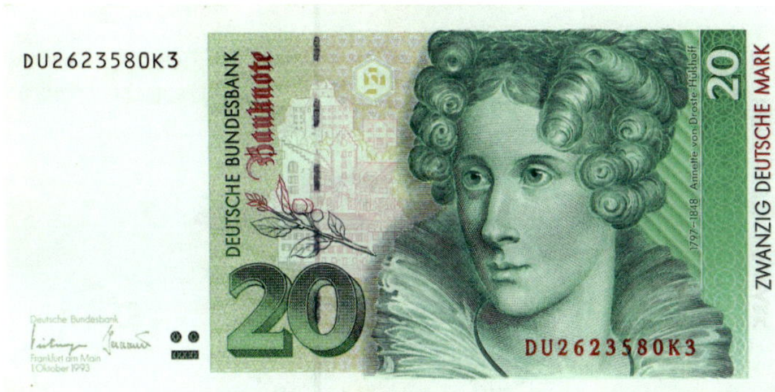

129 **20 DM,** 1991

MONEY IN UNITED GERMANY

Issuance of the new "BBk III" banknote series began almost simultaneously with the German monetary union. Like the DM coins, these notes remained in circulation until euro money was introduced in 2002.

FROM 1999 EUROPEAN MONETARY POLICY

On 1 January 1999 the euro was introduced as the single currency in Germany and ten other European Union (EU) countries, initially just as book money. Responsibility for monetary policy was transferred from the national central banks to the European level. Since then the Deutsche Bundesbank has been part of the Eurosystem, which comprises the euro-area national central banks and the European Central Bank (ECB). The Governing Council of the ECB is the supreme decision-making body. The President of the Bundesbank is a member of this Council.

In December 2012, the finance ministers of the European Union agreed upon the cornerstones of a joint European banking supervision regime under the aegis of the European Central Bank (ECB). Since 2014, the Bundesbank has worked within the "Single Supervisory Mechanism" (SSM). On 1 January 2013, the German Act on Monitoring Financial Stability came into force, giving the Bundesbank a "macroprudential mandate", or the legal task of helping to safeguard the stability of the financial system.

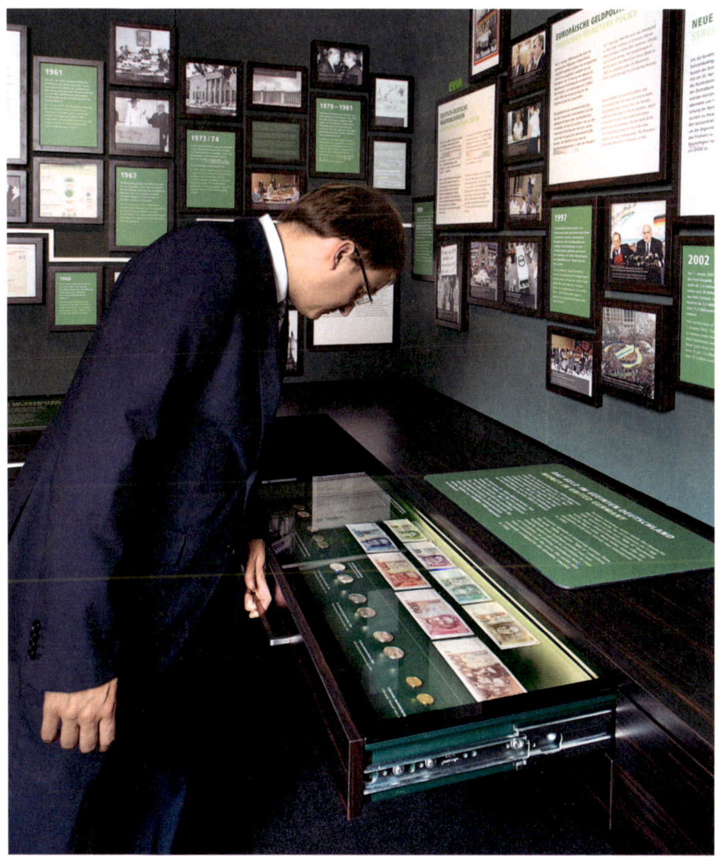

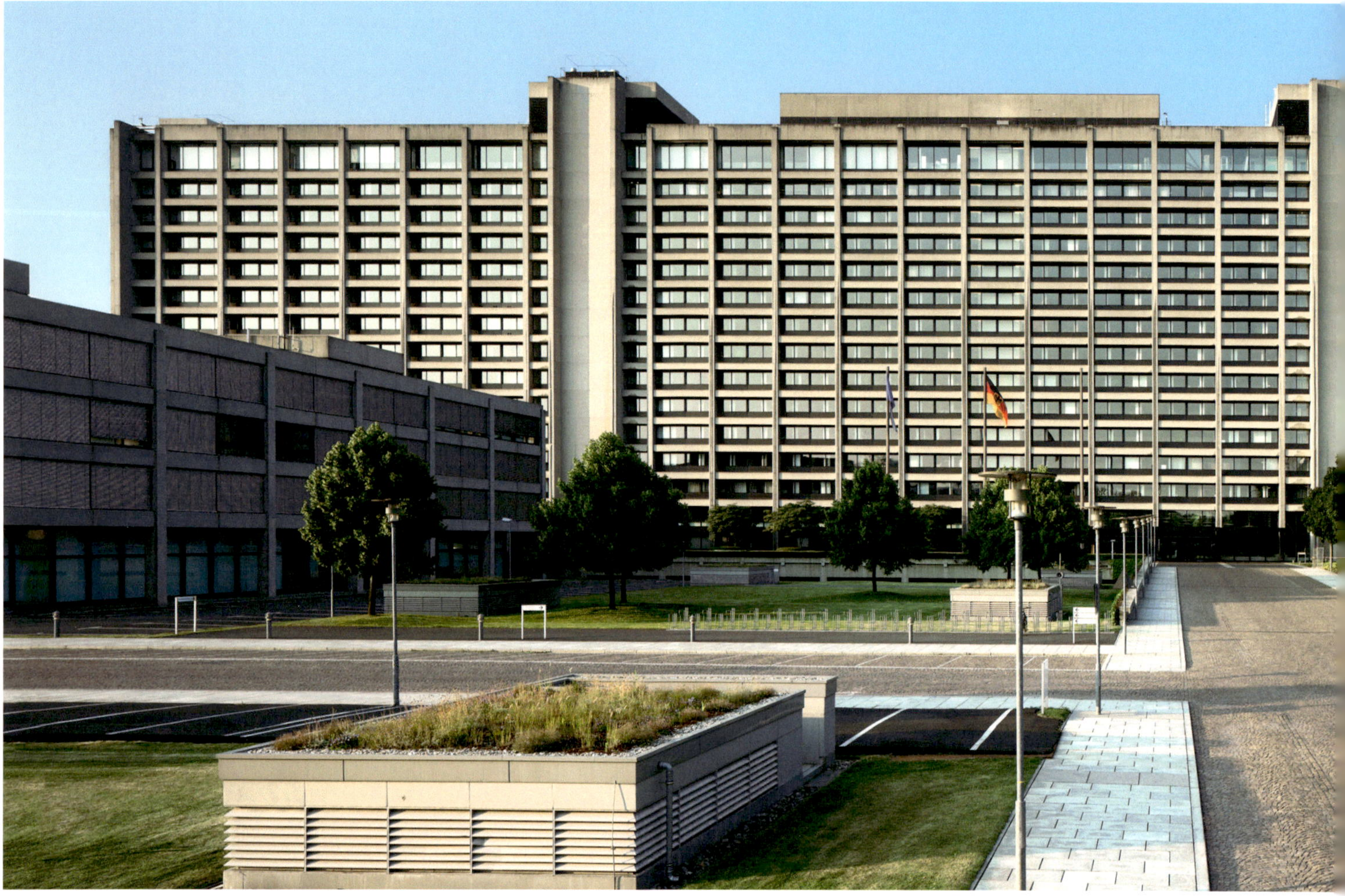

CENTRAL OFFICE

The Deutsche Bundesbank's Central Office is located in Frankfurt am Main. The Executive Board and around 3,000 employees work here. Besides administering the Bundesbank, Central Office is mainly responsible for policy issues and international tasks.

EXECUTIVE BOARD

The Executive Board governs and manages the Deutsche Bundesbank. The Federal Government nominates the president, deputy president and one further board member, while the Bundesrat nominates the remaining three members. The federal president generally appoints the Executive Board members for eight years.

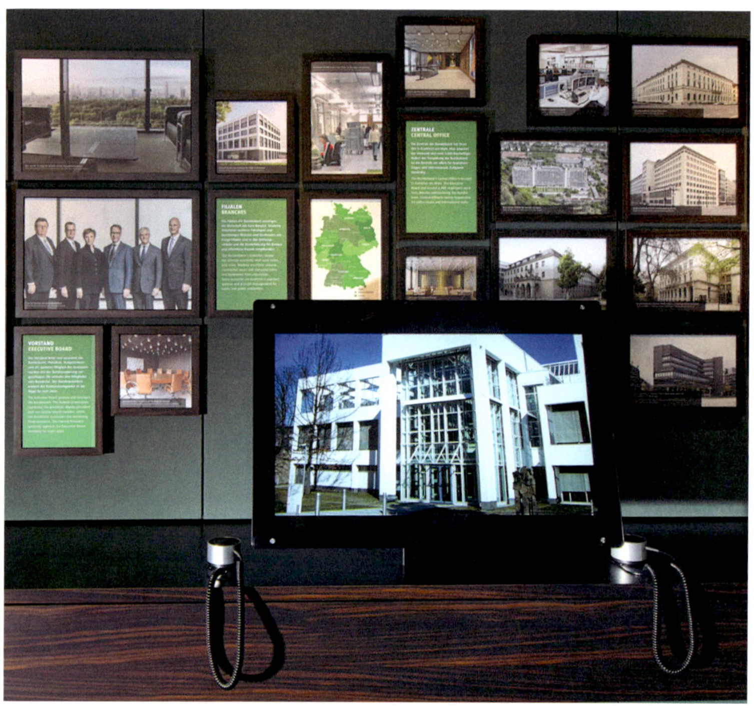

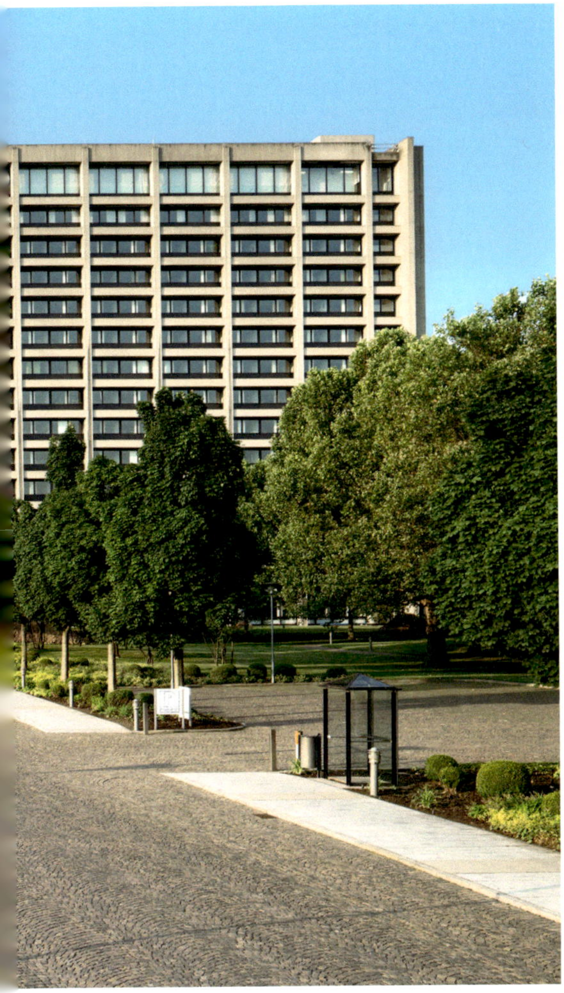

THE BUNDESBANK'S TASKS

The Deutsche Bundesbank is Germany's central bank. Together with the European Central Bank (ECB) and the central banks of euro-area countries, it is responsible for the euro and implements the monetary policy decisions in Germany. The Bundesbank ensures that cashless payments can be executed smoothly and puts cash into circulation via its branch network. Other tasks include cooperation in European banking supervision and supervising the financial and monetary system. It also manages Germany's foreign reserves and assumes the function of a "house bank" for central government. It collects data for statistics, conducts economic research and is a member of numerous international committees.

REGIONAL OFFICES

The Deutsche Bundesbank has regional offices in nine large cities, each being responsible for certain federal states. Their tasks include supervising the banks in their region and maintaining contact with local policymakers and the business community. They are also responsible for the branches.

BRANCHES

The Deutsche Bundesbank's branches supply the German economy with euro notes and coins. Modern machines remove counterfeit notes and damaged coins and banknotes from circulation. Some branches are involved in payment systems and account management for banks and public authorities.

AUFGABEN DER BUNDESBANK
TASKS OF THE BUNDESBANK

BARGELD
CASH MANAGEMENT

FINANZ- UND WÄHRUNGSSYSTEM
FINANCIAL AND MONETARY SYSTEM

GELDPOLITIK
MONETARY POLICY

BANKENAUFSICHT
BANKING SUPERVISION

UNBARER ZAHLUNGSVERKEHR
CASHLESS PAYMENTS

MITARBEIT IN INTERNATIONALEN GREMIEN UND INSTITUTIONEN
COOPERATION IN INTERNATIONAL COMMITTEES AND INSTITUTIONS

ÖKONOMISCHE FORSCHUNG, ERSTELLUNG VON STATISTIKEN
ECONOMIC RESEARCH, COMPILATION OF STATISTICS

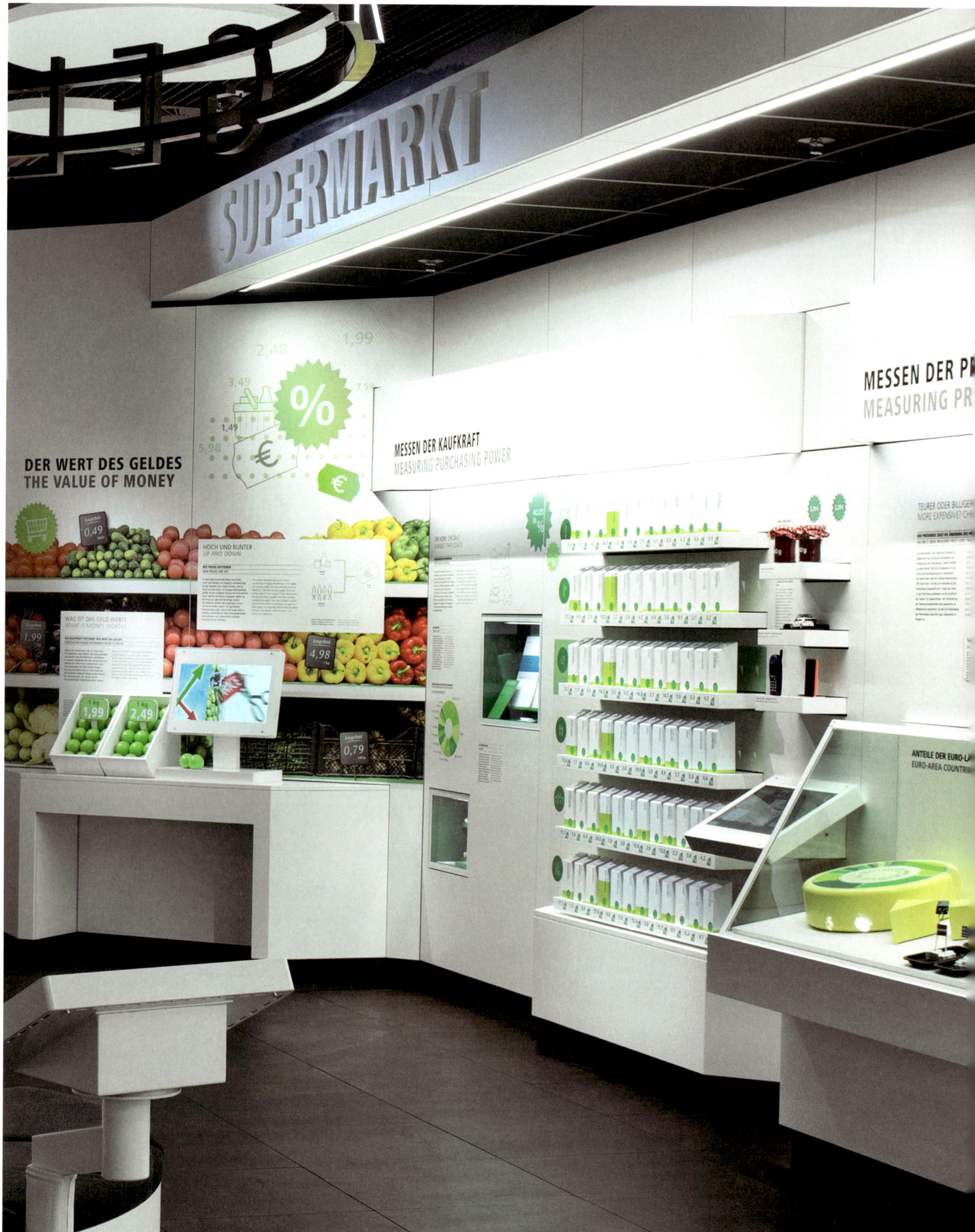
SUPERMARKT
DER WERT DES GELDES
THE VALUE OF MONEY
HOCH UND RUNTER
UP AND DOWN
WAS IST DAS GELD WERT?
WHAT IS MONEY WORTH?
MESSEN DER KAUFKRAFT
MEASURING PURCHASING POWER
MESSEN DER P
MEASURING PR
ANTEILE DER EURO-
EURO-AREA COUNTRI
Angebot
0,49
1,99
2,49
4,98
0,79
%
€

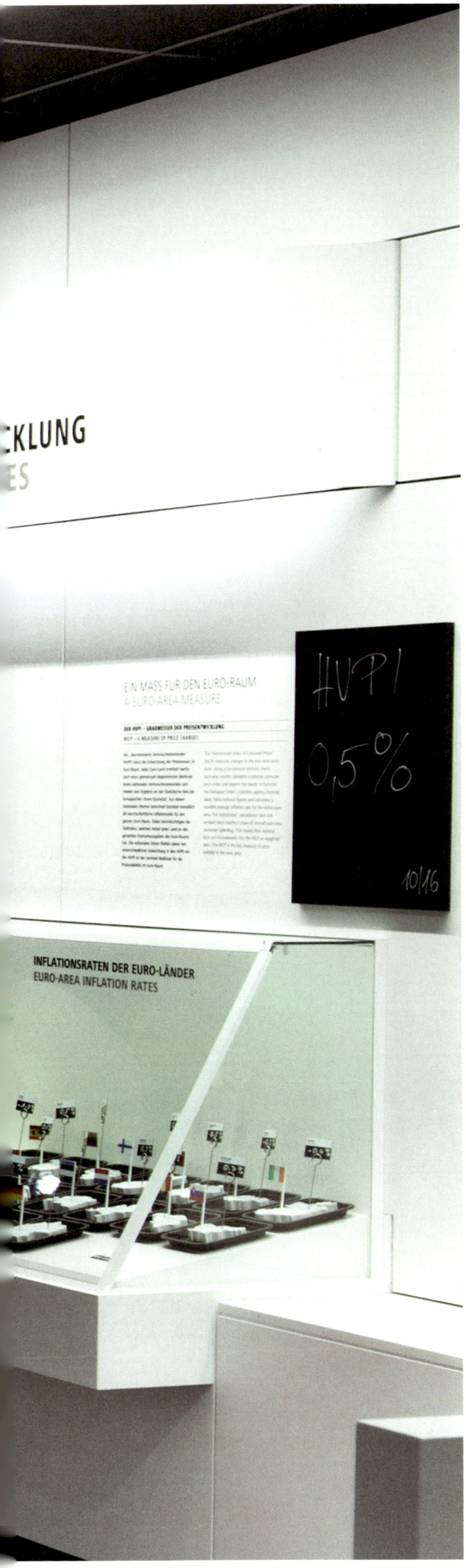

SUPERMARKET

Money's value lies in its purchasing power. If prices are stable, money retains its value. However, if price levels generally rise, money loses its value, and its purchasing power dips.

We can experience this cause-and-effect relationship every day when we go shopping. As an introduction to today's monetary policy, the visitor is therefore invited to walk through a simulated supermarket, where the produce section, dairy counter, refrigerated cabinets, newsstand and checkout counters show in true-to-life fashion what gives money its value and how prices are formed, how changes in purchasing power are measured and how inflation rates for Germany and euro area are calculated. Several media stations provide detailed information on the causes and effects of inflation and deflation and illustrate the importance of price stability. Both a continuous rise and a continuous fall in prices can wreck an economy. By contrast, stable money preserves incomes' purchasing power, safeguards savings and is a key prerequisite for employment, prosperity and a functional economy.

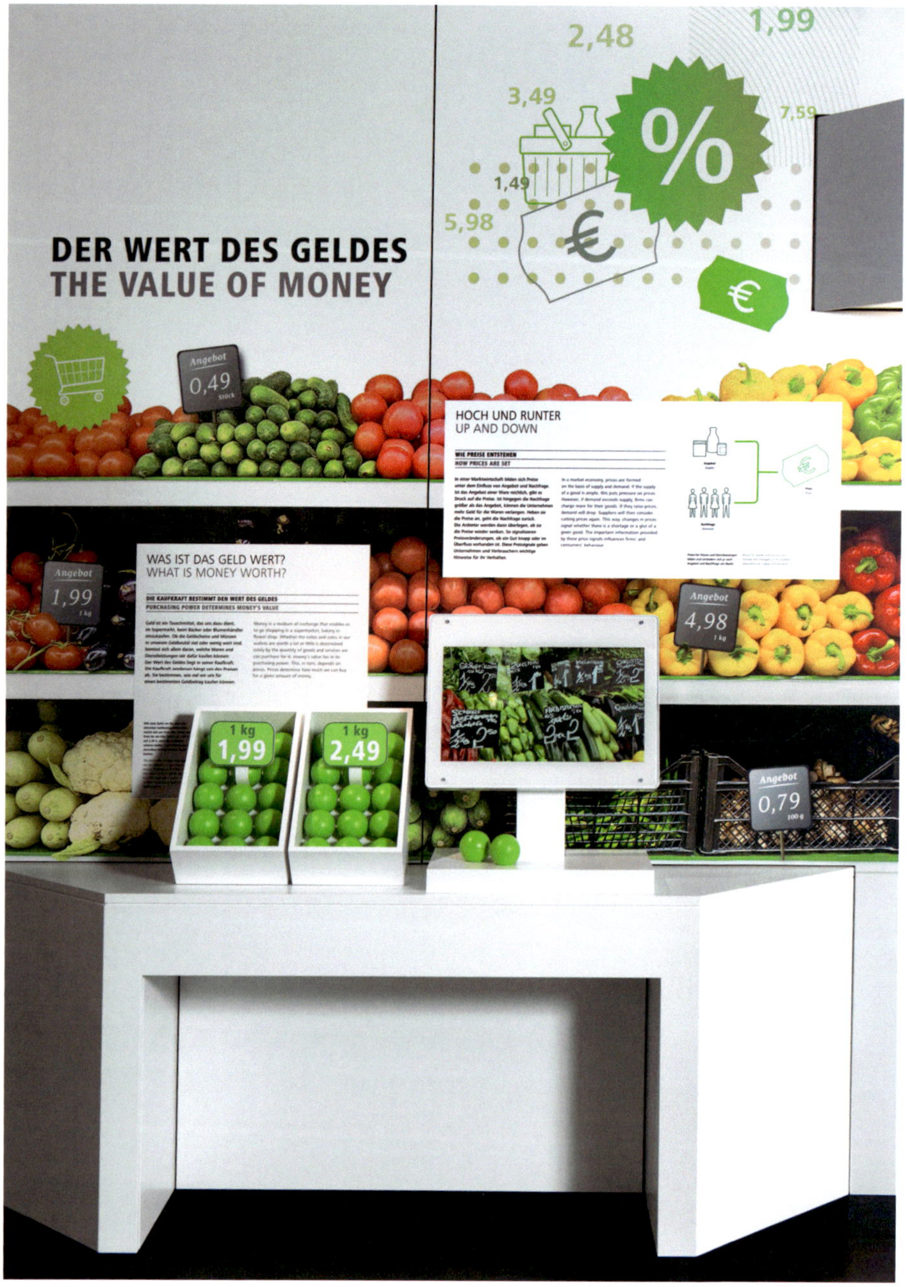

WHAT IS MONEY WORTH?

PURCHASING POWER DETERMINES MONEY'S VALUE

Money is a medium of exchange that enables us to go shopping in a supermarket, bakery or flower shop. Whether the notes and coins in our wallets are worth a lot or little is determined solely by the quantity of goods and services we can purchase for it: money's value lies in its purchasing power. This, in turn, depends on prices. Prices determine how much we can buy for a given amount of money.

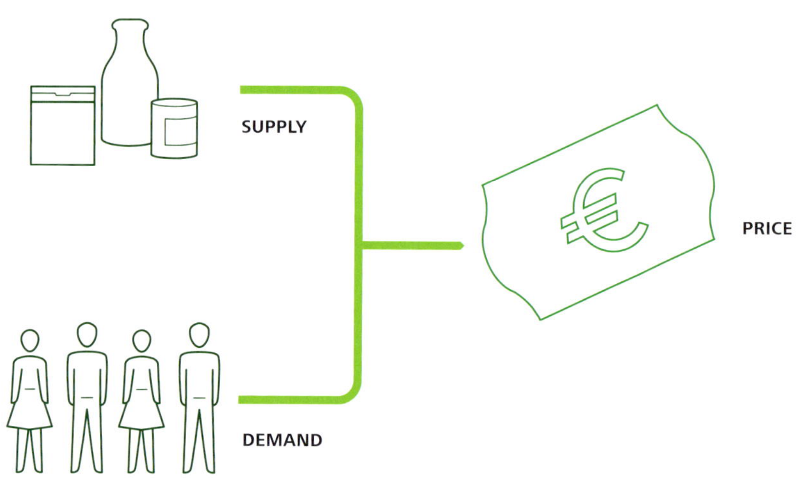

UP AND DOWN

HOW PRICES ARE SET

In a market economy, prices are formed on the basis of supply and demand. If the supply of a good is ample, this puts pressure on prices. However, if demand exceeds supply, firms can charge more for their goods. If they raise prices, demand will drop. Suppliers will then consider cutting prices again. This way, changes in prices signal whether there is a shortage or a glut of a given good. The important information provided by these price signals influences firms' and consumers' behaviour.

A BASKET THAT COUNTS

GOODS BASKET AND PRICES

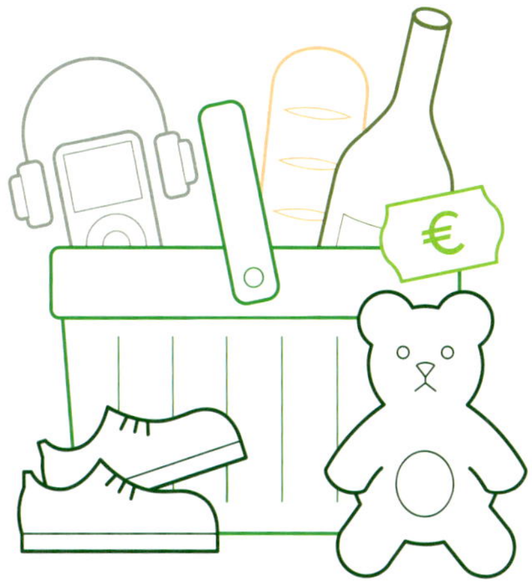

Purchasing power is measured not in terms of the movements of a select few prices but instead as the average change in all prices. However, as it is impossible to record millions of individual prices, for Germany the Federal Statistical Office uses a representative "basket of goods". Every month, statisticians use the prices of the selected goods and services to calculate the overall price of the basket of goods. This allows price level movements to be measured over time.

BASKET OF GOODS

The basket of goods contains some 600 types of goods which typify an average German household. It contains food and clothing, housing rents and insurance policies, services such as visits to the hairdresser and also infrequently purchased goods such as cars and washing machines. All in all, every month statisticians record over 300,000 individual prices at retailers, in catalogues and on the internet. The basket's components are updated continuously to reflect current purchasing trends.

WEIGHTING

Households spend their money in a variety of ways. Some spend a relatively large chunk of their money on a car, others on clothes, food or education. Every five years, the Federal Statistical Office therefore requests some 60,000 households to record their expenditure to the last cent. Statisticians use the average household's spending habits to derive the weights for the basket of goods.

HOW THE GERMAN BASKET OF GOODS IS WEIGHTED
AVERAGE PERCENTAGE SHARE OF CONSUMPTION EXPENDITURE

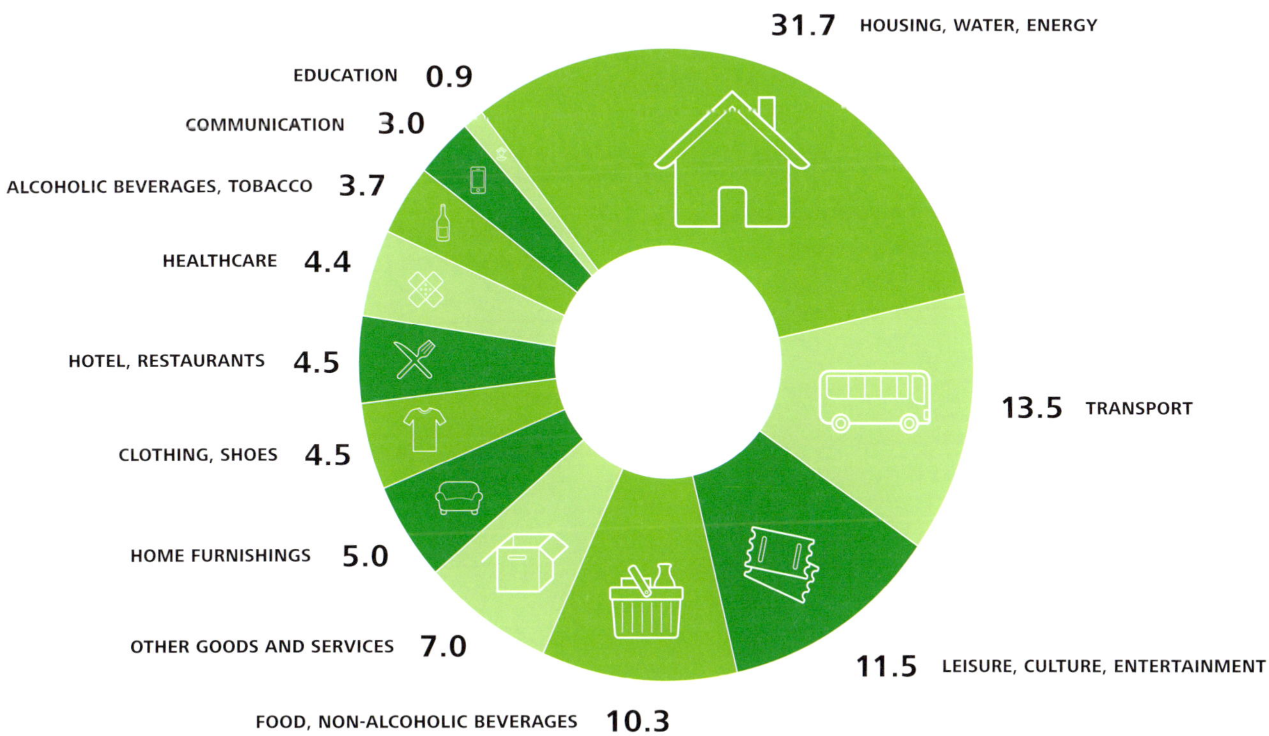

SOURCE: FEDERAL STATISTICAL OFFICE, BASE YEAR: 2010

MORE EXPENSIVE? CHEAPER?

THE PRICE INDEX MEASURES PRICE LEVEL CHANGES

In order to measure the stability of the value of money, the Federal Statistical Office monitors price level movements. It does so by collecting 300,000 individual prices of the goods and services that make up the basket of goods on a monthly basis. These prices are used to calculate the consumer price index (CPI), which measures changes in the price level. If the index goes up, prices have also gone up and the purchasing power of money has declined. The change in the CPI is generally referred to as the rate of inflation and measures the percentage change in the overall price level between two points in time.

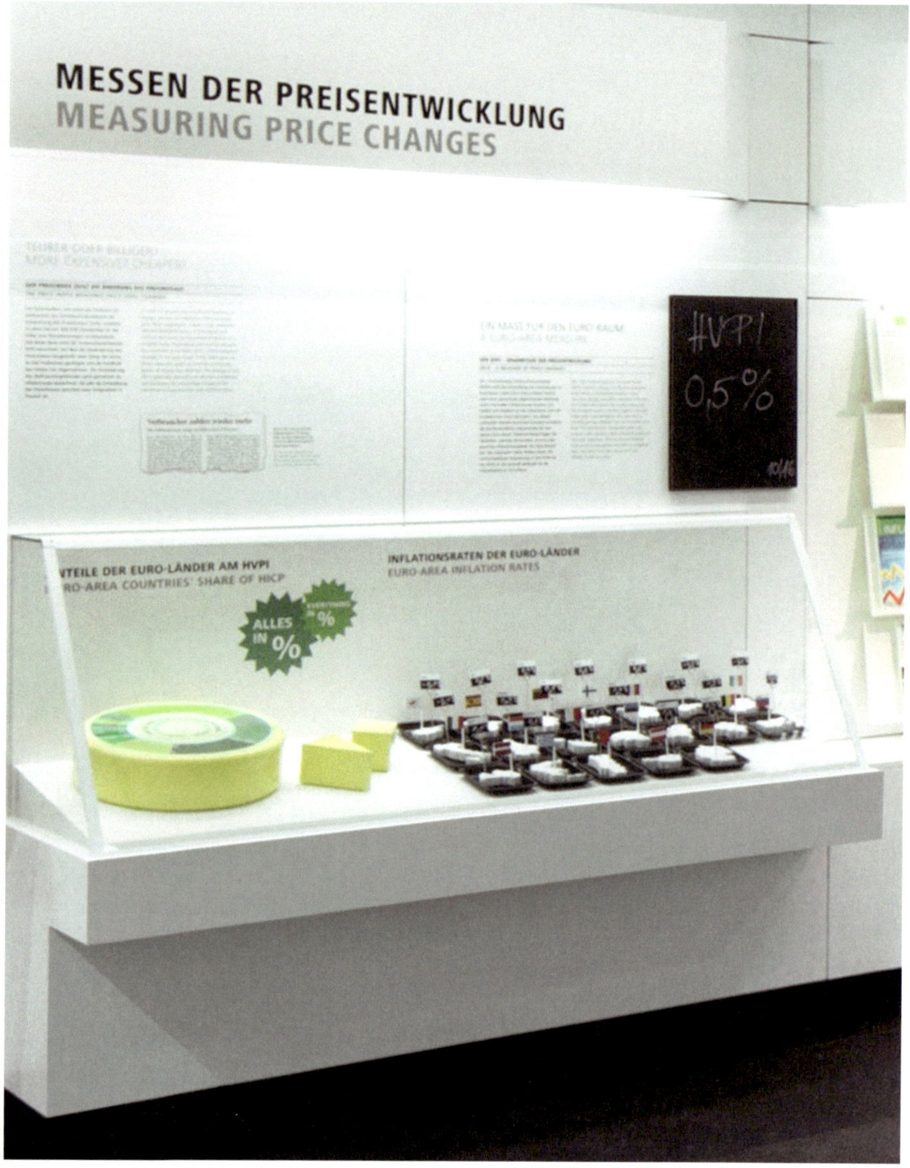

A EURO-AREA MEASURE

HICP – A MEASURE OF PRICE CHANGES

The "Harmonised Index of Consumer Prices" (HICP) measures changes in the euro-area price level. Using a harmonised method, every euro-area country calculates a national consumer price index and reports the results to Eurostat, the European Union's statistics agency. Eurostat takes these national figures and calculates a monthly average inflation rate for the entire euro area. The statisticians' calculations take into account each country's share of overall euro-area consumer spending. This means that national data are incorporated into the HICP as weighted data. The HICP is the key measure of price stability in the euro area.

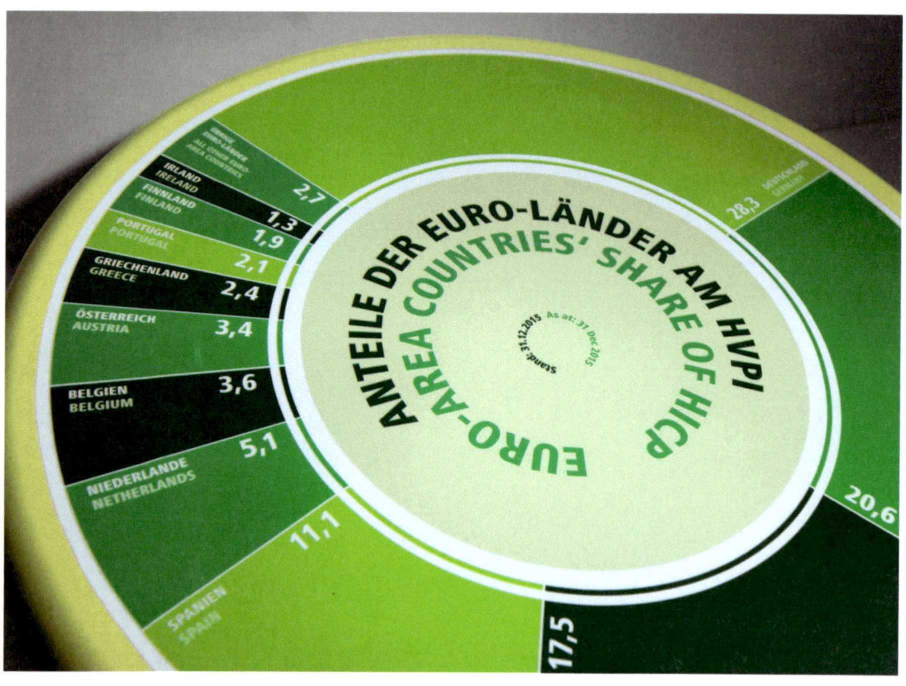

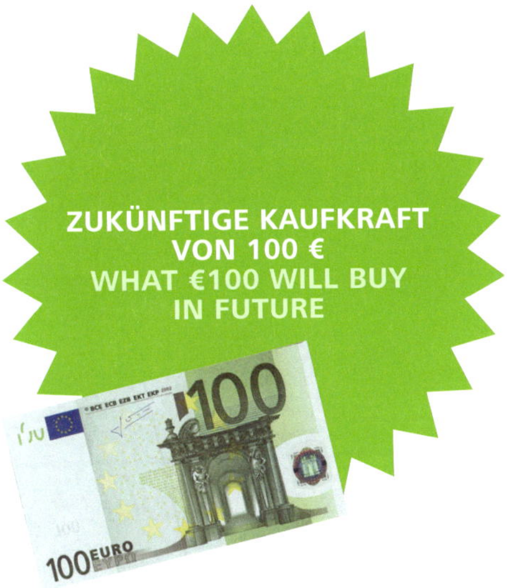

SMALL RATE – MAJOR IMPACT

MONEY LOSES VALUE
OVER THE YEARS

If prices are stable, money retains its value. However, if prices rise across the board, money loses its value: the same amount of money will buy us fewer goods and services. Even low rates of inflation over a relatively long period of time will erode purchasing power significantly: at a constant annual inflation rate of 4%, in ten years 100 euro will be worth only as much as just under 68 euro today.

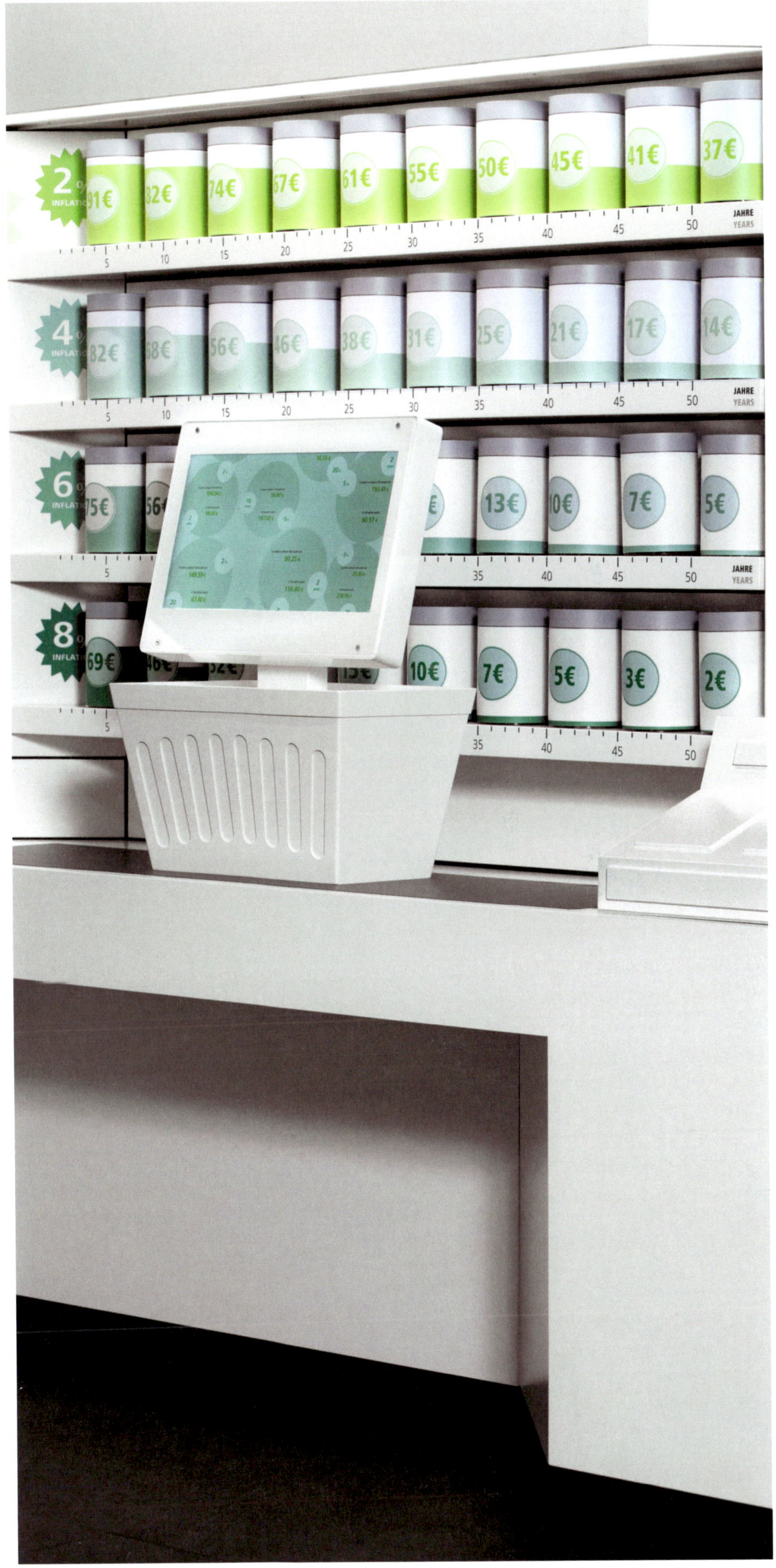

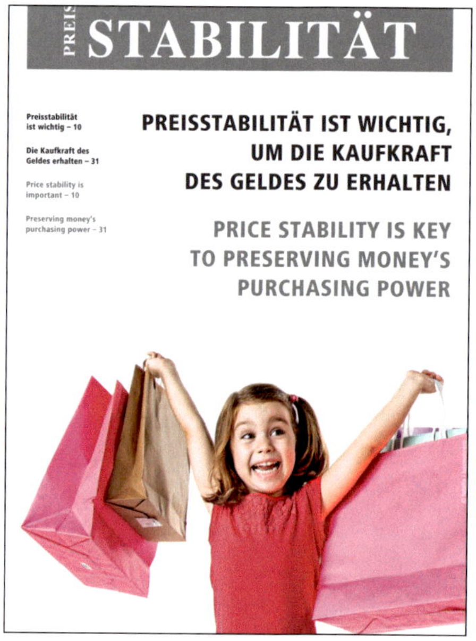
PREIS STABILITÄT
Preisstabilität ist wichtig – 10
Die Kaufkraft des Geldes erhalten – 31
Price stability is important – 10
Preserving money's purchasing power – 31
PREISSTABILITÄT IST WICHTIG, UM DIE KAUFKRAFT DES GELDES ZU ERHALTEN
PRICE STABILITY IS KEY TO PRESERVING MONEY'S PURCHASING POWER

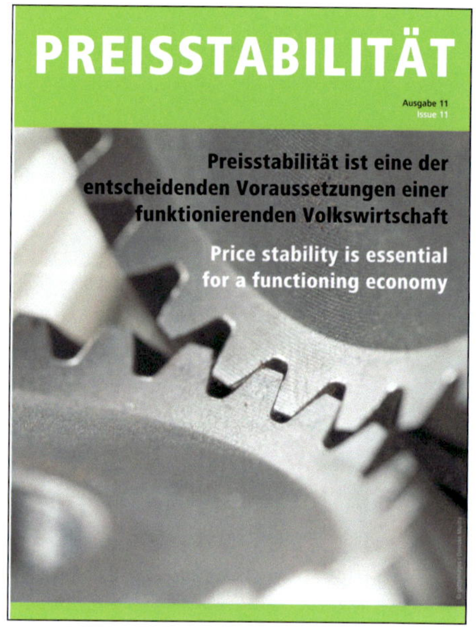
PREISSTABILITÄT
Ausgabe 11 Issue 11
Preisstabilität ist eine der entscheidenden Voraussetzungen einer funktionierenden Volkswirtschaft
Price stability is essential for a functioning economy

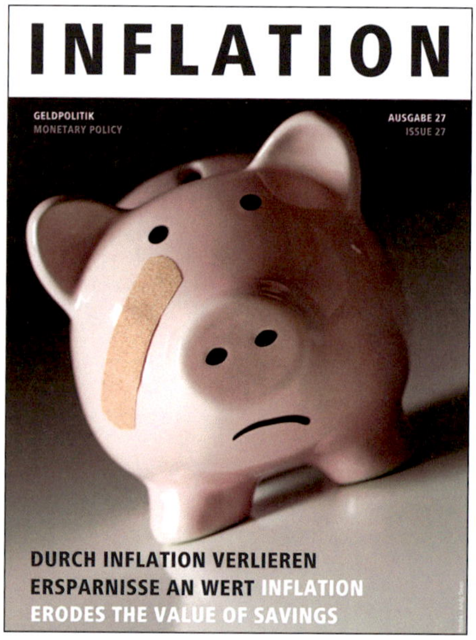
INFLATION
GELDPOLITIK MONETARY POLICY
AUSGABE 27 ISSUE 27
DURCH INFLATION VERLIEREN ERSPARNISSE AN WERT
INFLATION ERODES THE VALUE OF SAVINGS

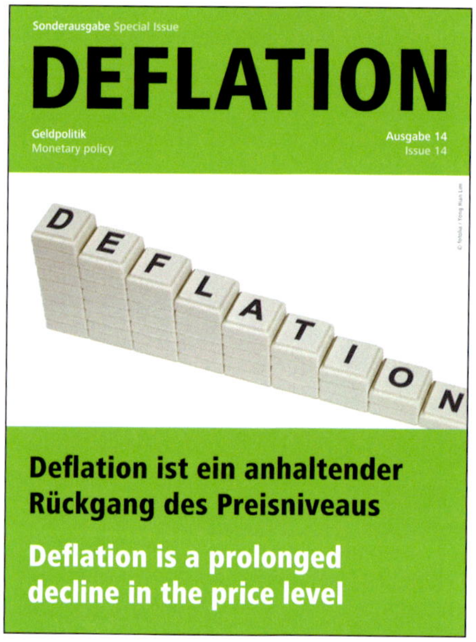
Sonderausgabe Special Issue
DEFLATION
Geldpolitik Monetary policy
Ausgabe 14 Issue 14
DEFLATION
Deflation ist ein anhaltender Rückgang des Preisniveaus
Deflation is a prolonged decline in the price level

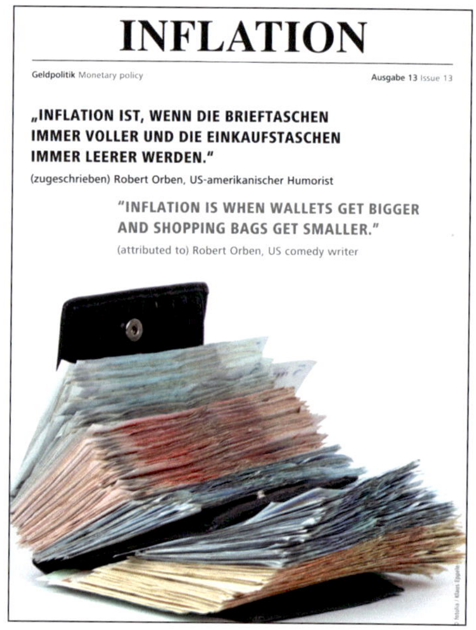
INFLATION
Geldpolitik Monetary policy
Ausgabe 13 Issue 13
„INFLATION IST, WENN DIE BRIEFTASCHEN IMMER VOLLER UND DIE EINKAUFSTASCHEN IMMER LEERER WERDEN."
(zugeschrieben) Robert Orben, US-amerikanischer Humorist
"INFLATION IS WHEN WALLETS GET BIGGER AND SHOPPING BAGS GET SMALLER."
(attributed to) Robert Orben, US comedy writer

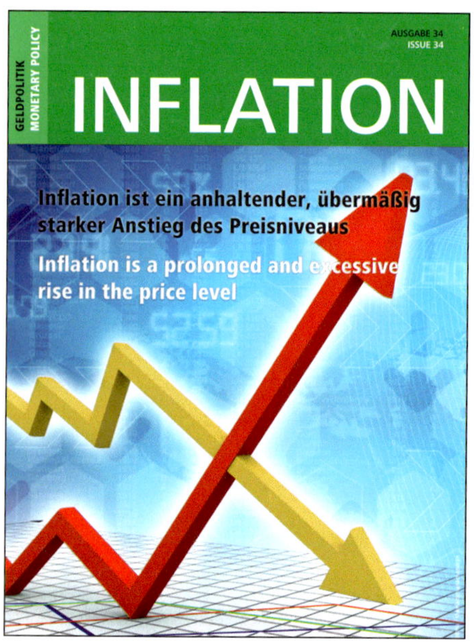
GELDPOLITIK MONETARY POLICY
AUSGABE 34 ISSUE 34
INFLATION
Inflation ist ein anhaltender, übermäßig starker Anstieg des Preisniveaus
Inflation is a prolonged and excessive rise in the price level

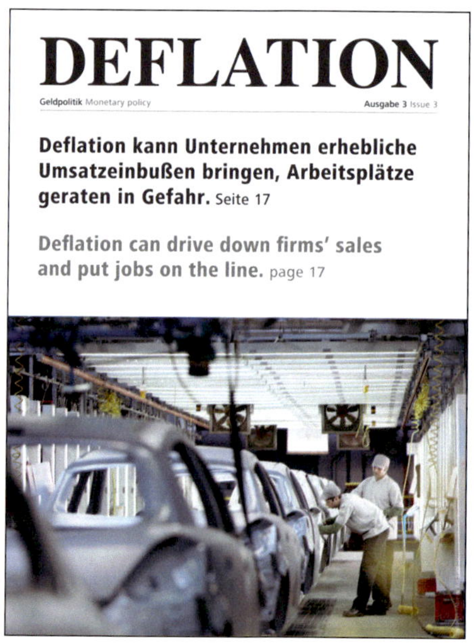
DEFLATION
Geldpolitik Monetary policy
Ausgabe 3 Issue 3
Deflation kann Unternehmen erhebliche Umsatzeinbußen bringen, Arbeitsplätze geraten in Gefahr. Seite 17
Deflation can drive down firms' sales and put jobs on the line. page 17

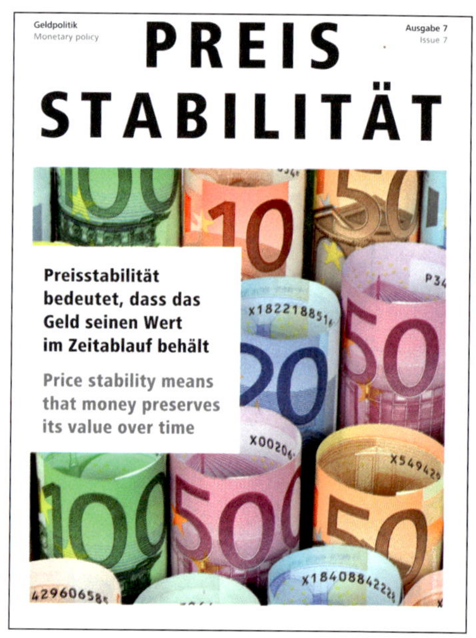
Geldpolitik Monetary policy
Ausgabe 7 Issue 7
PREIS STABILITÄT
Preisstabilität bedeutet, dass das Geld seinen Wert im Zeitablauf behält
Price stability means that money preserves its value over time

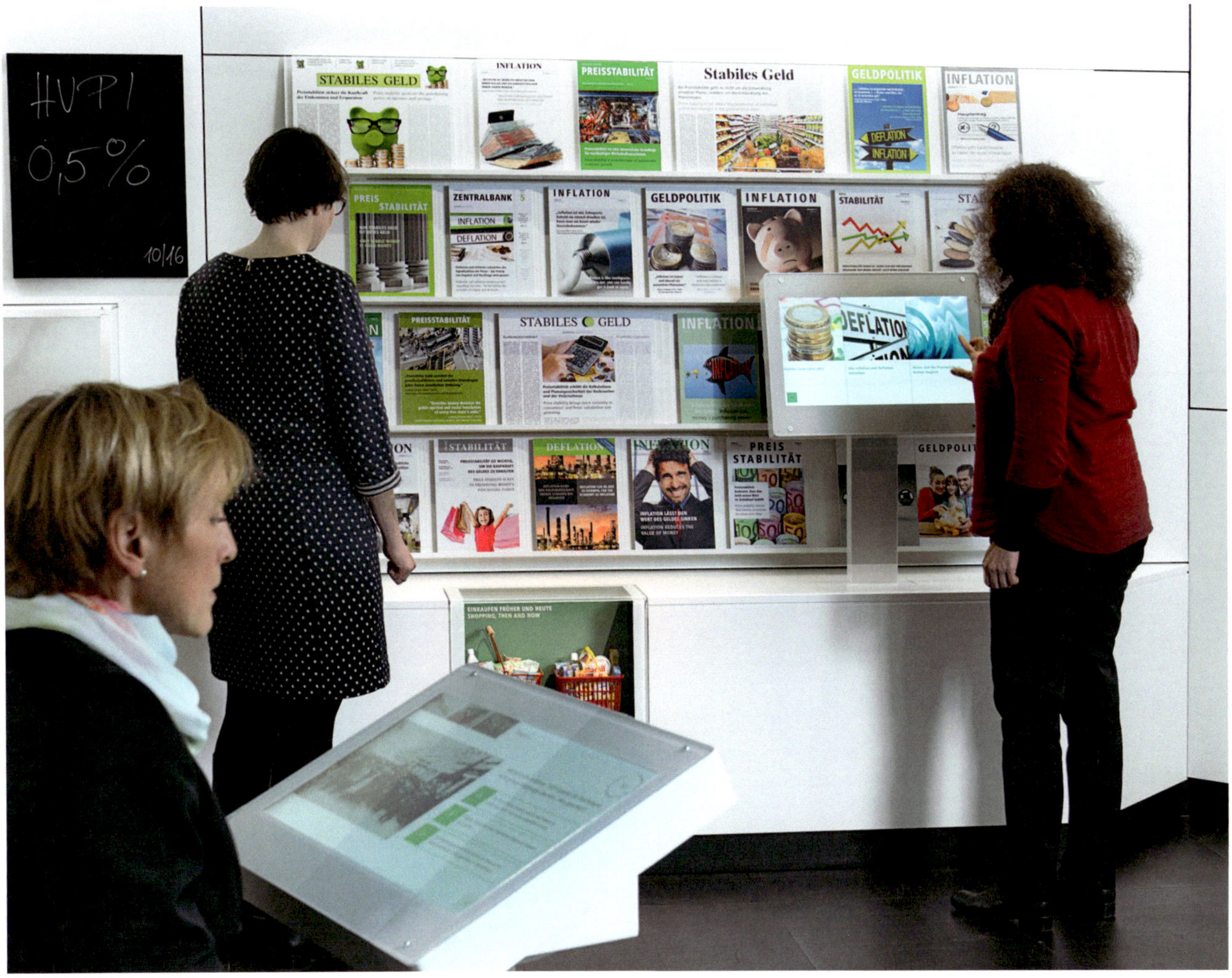

STABLE MONEY BENEFITS ALL

THE BENEFITS OF PRICE STABILITY

Price stability promotes growth, prosperity and social justice. Inflation, however, erodes purchasing power and devalues savings. Recipients of fixed incomes, pensions and social welfare benefits feel the pinch the hardest: they can afford less if their incomes are not adjusted to keep pace with price increases. Inflation and deflation alike also distort price signals, which provide key information on supply and demand. This disrupts the mechanisms used to steer a market economy. It is important to keep the value of money stable in order to avoid the harmful effects of inflation and deflation.

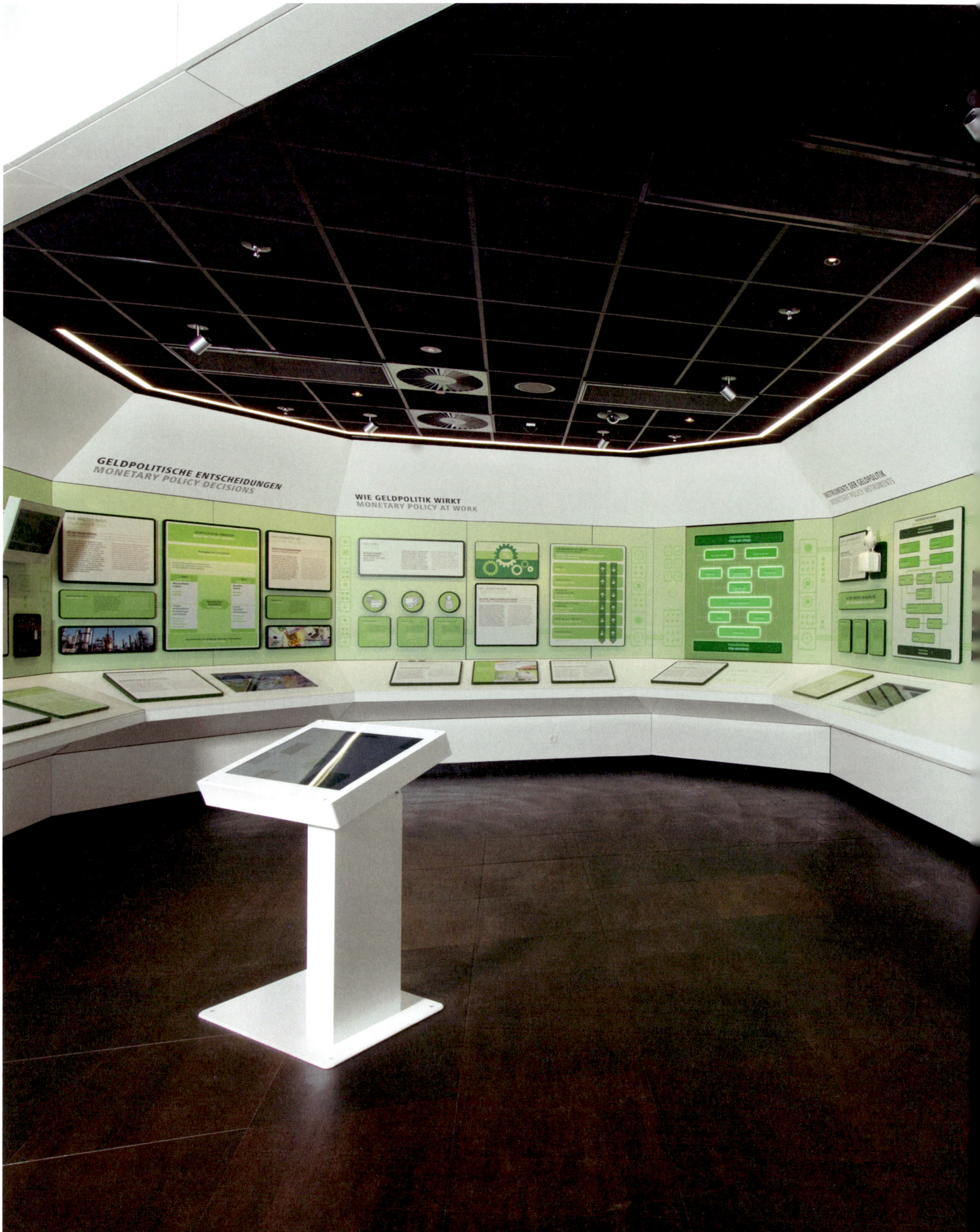
GELDPOLITISCHE ENTSCHEIDUNGEN
MONETARY POLICY DECISIONS
WIE GELDPOLITIK WIRKT
MONETARY POLICY AT WORK
INSTRUMENTE DER GELDPOLITIK
MONETARY POLICY INSTRUMENTS

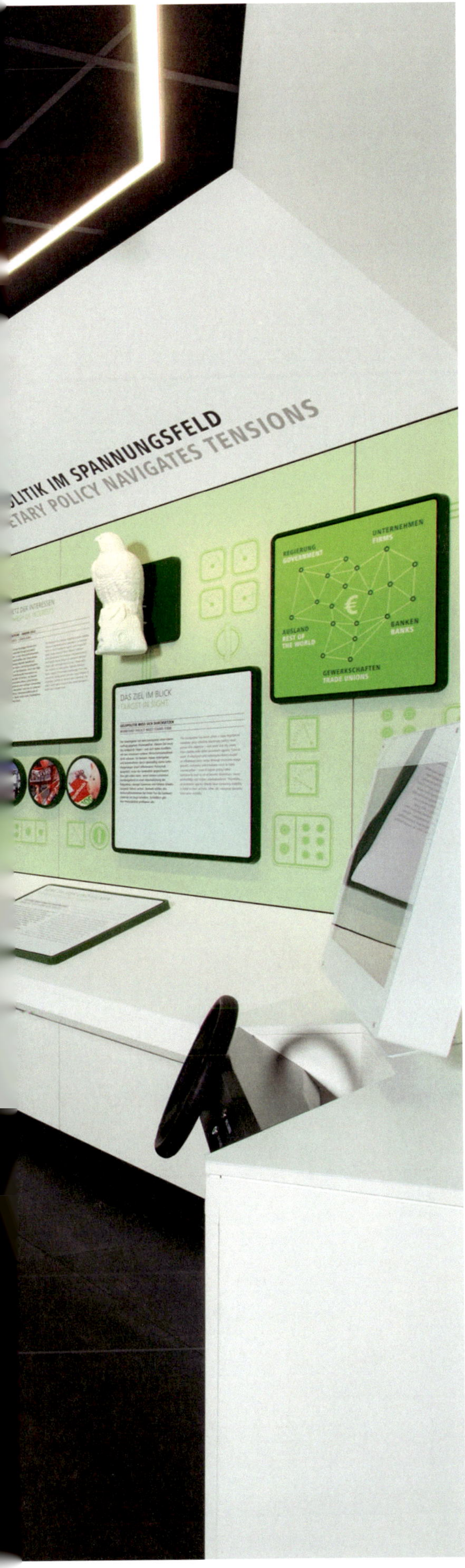

CONTROL ROOM

It is not by accident that the second room on current monetary policy is reminiscent of a control station: it is designed to show how monetary policy "steers" price movements.

Ensuring price stability is the primary monetary policy objective of the Eurosystem. Its highest decision-making body is the Governing Council of the ECB. Visitors will learn how it defines price stability and be acquainted with the two-pillar strategy as the basis of its monetary policy analyses and decisions. The exhibition will devote extensive coverage to the toolkit of instruments available to monetary policy makers to steer prices. Large display boards explain the cause-and-effect relationships involved with changes in policy rates or asset purchases. With these measures, monetary policy is often caught up in a web of different interests; central government, trade unions and firms are each pursuing an agenda of their own.

Historical experience has taught us that central banks have to be protected from external political influence in order to be able to act in a stability-oriented manner. This is why the Eurosystem's independence is enshrined in law.

2%

BELOW, BUT CLOSE TO, 2%

HOW THE ECB GOVERNING COUNCIL DEFINES PRICE STABILITY

The European Central Bank (ECB), the Bundesbank and the other national central banks in the euro area make up the Eurosystem. The ECB's supreme decision-making body is the Governing Council, of which the ECB President, the other members of the ECB's Executive Board and the governors of the national central banks are members. The Council decides on the euro area's monetary policy. Its primary objective is to maintain price stability, which it defines as an annual rise in the Harmonised Index of Consumer Prices of below, but close to, 2%. It pursues this objective over a medium-term horizon.

WHY NOT 0%?

WHY THE LEVEL WAS CHOSEN

It may come as a surprise that the ECB Governing Council's definition of price stability is not a 0% inflation rate but one of just under 2%. However, there are good reasons for this: a slightly positive overall euro-area inflation rate creates a "safety buffer" against deflation, which is tougher for monetary policymakers to fight than inflation. In addition, the selected definition ensures that individual euro-area countries whose inflation rate is below the average do not drift into deflation.

DECIDING TOGETHER

BUNDESBANK: AN ACTIVE MONETARY POLICY PLAYER

The Deutsche Bundesbank is part of the Eurosystem. Its experts prepare their own assessments of euro-area economic and monetary developments. These analyses are used by the President of the Bundesbank, who has a seat and a vote in the ECB Governing Council and thus has a say in the single monetary policy. Furthermore, the Bundesbank implements the ECB Governing Council's monetary policy decisions in Germany: it lends to commercial banks, administers the posted collateral and transacts purchases of securities where appropriate.

IN MAY 2003, THE ECB GOVERNING COUNCIL ANNOUNCED ITS DEFINITION OF PRICE STABILITY, WHICH STILL STANDS.

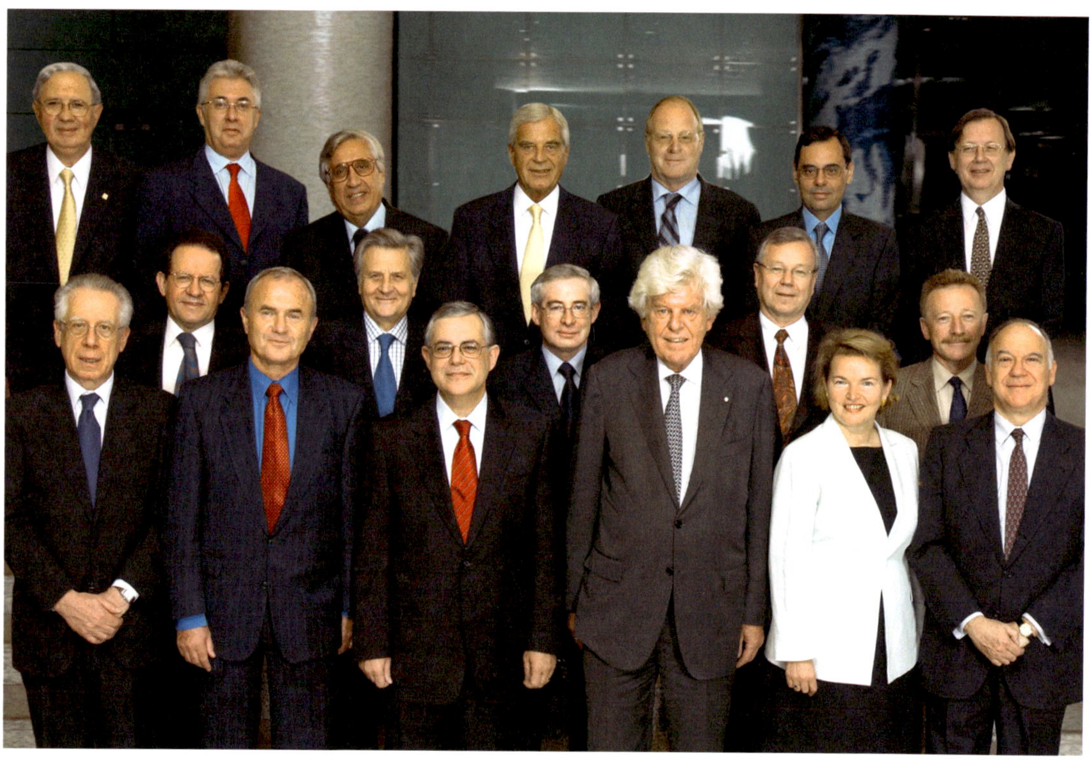

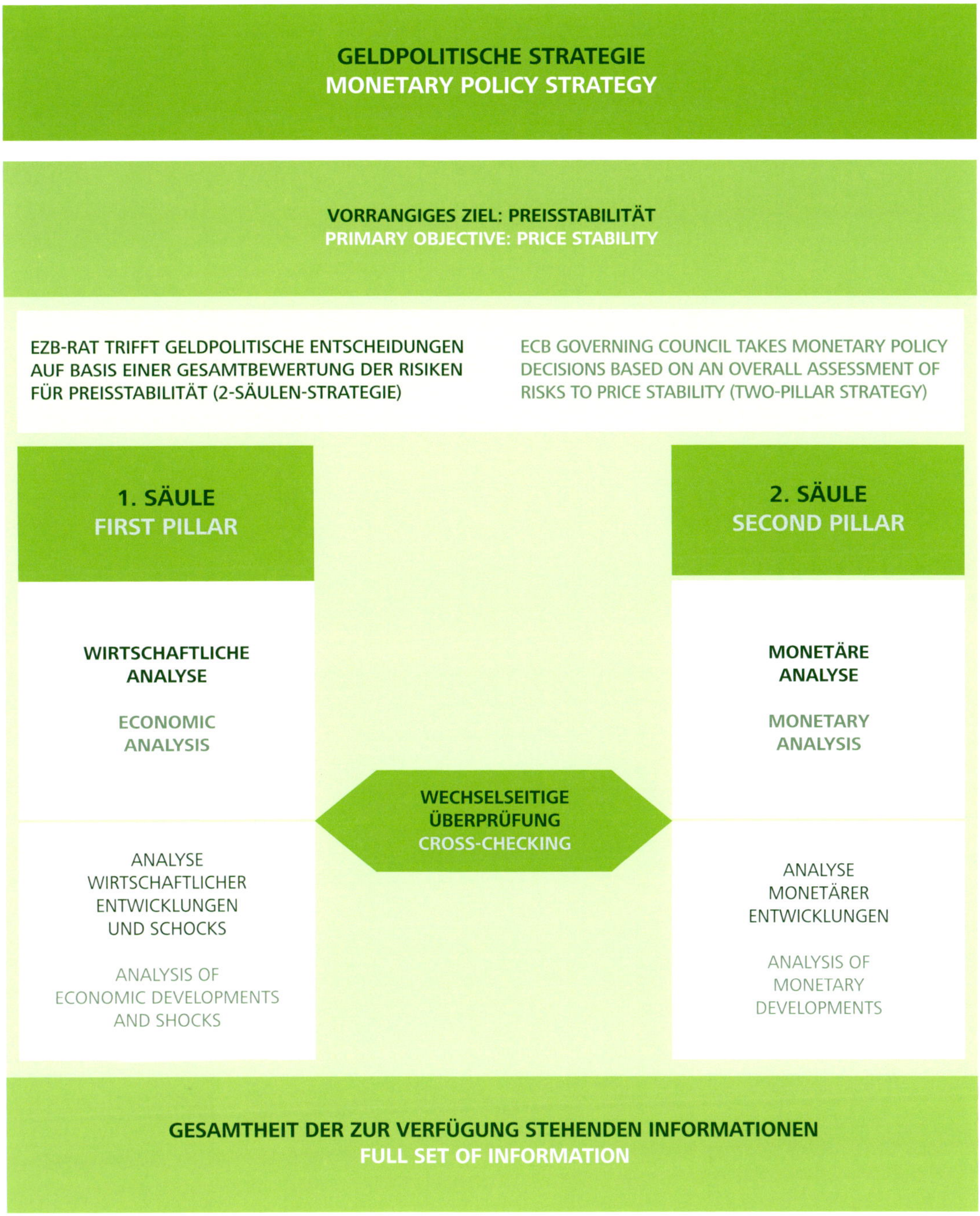

ON A BROAD BASE

THE TWO-PILLAR STRATEGY

The monetary policy of the ECB Governing Council is based on the "two-pillar strategy". The term denotes an extensive, two-pronged analysis of all factors which provide information regarding expected price developments. Experts at the central banks analyse economic developments in the euro area, and they also observe longer-term monetary factors, such as commercial banks' lending. They then cross-check the findings from the two "pillars". This strategy enables the ECB Governing Council to detect any potential risks to price stability at an early stage, and it is on this basis that it takes decisions on monetary policy measures.

"INTEREST RATE SCREW"

THE POLICY RATE – A KEY MONETARY POLICY INSTRUMENT

In order to cover banks' need for central bank money, the central bank typically provides loans, on which banks have to pay interest. The interest rate on these loans influences all other market interest rates. That is why it is called the policy rate. It is set by the ECB Governing Council. All changes to the policy rate influence the cost of credit for businesses and households. These costs, in turn, affect demand for capital and consumer goods. This is how the ECB Governing Council can influence aggregate demand and, ultimately, price developments. The process by which a change in the policy rate influences the economy is called the transmission mechanism.

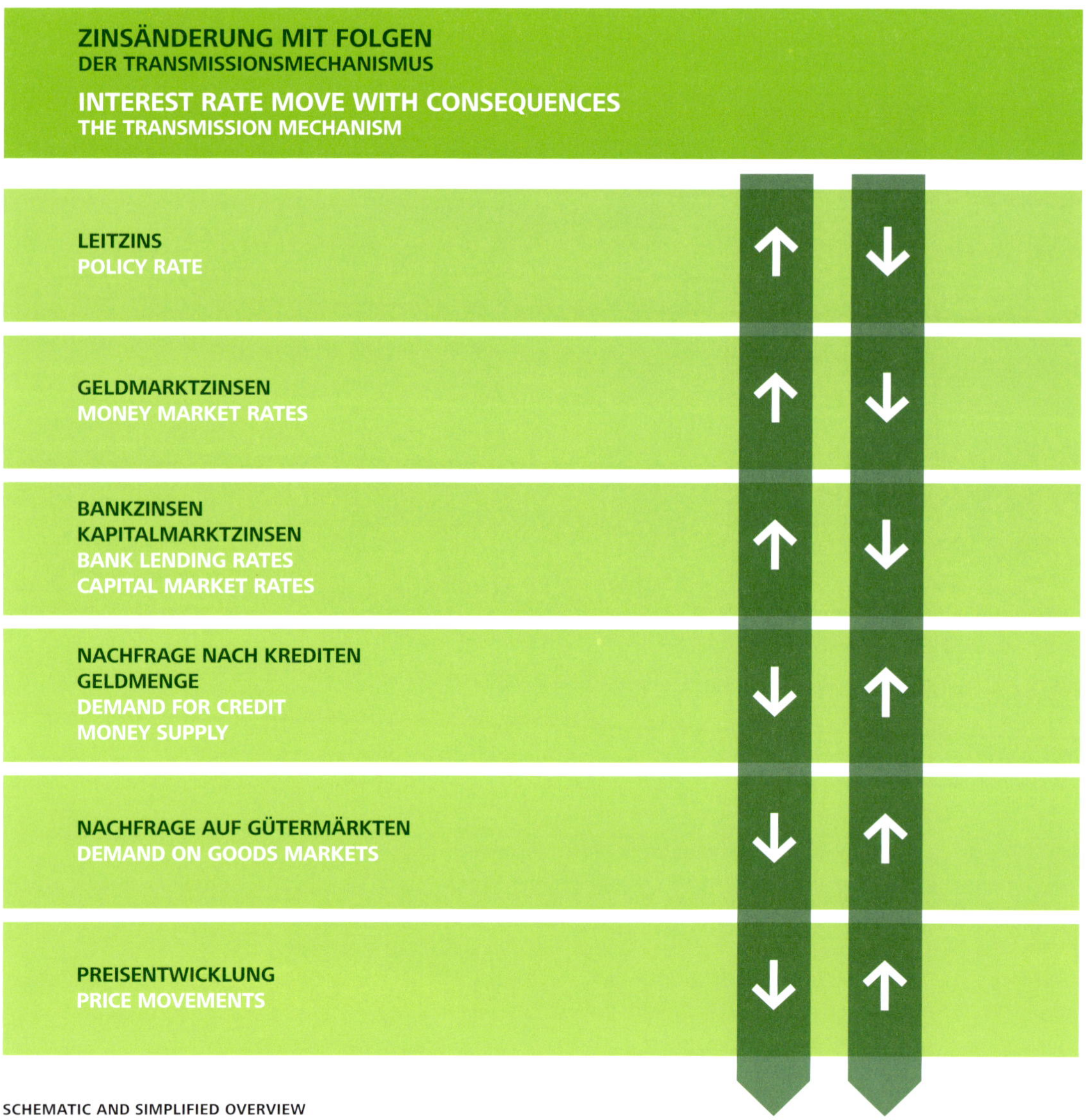

SCHEMATIC AND SIMPLIFIED OVERVIEW

SMALL TURN – MAJOR IMPACT

THE POLICY RATE INFLUENCES PRICE MOVEMENTS

If the ECB Governing Council fears that prices will rise too sharply, it "turns the interest rate screw", increasing the policy rate. This raises the interest rates at which commercial banks lend money to each other: the money market rates. Banks pass on the higher costs to their customers and bank lending rates go up. Firms and households therefore borrow less, which means less money goes into circulation and the demand for goods and services falls. This dampens upward price pressures. Conversely, the ECB Governing Council reduces the policy rate if prices are rising too slowly; loans are then cheaper, demand picks up and prices go back up.

THE THREE INTEREST RATES OF MONETARY POLICY

Policy rate adjustments are the main monetary policy tool. However, the policy rate on regular central bank lending to commercial banks (the "main refinancing rate") is not the only rate set by the ECB Governing Council. Two further interest rates can be used to influence prices.

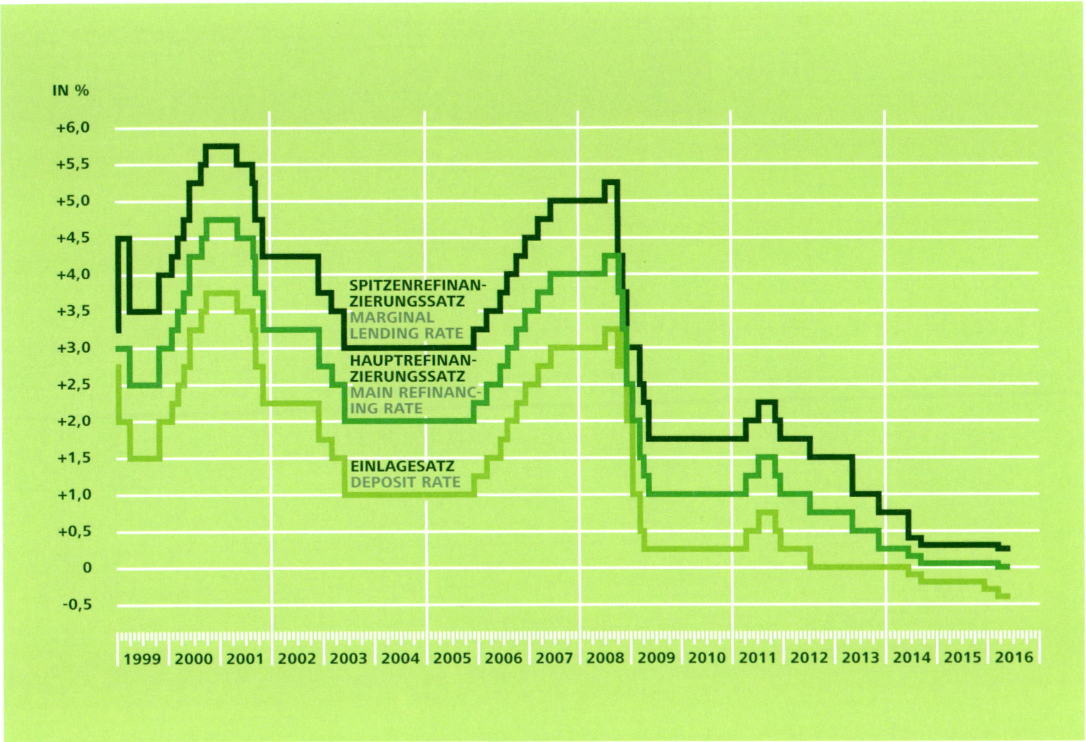

EURO-AREA MONETARY POLICY RATES

MARGINAL LENDING RATE

The "marginal lending facility" allows commercial banks to borrow central bank money overnight. They have to post collateral against this "overdraft facility". The interest rate paid on this loan is called the marginal lending rate, which is set by the ECB Governing Council. It is above the interest rate on the main refinancing operation (MRO) and forms the ceiling of the overnight interest rate at which commercial banks lend each other funds.

DEPOSIT RATE

The "deposit facility" allows commercial banks to deposit their surplus liquidity overnight at a special account held with the central bank. The rate of interest received by commercial banks is called the deposit rate, which is set by the ECB Governing Council. It is below the interest rate on the main refinancing operation and forms the floor for the overnight interest rate at which commercial banks lend to each other.

MAIN REFINANCING RATE

Every week, the Eurosystem settles a "main refinancing operation" (MRO), which allows commercial banks to borrow central bank money against collateral for a week. The interest rate on these loans, the main refinancing rate, is the key policy rate. It is set by the ECB Governing Council and indicates the monetary policy stance. An increase in interest rates is referred to as a "tightening" of monetary policy; a decrease is referred to as "loosening".

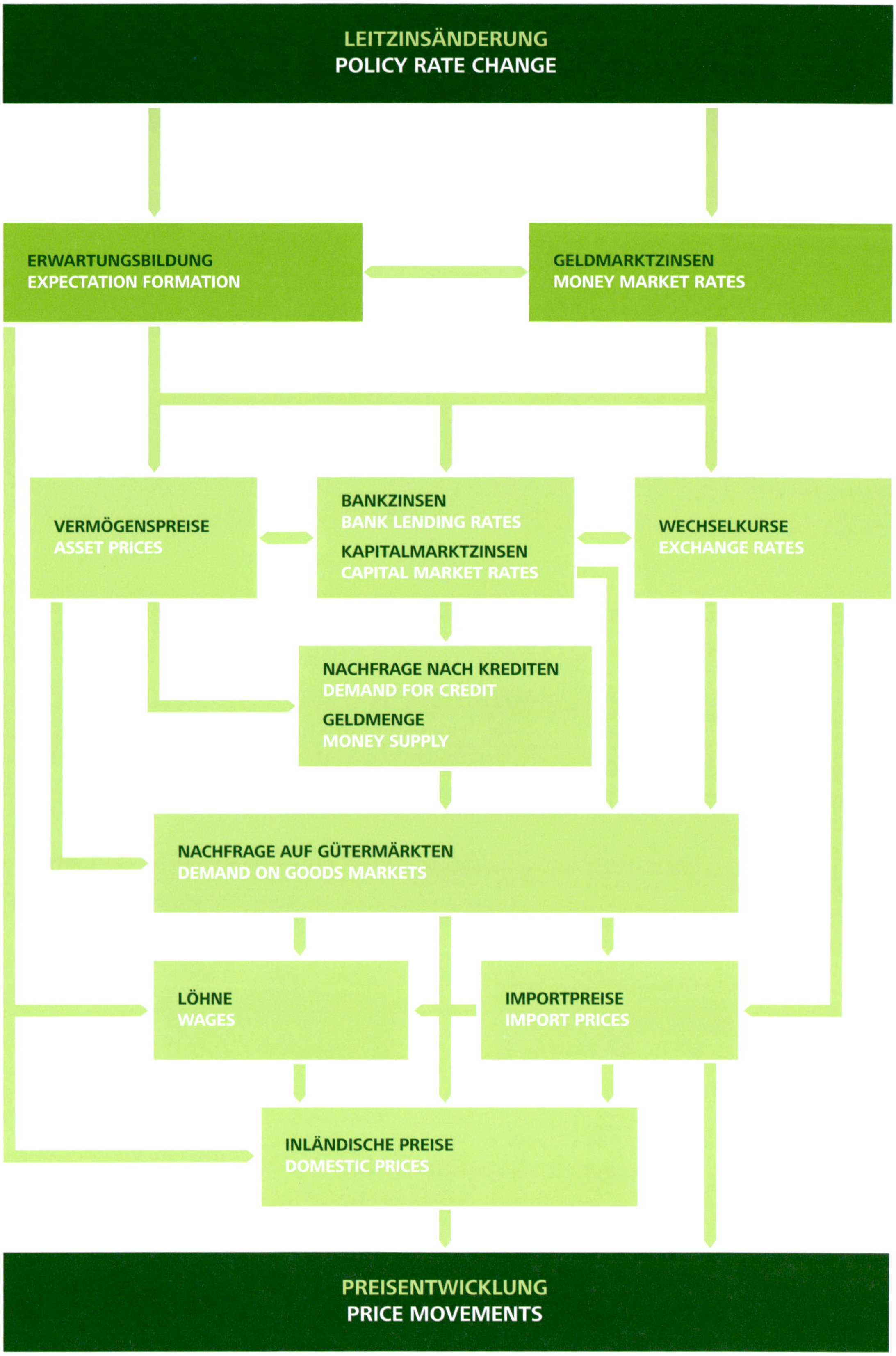

MANY PATHS

TRANSMISSION CHANNELS FOR RATE CHANGES

The ECB Governing Council's policy rate changes are transmitted to prices not only through the interest rate channel but also through several other "transmission channels", such as the asset price or exchange rate channels. This process is complex. Several chains of causality operate at the same time but at different speeds. Some are mutually reinforcing, while others are mutually weakening. In addition, the process can be influenced by external factors such as a change in commodity prices. There is generally a time lag between a change in the policy rate and its impact.

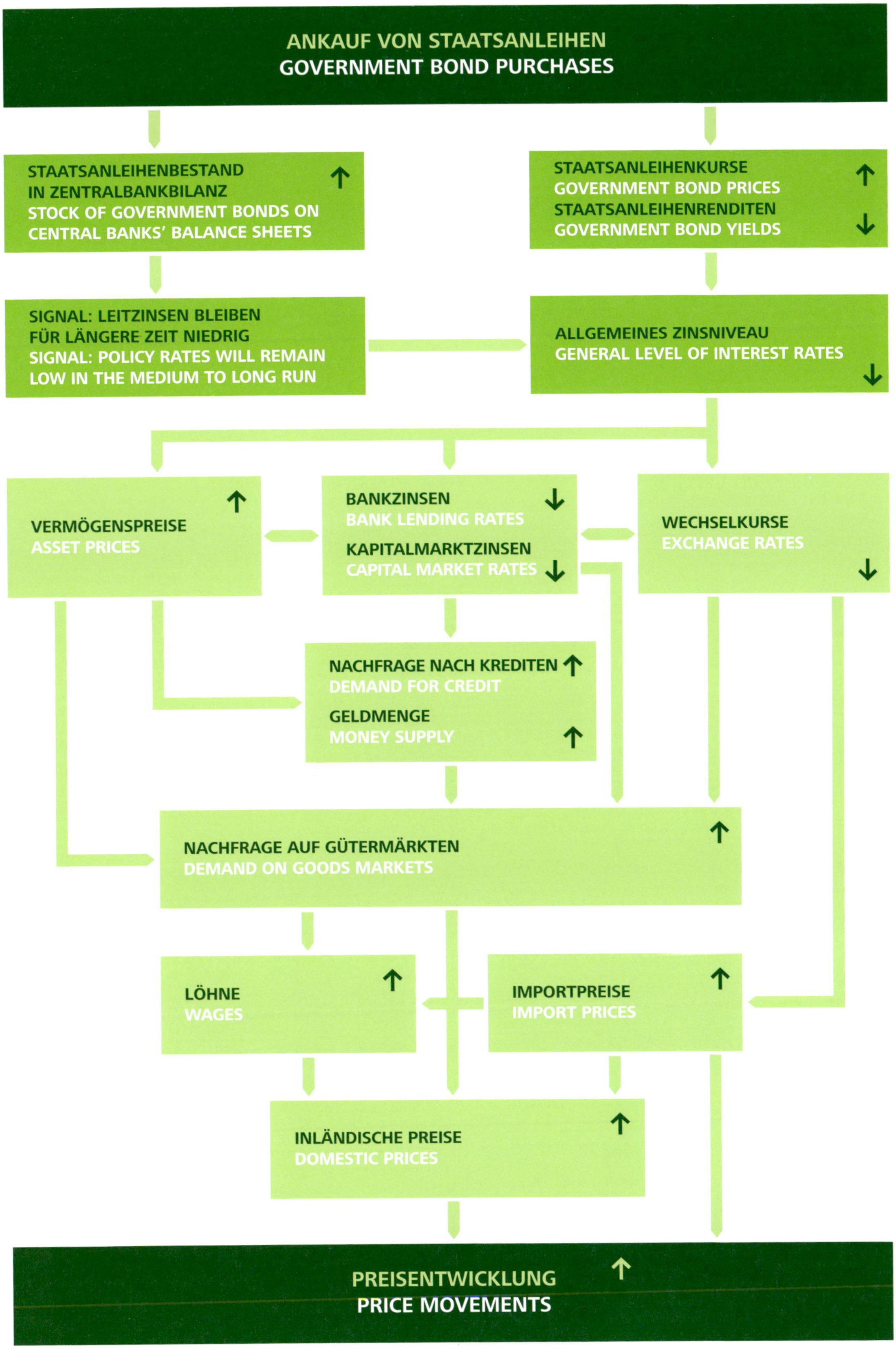

QUANTITATIVE EASING

MONETARY POLICY THROUGH ASSET PURCHASES

If all three of the rates are already nearly zero, interest rate policy approaches its limits. The ECB Governing Council can then take other measures, such as buying government bonds. This drives those assets' prices up, while market interest rates on the bonds fall. Consequently, the general level of interest rates falls as well. That, in turn, fuels credit demand, and the demand for investment and consumer goods rises. By purchasing assets, the central bank creates new central bank money; its quantity increases – hence the term "quantitative easing". This policy is designed to help push the inflation rate up again.

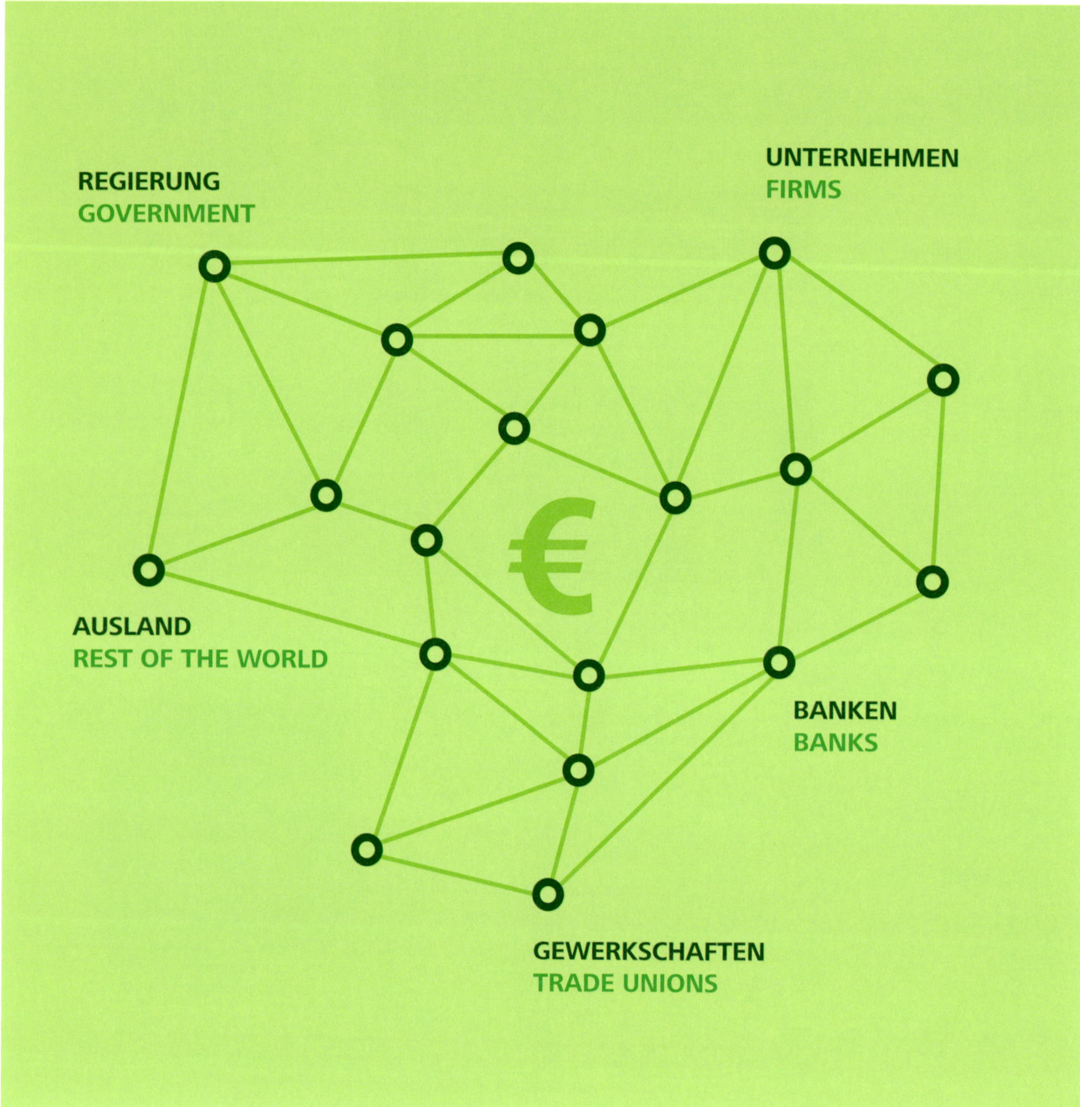

IN A MESH OF INTERESTS

OTHER AGENTS – OTHER AIMS

The Eurosystem's primary objective is price stability. However, monetary policy operates in an environment in which economic agents such as government, trade unions or firms likewise influence price movements. For instance, the government's fiscal policy has an impact on economic developments and consequently on prices. Wage policy also matters, as trade unions typically demand higher wages. If firms take sharp wage hikes into account by raising prices, this can cause inflation to accelerate. Conflicts of interest exist elsewhere, too: savers want higher interest rates, while borrowers want lower interest rates.

TARGET IN SIGHT

MONETARY POLICY MUST STAND FIRM

The Eurosystem has been given a clear legislative mandate: price stability. Monetary policy must pursue this objective – and must not shy away from clashes with other economic agents. Case in point: if employers and employees have caused an inflationary price surge through excessive wage growth, monetary policymakers need to take counteraction – even if higher policy rates temporarily lead to an economic downturn, lower profitability and higher unemployment. Therefore, all economic agents should bear monetary stability in mind in their actions. After all, everyone benefits from price stability.

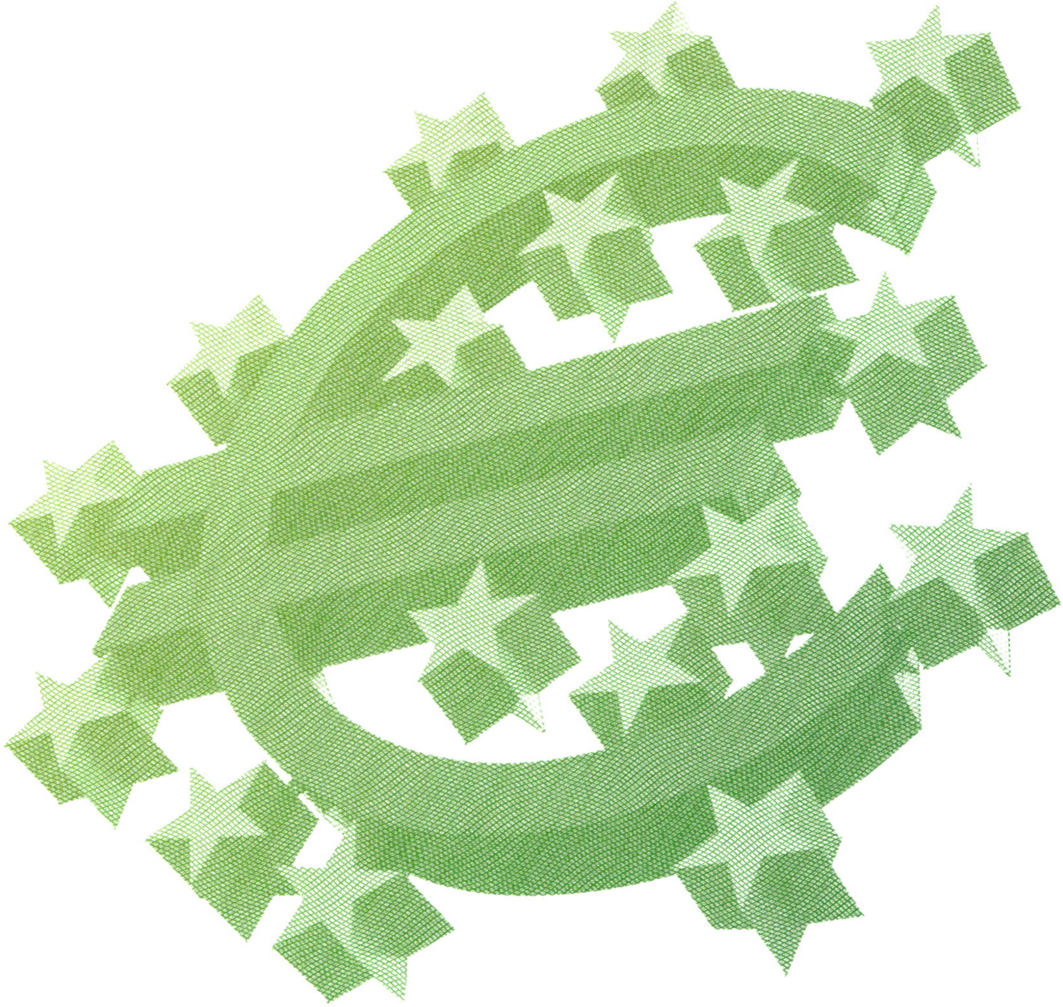

HISTORY'S LESSONS

MONETARY POLICY MUST BE INDEPENDENT

Modern monetary policy is based on confidence in the central bank's ability to keep the value of money stable. To do that, the central bank has to be independent of government instructions. After all, one of history's lessons is that monetary stability is in danger any time a government can hijack the central bank for its political objectives. For instance, politicians are occasionally tempted to finance government spending by "printing money", which can lead to inflation. This is why the independence of the European Central Bank (ECB) and the Eurosystem national central banks is enshrined in law: nobody is permitted to issue instructions to them or force them to take measures that run counter to their mandate.

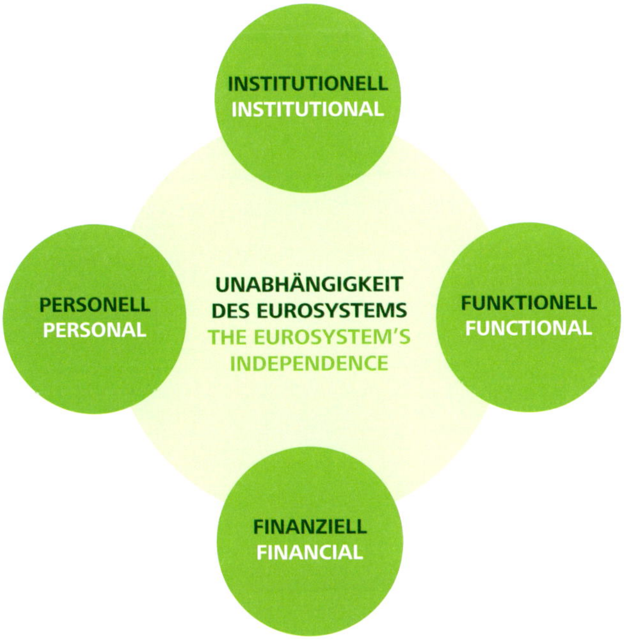

RIGHTS AND DUTIES

LIMITS OF INDEPENDENCE

The Eurosystem's independence is neither an end in itself nor a "blank cheque". It is intended to ensure that monetary policy actions are conducive to stability. In return for its independence, the Eurosystem is obligated to stay within its mandate – it is not allowed to pursue any other political objectives for which, by law, elected parliaments are responsible. It is precisely the political independence of the Eurosystem's central banks which requires them to be transparent: they are accountable to the public for their decisions and the success of their measures. The ECB president therefore regularly reports to the European Parliament and also holds press conferences.

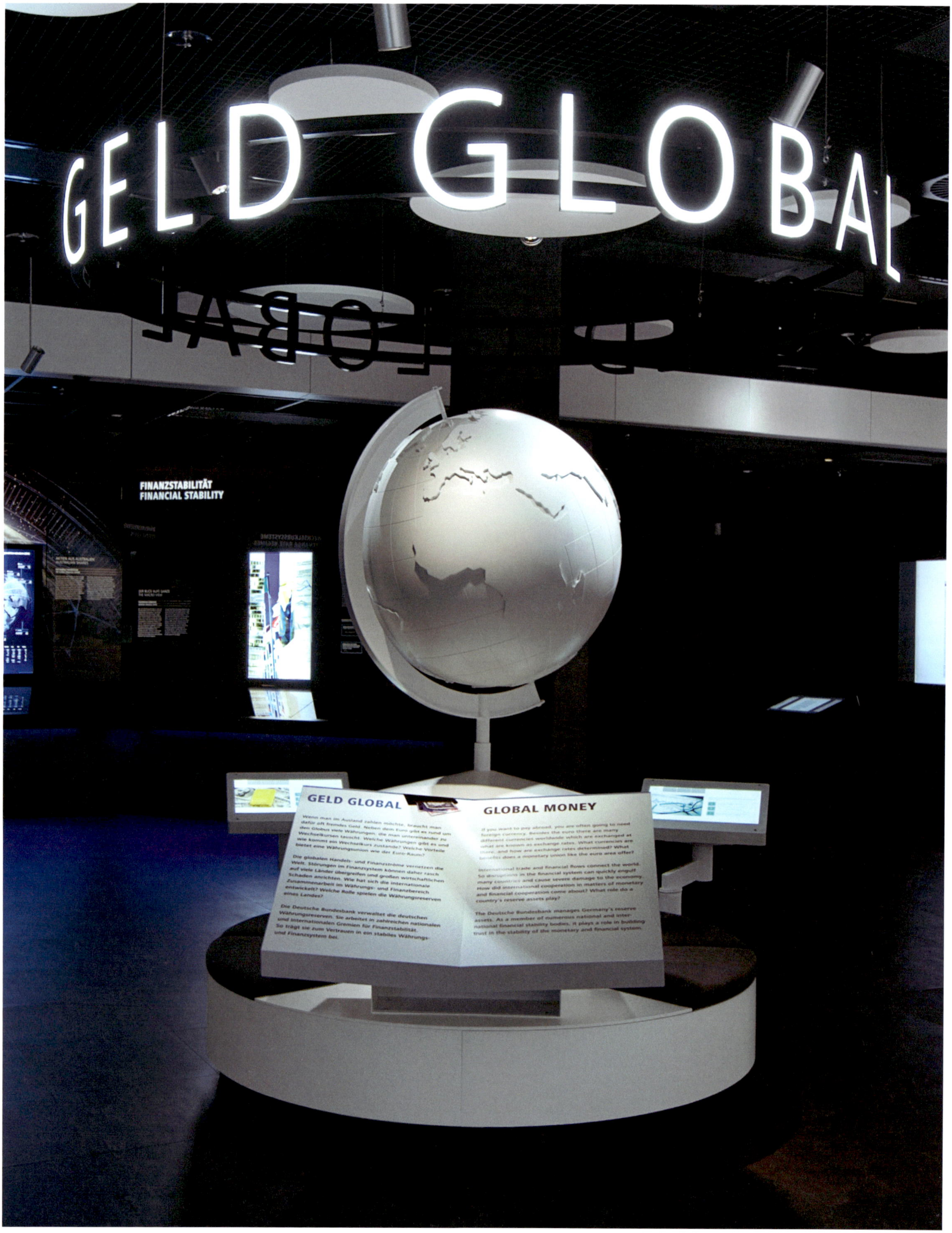
GELD GLOBAL
FINANZSTABILITÄT
FINANCIAL STABILITY
GELD GLOBAL
Wenn man im Ausland zahlen möchte, braucht man dafür oft fremdes Geld. Neben dem Euro gibt es rund um den Globus viele Währungen, die man untereinander zu Wechselkursen tauscht. Welche Währungen gibt es und wie kommt ein Wechselkurs zustande? Welche Vorteile bietet eine Währungsunion wie der Euro-Raum?
Die globalen Handels- und Finanzströme vernetzen die Welt. Störungen im Finanzsystem können daher rasch auf viele Länder übergreifen und großen wirtschaftlichen Schaden anrichten. Wie hat sich die internationale Zusammenarbeit im Währungs- und Finanzbereich entwickelt? Welche Rolle spielen die Währungsreserven eines Landes?
Die Deutsche Bundesbank verwaltet die deutschen Währungsreserven. Sie arbeitet in zahlreichen nationalen und internationalen Gremien für Finanzstabilität. So trägt sie zum Vertrauen in ein stabiles Währungs- und Finanzsystem bei.
GLOBAL MONEY
If you want to pay abroad, you are often going to need foreign currency. Besides the euro there are many different currencies worldwide which are exchanged at what are known as exchange rates. What currencies are there, and how are exchange rates determined? What benefits does a monetary union like the euro area offer?
International trade and financial flows connect the world. So disruptions in the financial system can quickly engulf many countries and cause severe damage to the economy. How did international cooperation in matters of monetary and financial cooperation come about? What role do a country's reserve assets play?
The Deutsche Bundesbank manages Germany's reserve assets. As a member of numerous national and international financial stability bodies, it plays a role in building trust in the stability of the monetary and financial system.

IF YOU WANT TO PAY ABROAD, YOU ARE OFTEN GOING TO NEED FOREIGN CURRENCY. BESIDES THE EURO THERE ARE MANY DIFFERENT CURRENCIES WORLDWIDE WHICH ARE EXCHANGED AT WHAT ARE KNOWN AS EXCHANGE RATES. WHAT CURRENCIES ARE THERE, AND HOW ARE EXCHANGE RATES DETERMINED? WHAT BENEFITS DOES A MONETARY UNION LIKE THE EURO AREA OFFER?

INTERNATIONAL TRADE AND FINANCIAL FLOWS CONNECT THE WORLD. SO DISRUPTIONS IN THE FINANCIAL SYSTEM CAN QUICKLY ENGULF MANY COUNTRIES AND CAUSE SEVERE DAMAGE TO THE ECONOMY. HOW DID INTERNATIONAL COOPERATION IN MATTERS OF MONETARY AND FINANCIAL COOPERATION COME ABOUT? WHAT ROLE DO A COUNTRY'S RESERVE ASSETS PLAY?

THE DEUTSCHE BUNDESBANK MANAGES GERMANY'S RESERVE ASSETS. AS A MEMBER OF NUMEROUS NATIONAL AND INTERNATIONAL FINANCIAL STABILITY BODIES, IT PLAYS A ROLE IN BUILDING TRUST IN THE STABILITY OF THE MONETARY AND FINANCIAL SYSTEM.

GLOBAL MONEY

"WAR, TRADE AND PIRACY ARE THREE IN ONE."

GOETHE, *FAUST II*

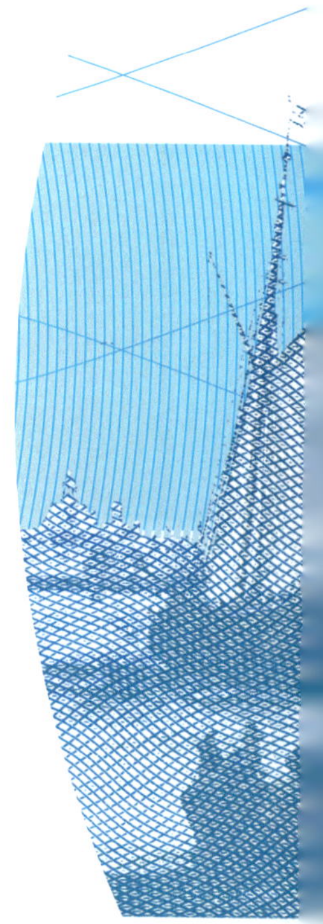

A LOOK BACK THROUGH HISTORY

Globalised trade has been said to exist since as early as the beginning of the 16th century, which heralded the onset of European colonialism. Powerful trading companies such as the Dutch East India Company – founded in 1602 in the Netherlands as the world's first publicly traded company – took control of overseas trade.

At the same time, the variety of currencies interfered with super-regional trade since the Middle Ages. As global trading and financial relations became increasingly interlaced, the need for international monetary cooperation became a matter of growing urgency.

Despite political efforts to create a stable monetary and financial system, time and again speculative bubbles burst, stock markets crashed and financial crises occurred. A detailed look at the financial and sovereign debt crisis triggered in 2007 by the US subprime mortgage crisis will guide the visitor back to the present.

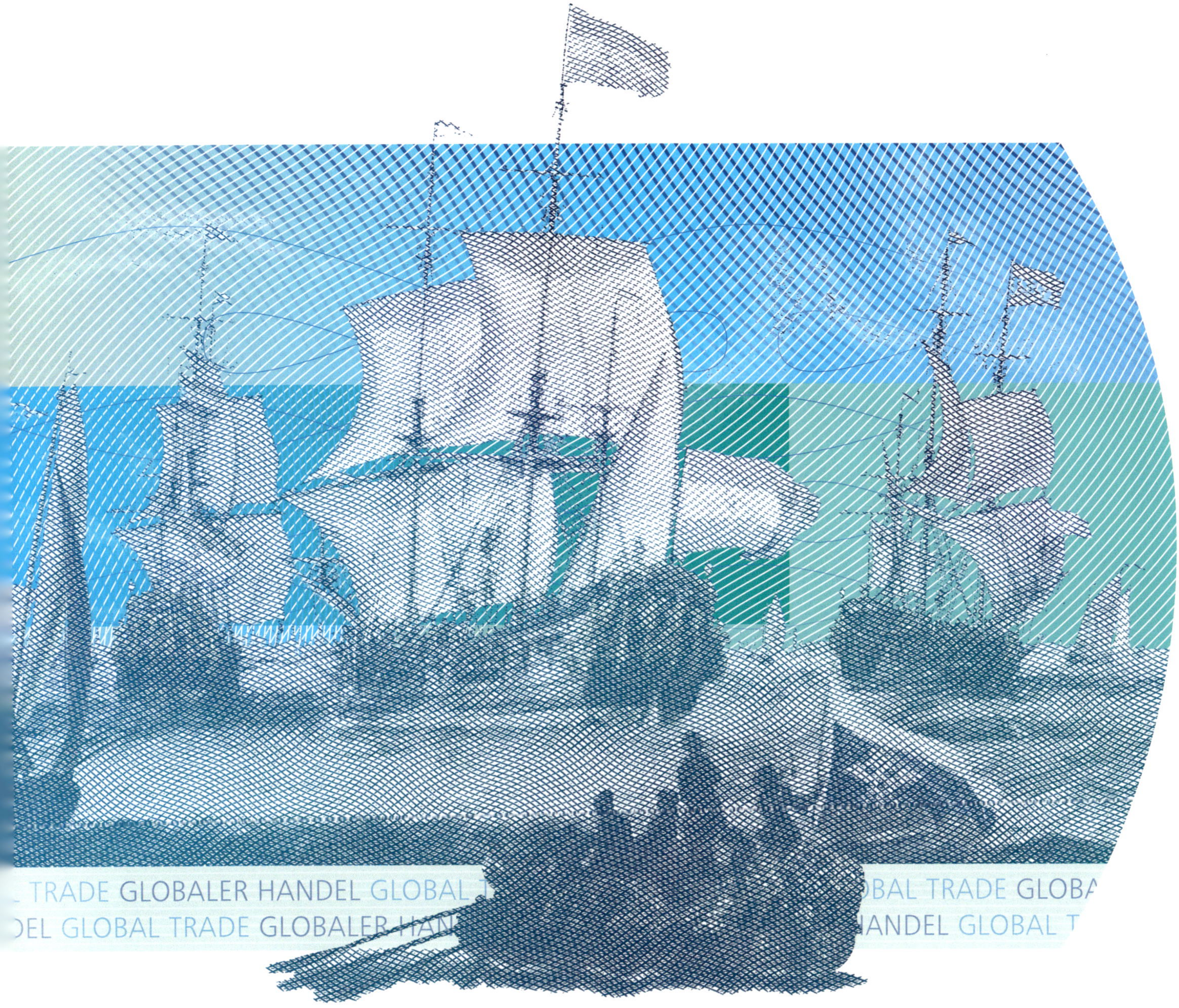
L TRADE GLOBALER HANDEL GLOBAL T
OBAL TRADE GLOBA
DEL GLOBAL TRADE GLOBALER HAN
HANDEL GLOBAL T

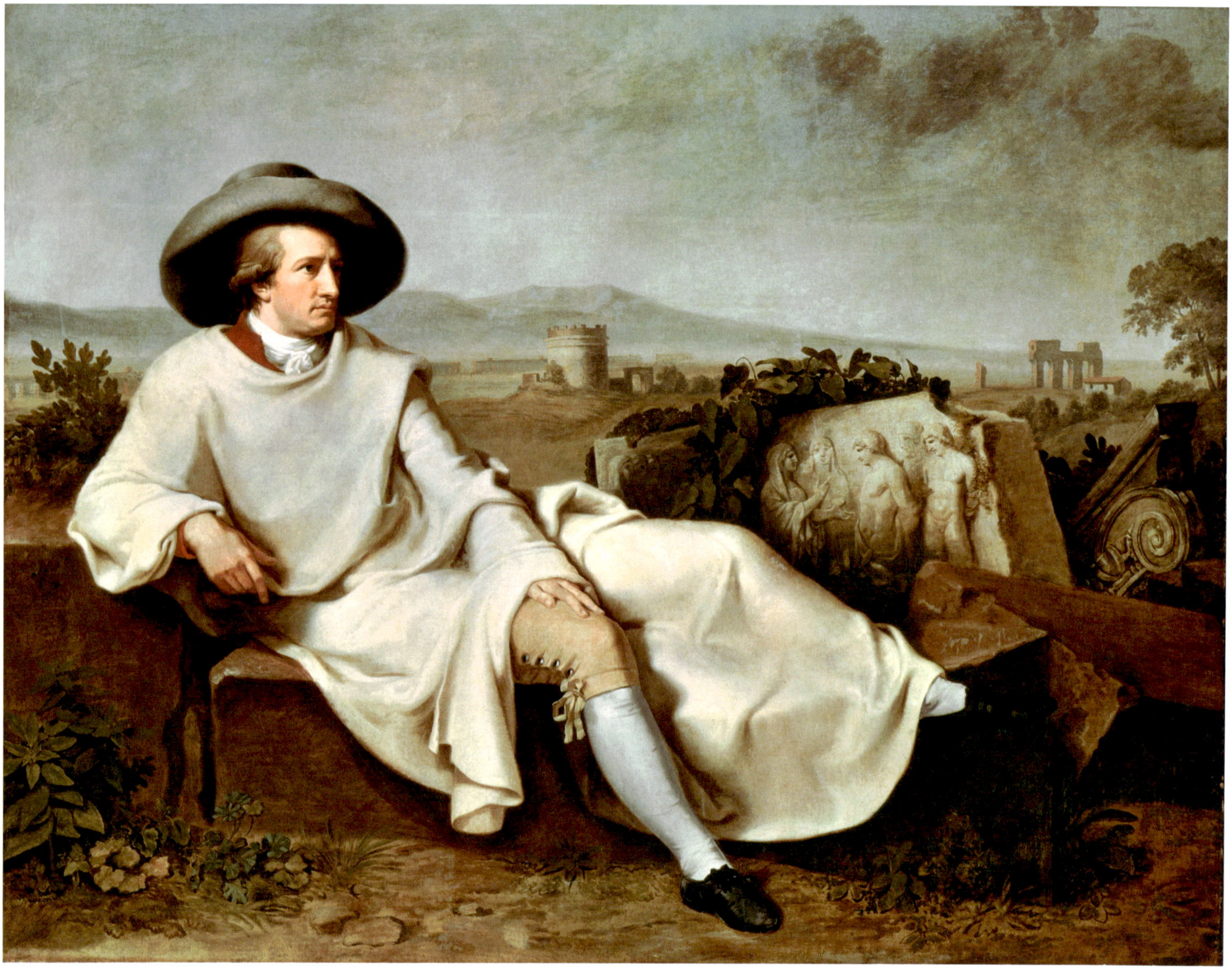

A NETWORKED WORLD

THE DEVELOPMENT OF WORLDWIDE TRADE

The discovery of America in 1492 and the sea route to Asia in 1498 marked the beginning of the age of global trade for Europeans. Spain, Portugal, the Netherlands, Great Britain and France established colonies and trading posts. Merchants formed trading companies to organise worldwide trade, using both diplomatic and military means to attain their economic goals. They imported luxury goods from Asia, such as spices, silk and porcelain. Atlantic triangular trade between Europe, Africa and America mainly involved weapons and metal goods (from Europe to Africa), slaves (from Africa to America) and sugar and tobacco (from America to Europe).

CHAOS IN GOETHE'S PURSE

MANY CURRENCIES MAKE TRAVEL DIFFICULT

In a report on his travels in Italy from 1786 to 1788, Johann Wolfgang von Goethe complained about having to change money daily. The many Italian states each had their own currency, and there were foreign coins in circulation as well. In fact, when Goethe checked his finances in Rome, he found seven different types of coins in his purse. Following the collapse of the Roman Empire, the variety of coins in Europe impaired not only travel, but, above all, trade. Money changers took advantage of this. Travellers and long-distance traders used them to exchange their coins from one currency to another – for a fee.

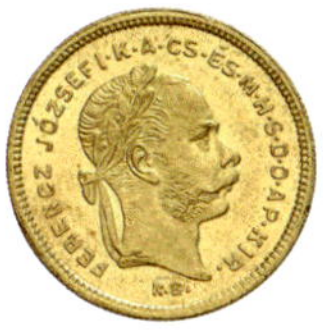

130

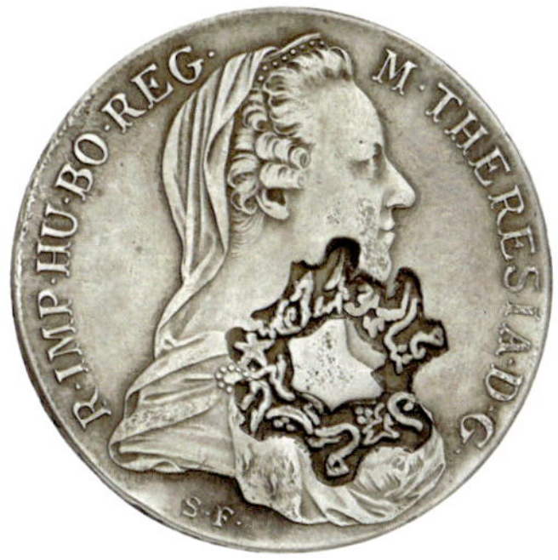

131

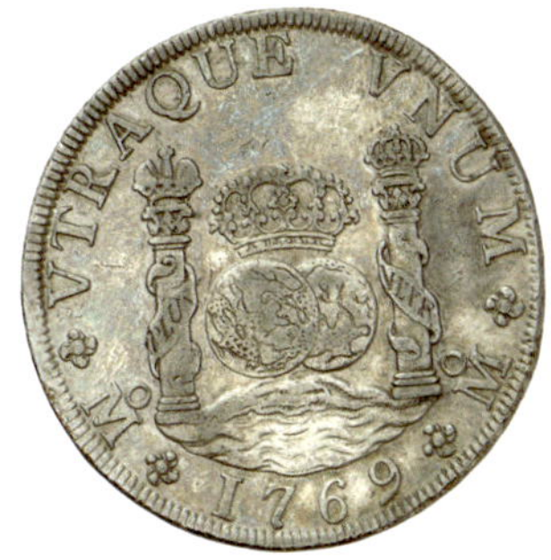

132

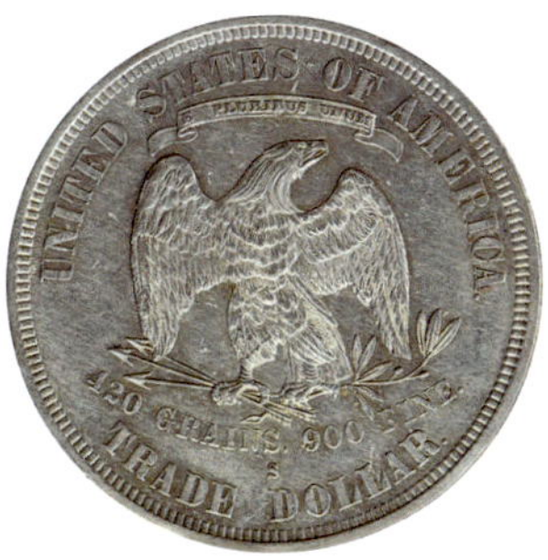

133

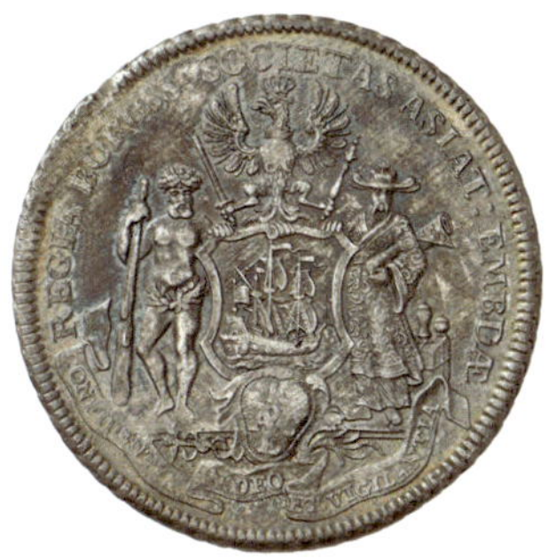

134

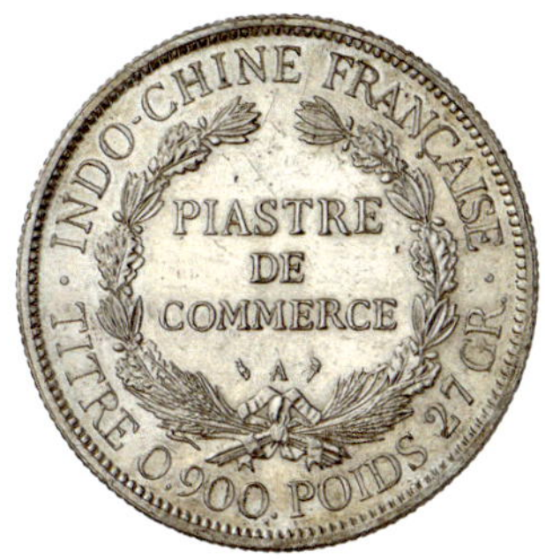

135

130 **DUCAT**
1877

131 **MARIA THERESA THALER**
1890/1892

132 **PIASTER (8 REALES)**
1769

133 **TRADE DOLLAR**
1877

134 **PRUSSIAN HANDELSPIASTER**
1751

135 **PIASTRE DE COMMERCE**
1901

INTERNATIONAL RECOGNITION

COINS FOR GLOBAL TRADE

The variety of coins worldwide made interregional trade difficult. Although exchanging European coins via money changers in Asia and Africa was possible, it was arduous and expensive. That is why from the 17th century some countries minted coins specifically for foreign trade. These trading coins corresponded to the weight and metal content of the coins that were circulating in the intended area of use. The issuing countries guaranteed their quality, which meant trading coins were widely recognised.

Some coins such as the ducat or the Maria Theresa thaler were so widely used that they were also recognised as a means of payment in international trade. New coins minted specifically for trade with East Asia such as the American trade dollar, the Prussian trade piaster and the French *piastre de commerce* were based on the most popular large silver coin at the time – the Spanish piaster (8-real coin).

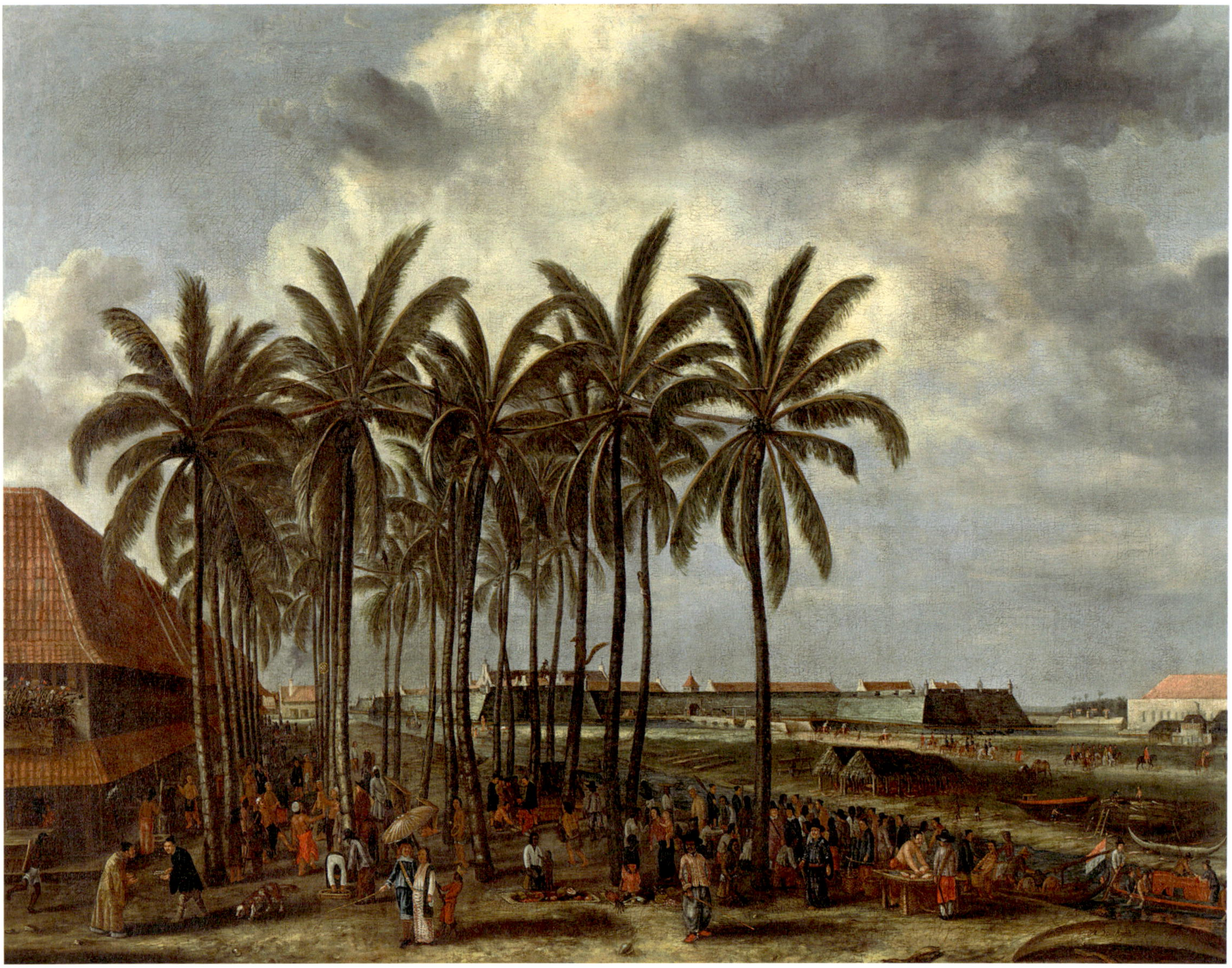

IN 1619, THE VOC CONQUERED THE CITY OF JAYAKARTA (NOW JAKARTA) AND, UNDER THE NAME BATAVIA, MADE IT ITS MOST IMPORTANT BASE IN ASIA.

THE FIRST JOINT STOCK COMPANY

THE VEREENIGDE OOSTINDISCHE COMPAGNIE (VOC)

In 1602, Dutch merchants founded the "Dutch East India Company" (VOC). It received a trade monopoly from the government for the entire Asia-Pacific region. Moreover, it was allowed to wage war in its trading area, and could acquire land and conclude treaties which were valid under international law. New ground was broken in the choice of business form, given that the VOC was the world's first joint stock company. In the 17th century, the VOC gained control over the lucrative trade in spices such as pepper, nutmeg, cloves and cinnamon. VOC shares were therefore a sought-after investment for decades. At the end of the 18th century, however, the VOC increasingly got into difficulties, and was finally dissolved.

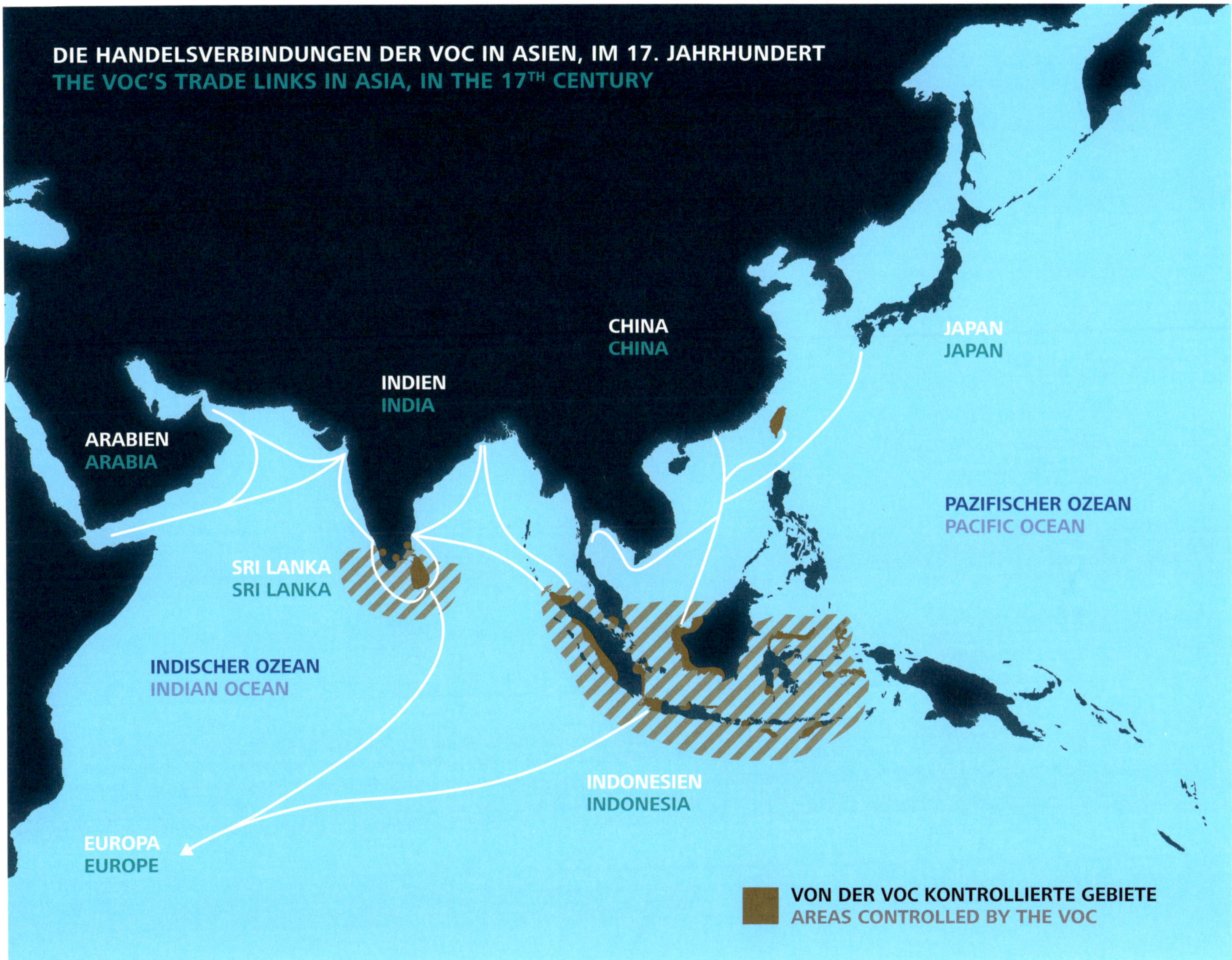

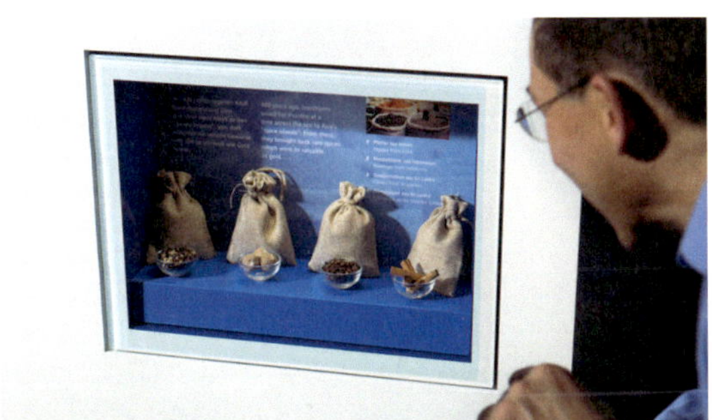

AS VALUABLE AS GOLD

400 YEARS AGO, MERCHANTS SAILED FOR MONTHS AT A TIME ACROSS THE SEA TO ASIA'S "SPICE ISLANDS". FROM THERE, THEY BROUGHT BACK RARE SPICES WHICH WERE AS VALUABLE AS GOLD.

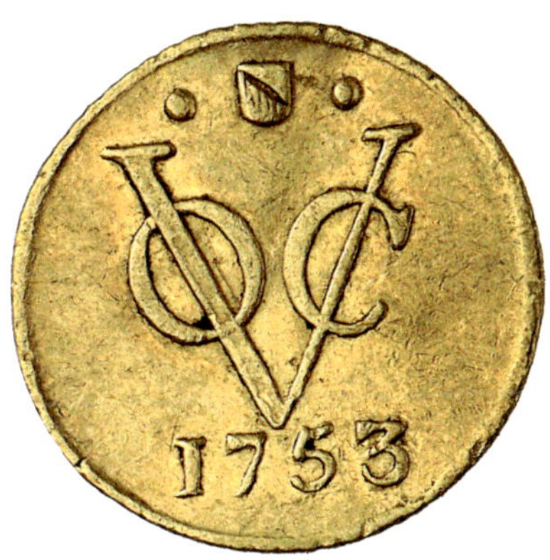

THE VOC HAD LARGE AMOUNTS OF GOLD, SILVER AND COPPER COINS MINTED FOR ITS TERRITORIES IN THE FAR EAST, PARTLY IN THE NETHERLANDS AND PARTLY IN ASIA ITSELF. MOST OF THE COINS BORE THE MONOGRAM VOC.

136 ½ **DUIT IN GOLD**
1753 (SCALE 3:1)

RHINEGOLD

THE RHENISH MONETARY UNION

In the Holy Roman Empire of the German Nation, there was a variety of currencies in circulation. This impaired trade. In order to create a stable common currency in their territories, the four Rhenish electoral princes joined forces in 1385 to form the "Rhenish Monetary Union". This monetary union was renewed time and again in subsequent contracts and occasionally also expanded. The last contract was concluded in 1515. The Rhenish Monetary Union became the most important monetary union in medieval Germany. The signatories harmonised their coinages. The goldgulden came to particular prominence: it was one of the most important coins in Europe in the Late Middle Ages.

MONEY BACKED BY GOLD

THE INTERNATIONAL GOLD STANDARD

In 1844, the United Kingdom introduced the gold standard by law to guarantee the value of Bank of England banknotes. The bank was permitted to print new banknotes only if the gold reserves were increased accordingly, since they had to be able to readily exchange their banknotes for gold coins. Numerous countries followed suit, including all major industrial nations, such as the USA, Germany, France and Japan. Hence, the international gold standard came into being. It was not based on contractually regulated cooperation, but solely on the currencies' link to gold. With the outbreak of World War I in 1914, the belligerent countries rescinded the legal obligation to redeem their banknotes for gold, thus ending the gold standard.

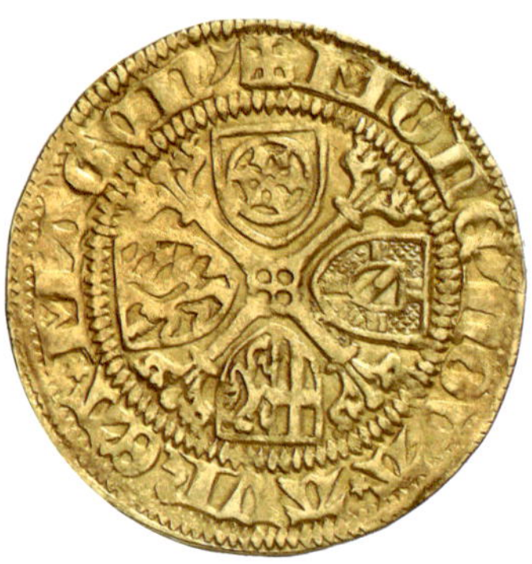

137 **GOLDGULDEN,** 1464/1465 (SCALE 2:1)

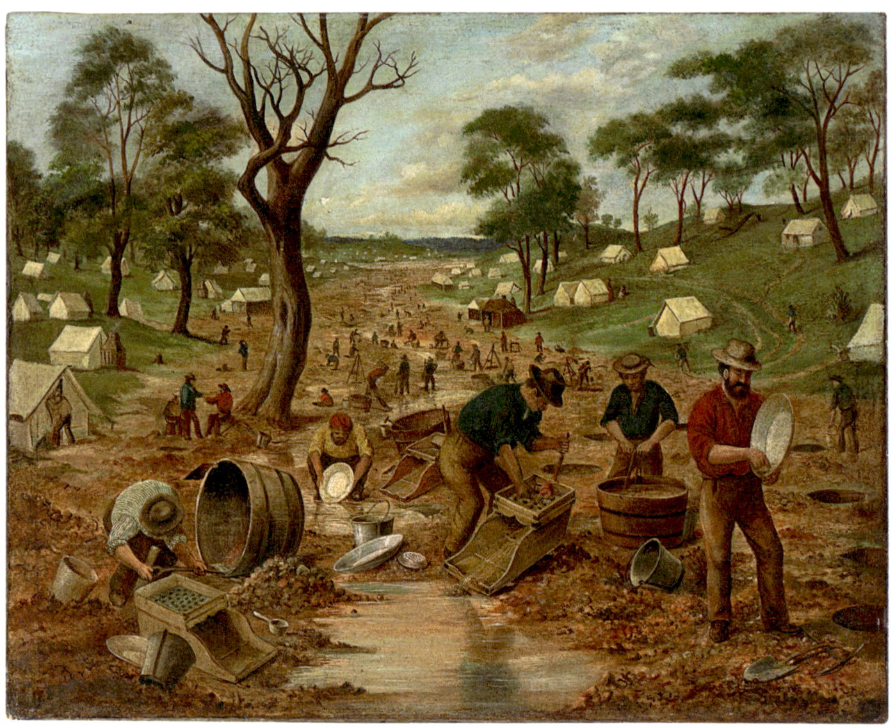

FROM THE MID-19TH CENTURY, LARGE GOLD DEPOSITS WERE DISCOVERED IN CALIFORNIA, AUSTRALIA, ALASKA AND SOUTH AFRICA – THE BASIS FOR THE GOLD STANDARD.

FIXED EXCHANGE RATES WORLDWIDE

THE BRETTON WOODS MONETARY SYSTEM

In July 1944, a United Nations conference took place in Bretton Woods (New Hampshire, USA). Delegates established a world monetary system with fixed exchange rates and the US dollar as its reserve currency. The United States central banking system guaranteed to redeem the member states' dollar reserves at a fixed rate in gold. The other central banks had to ensure the fixed exchange rate of their currency to the US dollar through their monetary policy. The new monetary system sought to facilitate world trade and promote reconstruction after World War II. West Germany joined the Bretton Woods system in 1952. Since the member states' economies developed differently, the fixed exchange rates had to be changed time and again. The Bretton Woods system finally collapsed in 1973.

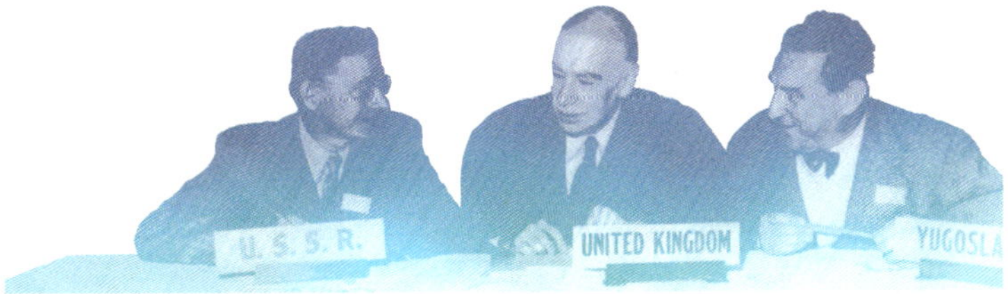

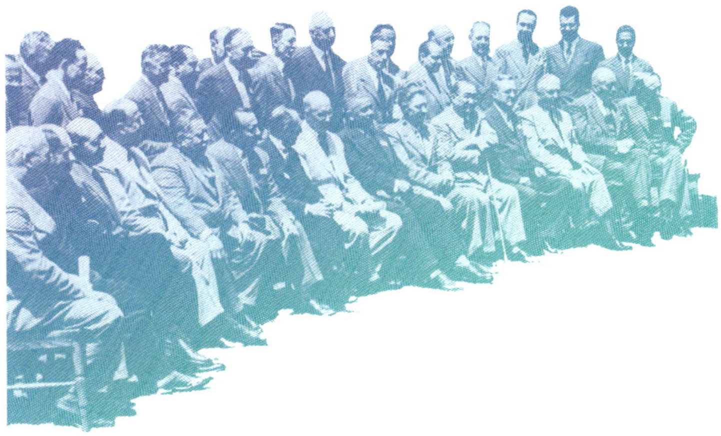

THE "INTERNATIONAL MONETARY FUND" (IMF) AND THE "INTERNATIONAL BANK FOR RECONSTRUCTION AND DEVELOPMENT" (WORLD BANK) WERE CONCEIVED DURING THE BRETTON WOODS CONFERENCE.

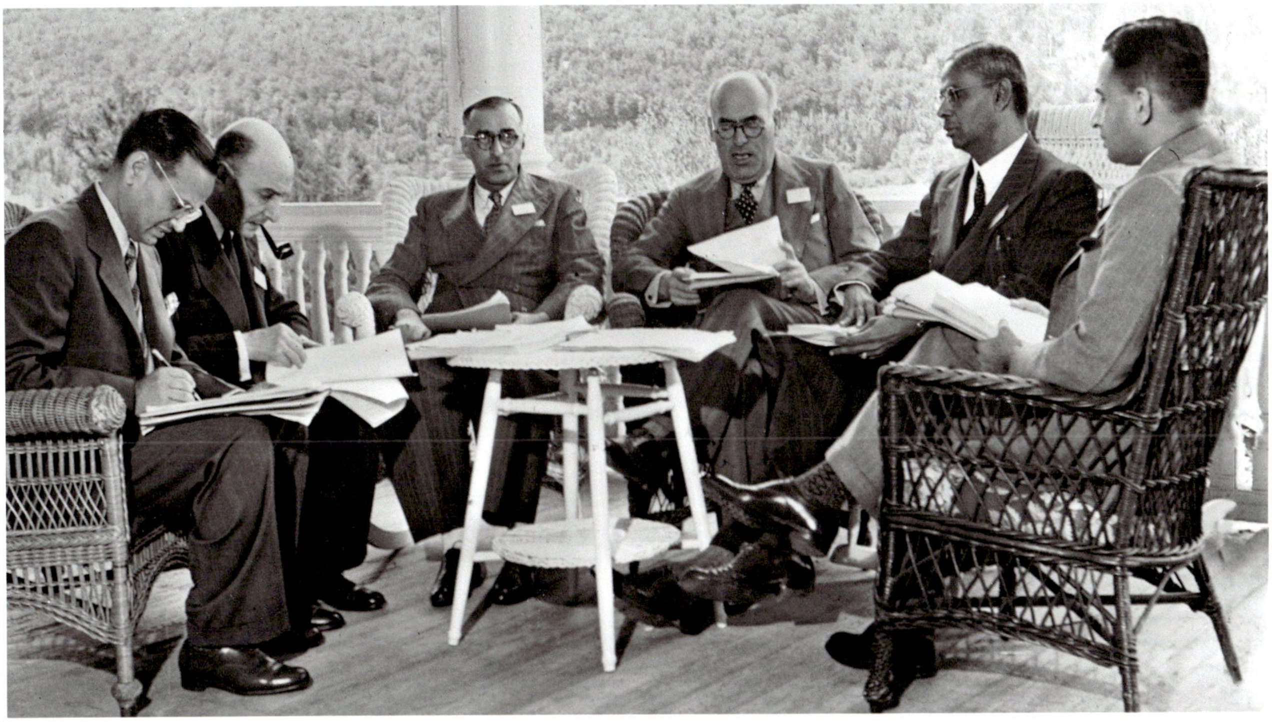

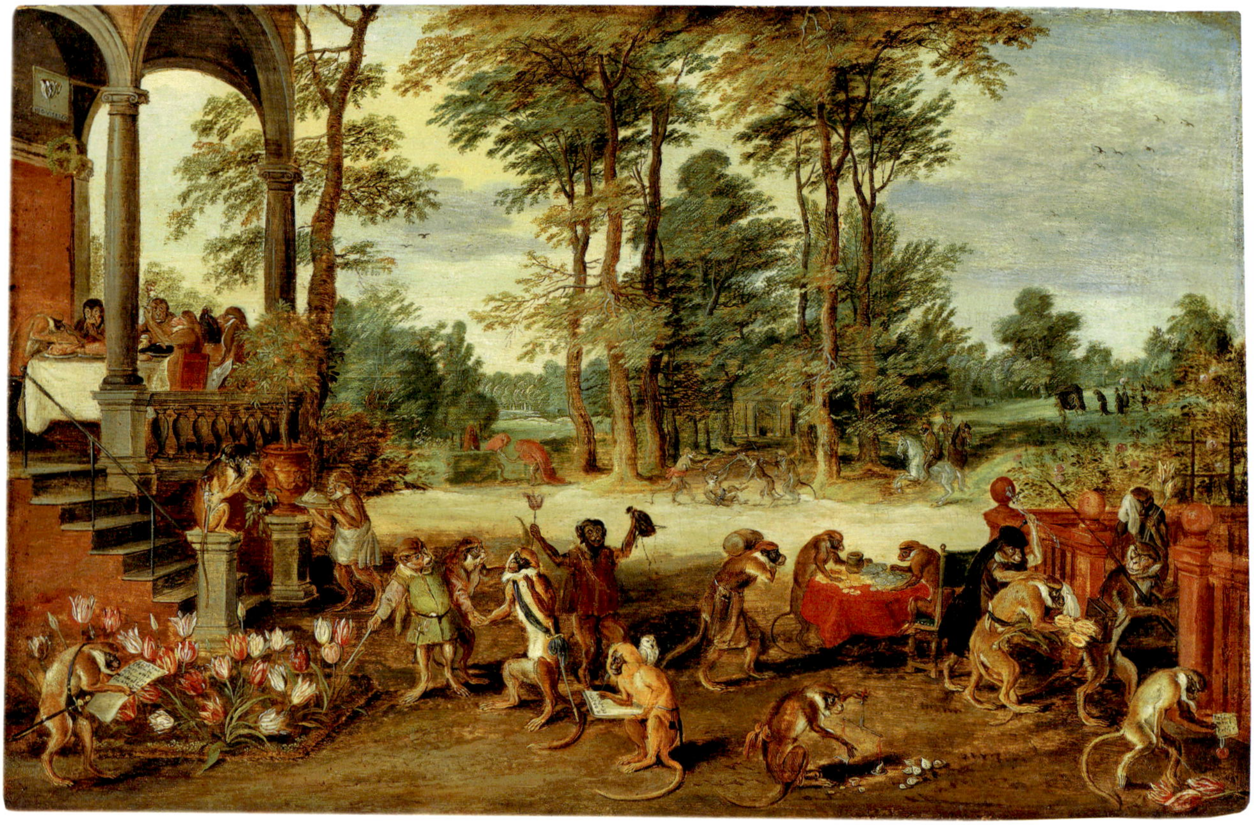

WITH HIS SATIRE ON TULIP MANIA, JAN BRUEGHEL THE YOUNGER MOCKED THE FOOLISHNESS OF HIS CONTEMPORARIES. HE PORTRAYED THE TULIP SPECULATORS AS MONKEYS.

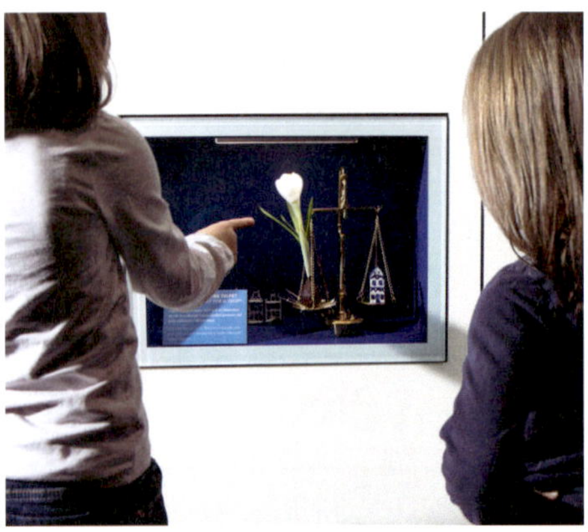

THAT MUCH MONEY FOR A TULIP?

UNBELIEVABLE: IN 1637, THERE WERE PEOPLE WHO PAID JUST AS MUCH MONEY FOR A SINGLE TULIP BULB AS FOR A HOUSE.

WHEN BUBBLES BURST

FROM SPECULATION TO CRISIS

As global trade increased and financial markets became more networked, the risk of financial crises also grew. They were frequently triggered by waves of speculation: the prices of certain goods or securities rose rapidly. The prospect of quick profits attracted more and more investors to the market and prices skyrocketed. However, as soon as doubt arose as to the further advancement of price growth, investors tried to sell as quickly as possible. This caused prices to fall. The speculative bubble burst – often with serious implications for the entire economy. This pattern is not only typical of modern stock market crashes and financial crises, but could also be observed back in the 17th century with "tulip mania".

BETTING ON GROWTH

THE TULIP BUBBLE IN THE NETHERLANDS

The tulip, which originated in Asia, was first brought to Europe in the 16th century. In the Netherlands, the exotic plant quickly became an object of prestige for wealthy flower lovers. Botanists cultivated more and more new varieties and dealers developed an elaborate auction system. "Tulip mania" swept the country. In the 1630s, speculators – who were only interested in the profitable reselling – heated up the market with option transactions. It was no longer the tulips themselves which were traded, but instead the purchase right for flowers which still had to grow from the bulbs in the ground. The prices skyrocketed – until they suddenly crashed at an auction in Haarlem in February 1637. The speculative bubble had burst.

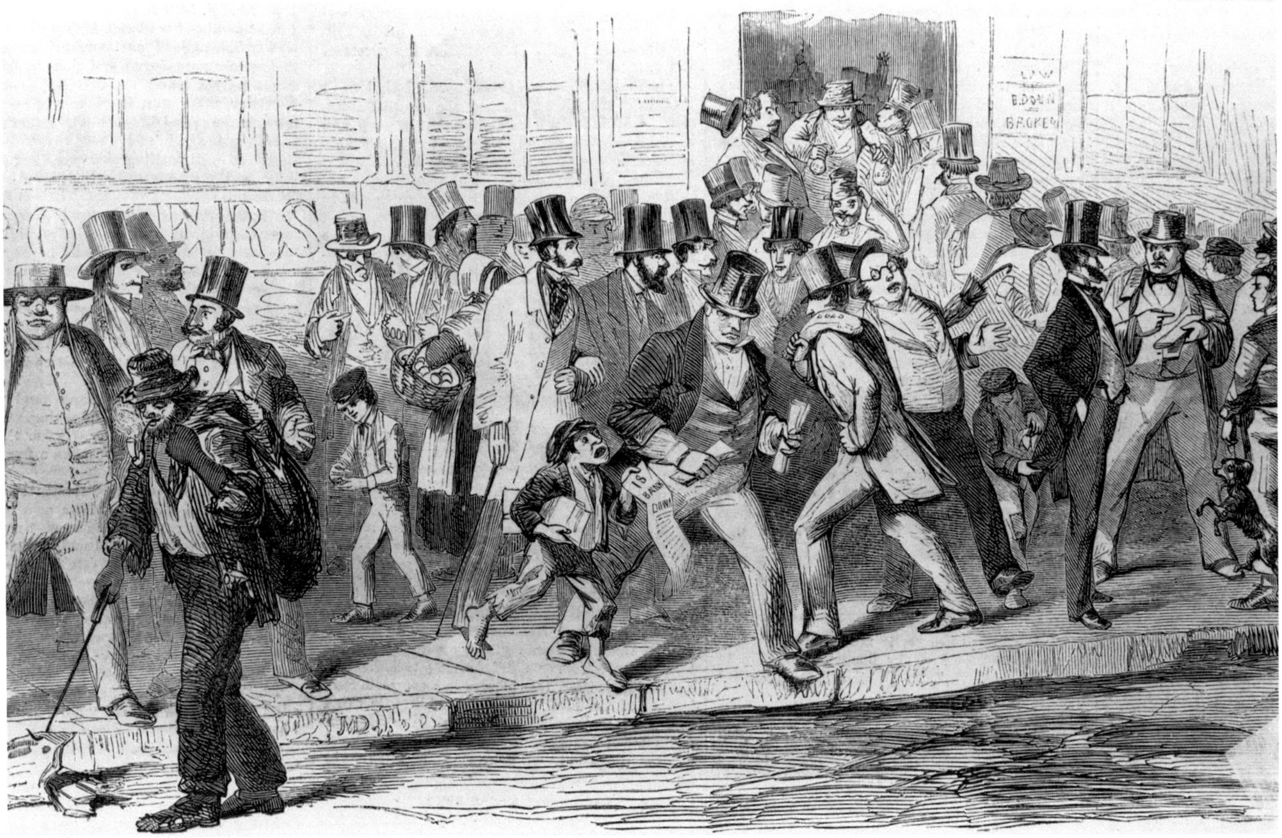

IN AUTUMN 1857, THERE WERE BANK RUNS IN MANY CITIES ACROSS THE USA: AFRAID THAT BANKS MIGHT BECOME INSOLVENT, INVESTORS STORMED THE COUNTERS AND WITHDREW THEIR MONEY.

FIRST OF ITS KIND

GLOBAL DEPRESSION 1857–1859

The bankruptcy of the Ohio Life Insurance and Trust Company triggered the first worldwide economic crisis. On 24 August 1857, the financial institution had to stop its payments following failed investments in railway shares. Banks which had provided loans to Ohio Life got into difficulties themselves – and pulled their own investors into the downward spiral with them. On 13 October 1857, the banks in the financial centre New York ran out of money. Thousands of companies in the USA collapsed. Within weeks the crisis reached Europe: first the United Kingdom, then Germany, where, particularly in Hamburg, numerous trading houses went bankrupt. Soon after, it hit South America and India. The economy did not recover again until 1859.

THE WALL STREET CRASH

THE GREAT DEPRESSION 1929–1933

In autumn 1929, the economic boom of the 1920s ended with a massive slump in prices on the New York Stock Exchange. America entered a deflationary downward spiral. Because of economic interlinkages between the industrial nations, the crisis spread around the globe. World trade fell by two-thirds. Germany was particularly affected by this: industrial production sank by more than 40 per cent and the unemployment rate rose to over 30 per cent. After the Great Depression peaked in 1932, the economy did recover, but the effects of the crisis persisted for quite some time.

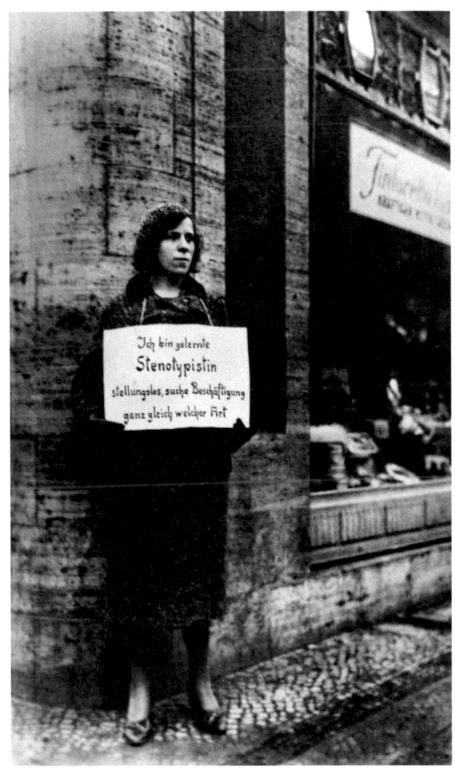

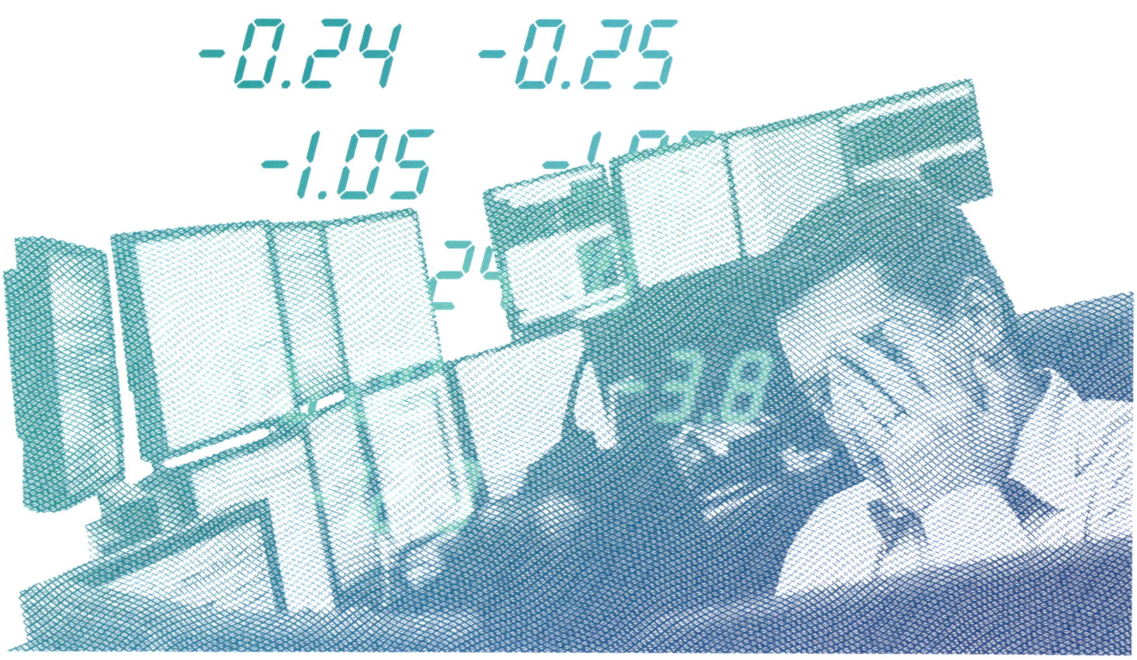

NO END TO THE CRISES?

SUBPRIME CRISIS IN THE USA IN 2007

The most severe post-war financial and economic crisis to date broke out in the summer of 2007, triggered by US banks' overly generous mortgage lending to low-income customers (subprime loans). Many borrowers were unable to afford the interest and principal payments on their properties and were forced to sell up. This caused prices to collapse, triggering a downward spiral: falling property prices led to rising unemployment in the construction industry, bankruptcies in the real estate sector and losses among banks. Further panic selling in the US real estate market ensued. Many households suffered financially and had to limit their consumption. The crisis spread ever further.

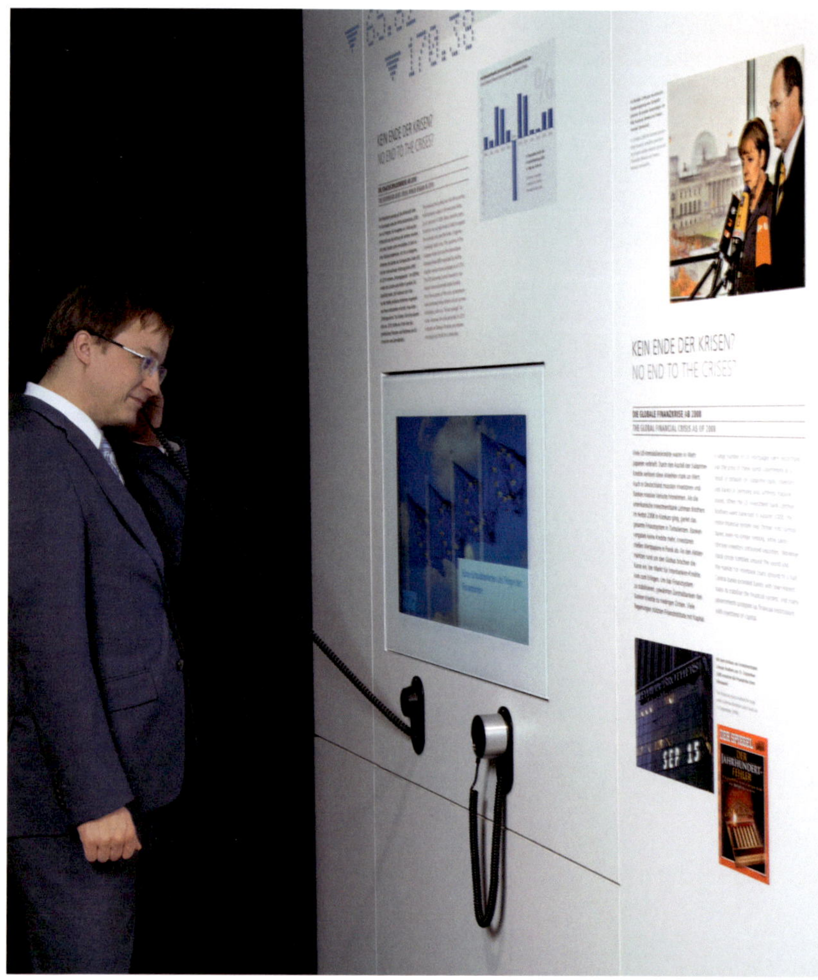

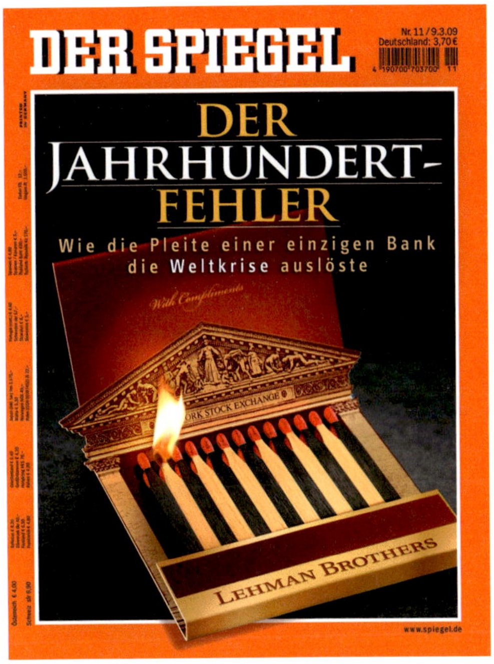

NO END TO THE CRISES?

THE GLOBAL FINANCIAL CRISIS AS OF 2008

A large number of US mortgages were securitised, and the price of these bonds plummeted as a result of defaults on subprime loans. Investors and banks in Germany also suffered massive losses. When the US investment bank Lehman Brothers went bankrupt in autumn 2008, the entire financial system was thrown into turmoil. Banks were no longer lending, while panicstricken investors jettisoned securities. Moreover, stock prices tumbled around the world and the market for interbank loans ground to a halt. Central banks provided banks with low-interest loans to stabilise the financial system, and many governments propped up financial institutions with injections of capital.

GROSS DOMESTIC PRODUCT (GDP) IN GERMANY, PERCENTAGE CHANGE

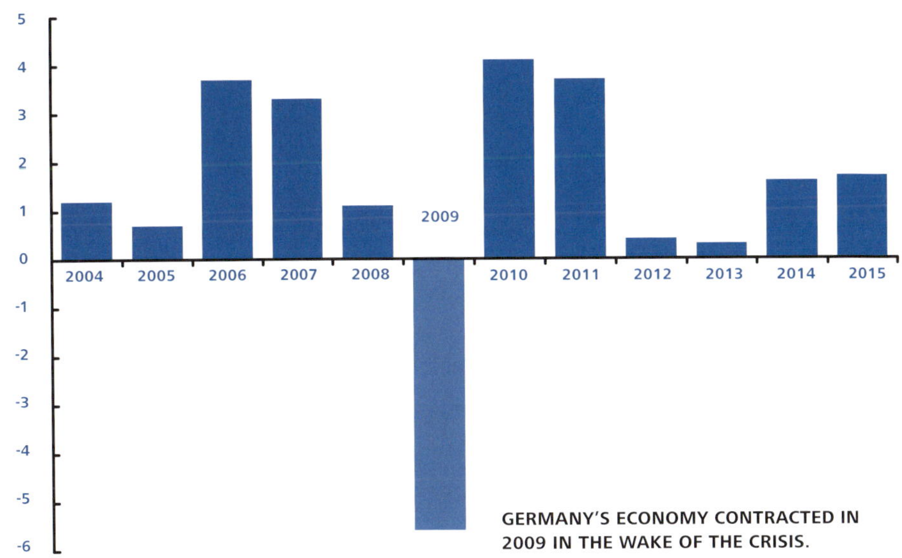

NO END TO THE CRISES?

THE SOVEREIGN DEBT CRISIS WHICH BEGAN IN 2010

The financial crisis spilled over into the economy, with economic output in the euro area falling by 4.5 per cent in 2009. Many countries were forced to rack up high levels of debt to support the economy and save the banks, triggering a sovereign debt crisis. The countries of the European Union (EU) and the International Monetary Fund (IMF) responded by putting together several rescue packages as of 2010. The ECB Governing Council lowered its key interest rate and provided ample liquidity. Since the outbreak of the crisis, governments have introduced many reforms and set up new institutions, such as a "rescue package" for states. However, the crisis persisted. In 2015 a dispute on Greece's finances and reforms once again put the EU to a severe test.

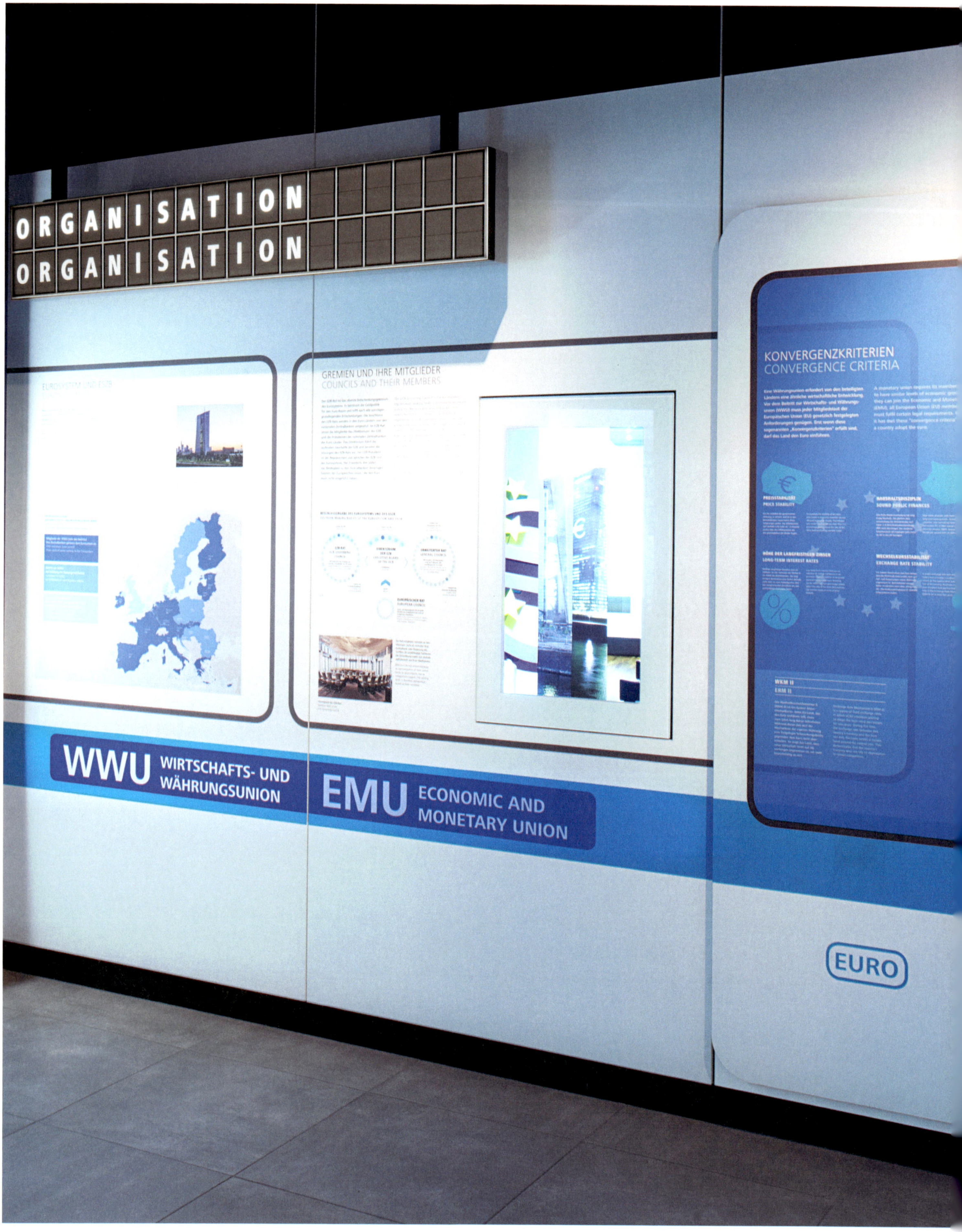
ORGANISATION
ORGANISATION
GREMIEN UND IHRE MITGLIEDER
COUNCILS AND THEIR MEMBERS
KONVERGENZKRITERIEN
CONVERGENCE CRITERIA
WWU WIRTSCHAFTS- UND WÄHRUNGSUNION
EMU ECONOMIC AND MONETARY UNION
EURO

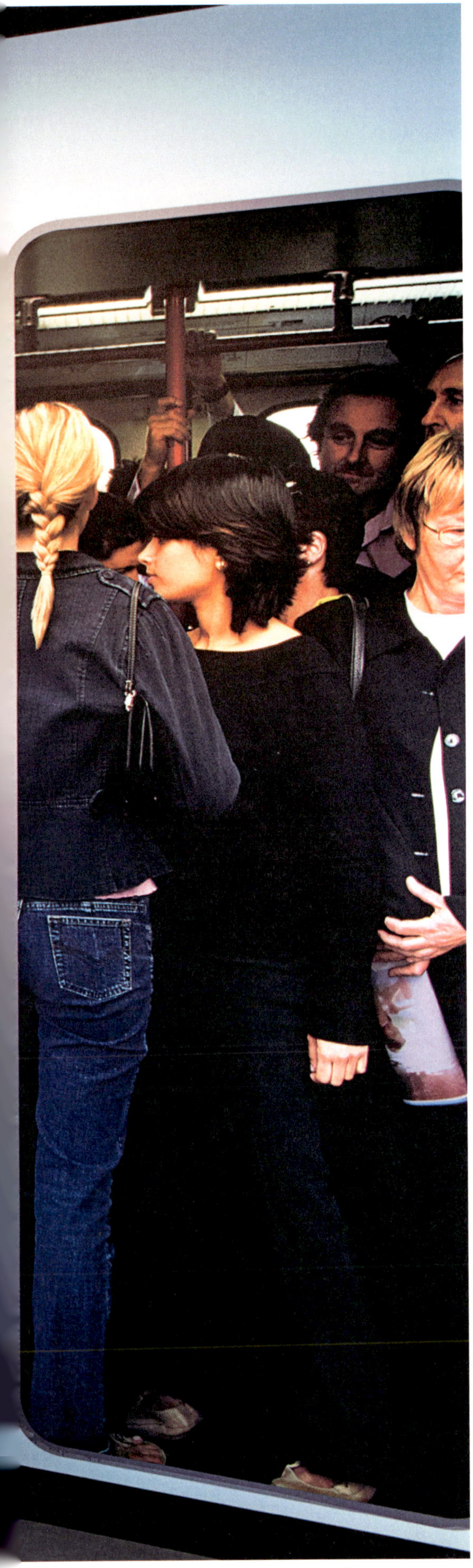

ECONOMIC AND MONETARY UNION (EMU)

A jumble of voices and announcements on loudspeakers, trains screeching along tracks, the hissing of brakes – these sounds, typical of railway stations, form the atmospheric background to this cabinet, which will take the visitor on a grand European voyage to economic and monetary union.

The visitor can already interactively call up the individual stops on the long journey to the single currency, from the establishment of the European Coal and Steel Community in 1951 to the introduction of the euro in 1999 as book money and in 2002 in physical form. The newsstand displays the front pages of newspapers from all over Europe on the day the euro was introduced in each respective country; the newsagent recounts his memories of the currency changeover.

The Deutsche Bundesbank's political independence and commitment to price stability served as a blueprint when designing the European Central Bank and the Eurosystem. The charts and monitors discuss in detail the contractual regulatory framework and the institutional structure of Europe's institutions, highlight their benefits – but also critically address the political and economic challenges.

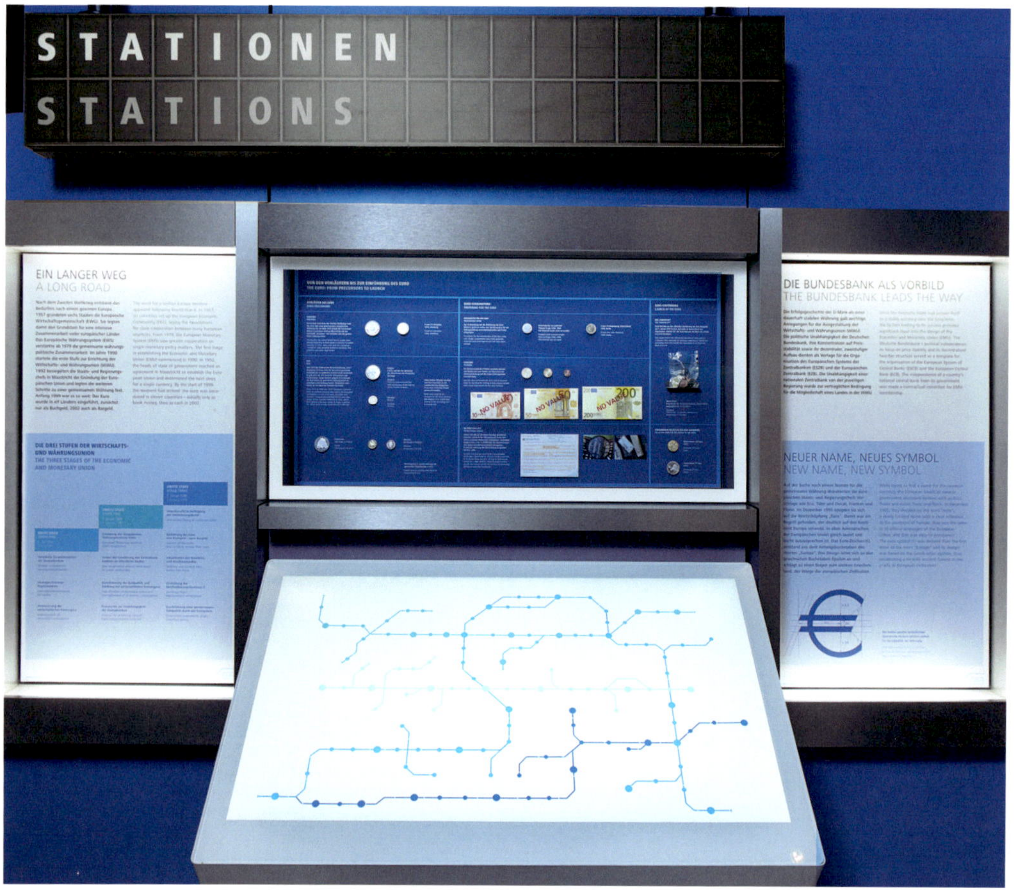

A LONG ROAD

The need for a unified Europe became apparent following World War II. In 1957, six countries set up the European Economic Community (EEC), laying the foundations for close cooperation between many European countries. From 1979, the European Monetary System (EMS) saw greater cooperation on single monetary policy matters. The first stage in establishing the Economic and Monetary Union (EMU) commenced in 1990. In 1992, the heads of state or government reached an agreement in Maastricht to establish the European Union and determined the next steps for a single currency. By the start of 1999, the moment had arrived: the euro was introduced in eleven countries – initially only as book money, then as cash in 2002.

ON 25 MARCH 1957, FEDERAL CHANCELLOR ADENAUER SIGNED THE EEC TREATY ESTABLISHING THE EUROPEAN COMMUNITY WITH THE AIM OF CREATING A COMMON MARKET.

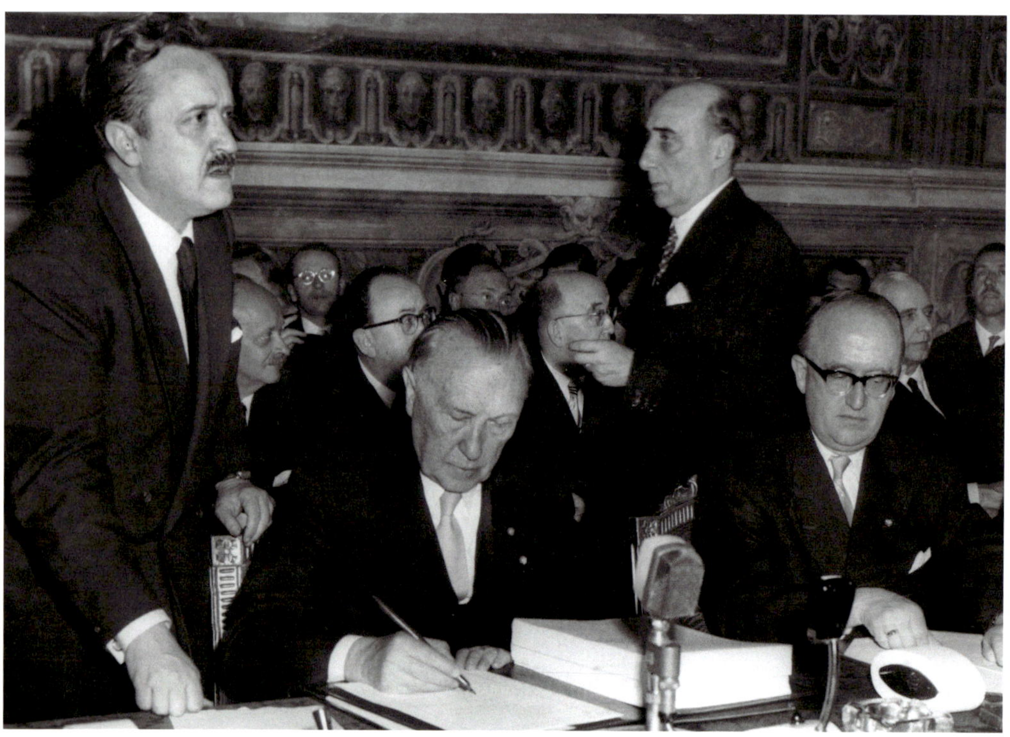

EUROPINO

Shortly after the end of World War II, people were already beginning to think about a common European currency. In 1952, silver coins with the inscription "europino" were privately minted in Hamburg. The europino was never legal tender.

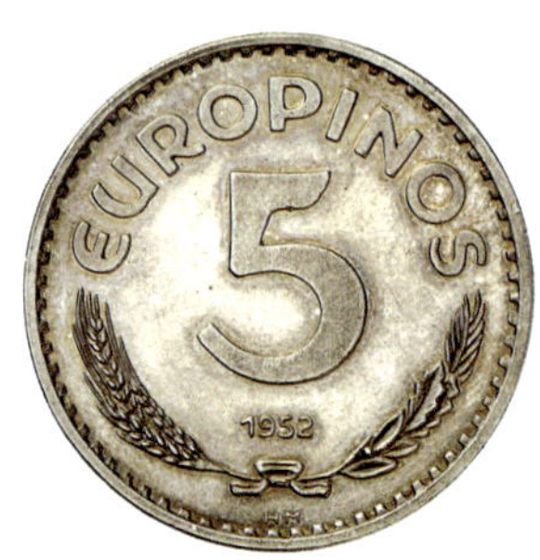

138 **5 EUROPINO,** 1952

ECU

From 1979 to 1998, the "ECU" (European Currency Unit), an artificial currency, was used in the European Community as a unit of account. Securities and travellers' cheques denominated in ECU were also issued. A few countries minted ECU coins, which were theoretically legal tender in these countries but which were actually mainly aimed at collectors.

139 **FRANCE, 15 ECU**

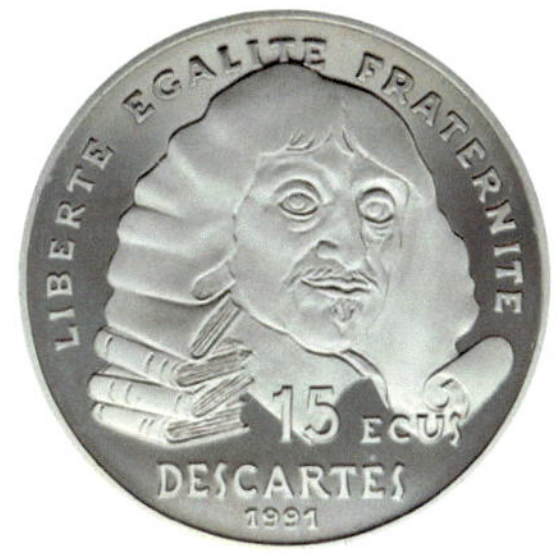

139

THE BUNDESBANK LEADS THE WAY

Since the Deutsche Mark had proven itself as a stable currency over the long term, the factors leading to its success provided significant input into the design of the Economic and Monetary Union (EMU). The Deutsche Bundesbank's political independence, its focus on price stability and its decentralised two-tier structure served as a template for the organisation of the European System of Central Banks (ESCB) and the European Central Bank (ECB). The independence of a country's national central bank from its government was made a contractual condition for EMU membership.

140 **COLLECTOR COIN FOR THE LAUNCH OF THE EURO 2002: GERMANY, 100 EURO (SCALE 2:1)**

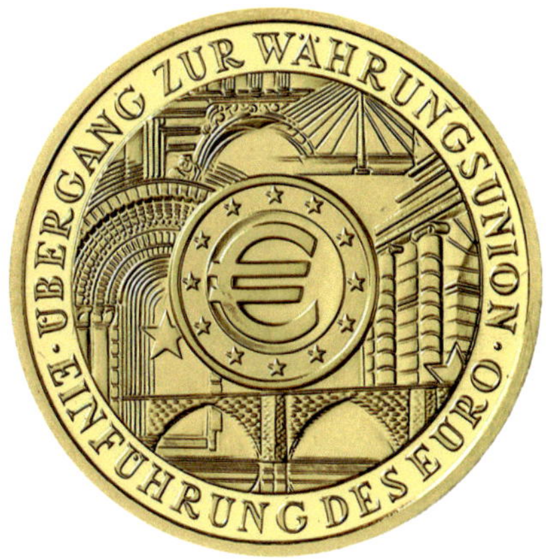

140

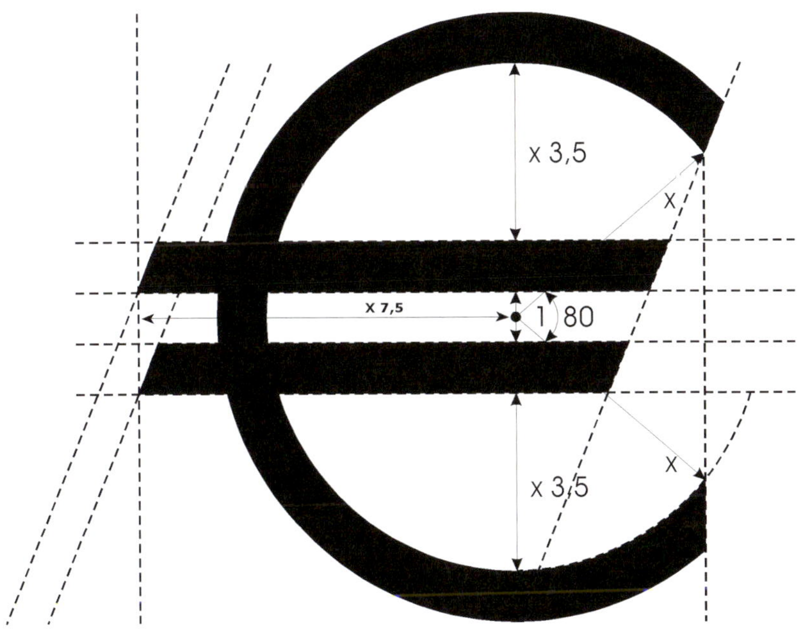

THE TWO PARALLEL LINES ACROSS THE CENTRE OF THE EURO SYMBOL REPRESENT THE CURRENCY'S STABILITY.

NEW NAME, NEW SYMBOL

While trying to find a name for the common currency, the European heads of state or government discussed options such as ECU, thaler and ducat, franc and florin. In December 1995, they decided on the term "euro", a newly created name with a clear reference to the continent of Europe, that was the same in all official languages of the European Union, and that was easy to pronounce. The euro symbol (€) was derived from the first letter of the word "Europe" and its design was based on the Greek letter epsilon, thus establishing a tie with ancient Greece as the cradle of European civilisation.

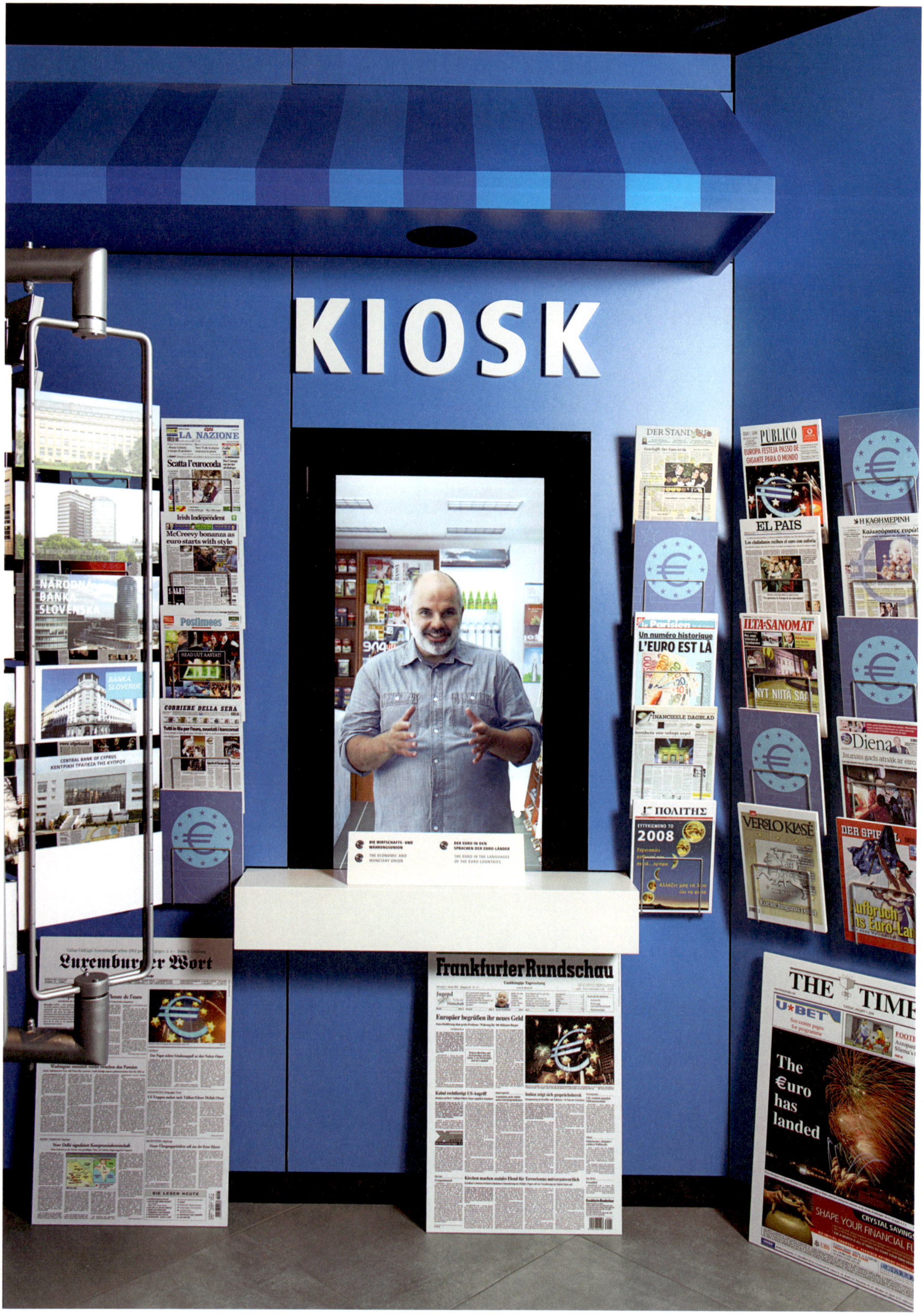
KIOSK
LA NAZIONE
Scatta l'eurocoda
Irish Independent
McCreevy bonanza as euro starts with style
NÁRODNÁ BANKA SLOVENSKA
Postimees
BANKA SLOVENIJE
CORRIERE DELLA SERA
CENTRAL BANK OF CYPRUS
PUBLICO
EL PAIS
Η ΚΑΘΗΜΕΡΙΝΗ
Le Parisien
Un numéro historique
L'EURO EST LÀ
ILTA-SANOMAT
FINANCIEELE DAGBLAD
Diena
ΠΟΛΙΤΗΣ
2008
VERSLO KLASĖ
FrankfurterRundschau
Europäer begrüßen ihr neues Geld
The €uro has landed

HELLO...

Would you like to buy a postcard or a newspaper? They're from all over Europe. When it comes to culture, I value variety. But do you still remember when each country in Europe had its own currency? Whenever you went on holiday in Europe, you had to exchange money, work out what things cost, exchange rates changed ... European politicians had been thinking about a common currency in Europe for quite some time before they finally drew up the Maastricht Treaty, which they signed in 1992. It was in this treaty that the Economic and Monetary Union was agreed upon. But it wasn't until 1999 that 11 countries introduced the euro as their common currency, at first only as book money and then, from 2002, also as cash. From one day to the next we all got new notes and coins. I can still remember: for a while everybody converted prices back to their old currency in their head. But now we've all got used to using the euro, and many other European countries have introduced the euro as their currency since then.

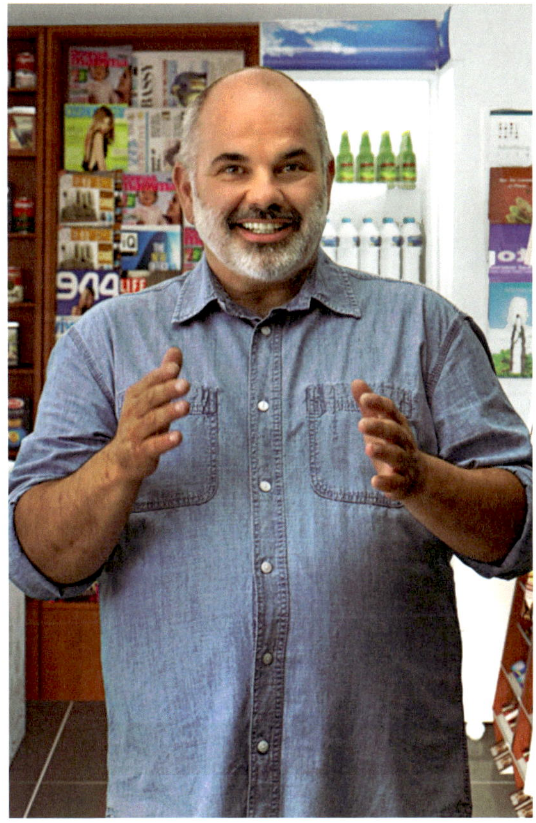

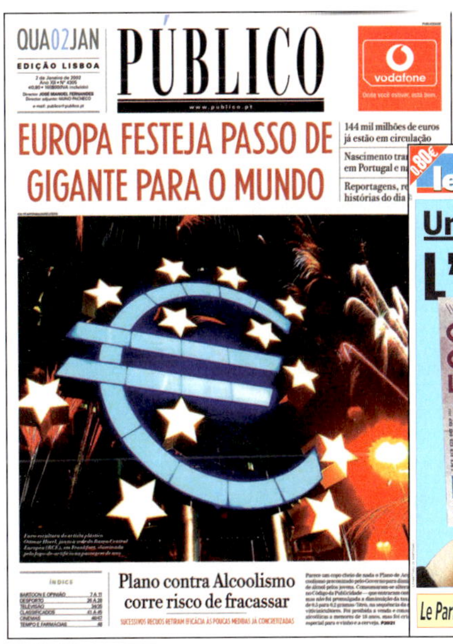

PORTUGAL, 2002

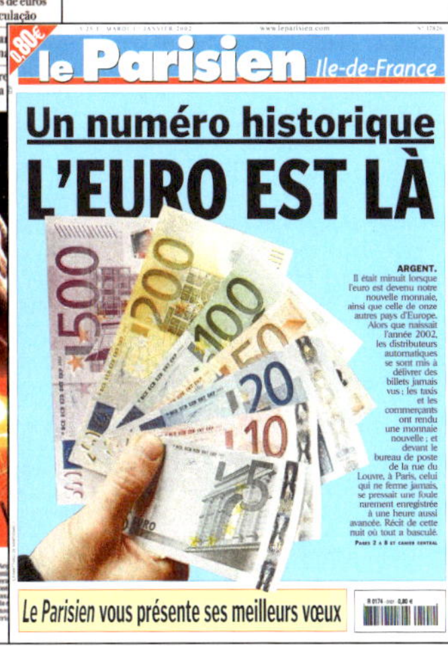

FRANCE, 2002

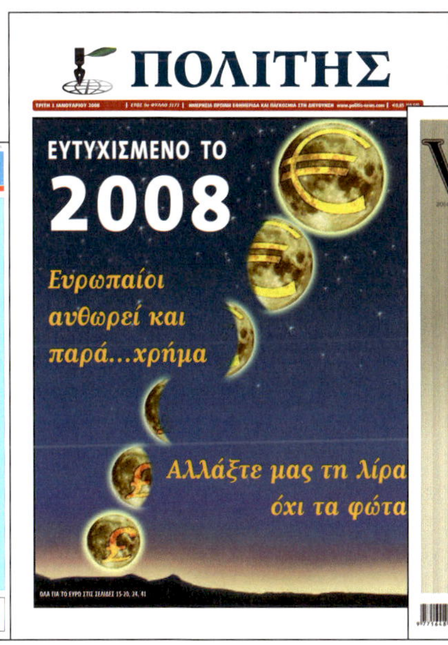

CYPRUS, 2008

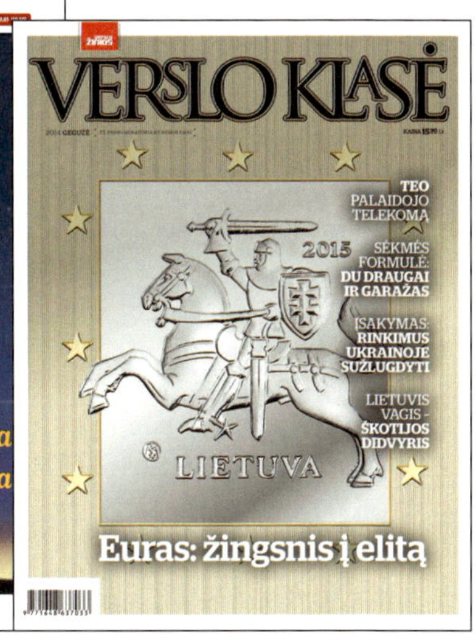

LITHUANIA, 2015

GERMAN TRADING PARTNERS

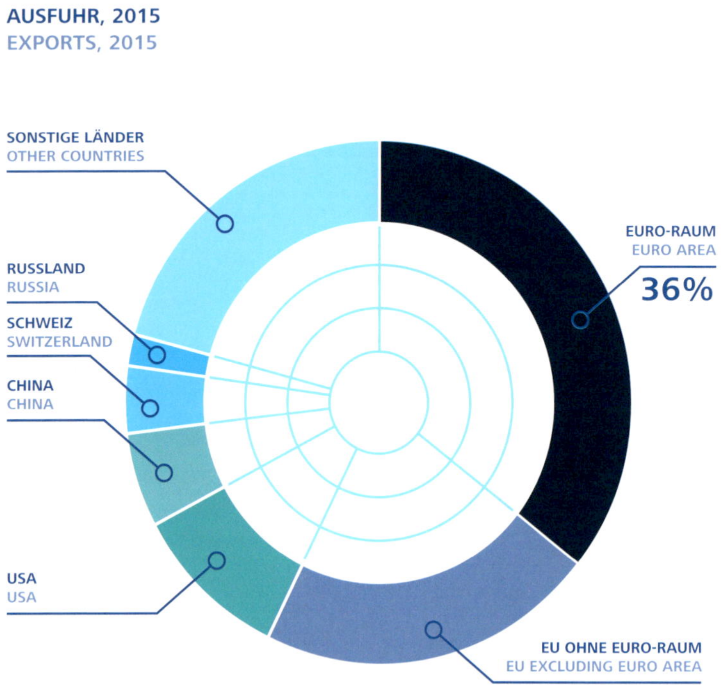

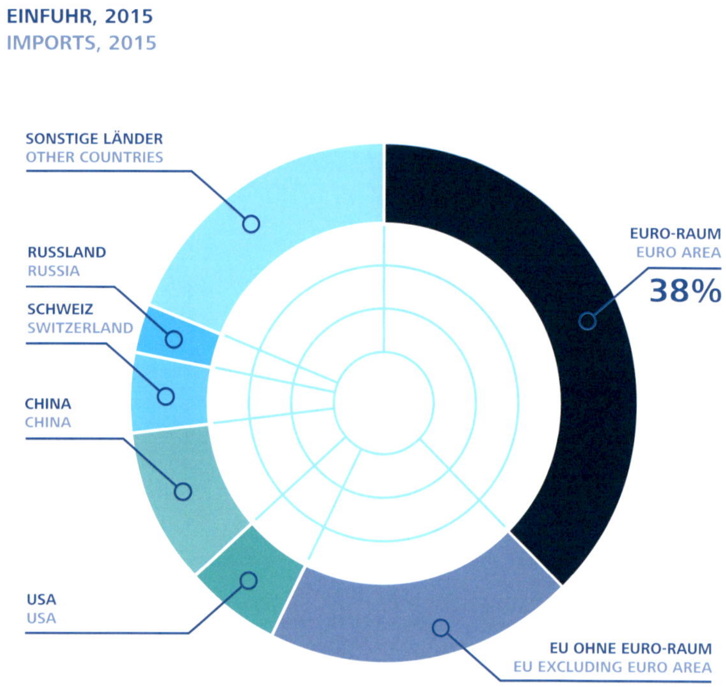

THE OTHER EURO-AREA COUNTRIES ARE KEY TRADING PARTNERS FOR GERMANY. THE GERMAN ECONOMY PROFITS FROM THE FACT THAT EXCHANGE RATES NO LONGER FLUCTUATE WITHIN THE EURO AREA.

EXCHANGE-FREE TRAVEL

Francs, lire, pesetas or schillings – until the euro was introduced, each European country had its own currency. Today, most countries in the European Union belong to the euro area. Major advantages of the single currency include no longer having to exchange currency when travelling between euro-area countries and not having to pay foreign exchange fees or convert prices. It is now much simpler to make purchases abroad and compare the prices of hotels, restaurants and goods. This, in turn, promotes both tourism and economic competition in general.

FEWER ECONOMIC HURDLES

A sizeable market was created when the euro was launched, with more than 300 million people using the single currency. Obstacles to trade, such as costly currency conversion, no longer exist in the euro area, meaning no more uncertainty about which way exchange rates are likely to move in future. Enterprises thus have fewer costs as well as more security when it comes to planning, which strengthens cross-border trade and promotes growth and employment. In addition, the euro led to the creation of a harmonised financial market, making it easier for enterprises to raise capital and for investors to invest. Owing to its economic strength, the euro area is a key player in the global economy.

A DRIVER OF CONVERGENCE?

The euro was conceived as more than just a common currency for the euro area countries. It has another purpose: to be the engine driving greater convergence in Europe.
The members of the Economic and Monetary Union (EMU) relinquished their national currencies, thus also surrendering their monetary policy decisionmaking powers in favour of a single European monetary policy.

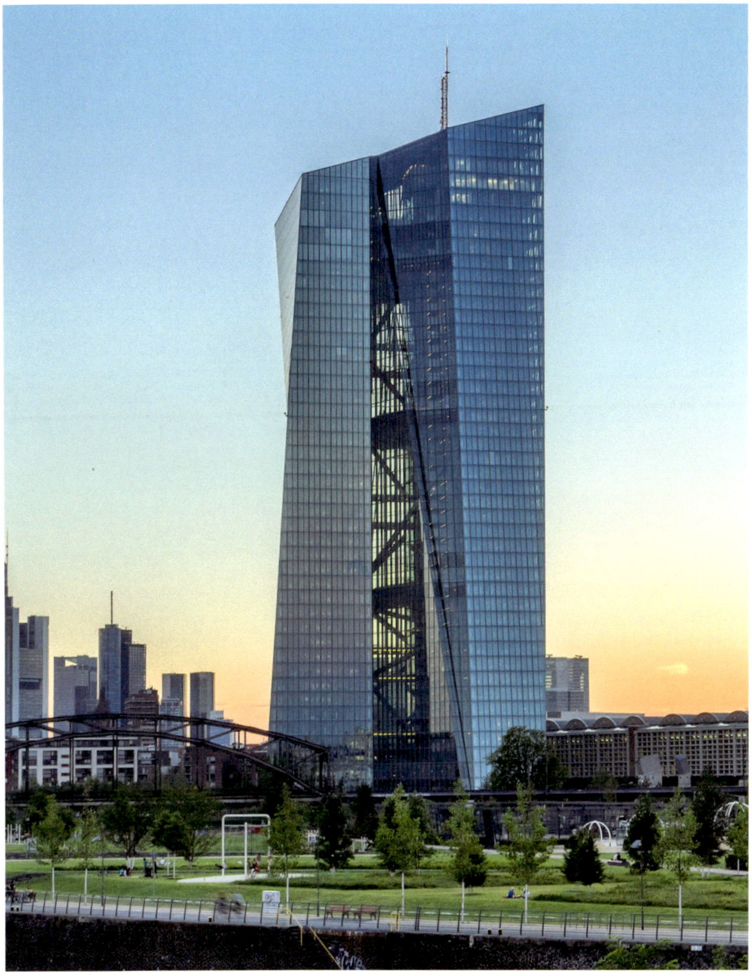

THE EUROSYSTEM AND THE ESCB

Not all countries in the European Union (EU) have joined the Economic and Monetary Union yet. Therefore, a distinction is made between the European System of Central Banks (ESCB) and the Eurosystem. The ESCB is composed of the European Central Bank (ECB) and the national central banks of all the EU countries. The Eurosystem, on the other hand, comprises the ECB and the central banks of the states which have adopted the euro. The Eurosystem is responsible for the single monetary policy in the euro area.

COUNCILS AND THEIR MEMBERS

The ECB Governing Council is the Eurosystem's top decision-making body. It formulates monetary policy for the euro area and makes all other major decisions. The national central banks implement the ECB Governing Council's decisions in the euro-area countries. The Governing Council consists of the members of the ECB's Executive Board plus the governors of the euro-area national central banks. The Executive Board manages the day-to-day business of the ECB and prepares Governing Council meetings. The ECB President is the representative and spokesperson of both the ECB and the Eurosystem. The General Council forges a link between the Eurosystem and the central banks of the EU countries that have not yet adopted the euro.

THE EUROPEAN CENTRAL BANK (ECB) IN FRANKFURT AM MAIN.

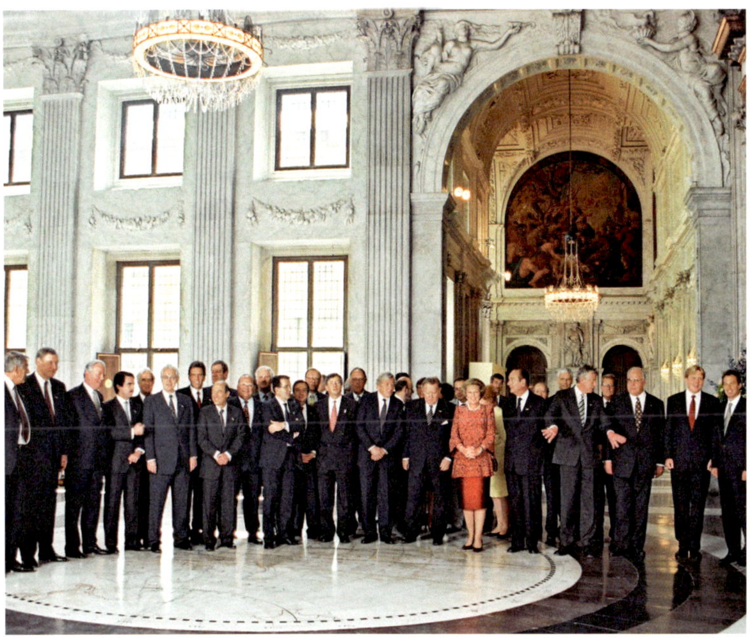

STABILITY AND GROWTH PACT

The "Stability and Growth Pact" was adopted in 1997 and has been amended several times since. It requires member states to adhere to specific budgetary rules in order to ensure sound public finances. The euro-area countries commit to a medium-term objective of a broadly balanced budget, even after adopting the euro. The upper limit for annual new borrowing is 3% of national gross domestic product (GDP) and the ceiling for public debt is 60% of national GDP.

THE HEADS OF STATE OR GOVERNMENT OF THE EUROPEAN UNION ADOPTED THE STABILITY AND GROWTH PACT AT THEIR SUMMIT IN JUNE 1997 AS PART OF THE "TREATY OF AMSTERDAM".

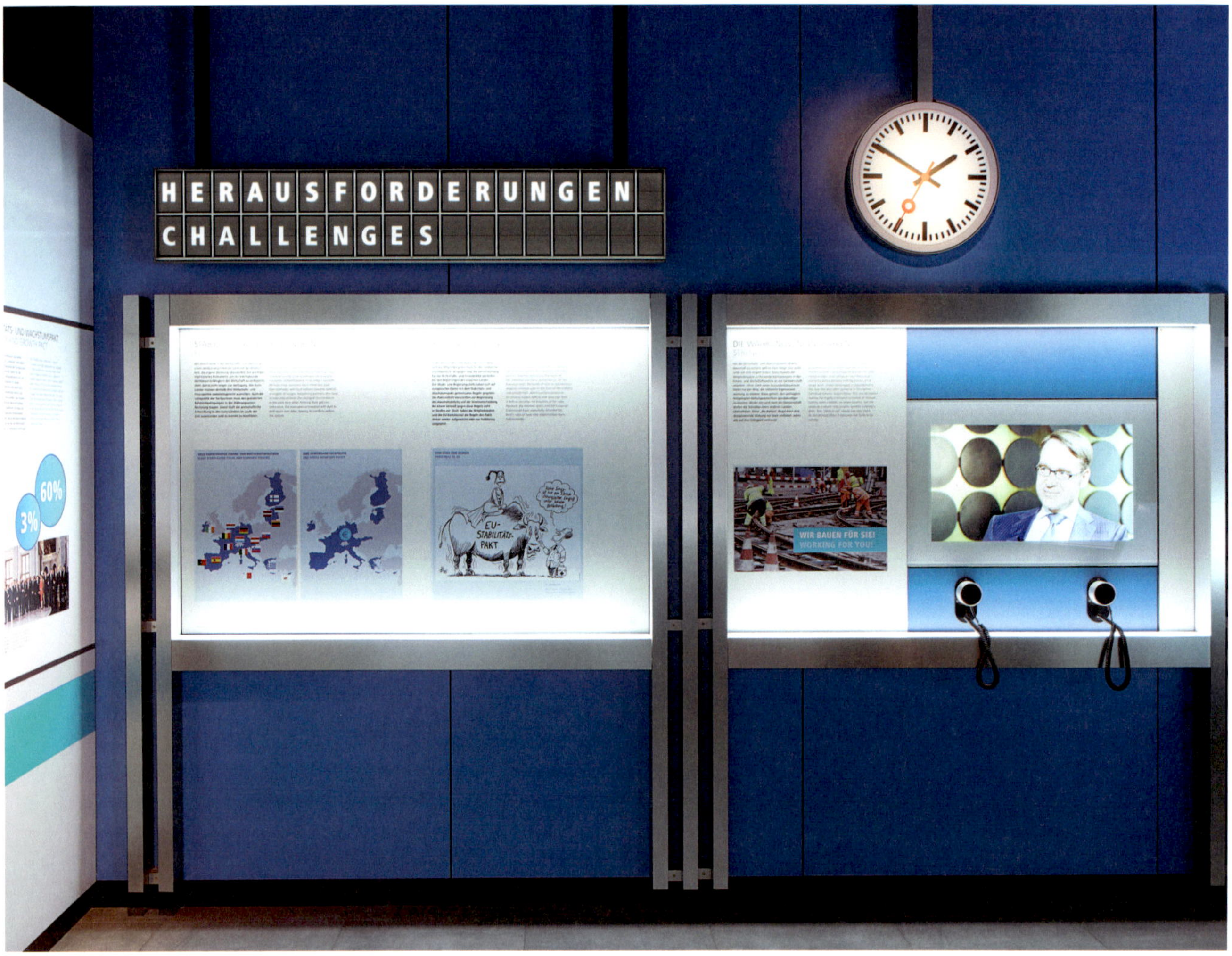

FOCUSED ON STABILITY

Upon joining the Economic and Monetary Union (EMU), countries forfeit their ability to devalue their own currencies. This means that one major tool traditionally used to enhance international economic competitiveness is no longer available. All euro-area countries must therefore gear their economic and fiscal policies towards stability. In respect of wages, bargaining partners also need to take into account the changed circumstances in the euro area when forming their policies. Otherwise, the euro-area economies will start to drift apart over time, leading to conflicts within the system.

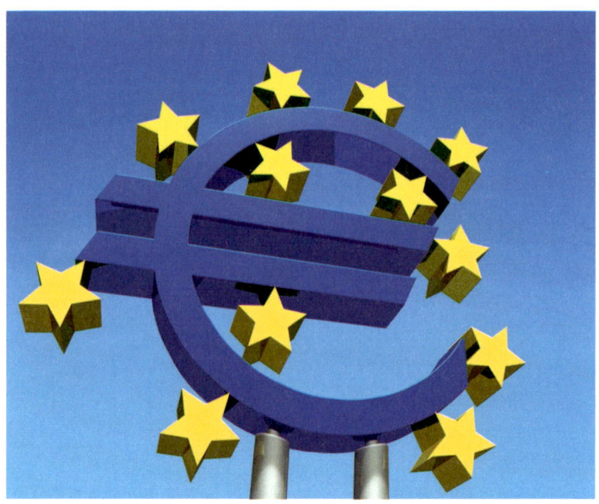

MANY STAND-ALONE FISCAL AND ECONOMIC POLICIES

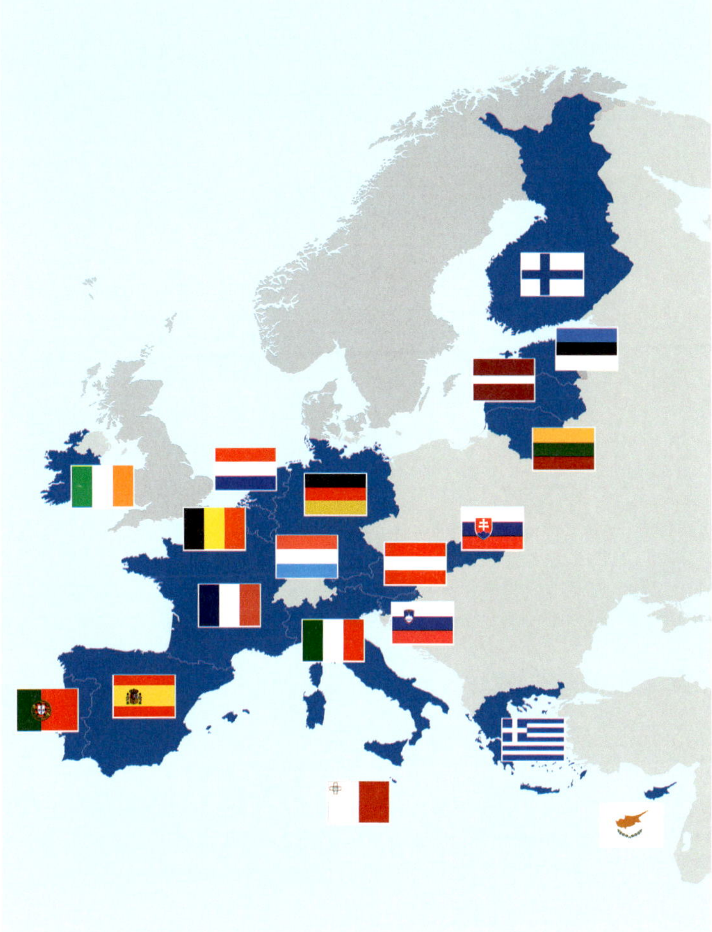

ONE SINGLE MONETARY POLICY

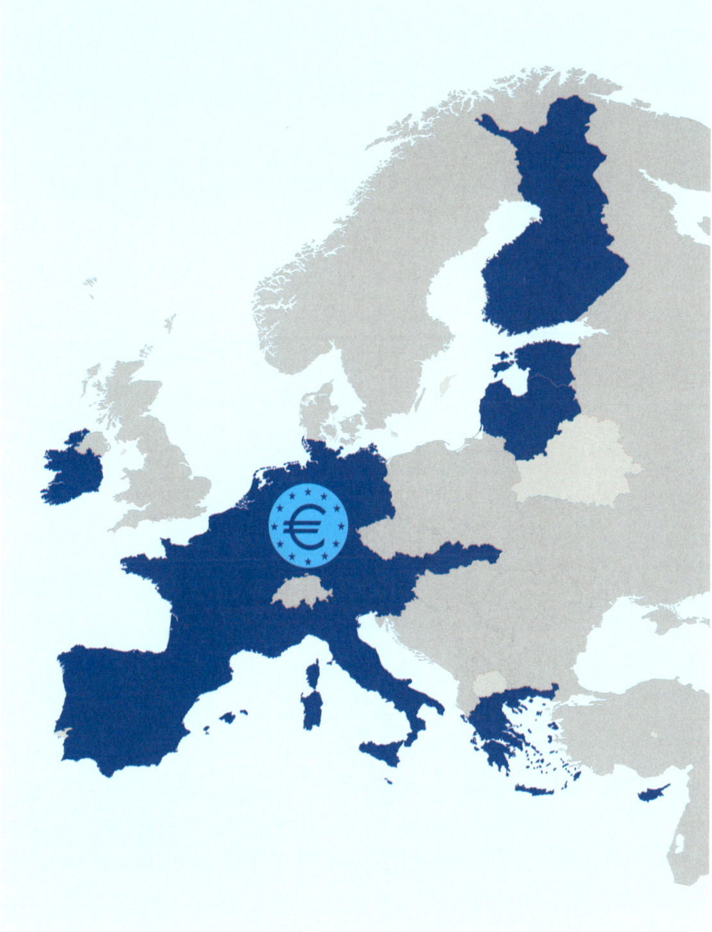

OBSERVING THE RULES

In the Economic and Monetary Union (EMU), the members are jointly responsible for monetary policy. Accountability for economic and fiscal policies, however, remains in the hands of the individual countries' governments. At the European level, the heads of state or government adopted common rules in the form of the Stability and Growth Pact, which contains provisions for limiting budget deficits and sovereign debt. It defines penalties for breaches of the rules. However, the member states and the European Commission have repeatedly softened the Pact's rules or have only implemented them half-heartedly.

STRENGTHENING THE MONETARY UNION

There are two ways to safeguard the Economic and Monetary Union (EMU) over the long term. The fi rst is with a more integrated union: for this, member states must relinquish their fiscal and economic policy decision-making powers on a broad scale. Unless sovereignty is surrendered in this way, the only other option is to strengthen individual national responsibility. This would involve making the legally enshrined exclusion of mutual liability more credible: no single country, nor the union as a whole, may assume another country's debt. This "no-bail-out" clause can only exert its disciplining effect if everyone has faith in its validity.

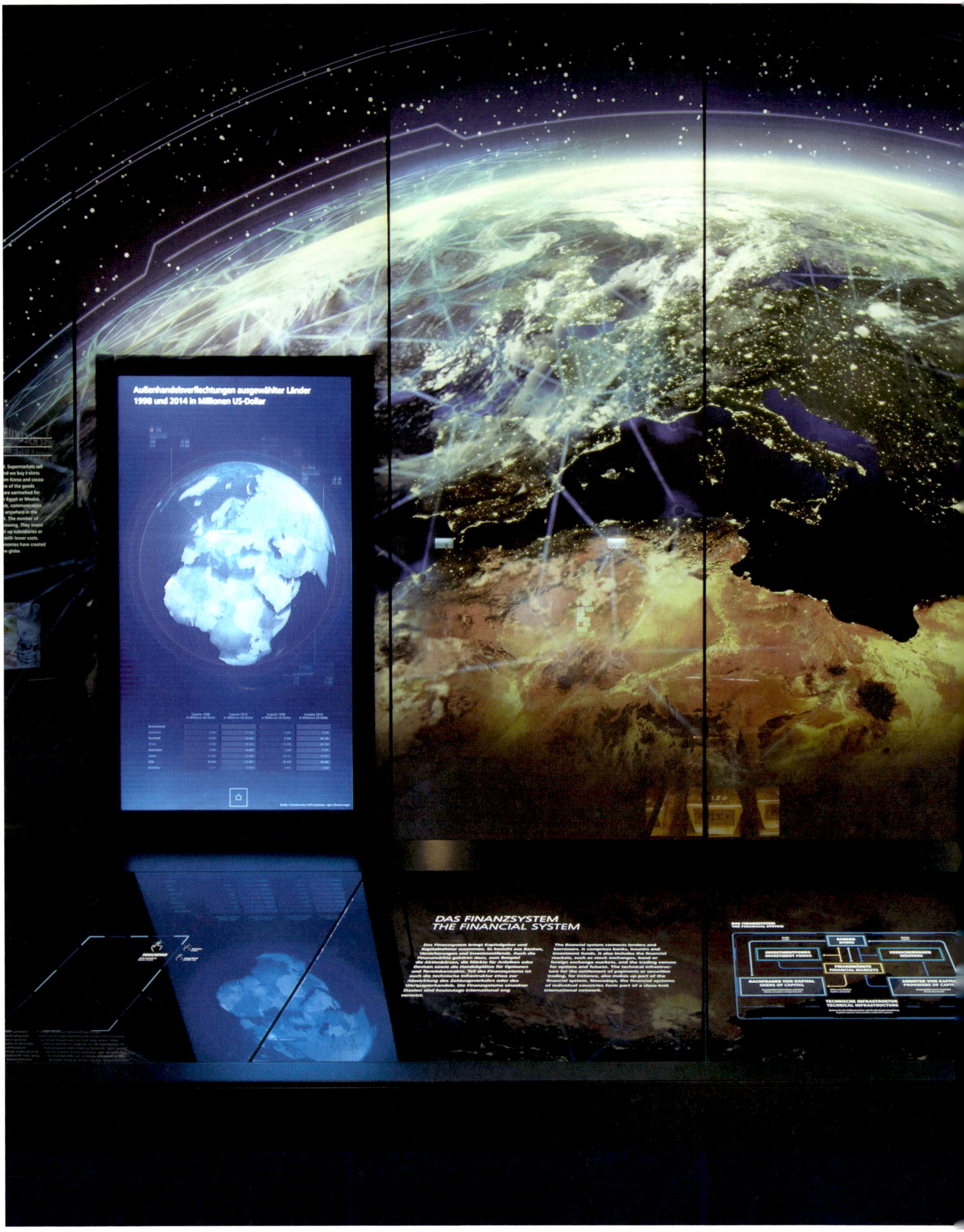
Außenhandelsverflechtungen ausgewählter Länder 1998 und 2014 in Millionen US-Dollar
DAS FINANZSYSTEM
THE FINANCIAL SYSTEM
Das Finanzsystem bringt Kapitalgeber und Kapitalnehmer zusammen. Es besteht aus Banken, Versicherungen und Investmentfonds. Auch die Finanzmärkte gehören dazu, zum Beispiel die Aktienbörsen, die Märkte für Anleihen oder Devisen sowie die Handelsplätze für Optionen und Terminkontrakte. Teil des Finanzsystems ist auch die technische Infrastruktur etwa zur Abwicklung des Zahlungsverkehrs oder des Wertpapierhandels. Die Finanzsysteme einzelner Staaten sind heutzutage international eng vernetzt.
The financial system connects lenders and borrowers. It comprises banks, insurers and investment funds. It also includes the financial markets, such as stock exchanges, bond or foreign exchange markets, and the trading venues for options and futures. The technical infrastructure for the settlement of payments or securities trading, for instance, also makes up part of the financial system. Nowadays, the financial systems of individual countries form part of a close-knit international network.

TOWER

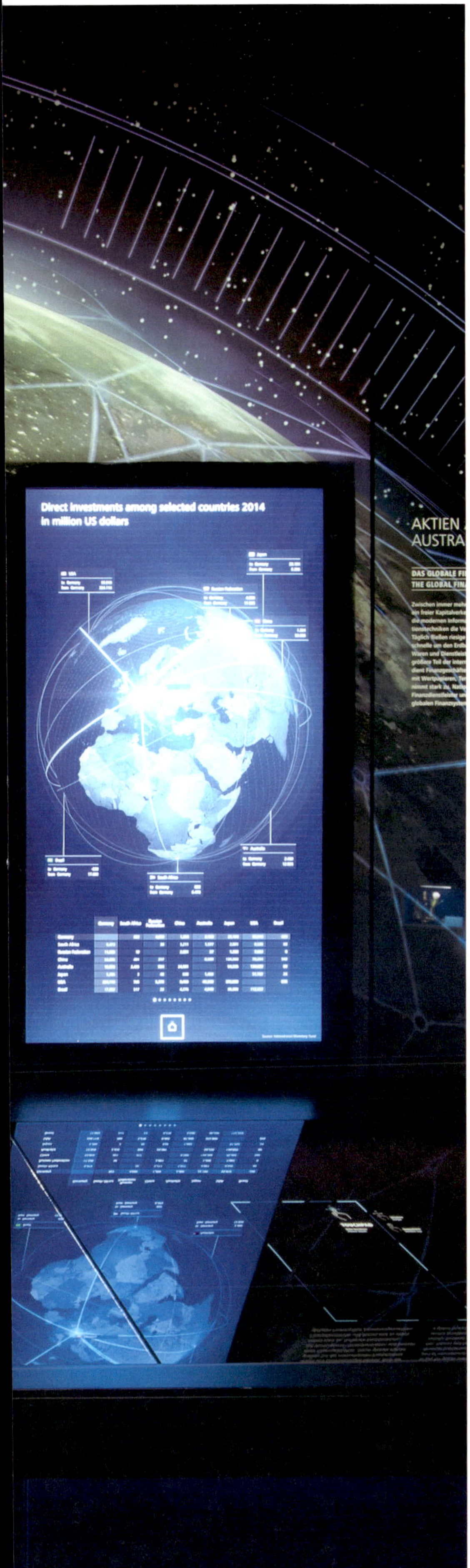

The tower overlooks the entire globe. From the world's currencies to exchange rate regimes and reserve assets to the globe-spanning trade and financial flows and international cooperation in the field of financial stability: we are taking a global view of money here.

An interactive exchange bureau provides an introduction to the topic of currencies and exchange rates. A visual experience of the global variety of currencies is rendered by the "swarm of banknotes": more than 170 valid banknotes from all over the world are on display between high, angular glass walls. In the centre of the room, visitors' attention is drawn to a bar of gold from Germany's holdings of reserve assets. Visitors can touch the 12.5 kilogramme bar of gold and try to lift it.

A multimedia presentation in front of a giant globe introduces global trade and capital flows. In the light of the global interrelationships and their risks, the Deutsche Bundesbank is active in numerous national and international bodies which monitor the networked financial system and safeguard monetary and financial stability.

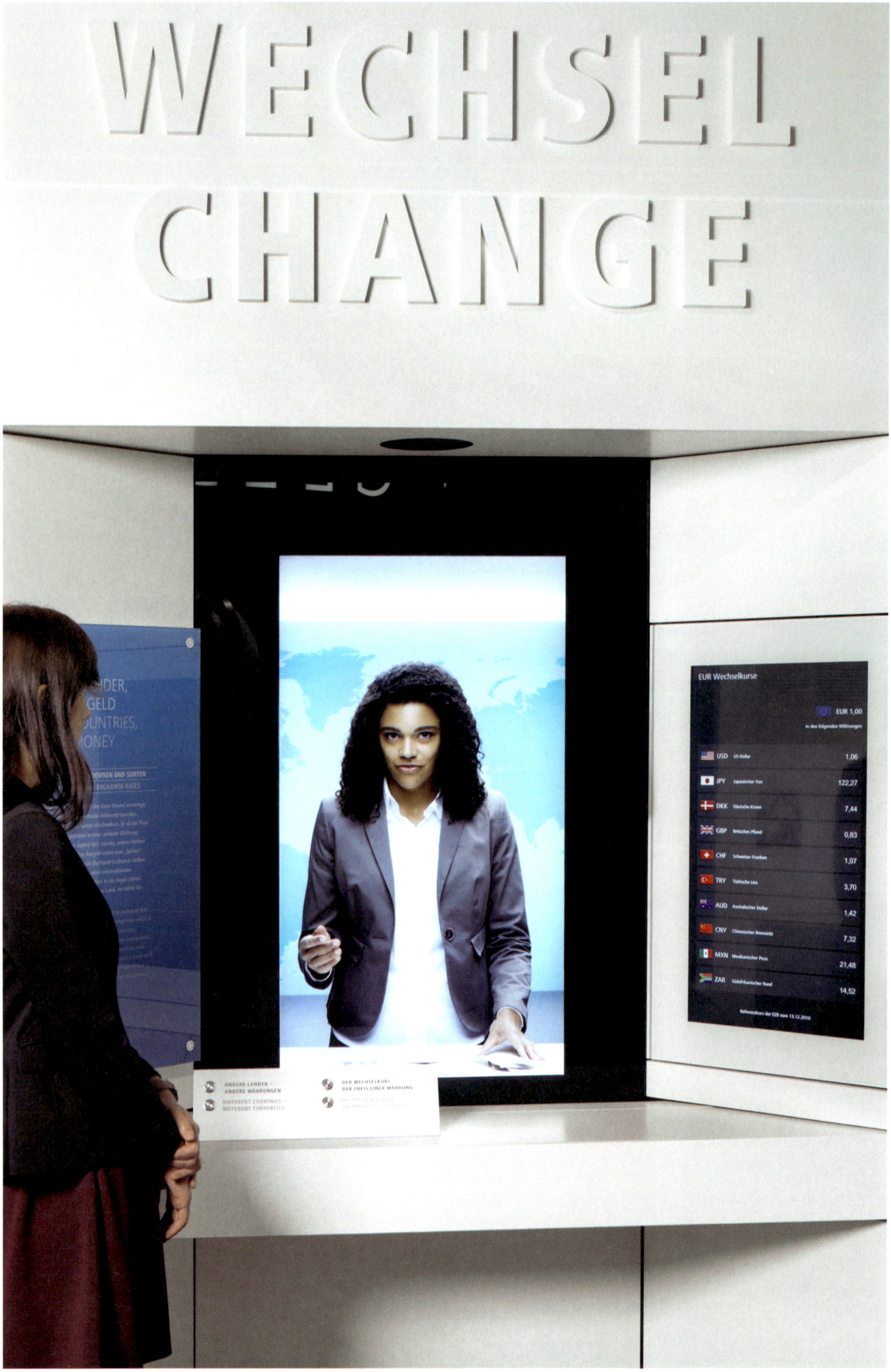
WECHSEL
CHANGE
EUR Wechselkurse
EUR 1,00
in den folgenden Währungen
USD US-Dollar 1,06
JPY Japanischer Yen 122,27
DKK Dänische Krone 7,44
GBP Britisches Pfund 0,83
CHF Schweizer Franken 1,07
TRY Türkische Lira 3,70
AUD Australischer Dollar 1,42
CNY Chinesischer Renminbi 7,32
MXN Mexikanischer Peso 21,48
ZAR Südafrikanischer Rand 14,52
Referenzkurs der EZB vom 13.12.2016

OTHER COUNTRIES, OTHER MONEY

FOREIGN CURRENCY AND EXCHANGE RATES

Holidaymakers outside the euro area need to exchange their money for foreign currency at a given exchange rate, which is the price of a currency expressed in another currency. Some exchange rates change constantly, others remain static over a long period of time. Foreign currency exists as cash and book money alike. Each currency is allocated a three-letter international currency code. As a rule, the first two letters indicate the country and the third stands for the currency (eg USD for US dollar).

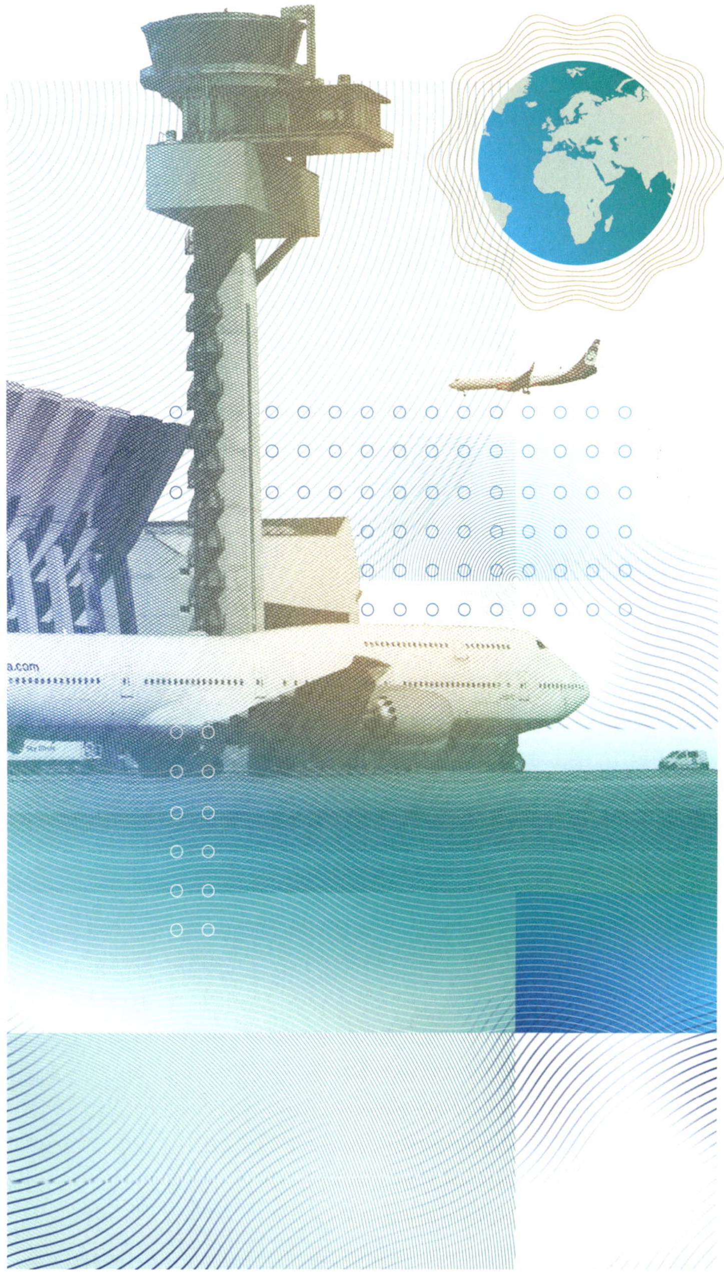

FIXED OR FLOATING?

HOW EXCHANGE RATES COME ABOUT

The exchange rate between two currencies is dictated by supply and demand in the foreign exchange market (forex market). If demand for a currency increases, so, too, does its price. The currency "appreciates". As soon as demand subsides, the exchange rate falls and the currency "depreciates". The euro and other major currencies have "floating" exchange rates with other currencies which are formed freely in the market without state intervention and can vary from day to day, even from second to second. In a "fixed" exchange rate regime, the exchange rate is pegged by the state and is maintained through intervention, ie purchases and sales in the forex market.

THE BIG MAC INDEX

The popular Big Mac Index is a highly simplified way of comparing the purchasing power of various currencies. The Big Mac, which is produced in the same way in over 120 countries, is the unit of measurement. The local price of a Big Mac is converted at the current exchange rate into euro, for example. That way, the euro price of a Big Mac can be compared from one country to the next.

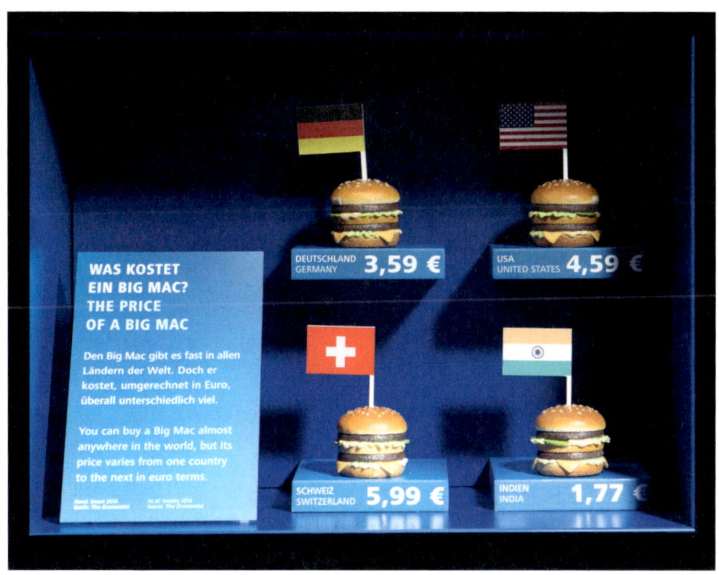

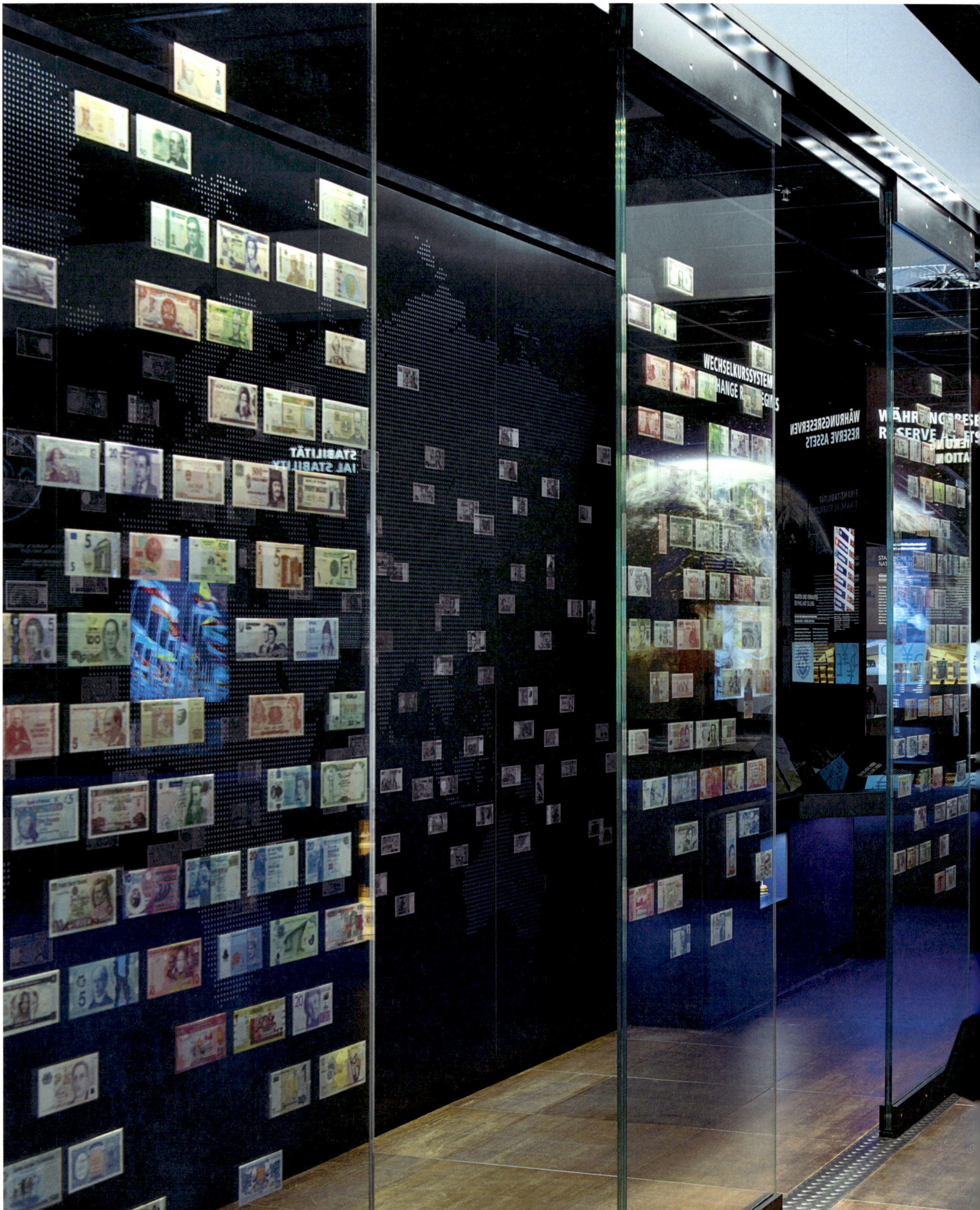
WECHSELKURSSYSTEM
WÄHRUNGSRESERVEN
RESERVE ASSETS

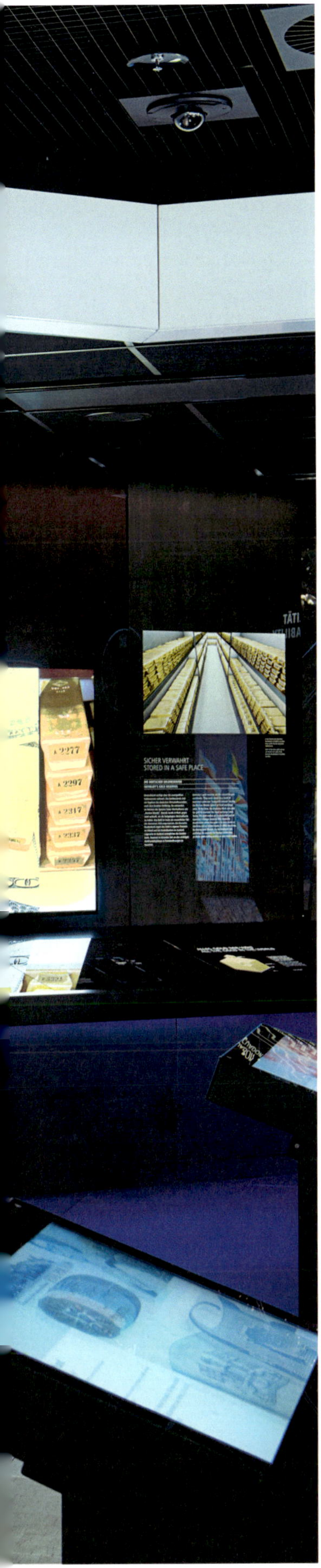

A COUNTRY'S TRADEMARK

CURRENCIES ARE SYMBOLS OF NATIONAL IDENTITY

Most countries in the world have their own currencies. The exception are currency unions such as the euro area, where several countries have agreed on a single monetary system. At present, there are over 160 currencies worldwide. A currency is always closely linked to the history of a given country or territory and makes up part of its identity. Banknotes and coins usually depict national icons and symbols or motifs which reflect the country's history and culture or its flora and fauna.

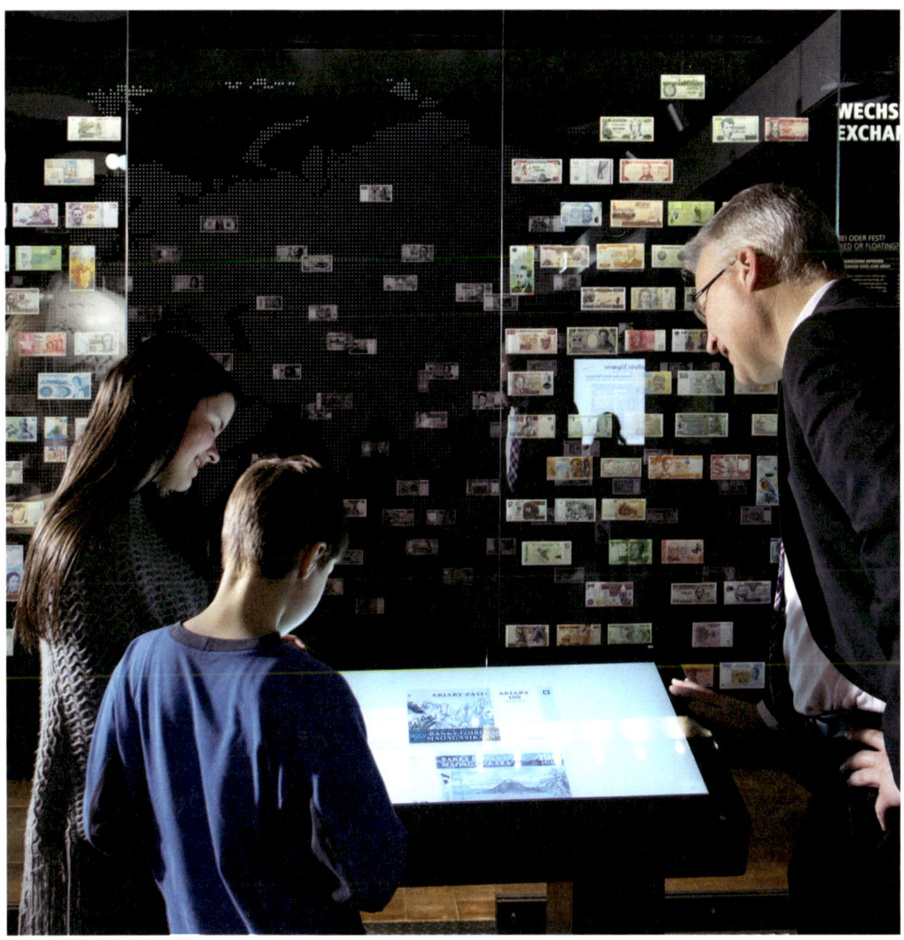

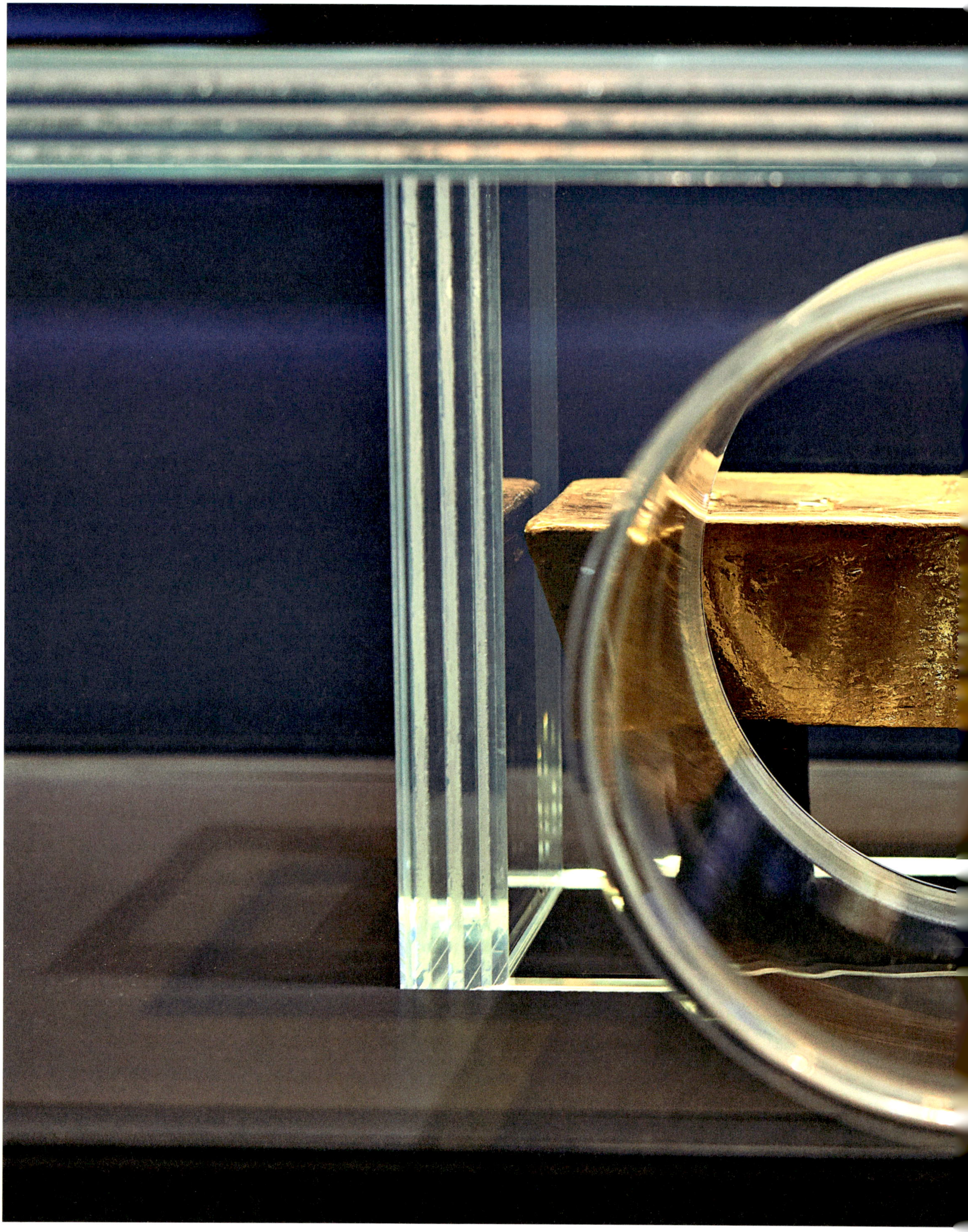

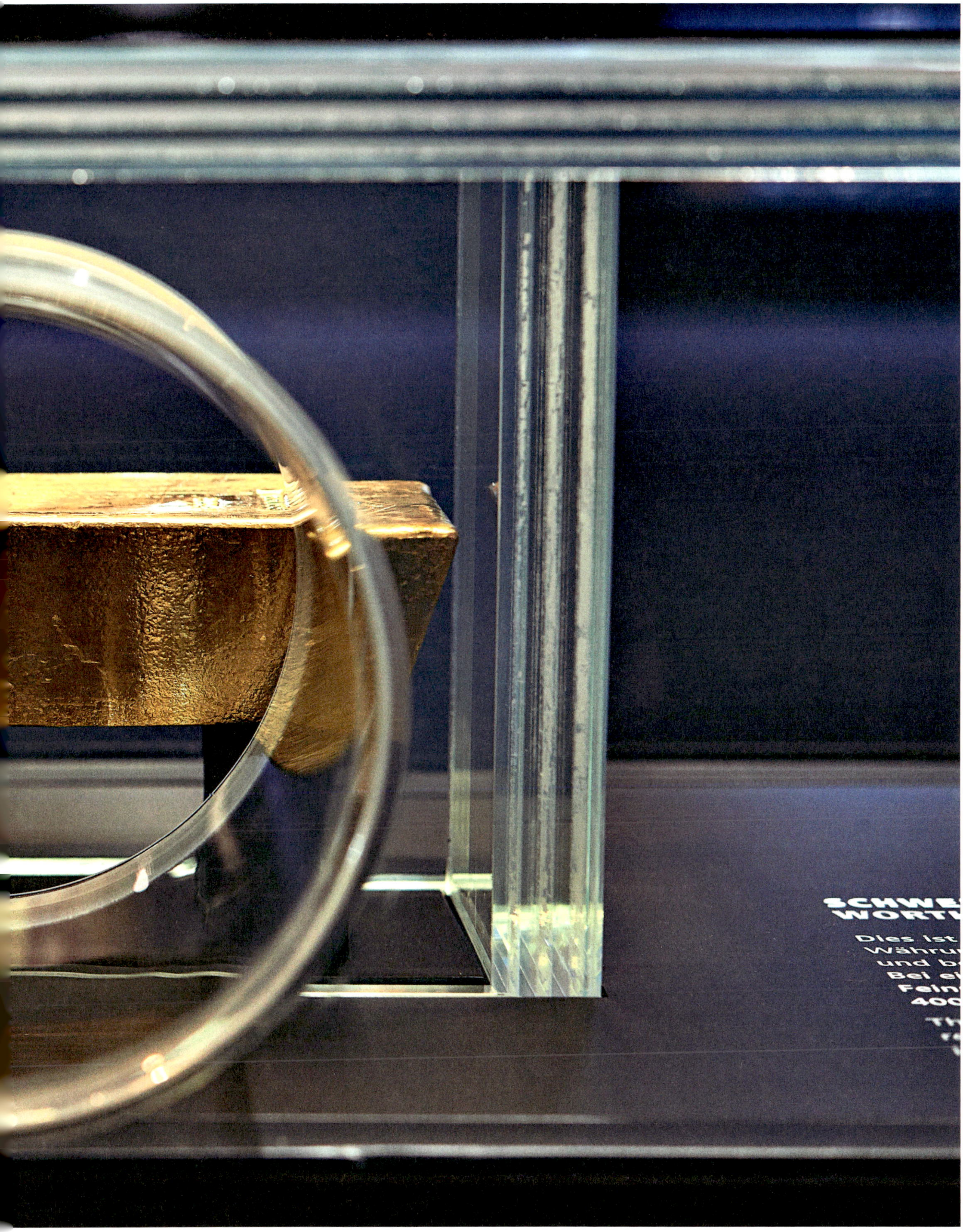
Dies ist

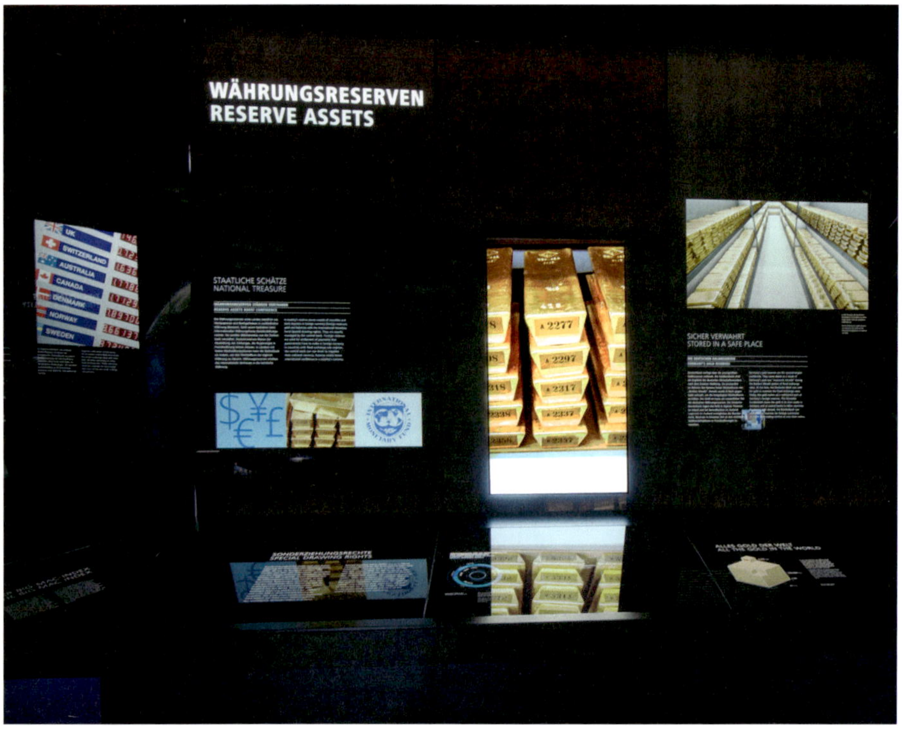

NATIONAL TREASURE

RESERVE ASSETS BOOST CONFIDENCE

A country's reserve assets consist of securities and bank deposits in foreign currency (foreign reserves), gold and balances with the International Monetary Fund (special drawing rights). They are usually managed by the central bank. Foreign reserves are used for settlement of payments that governments have to make in foreign currency. In countries with fixed exchange rate regimes, the central bank can use them to regulate their national currency. Reserve assets boost international confidence in a country's currency.

WORTH ITS WEIGHT

This gold bar belongs to Germany's reserve assets. It weighs 12.495 kg and is 99.99 % pure gold. At a gold price of 1,000 euro per fine ounce (31.1 g), it is worth around 400,000 euro.

141 **GOLD BAR OF GERMANY'S RESERVE ASSETS**

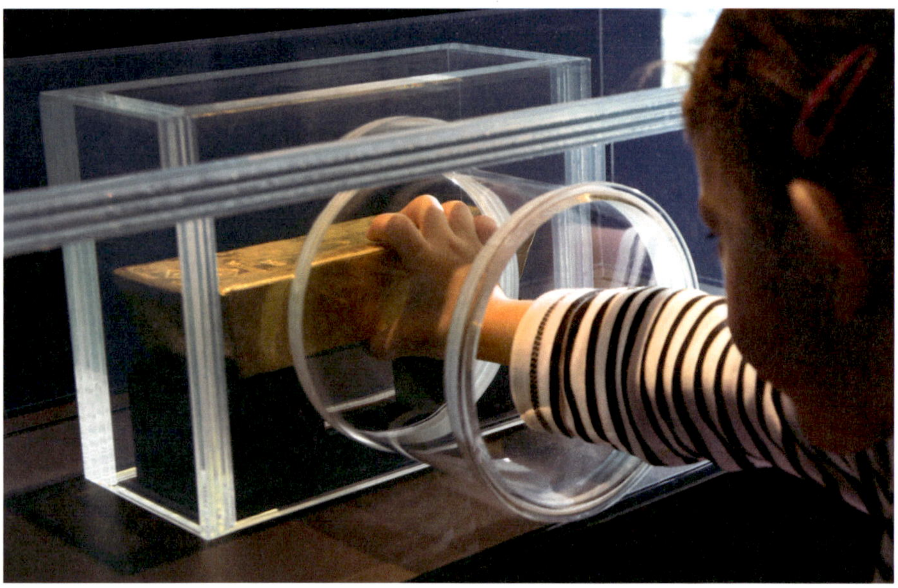

STORED IN A SAFE PLACE

GERMANY'S GOLD RESERVES

Germany's gold reserves are the second-largest worldwide. They came about as a result of Germany's post-war "economic miracle" during the Bretton Woods system of fixed exchange rates. At the time, the Deutsche Mark was sold for gold to maintain the fixed exchange rates. Today, this gold makes up a substantial part of Germany's foreign reserves. The Deutsche Bundesbank stores the gold in its own vaults in Germany and at central banks in other countries. By storing gold abroad, the Bundesbank can exchange its reserves for foreign currencies at major gold trading centres at very short notice.

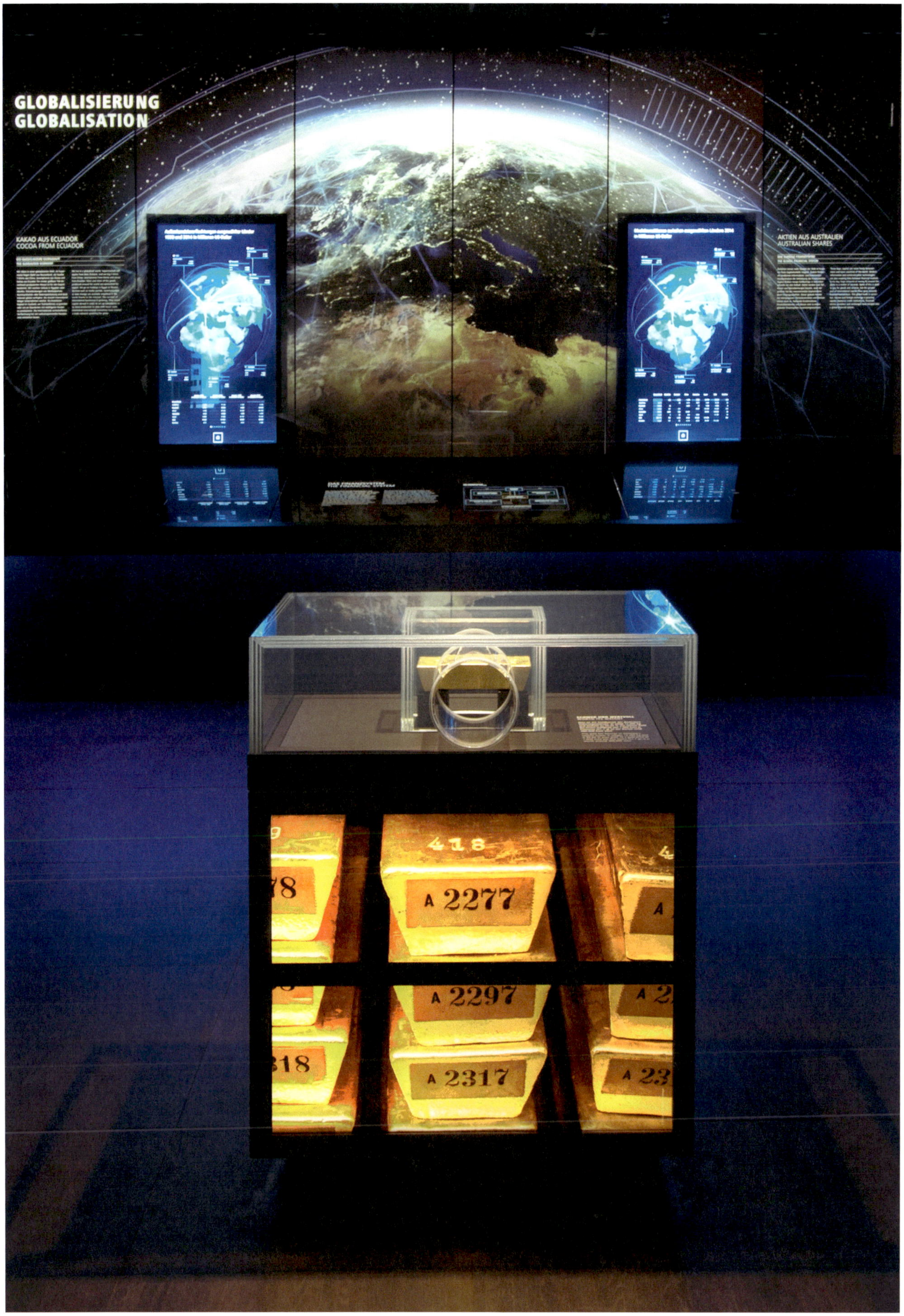
GLOBALISIERUNG
GLOBALISATION
KAKAO AUS ECUADOR
COCOA FROM ECUADOR
AKTIEN AUS AUSTRALIEN
AUSTRALIAN SHARES
A 2277
A 2297
A 2317

COCOA FROM ECUADOR

THE GLOBALISED ECONOMY

We live in a globalised world. Supermarkets sell apples from New Zealand, and we buy T-shirts from China, smartphones from Korea and cocoa from Ecuador. More and more of the goods produced around the world are earmarked for export. We go on holidays in Egypt or Mexico. Services such as media portals, communication or data storage are available anywhere in the world thanks to the internet. The number of international businesses is growing. They invest capital abroad in order to set up subsidiaries or to move production to sites with lower costs. Interlinked international economies have created a trade network spanning the globe.

AUSTRALIAN SHARES

THE GLOBAL FINANCIAL SYSTEM

These days, capital can move freely between more and more countries of the world. Modern information and communication technologies are also creating links between financial markets. Every day, huge amounts of money fly around the globe in a matter of seconds. Some of this is used to pay for goods and services, but the greater part of international capital flows goes towards financial transactions. This global trade in securities, futures and foreign exchange is growing rapidly. National credit institutions, financial service providers and exchanges have merged into a global financial system.

THE FINANCIAL SYSTEM

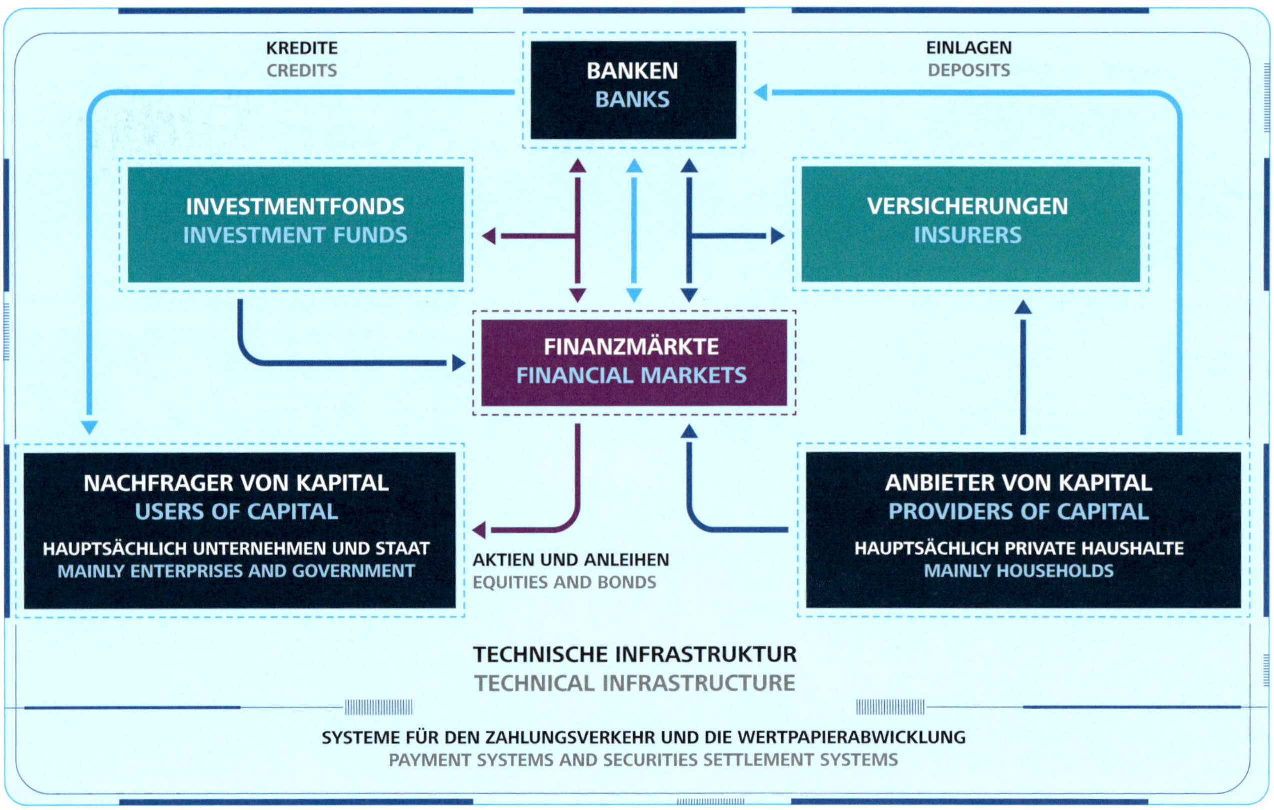

THE FINANCIAL SYSTEM CONNECTS LENDERS AND BORROWERS. NOWADAYS, THE FINANCIAL SYSTEMS OF INDIVIDUAL COUNTRIES FORM PART OF A CLOSE-KNIT INTERNATIONAL NETWORK.

THE MACRO VIEW

AVOIDING FINANCIAL CRISES

Financial transactions can only be settled securely and efficiently when the financial system is stable. Failed speculations, non-performing loans, ailing banks and over-indebted governments – any of these unwanted developments can have domino effects, not just nationally but inter nationally. This can trigger financial crises and cause severe damage to the economy. These disruptions also hinder the transmission of monetary policy. In order to identify risks early on, national and international supervisory authorities have a "macroprudential" mandate: they monitor the entire financial system, with all its interconnections. If need be, they can intervene to provide regulation and support.

ANALYSE, WARN, PREVENT

THE BUNDESBANK MONITORS THE FINANCIAL SYSTEM

Germany's Financial Stability Committee (Ausschuss für Finanzstabilität, AFS) is responsible for the macroprudential monitoring of the German financial system. As an AFS member, the Deutsche Bundesbank has the legal mandate to analyse risks to the stability of the financial system, flag threats at an early stage and develop any countermeasures. Based on this, the AFS decides on warnings and recommendations to be given to public sector entities in Germany. Recommendations can entail binding government measures. The Bundesbank also publishes its assessments and analyses of the German financial system in an annual Financial Stability Review.

COMPOSITION OF THE FINANCIAL STABILITY COMMITTEE (AFS)

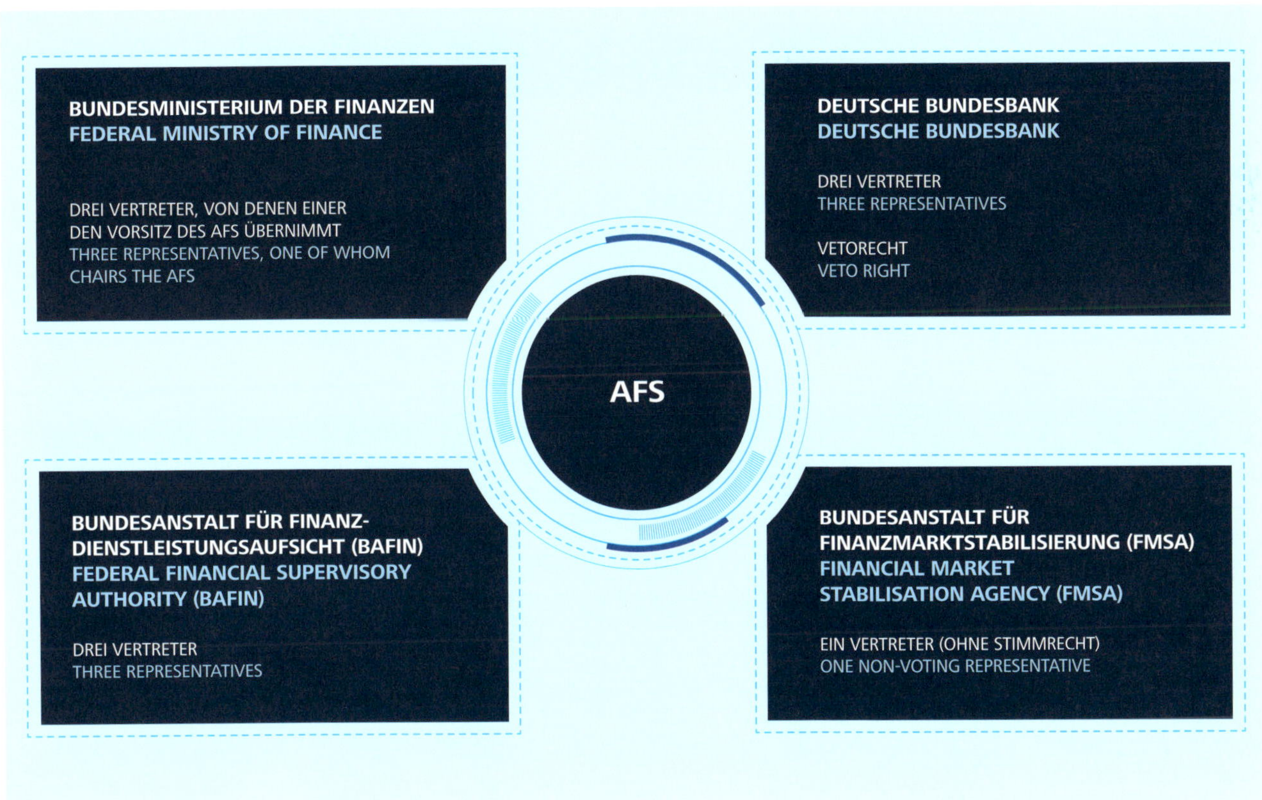

ACTING TOGETHER

INTERNATIONAL COOPERATION

On their own, individual states cannot adequately respond to crises in the globally interconnected financial system. This is why international bodies are needed, as well as national authorities. They agree on rules and monitor the financial and monetary system in order to prevent unwanted developments and combat crises. The Deutsche Bundesbank plays a role in numerous bodies and institutions which safeguard financial and monetary stability at the national, European and global levels.

KEY BODIES AND INSTITUTIONS FOR FINANCIAL STABILITY

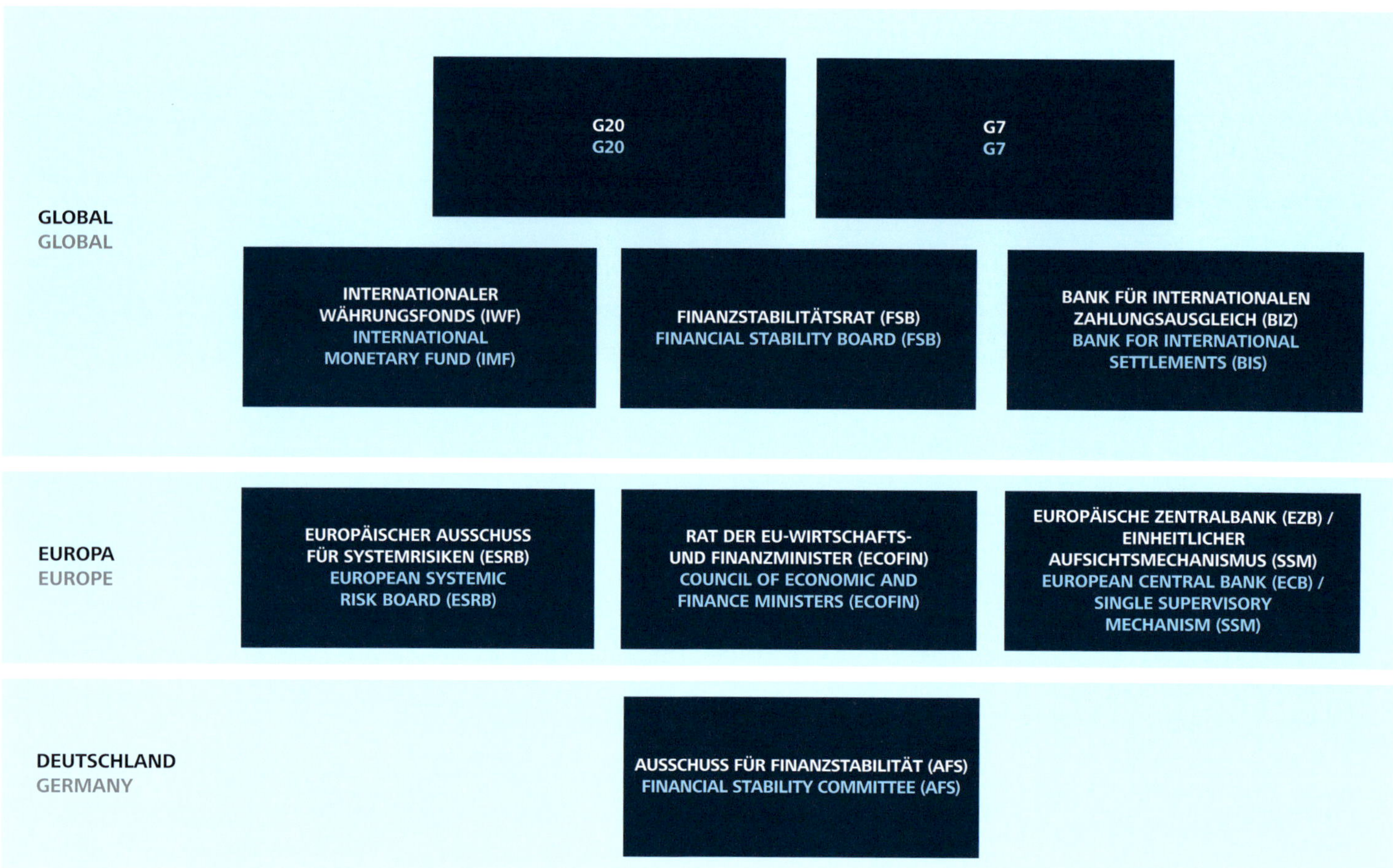

THE DEUTSCHE BUNDESBANK CONTRIBUTES ITS RISK ANALYSES AND POSITIONS ON FINANCIAL STABILITY POLICY TO THESE BODIES AND INSTITUTIONS.

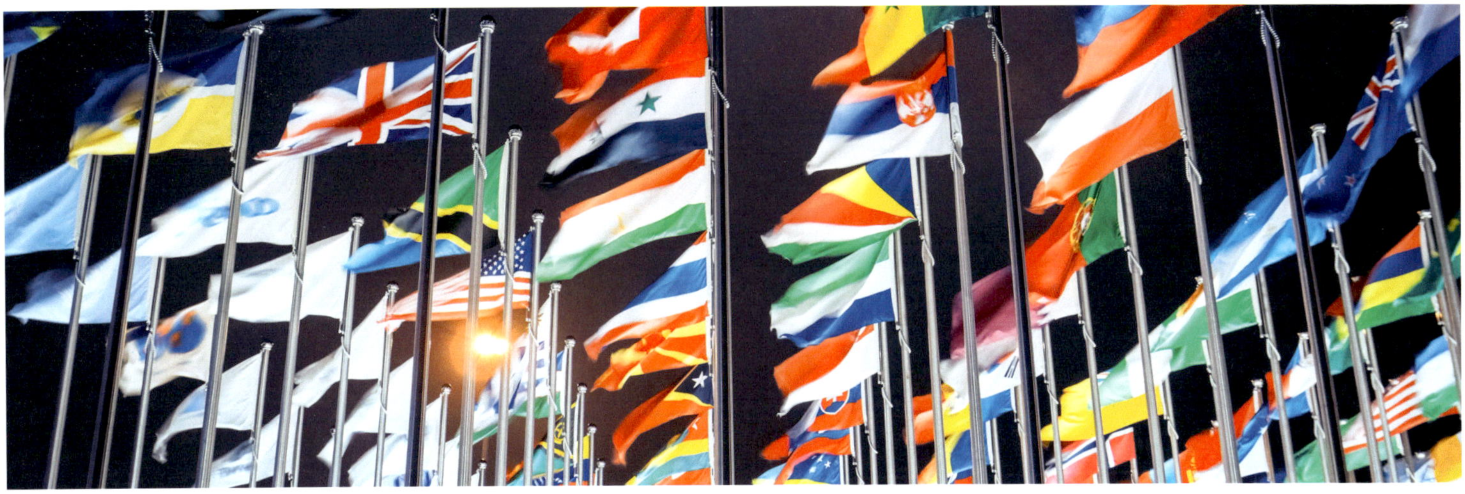

EUROPEAN SYSTEMIC RISK BOARD (ESRB)

The ESRB is responsible for macroprudential oversight in the European Union and is tasked with identifying and curbing risks that could pose a threat to the financial system. The ESRB brings together financial market experts from throughout the EU. The President of the Bundesbank is a voting member of the General Board, the ESRB's decision-making body.

FINANCIAL STABILITY BOARD (FSB)

At the international level, the Financial Stability Board (FSB) coordinates the work of the national authorities, international institutions and standard-setting bodies that are responsible for financial stability. The FSB identifies systemic risks in the financial sector, develops measures to counteract them and oversees their implementation. The Bundesbank is a member of the FSB.

IMF

The International Monetary Fund (IMF) was established at the Bretton Woods Conference in 1944 and currently has 189 member countries. Germany joined the IMF in 1952. The overarching aim of the IMF is to promote economic cooperation and stability in the international monetary system. The President of the Bundesbank represents Germany on the IMF Board of Governors.

BIS

The Bank for International Settlements (BIS), based in Basel, is home to significant standing committees of which the Bundesbank is a member, such as the Committee on the Global Financial System and the Basel Committee on Banking Supervision. The regular meetings at central bank governor level deal with economic, financial market and financial stability issues. The Bundesbank President automatically has a seat on the BIS Board of Directors.

G7

The Group of Seven (G7) was established in 1976 and is a club of the world's seven most advanced industrial economies: the United States, Japan, Germany, France, Italy, the United Kingdom and Canada. The G7's finance ministers and central bank governors regularly discuss current economic and monetary policy topics. In the discussions held by G7 finance ministers and central bank governors, the Bundesbank is represented by its president.

G20

The G20 includes the G7 countries, Australia, eleven economically significant emerging market economies and the EU. Since its inception in 1999, the G20 has focused mainly on the resolution of financial crises, but also on promoting robust and sustainable global economic growth. The German government and the Bundesbank are independent members of the G20 and cooperate closely.

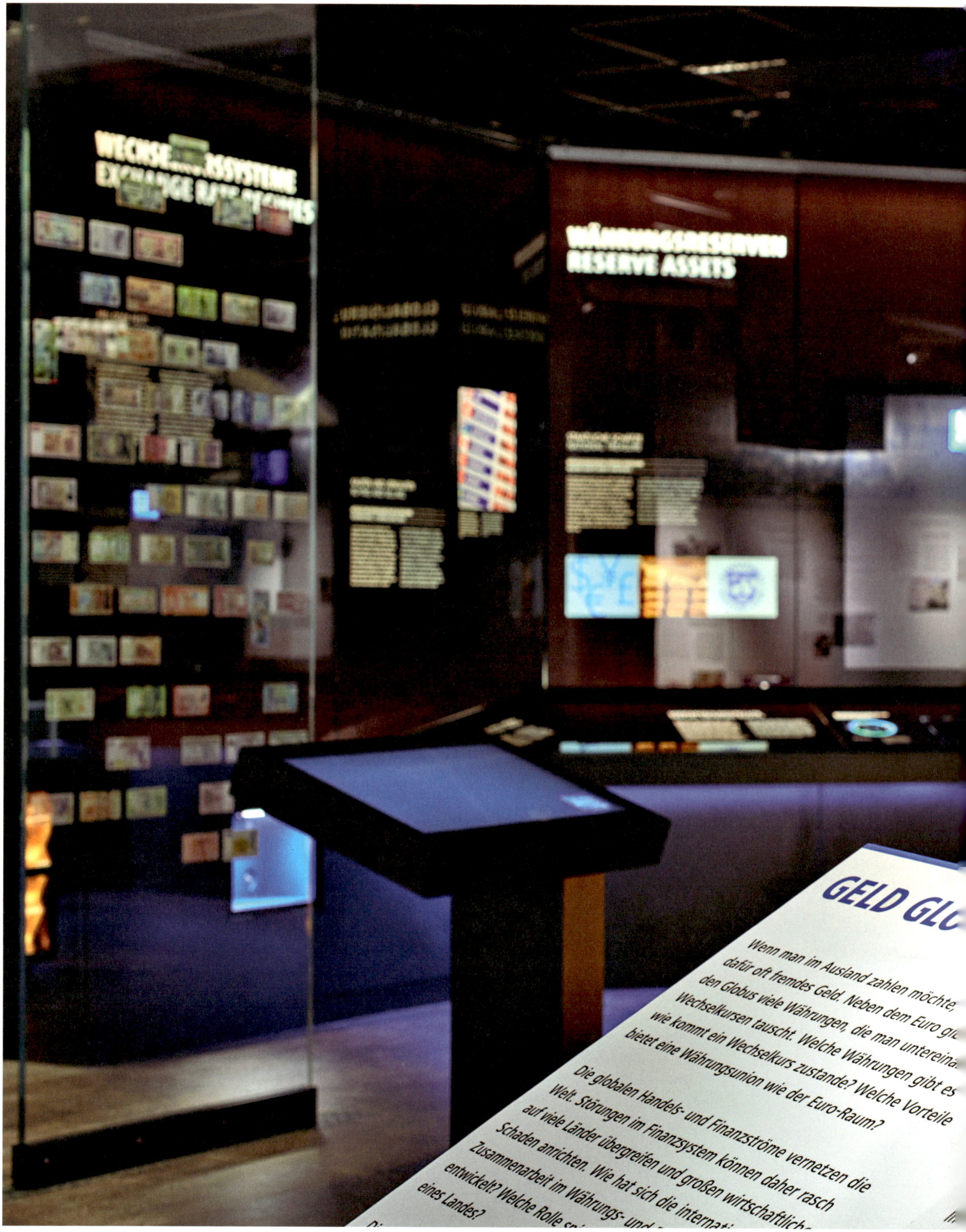
WÄHRUNGSRESERVEN
RESERVE ASSETS

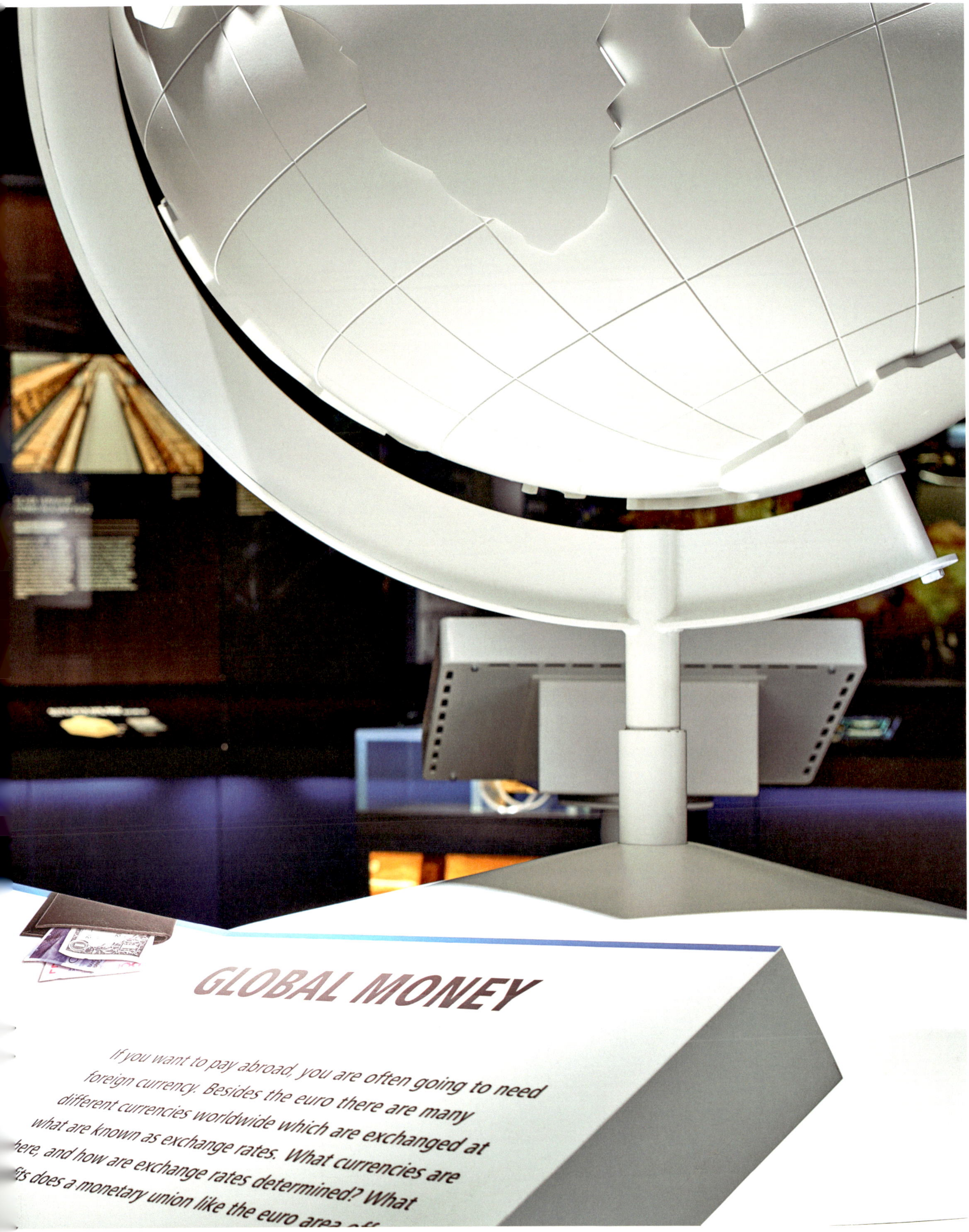
GLOBAL MONEY
If you want to pay abroad, you are often going to need
foreign currency. Besides the euro there are many
different currencies worldwide which are exchanged at
what are known as exchange rates. What currencies are
here, and how are exchange rates determined? What
fits does a monetary union like the euro area

LECTURES AT THE MONEY MUSEUM

The Bundesbank's Money Museum offers lectures to educational institutions and other groups of visitors free of charge. These lectures are held Monday to Friday at the Money Museum.

Lecture topics (held in German):

- **The Deutsche Bundesbank – Objectives and tasks:**
  This lecture provides an overview of the German central bank and the institution's most important tasks in a European context.

- **Monetary policy in the Eurosystem:**
  This lecture focuses on the objectives, instruments and strategy of the Eurosystem's monetary policy, with reference also being made to current developments.

- **Euro currency:**
  This lecture provides information about the design and the appearance of euro banknotes and coins as well as about how to identify counterfeits.

There is also one lecture in English entitled "The Deutsche Bundesbank – Information about the German central bank".

The lectures are suitable for groups of between 10 and 55 participants. Prior registration is required. Further information is available at www.geldmuseum.de.

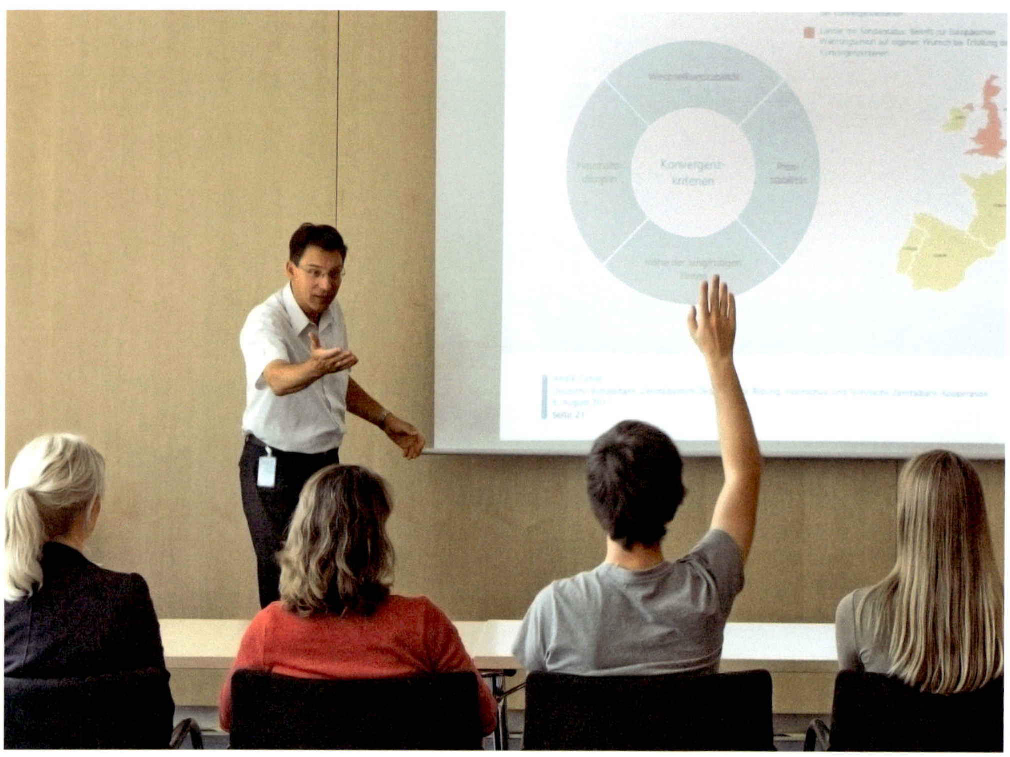

EDUCATIONAL SERVICES PROVIDED BY THE MONEY MUSEUM

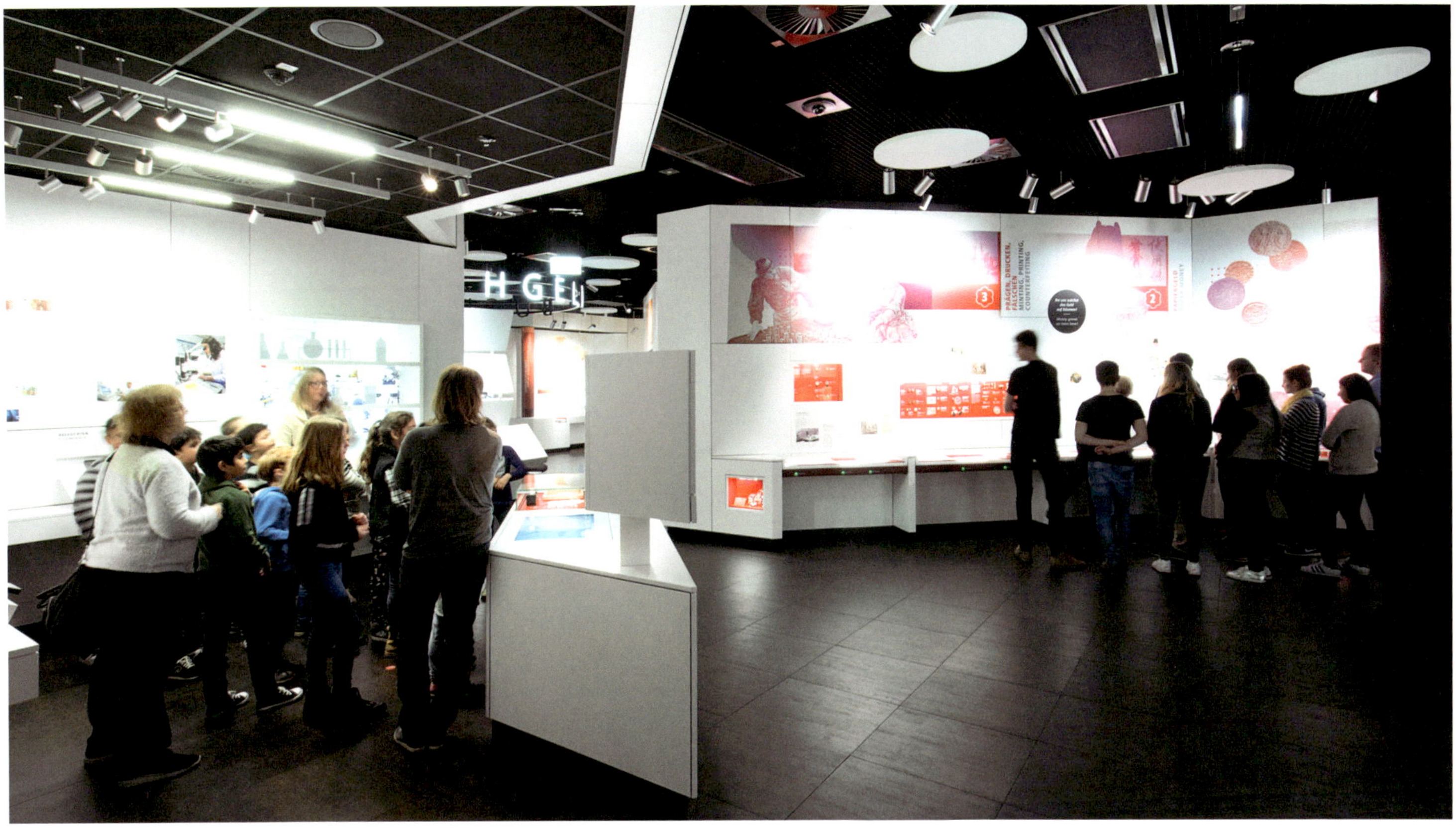

Guided tours

The museum is a unique place to learn and experience all there is to know about money. Guided tours are offered free of charge in German for groups of between 10 and 30 participants on the following topics.

- **A history of money in ten objects:**
  Ten carefully selected objects – coins, banknotes and other forms of money – bring the history of money to life. Learn more about the origin of paper money and coins as well as the vast range of different coins and other exotic means of payment.

- **Only stable money is good money – dangers of inflation and deflation:**
  Stable money is of great economic and political importance. Learn more about the dangers of inflation and deflation and how a central bank keeps money stable.

- **Money's what you can count on:**
  Money is round and made of metal or rectangular and made of paper, isn't it? See just how many different forms money can take, be it as a stone, a snail or completely beyond materiality in the form of book money, which only exists on bank accounts.

Workshops

For children and young people, we offer a number of different workshops, all of which are held in German:

- **Banknote detectives on the case (for young people aged 10 to 15):**
  How can you spot the difference between genuine and counterfeit money? This workshop takes a playful approach to counterfeit detection. Once armed with the necessary know-how, participants are let loose as banknote detectives.

- **The world of coins (for children aged 6 to 10 and young people aged 10 to 15):**
  Where did coins come from, how were they made, and how are they made today? This workshop provides age-appropriate answers to these and many other questions relating to the topic of coins. Participants are also given the opportunity to design their own coins.

- **Design your own banknote (for children aged 6 to 10):**
  By designing their own banknotes, children learn and become familiar with the design elements and security features of banknotes.

MONEY MUSEUM OPENING HOURS

Monday and Tuesday	9 am to 5 pm
Wednesday	9 am to 8 pm
Thursday and Friday	9 am to 5 pm
Saturday	Closed
Sunday / public holiday	9 am to 5 pm

Closed on 1 January, Easter, 1 May, 24, 25 and 31 December.

Admission is free.

ACCESSIBILITY

The Money Museum is accessible for visitors who are in a wheelchair. A ramp is available to help you access the Money Museum building from the street. Once inside the building, an easily accessible lift is available for you to access the exhibition area. The exhibition rooms and the café are located on the same floor. The museum's lecture rooms are located on the first floor and can be reached by lift.

People with visual impairments are advised to bring someone along to accompany them. Audio guides are also available for people with visual impairments.

GETTING HERE

The Money Museum is located on the premises of the Bundesbank's Central Office in the Ginnheim district of Frankfurt.

Travelling by public transport from the main train station ("Hauptbahnhof"):
Take underground line U4 (direction "Seckbacher Landstrasse") or U5 (direction "Preungesheim") to "Willy-Brandt-Platz"; change to lines U1 (direction "Ginnheim"), U2 (direction "Bad Homburg-Gonzenheim"), U3 (direction "Oberursel-Hohemark") or U8 (direction "Riedberg") and get off at "Dornbusch". From there, you can either take bus number 34 (direction "Mönchhofstrasse") and get off at the "Deutsche Bundesbank" stop or, alternatively, you can walk roughly 500 metres down the street "Am Dornbusch".

Travelling by car:
Take the A5 motorway to "Nordwestkreuz Frankfurt", where you turn onto the A66 towards "Miquelallee/Stadtmitte". After taking the exit "Miquelallee", follow the signs for "Deutsche Bundesbank". The entrance to the Money Museum is located approximately 100 metres away from the Bundesbank's main gate. A limited number of visitor car parking spaces are available in front of the museum building as well as parking spaces for coaches.

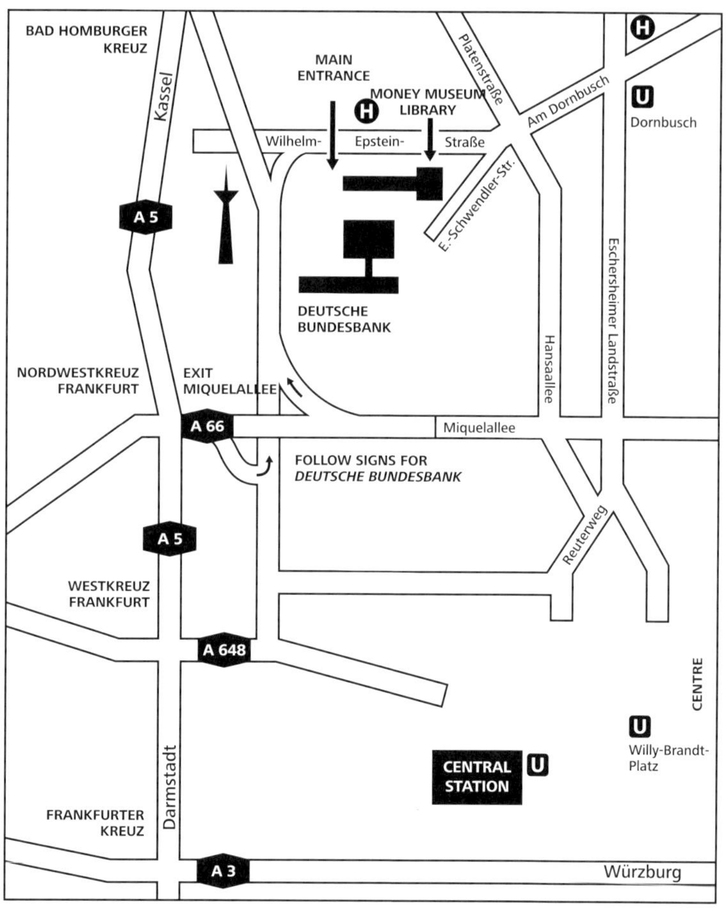

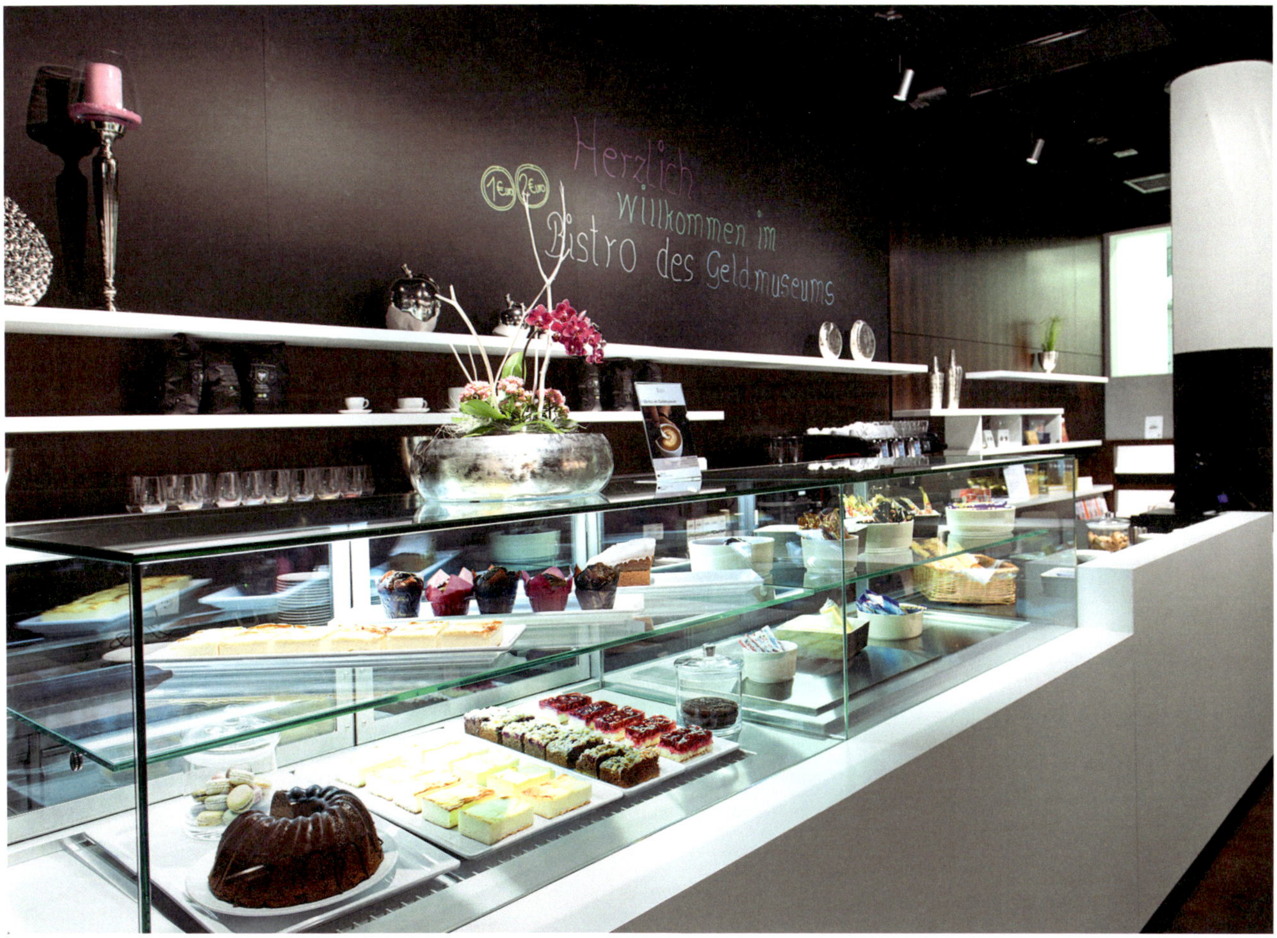

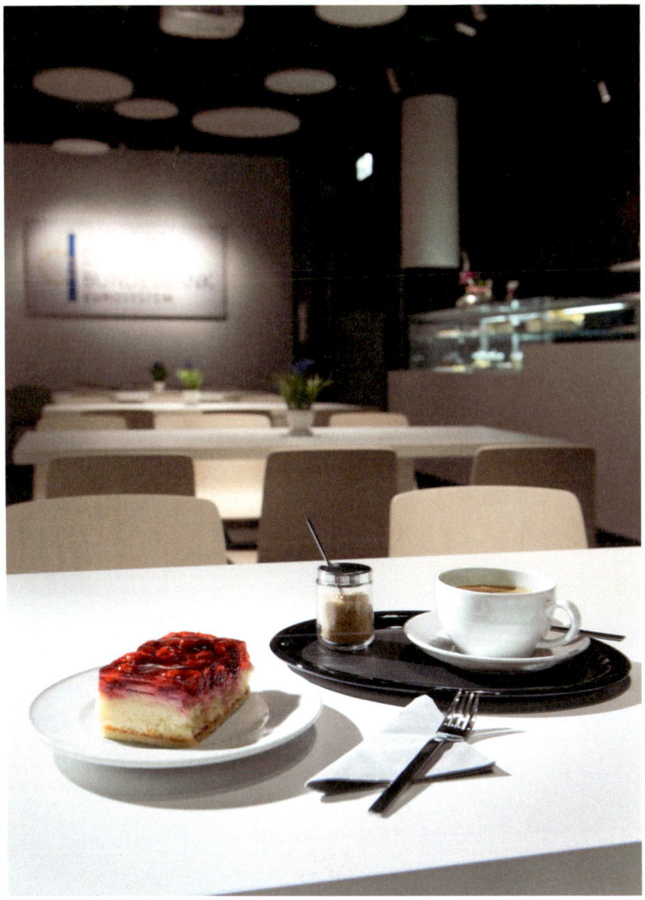

CAFÉ

The museum's café serves hot and cold drinks as well as light snacks. The café is open from 9.30 am to 4.30 pm on Monday, Tuesday, Thursday, Friday and Sunday, and from 10 am to 7 pm on Wednesday.

LIST OF EXHIBITS

42
p 39
Jerusalem, King Amalric, denier, 1163–1174

43
p 39
Order of St John on Rhodes, Fra' Robert de Juliac, gigliato, 1374–1376

44
p 40
Emperor Maximilian I, schauguldiner, 1509

45
p 40
Electorate of Saxony, klappmützenthaler ("flat cap thaler"), 1500

46
p 40
Duchy of Friedland, Duke Albrecht of Wallenstein, reichsthaler, 1629

47
p 40
Imperial city of Regensburg, ½ konventionsspeziesthaler, 1782

48
p 40
Hoard of coins found in Walle

49
p 41
Japan, feudal era, Tsūhō, 1768–1788

50
p 41
Japan, Meiji dynasty, Mutsuhito Tenno, 20 yen, 1870

51
p 41
Japan, feudal era, Ōban, 1725–1743

52
p 41
Japan, Meiji dynasty, Mutsuhito Tenno, Bank of Japan, 1 yen, 1889

53
p 42
East India Company, minted in the name of Queen Victoria, mohur, 1841

54
p 42
India, Mughal dynasty, Muhammad Akbar, mohur, 1568/1569

55
p 42
Danish India (Tranquebar), King Christian VI, 4 kas, 1730–1746

56
p 42
Kingdom of Mysore, rupee, 1787

57
p 42
Republic of Central America, 4 escudos, 1837

58
p 42
Mexico, King Ferdinand VI of Spain, 8 reales, 1755

59
p 42
USA, 1 dollar, 1880

60
p 42
Wass, Molitor & Co, 50 dollars, 1855, San Francisco, minted from the proceeds of the California Gold Rush

61
p 43
Principality of Waldeck and Pyrmont, double thaler, 1842

62
p 43
Free city of Frankfurt, double union thaler, 1862

63
p 43
Kingdom of Saxony, King Johann, siegesthaler, 1871

64
p 43
German Reich, 1 Mark, 1896

65
p 44
Saxony, Churfürstlich-Sächsische Cassen, 1 reichsthaler, 6 May 1772

66
p 44
Sweden, Stockholms Banco, 10 dalers, 17 April 1666

67
p 44
USA, 1 dollar, 1 August 1862

68
p 44
Fiji, 1 penny, 1 July 1942

69
p 44
Germany, Bank deutscher Länder, 20 DM, 20 June 1948

70
p 44
Romania, 10 bani, 1917

71
p 44
China, Ming dynasty, 1 kuan = 1,000 cash, 1368–1399

72
p 45
Seychelles, 50 rupees, 1 August 1973

73
p 45
German East Africa, Deutsch-Ostafrikanische Bank, 100 rupees, 15 June 1905

74
p 45
Yugoslavia, 500,000,000,000 dinar, 1993

75
p 45
German Reich, Reichsbank, 100 trillion Mark, 15 February 1924

76
p 45
Nicaragua, 1 peso, 1894

77
p 45
Union of Soviet Socialist Republics (USSR), 25 roubles, 1947

78
p 45
Australia, 10 dollars, 26 January 1988

79
p 45
German Reich, 10-pounds counterfeit, 1942–1945

80
p 46
Oceania, island of Yap, rai (stone money), until ca 1910, aragonite, 69 kg, 77 cm

81
p 47
Cowrie snail money chain, Papua New Guinea

82
p 47
Bar of salt (Amoli), Ethiopia

83
p 49
Roman Republic, Marcus Junius Brutus, mint master L Plaetorius Cestianus, aureus, 43/42 BC, Brutus' mobile military mint

84
p 49
Italy, Lorenzo di Pierfrancesco de' Medici, medallion commemorating the assassination of his cousin Alessandro, 1537

85
p 49
France, Henry II, medallion commemorating the alliance with the German protestant princes, 1552

86
p 50
World War I, German East Africa, 15 rupees, 1916

87
p 50
Siege of Vienna, ducat (klippe), 1529

88
p 50
German New Guinea, New Guinea Company, 20 Mark, 1895

89
p 51
German Reich, coin-decorated tankard, 1873, prussian goldsmith company Sy & Wagner, Berlin

90
p 55
Draft design of the German reverse of the 1-cent coin by Rolf Lederbogen

91
p 55
The master dies for the 1-cent coin

92
p 55
Upper and lower dies for the 1-cent coin

93
p 56
Stamping die with the watermark motif

94
p 65
Banknotes damaged by fire

95
p 65
50-euro banknote, damaged by a parrot

96
p 72
Mesopotamia, cuneiform tablet, 1799 BC

97
p 73
Bill of exchange for 150 gulden dated 25 January 1833

98
p 79
China, abacus, from ca 1900

99
p 107
Prussia, King Frederick II, 8 gute groschen, 1753

100
p 107
Prussia, King Frederick II, 8 gute groschen, 1759, war money, minted with a 41% reduced silver content

101
p 107
Poland, King August III, August d'or, 1754

102
p 107
Poland, King August III, new August d'or, 1758 (minted 1761/1762 as war money by Frederick II)

103
p 109
Coin scale (ca 1620, design probably augmented in 1729), Cologne, Scale and weight designer: Philipp Wilhelm Marx

104
p 109
Austria, Ferdinand II, groschen, 1626

105
p 109
Austria, Ferdinand II, groschen (debased coin), 1623

106
p 110
Zimbabwe, Reserve Bank of Zimbabwe, 100 trillion Zimbabwean dollars, 21 January 2009

107
p 113
USA, Federal Reserve Board, 5 dollars, 1914

108
p 113
USA, Federal Reserve Board, 5 dollars, 2013

109
p 117
German Reich, Reichsbank, 10,000 Mark, 19 January 1922

110
p 117
German Reich, Reichsbank, 2 trillion Mark, 5 November 1923

111
p 117
District savings bank Traunstein, 500 billion Mark, 9 November 1923

112
p 117
Heilbronn (Württemberg), 200 billion Mark, 1923

113
p 117
Medallist unknown, satirical ducat, 1923

114
p 123
German Reich, Reichsbank, 1,000 Mark, 1884

115
p 123
German Reich, Reichsbank, 100 Mark, 1883

116
p 124
German Reich, Reichsbank, 50 Mark, 1919

117
p 124
German Reich, 5 Rentenmark, 1926

118
p 124
German Reich, Reichsbank, 10 Reichsmark, 1924

119
p 125
German Reich, Reichsbank, 20 Reichsmark, 1939

120
p 125
German Reich, Reich treasury office, 20 Reichsmark 1939–1944

121
p 125
Allied military authorities, 100 Mark, 1944

122
p 126
Germany, Bank deutscher Länder, 10 DM, 1948

123
p 127
Coupon Mark from the Soviet occupation zone, 1948

124
p 127
German Democratic Republic, 100 Mark, 1964

125
p 127
German Democratic Republic, 100 Mark, 1975

126
p 128
Germany, Deutsche Bundesbank, "BBK I" banknote series, 10 DM, 1989

127
p 128
Germany, Deutsche Bundesbank, "BBK I" banknote series, 20 DM, 1991

128
p 129
Germany, Deutsche Bundesbank, "BBK III" banknote series, 10 DM, 1989

129
p 129
Germany, Deutsche Bundesbank, "BBK III" banknote series, 20 DM, 1991

130
p 155
Austria-Hungary, Emperor Franz Joseph I, ducat, 1877

131
p 155
Habsburg lands, Maria Theresa Thaler, 1780, Günzburg (restruck in Vienna, from 1820), counterstamp of the port town of Obock (Djibouti / French Somaliland), 1890/1892

132
p 155
Mexico, King Charles III of Spain, Piaster (8 reales), 1769

133
p 155
USA, trade dollar, 1877

134
p 155
Prussia, King Frederick II, handelspiaster, 1751

135
p 155
French Indochina, piastre de commerce, 1901

136
p 157
City of Utrecht, gold strike of ½ duit, 1753

137
p 158
Mainz, Archbishop Adolf II, goldgulden, 1464/1465

138
p 166
5 europino, 1952

139
p 167
France, 100 francs ≈ 15 ECU (values in local currency with rounded equivalents in ECU)

140
p 167
Germany 100 euro, 2002, collector coin for the launch of the euro

141
p 182
Gold bar

PHOTO CREDITS

Leo Seidel, Berlin:
pages 4/5, 11, 13, 22/23, 34/35, 38, 40, 43, 46, 48, 48, 48, 50, 52/53, 54, 55, 55, 58, 60/61, 62, 63, 64, 64, 66, 70/71, 73, 74, 76/77, 79, 82, 84/85, 87, 88, 89, 91, 95, 96, 98, 99, 100, 104, 109, 114/115, 116, 119, 120/121, 129, 130, 132/133, 134, 136, 136, 137, 139, 140/141, 150, 157, 160, 162, 164/165, 166, 168, 172, 174/175, 176, 177, 178/179, 179, 182, 182, 183, 191, 193, 193

p 9: Gaby Gerster
p 12: Frank Rumpenhorst
p 18: Uwe Nölke
p 21: bpk | RMN – Grand Palais | Hervé Lewandowski
p 24/25 (Charlemagne): akg-images
p 26: ullstein bild - Granger, NYC
p 27: Bayerische Staatsbibliothek, Hbks/F 105 f-1, Fig. 54
p 28: BBB, Mss.h.h.l.16, p 222/ photo: Codices Electronici AG
p 29: Giesecke & Devrient GmbH, München
p 29: Photo-Design Herbert Boswank/ Kupferstich-Kabinett Dresden
p 33: ullstein bild
p 36, p 37, p 38, p 39, p 40, p 41, p 42, p 42, p 43: Team Uwe Nölke
p 46: Mary Evans
p 46: Bayerische Staatsbibliothek München/ Bildarchiv
p 47: RCS Y3045T/11, Cambridge University Library
p 49: Team Uwe Nölke
p 55: Bundesbank/Rumpenhorst
p 56: EZB
p 57: Bundesbank/Christian Thiel
p 62: fotolia/stryjek
p 65: Bundesbank/Bostelmann
p 69: Fundación Museo de Bellas Artes de Bilbao
p 69: Rheinisches Landesmuseum Trier, Foto: TH. Zühmer
p 72: BnF/Le Chevalier errant, fol. 167
p 73: akg-images/Quint & Lox
p 74: The British Library Board Stowe 594 f7v
p 75: Axel Springer Syndication GmbH
p 75: ullstein bild – dpa
p 78, p 79: akg-images
p 79: Interfoto/Alinari
p 80: akg-images
p 81: ullstein bild – Imagno
p 81: bpk | Scala – courtesy of the Ministero Beni e Att. Culturali
p 83: akg-images
p 83: SLUB Dresden/Deutsche Fotothek
p 86: Visio
p 86: fotolia/M. Schuppich
p 92: fotolia/zinkevych
p 92: fotolia/Idprod
p 92: fotolia/Piotr Adamowicz
p 93: masterfile/Leaf
p 94: fotolia/corbis_fancy
p 96: Kostas Koufogiorgos
p 97: Bundesbank/roosen photography
p 103, p 105: akg-images
p 105: BnF
p 106: Staatliche Münzsammlung München
p 106: The Goldsmiths' Company. Photography by Richard Lea-Hair
p 107: bpk | Stiftung Preußische Schlösser und Gärten Berlin-Brandenburg | Jörg P. Anders
p 108: akg-images
p 108: Deutsches Historisches Museum, Berlin
p 110: dpa picture alliance
p 111: Scherl/SZ Photo
p 111: ullstein bild
p 112: National Library of Sweden
p 113: The Governor and Company of the Bank of England
p 118: Science Photo Library/akg-images
p 118: BArch, Bild 102-00104/Photography: Georg Pahl
p 118: ullstein bild – Roger-Viollet/ Albert Harlingue
p 123: BArch, Bild 146-1970-047-37
p 124: akg-images
p 126: Bundesregierung/Puck-Archiv
p 127: akg-images/Paul Almasy
p 128: ullstein bild – dpa
p 138: fotolia/luismolinero
p 138: gettyimages/Daisuke Morita
p 138: fotolia/Andy Dean
p 138: fotolia/Yong Hian Lim
p 138: fotolia/Klaus Eppele
p 138: fotolia/sheelamohanachandran
p 138: gettyimages/Monty Rakusen
p 138: fotolia/nmann77
p 142: EZB
p 149: Juergen Moers/DJV Bildportal
p 153: Het Scheepvaartmuseum, Amsterdam
p 154: akg-images
p 156: Rijksmuseum, Amsterdam
p 158: Edwin Roper Stocqueler, An Australian gold diggings, c.1855, National Gallery of Australia and the National Library of Australia, Rex Nan Kivell Collection
p 159: AP/dpa/SZ Photo
p 159: IMF
p 159: National Archives (208-MO-78A-N29535-FO)
p 160: Frans Hals Museum, Haarlem, purchased with support of the Rembrandt Society. Photo: Tom Haartsen
p 161: Library of Congress
p 161: bpk
p 162: picture alliance/dpa
p 163: DER SPIEGEL 11/2009
p 166: UPI/Süddeutsche Zeitung Photo
p 169: Público, Portugal; Le Parisien; Politis; Verslo Klase
p 171: fotolia/thomasmuessig

p 171: Bundesregierung/Christian Stutterheim

p 172: fotolia/bluedesign

p 177: Fraport AG

p 177: iStock.com/iconeer

p 180/181: Uwe Nölke

p 187: fotolia/chungking

p 188/189: Uwe Nölke

All other illustrations:
Deutsche Bundesbank

All attempts have been made by the editors and publisher to locate the holders of the rights to the works in this publication. Should any have been overlooked, please do not hesitate to contact us.

IMPRINT

The Money Museum of the Deutsche Bundesbank
www.geldmuseum.de

Publisher
Deutsche Bundesbank

Design, editorial work and author of the introductory texts
Sylvia Obst

Translation, copyediting of the English texts
Language Services Division of the Deutsche Bundesbank

Design
Martin Kaufmann, Sign Kommunikation, Frankfurt

Project management publisher
Kerstin Ludolph

Production
Peter Grassinger

Lithography
Reproline Genceller, Munich

Printing and binding
Passavia Druckservice, Passau

ISBN 978-3-7774-2807-9

Bibliographical data of the Deutsche Nationalbibliothek
The Deutsche Nationalbibliothek lists this publication in the Deutschen Nationalbibliografie; detailed bibliographic information is available on the Internet at http://www.dnb.de.

www.hirmerpublishers.com